European Architecture
1750–1890

W9-BTD-205

Oxford History of Art

Barry Bergdoll is Professor of Art History at Columbia University, New York, and the author of numerous works on nineteenth- and twentieth-century architecture, including *Léon Vaudoyer: Historicism in the Age of Industry* (1994), *Karl Friedrich Schinkel: An Architecture for Prussia* (1994), and *Mastering McKim's Plan* (1997). He has also curated exhibitions on architecture, notably 'Le Panthéon: Symbole des Révolutions', held in 1989 in Paris and Montreal, and the forthcoming 'Mies van der Rohe in Berlin', to be held in 2001–2 in New York and Berlin.

Oxford History of Art

Titles in the Oxford History of Art series are up-to-date, fully-illustrated introductions to a wide variety of subjects written by leading experts in their field. They will appear regularly, building into an interlocking and comprehensive series. In the list below, published titles appear in bold.

Oxford History of Art

European Architecture 1750–1890

Barry Bergdoll

OXFORD
UNIVERSITY PRESS

OXFORD
UNIVERSITY PRESS

Great Clarendon Street, Oxford OX2 6DP

Oxford New York

Athens Auckland Bangkok Bombay Calcutta
Cape Town Dar es Salaam Delhi Florence Hong Kong Istanbul
Karachi Kuala Lumpur Madras Madrid Melbourne Mexico City Mumbai
Nairobi Paris São Paulo Singapore Taipei Tokyo Toronto Warsaw

and associated companies in Berlin Ibadan

British Library Cataloguing in Publication Data
Data available

Library of Congress Cataloguing in Publication Data

ISBN 0-19-284222-6

10 9 8 7 6 5 4 3 2 1

Library of Congress Cataloguing-in-Publication Data

Bergdoll, Barrry
European architecture 1750–1890/ Barry Bergdoll.
(Oxford history of art)
Includes bibliographical references and index.
1. Architecture–Europe 2. Neoclassicism (Architecture)–Europe. 3. Architecture,
Modern–19th century–Europe. I. Title. II Series.
NA956 .B47   2000   724'.19-dc21   00-036747
ISBN 0-19-284222-6

Picture research by Elisabeth Agate
Design by John Saunders

Printed in Hong Kong
on acid-free paper by C&C Offset Printing Co. Ltd.

Contents

Acknowledgements

Many people have contributed to this book in the long period of its gestation, on every level from moral support—when courage lagged to tackle such a daunting subject and time frame in such a succinct format—to ready answers for points of information or advice. My first thanks go to Simon Mason who commissioned this volume and encouraged me with a firm but knowing hand through the stages of writing, cutting, and refining. A residency at the Liguria Study Centre for the Arts and Humanities provided much needed solitude in late spring 1997 during the drafting of the early chapters, and I am grateful to James Harrison of the Bogliasco Foundation, as well as Alan Rowlin and Anna Maria Quiat, Resident Director of the Centre, for making my stay in Bogliasco, near Genoa, such a useful and agreeable time; and my thanks go too to other fellows for advice, notably Hayden Herrera, Jonathan Shahn, Julia Pryzbos, and David Del Tredici. The staff of Columbia's Avery Library has been, as always, most helpful, and Columbia University's Reid Hall, Paris, where the final stages of corrections and proof-reading took place are also to be thanked, in particular Brune Biebuyck, Christine Babeuf, and Danielle Haase-Dubosc. Friends and colleagues who contributed in one way or another, often unwittingly, to this book's success include Eve Blau, Karen Bowie, Robert Bruegman, Jean Castex, Jean-Louis Cohen, Alan Colqhoun, Stefano Fera, Jane and Steven Garmey, Bertrand Gautier, Catherine Healey, Michael Lewis, Harry Francis Mallgrave, Robin Middleton, Nicholas Olsberg, Janet Parks, Antoine Picon, Carmen Popescu, Joszef Sisa, Carl Strehlke, Daniel Rabreau, Terence Riley, William Ryall, Suzanne Stephens, Caroline van Eck, and Dora Wiebenson. I have had the good fortune of working with an exceptional group of graduate students in the last few years at Columbia University and thank in particular Christopher Armstrong, Jean-François Bédard, Terry Kirk, Sean Sawyer, Edward Wendt, Leila Wittemore, and Richard Witman. The book has gained enormously by the unflagging enthusiasm and interest of Lisa Agate, who tirelessly searched down images, as well as the skilful editing of Elizabeth Teague and Katherine Reeve, and the advice of Paul Manning. Needless to say any omissions—and there are, obviously, many that I am aware of and many more of which I am probably not—and errors are entirely my own.

Introduction

Viewed as a period of transition, European architecture between 1750 and 1890 was, until the mid-1960s, routinely examined principally to discern the roots of twentieth-century modernism. Both the ideal of imitation proffered by Neoclassicism of the 1750s–1820s and the plurality of stylistic imagery of mid-nineteenth-century historicism were taken as evidence that, from the mid-eighteenth century to the dawn of the twentieth century, architecture lacked not only originality but also both stylistic and cultural unity and direction. No convenient label adhered easily to a period which opened with self-conscious attacks on the Baroque and Rococo and closed with a renewed appreciation of those very same styles as the last great unified cultural expressions. While some art historians of the late nineteenth and early twentieth centuries sought to extend the pattern of stylistic unities to include the Neoclassicism of the second half of the eighteenth century, the widespread appearance by 1800 of structures evoking nearly every period in western art history—and many exotic 'oriental' styles as well—signalled the end of the narrative mapped out with the tools available to the young academic discipline of art history.

Faced with this seeming breakdown of stylistic coherence, architectural historians sought to isolate pioneering strands of a nascent modernity, sometimes in the purist geometries and severe articulations of some of the late eighteenth century's most radical experiments with an elemental architectural vocabulary, sometimes in the frank deployment, particularly by the newly distinct profession of the engineer, of such new materials as iron and glass, and later concrete. These modernist scenarios, alternatively formalist and materialist, were potently formulated by Emil Kaufman, Sigfried Giedion, and Sir Nikolaus Pevsner from the 1930s to the late 1950s.[1] The vast majority of architectural production of the century and a half preceding the modern movement was dismissed as unproductive chaff, from which only the germinating seeds of modernism were to be isolated for study and criticism. European architecture from the Enlightenment through to the Second Industrial Revolution of the 1870s and 1880s thus became the victim of one of its own most characteristic attitudes: historical judgement and hindsight. The texture of the period itself, its imperatives, its issues, its evolving definition of architecture, were all obscured from view in the process.

While Pevsner's and Giedion's views have been vehemently attacked and critiqued, and have themselves become objects of historical study, very few overarching interpretations of the period 1750–1890 have been offered to fill the void left by these discredited polemical histories, although studies of key figures, buildings, and aspects of the period have proliferated. Synthetic studies have largely been formulated as national histories of architecture, thus confirming over and over again one of the most characteristic constructs of the nineteenth century: the nation-state as the organizer of experience and identity. It is certainly a daunting task to attempt to break out of that scenario, with all its conveniences of ready-made historical subdivisions as well as a certain parallelism between political, social, and artistic events. Even as Europe struggles in our time to reinvent itself, it might seem foolhardy to use such a continental scope in an account of architecture in the eighteenth and nineteenth centuries, riven as those centuries were by political, economic, and cultural rivalries. And it is certainly beyond the scope of these introductory volumes to venture a new account with the rich texture of details of national surveys, or even the much longer survey books of the 1960s and 1970s that set out to map this period more objectively as the modernist project came under attack in both architecture and historiography. I think here of Henry-Russell Hitchcock's *Architecture: Nineteenth and Twentieth Centuries* in the Pelican History of Art, last revised in 1977, and Robin Middleton and David Watkin's lively *Neoclassical and Nineteenth Century Architecture*, first issued in Italian in the same year, both of which remain valuable reference tools even if they were composed more as a collage of national chapters. The approach here is thematic, and it is hoped that this book will offer a reading of the period under study that will prove stimulating not only for those studying it for the first time, but for the many engaged in its ongoing reappraisal.

Key themes and issues

The fundamental hypothesis might be summarized thus: ushered in by the great period of intellectual questioning which historians have called the Enlightenment and fuelled by the social, political, and economic upheavals and challenges of a century and a half continually made aware, anxious even, of the changes that separated it from the past, architecture after 1750 became self-consciously experimental as never before. Continually testing its own limits, the possibilities and capacities of architecture were questioned, expanded, and debated as an integral part of those processes of secular human reason, of scientific observation and experimentation, that characterized the Enlightenment in philosophy and in science. This led to an unprecedented range of architectural solutions and experiments, of competing visions and theories, even of bold blueprints. Far from being an era of stodgy 'revivalism' as it was so often characterized by modernists seeking to exorcize one of the period's greatest legacies to our own—cultural anxiety—this period was one of continual experimentation on the very nature of architecture, its capacity to represent and to communicate, even its capacity to affect and mould behaviour. By its very diversity, architecture in the nineteenth century sought to expand its capacity to accommodate new demands of a rapidly evolving society and societal consciousness, and its flexibility to respond to new visions and insights of a society's place in the larger order of things, whether historical, natural, or social.

Three interlocking themes characterize the architecture of this period and will structure its assessment here: (1) a fundamentally new vision of the relationship of architecture to the historical past, (2) architecture's response to the explosion of scientific inquiry, not simply into the natural realm, but into humanity itself, as the sciences of man sought an equivalent status to the emerging natural sciences—a term itself invented over the course of the period, and (3) the emergence of new publics for architecture in a period of social and economic revolution and nation-building.

Architecture and history

It is characteristic of the new historical consciousness ushered in by such pioneering works as Montesquieu's *The Spirit of the Laws* (1747) and Voltaire's *The Century of Louis XIV* (1751) that the attempt to understand the nature of historical time as a process of lawful evolution and change was continually motivated by a desire to change the present. The great revolution in archaeological studies, themselves the bedrock upon which the stylistic experiments generally referred to as Neoclassicism were grounded, was fuelled by a longing for fundamental laws for making and criteria for judging architecture. More than any other medium, architecture embodied poignantly the period's quest to combine an understanding of progress and change with a consensus on truth, a relating of the eternal and relative that remained one of the fundamental quests of the period's myriad philosophies of human, and even natural, history. Although the vision of the shape of time was to change radically over the course of the period, the fundamental belief that an understanding of the place of the present in a larger orderly progress of time was a prerequisite to creating an appropriate ethics, be it of government, society, or architecture, was held in common throughout the late eighteenth and nineteenth centuries. In the pages that follow the phenomena of revivalism and eclecticism, the self-conscious examination of the historical category of style in architecture, will be examined as a by-product of this great revolution in the status of historical knowledge.

Architecture and scientific inquiry

From the publication in 1749 of the first volume of Buffon's *Natural History*, even inquiry into the natural realm was to be framed historically. While the nineteenth century would explore at length the relations between systems of classification and analysis in the natural sciences, the eighteenth century, in its great admiration for the Newtonian revolution in scientific reasoning, was most eager to put a whole range of 'sciences of man' on an equal footing with the new standards of objectivity, observation, and lawfulness which characterized investigation of the universe and its workings. Built on Locke's premise that all knowledge was derived through the sensations, sensationalist philosophy opened up the whole realm of human emotional response, knowledge, and ultimately even morality to scientific experimentation and inquiry. This was to cause a profound reconsideration of the domain of the aesthetic. Natural philosophy, as science was still called early in the period, thus framed a whole new 'objective' basis for exploring the nature of architectural form, its effect on the senses, and ultimately on behaviour. From this descriptive ethos of contemporary 'Newtonian' social science, the political and social potential of the malleability of human behaviour was postulated. Sensationalist man, objectively described, became the premise for behavioural, social, and even political reform. In the context of the economic, technological, and political revolutions of the late eighteenth century, this new instrumental potential of architecture was a powerful legacy to be studied throughout the nineteenth century as science increasingly came to rival history in explanations of both the natural and the social realm. Only at the end of the nineteenth century did new theories of subjectivity lead to a fundamental re-evaluation of both architectural form and its audience.

A new audience for architecture

If architects came to frame investigation of their work in terms that placed architectural design as one of the constituent elements both shaping and shaped by events, debates, and ideologies, this was a period, too, which saw an ever-widening public for architecture. In a burgeoning world of printed pamphlets, expanding salon and coffee-house culture, and open debate over the nature of authority and citizenship, architecture was subject for the first time to professional criticism, framed outside the traditional power of rulers, aristocrats, and the church. The increased political, social, and intellectual freedom and power of a burgeoning bourgeoisie in Western Europe, as well as the engagement of any number of rulers from the German states to Russia with the Enlightenment's open questioning of the limits and nature of autocratic rule, both fostered and in turn responded to a revolution in the history of architectural programmes. Not only did architects turn their attention to a much wider range of buildings, but new and unprecedented building types and tasks developed with increasing rapidity. Museums, public theatres, public libraries, halls of legislative assembly, and later railway stations, department stores, and buildings for exhibitions and fairs, all made their appearance for the first time during this period. The invention of the building type and its public went hand in hand. Although this was the first period to create a theory of architecture as one of the most immediate reflections of the specificity of historical and geographical setting, it was also one of the first to confront self-consciously the challenges of solving architectural programmes that had never before been formulated. Not surprisingly, in doing so the joint concerns of following historical law and learning from the methods of science were enlisted. None of the themes singled out here, from the intellectual revolution of historical studies to the rise of a new public consciousness, can be pursued in isolation.

In the two decades since the last significant attempt to take stock of this complex period was published, a veritable avalanche of research has continually expanded the canon of architects, buildings, and even countries which contribute to the vibrant culture of architecture in late eighteenth- and nineteenth-century Europe. An attempt has been made to represent this wealth in the bibliography at the end of this volume. More importantly, efforts to view the period through new methodological lenses offered by an increasingly self-questioning discipline of art history have been sketched in various thematic studies, many taking their questions for the first time from outside the discipline of architecture itself. From the social history of art of the late 1960s and 1970s to analyses of architecture itself as an ideological instrument in the wake of the vivid interest of architectural historians in the work of post-structuralists, the period's transitional status has become rich for analysis rather than a roadblock to understanding. It is hoped that this book is at once a record of some of the shifts of emphasis and interpretation that have been opened up both within and adjacent to the field of architectural history and criticism, and a suggestive charting of a new set of themes for further work.

The chapters that follow are organized both thematically and chronologically. There is therefore inevitably a certain amount of moving back and forth in time as the chapters sometimes pursue a theme over several decades. An individual architect's work will at times be discussed in more than one chapter and cross-references to illustrations will encourage readers to pursue themes and comparisons that cannot be fully taken up in this introduction to the period. Each chapter seeks to elucidate in some depth one or two seminal buildings, considered not only as masterpieces of an architectural author, but as diverse mirrors of the social, political, and cultural situation of a given moment and place.

Part I

Progress, Enlightenment, Experiment

Neoclassicism: Science, Archaeology, and the Doctrine of Progress

1

Architecture and the Enlightenment

In the mid-eighteenth century, antiquity was upheld as a standard for architecture as never before. At first glance the quest to extend both the scope and the depth of understanding of the classical language which had dominated European architectural expression since the fifteenth century might seem a fulfilment of Renaissance ideals rather than a critical new departure. But the Europe-wide movement, often labelled Neoclassicism, was anything but a revival; it represented rather a fundamental investigation of the very bases of architectural form and meaning. Debates over the origins and authority of the Classical orders were given a new impetus by the climate of analytical inquiry initiated both by the Newtonian revolution in science and by the probing deployment of reason in the fields of philosophy, history, and social critique in Enlightenment thought. This fascination with origins would motivate two, sometimes contradictory, lines of investigation, one philosophical and best exemplified by the rigorist writings and teachings of the Abbé Laugier in Paris and of Fra Carlo Lodoli in Venice, the other historical and motivating a new zeal for recording at first hand the physical remains of antiquity. In the 1750s an alliance between archaeological exploration and architectural theory was inaugurated which would continue through the nineteenth century.

France, largely through the prestige of its national Academy of Architecture, gained a new primacy in architectural theory during these years. Two events set the stage intellectually for architectural debate in the middle decades of the century when built production was slowed first by the War of Austrian Succession (1740–48) and then the Seven Years' War (1756–63): the publication in 1750 of the prospectus for Diderot and d'Alembert's *Encyclopédie*, and the lectures in the same year at the Sorbonne given by the encyclopaedist, philosopher, and physiocrat Anne-Robert Turgot, notably his *Philosophic Panorama of the Progress of the Human Mind*. Diderot's hesitation over the place architecture should occupy in the system of knowledge which organized the encyclopaedia—whether it was more properly placed under the faculty of reason or that of imagination—reopened an ancient debate that subsequent generations would play out as they sought to align architecture's power to move and shape users' responses alternately with rhetoric and poetry or the growing prestige of science. The explosion of architectural research, travel, and publishing after 1750 was launched in the spirit of Diderot's determination to examine every domain freed from the shackles of tradition, of church dogma, and of received superstition. In the spirit of Voltaire and of Turgot, whose commitment to progress would colour the entire period, architects grappled with the overarching challenge of Enlightenment philosophy: how to reconcile the quest for primary eternal truths with a growing awareness of the relativity and contingency of man's cultural expressions. How could one conceive an architecture which responded both to reason and to that spirit of progress and, additionally, to that of cultural relativity articulated by Montesquieu who, in his widely read *Spirit of the Laws* of 1747, had established that societies were as much the products of local laws of climate, system of government, and traditions as they were of unchanging human nature?

Battles over relative and absolute truths and the respective merit of ancient models and modern innovations had erupted periodically in the French Academy of Architecture since its founding in 1671, most famously in the debates over Claude Perrault's challenge to the authority of the Classical orders and their systems of proportion, set down in the commentaries to his 1673 French translation of Vitruvius's *Ten Books on Architecture*. By the 1750s the decades-old 'quarrel of the ancients and moderns' was being played out in the lively arena of essays, pamphlets, and journals, breaching the walls of the Academy to find a place in the literary salons and coffee houses that were new centres of debate among a limited, but expanding, reading public.

The battle of the ancients vs the moderns and Laugier's rationalist theory

In publishing his polemical *Essay on Architecture* (1753) as an anonymous pamphlet, the Jesuit priest and amateur aesthetician Marc-Antoine Laugier (1713–69) divorced these debates from antiquarian exchange and introduced them into a Parisian marketplace of ideas already abuzz with challenges to prevailing tastes, both for the decorative Rococo in aristocratic interiors and an Italianizing academic Baroque tradition in church design. These fashions were attacked not in the name of taste alone, but primarily of reason. Signing a second edition in 1755—by

Frontispiece for the second edition of Marc-Antoine (Abbé) Laugier's *Essay on Architecture*, Paris, 1755
Clutching a compass and right angle, and reclining on the elements of an Ionic order, the muse of architecture directs attention away from the preoccupation of earlier treatises with harmonious proportions and towards a more essential truth of structural clarity embodied in mankind's first structure.

which time an English translation had appeared and a German version was in preparation—Laugier answered his critics and added the famous frontispiece [1] of the primitive hut which encapsulated his theory in allegorical form. The hut had been a standard feature of architectural theory since Vitruvius; but never before had it been proposed as anything more than a fanciful story of the primitive origins of architecture.

Laugier's radical step was to propose this origin as a moment of higher truth: 'All the splendors of architecture ever conceived have been modeled on the little rustic hut I have just described. It is by approaching the simplicity of this first model that fundamental mistakes are avoided and true perfection is achieved'[1] An irreducible construct of logic, the hut was to be emulated, not copied. It provided a norm of procedure rather than a model, an answer to the quest for what Laugier calls 'fixed and unchanging laws'.

Laugier's thought was deeply affected by recent philosophy, not only in his constant appeal to reason, but in his belief that the hut itself, although a first construct of man, could be accorded the status almost of a natural law. His work parallels in striking ways the contemporary development of Jean-Jacques Rousseau's early work in which nature was lauded as a corrective to the artifice of evolved society, most famously in the 1755 *Discourse on the Origin of Inequality*, with its figure of the noble savage as the type of man in a natural, almost secular, state of grace. Rousseau himself admitted that this original man was purely imaginary, just as Laugier was unconcerned to document the real existence of the hut. Laugier's was not a work of archaeology, history, or even of allegory, but rather of philosophical aesthetics. The first hut embodied in its simplicity a process of imitation that could reform architecture and ground it again in reason. It already comprised all the elements of architecture: upright column, spanning entablature and protective sloping roof. All else was licence, the products of civilization rather than nature. Such elements as walls, necessary for protection but not for structural support, were never to be employed unaware of their artifice or without deference to these primary elements. His notion of function was strictly one of construction rather than of use or programme. 'By imitating the natural process, art was born,'[2] Laugier asserted, dismissing what he viewed as the superficial imitations of the outward appearances of nature in the Rococo and establishing the Greek temple as the first example of the application of a natural law of structural reasoning. Columns, for instance, taper because plants do, as well as in relation to the load they carry. 'Let us keep to the simple and the natural, it is the only road to beauty,'[3] Laugier concludes, establishing ethical criteria of truth which would have a long life in modern architectural theory.

The *Essay* unleashed a fury of rebuttals; but as a revolutionary tract it was heralded immediately. Even that great advocate of moderation, Jacques-François Blondel (1705–74), whose influential private school of architecture, founded in 1743, was to foster many of the most innovative talents of the next generation, notably C.-N. Ledoux and William Chambers, recommended it to his students. Although accessible to a broad audience, Laugier underscored that his main aim was to form the taste of architects. Coupled with Blondel's use of site visits to hone visual judgements, Laugier's logic became a form of operable criticism. His principles were endowed with the simplicity that the Enlightenment associated with nature's laws. Pilasters were proscribed as 'bizarre', arcades as 'vicious', and columns on pedestals as 'against nature'. Pediments were to be used only when they corresponded to a sloping roof, never as a mere device for crowning a façade. Superimposed orders should never represent several storeys on the exterior when this is not the case within.

Not that Laugier advocated the application of free-standing temple fronts to all classes of buildings. The *Essay* upheld the academic decorum of *convenance* or appropriateness, and its sense of a hierarchy of building types by function and social class. And Laugier postulates beautiful buildings even without orders, for as he admits, not everyone can afford columns! Only the three Grecian orders were condoned, although he hinted that in the future new orders might be devised. A return to origins was by no means an impediment to progress; rather it was an essential first step. Although his normative vision of nature parallels Rousseau's, Laugier did not envision an architecture critical of the reigning social order. His was the more limited agenda of reforming taste and allowing the light of reason to illuminate a subject that had, he felt, become encumbered by tradition and rules.

The Graeco-Gothic synthesis and the debate over the ideal church

As Laugier sought to accommodate the Grecian model to modern demands, he was led to the challenging idea that French Gothic architecture, for which he otherwise shared the period's disdain, might none the less offer lessons for achieving a light and airy structural aesthetic. The notion of a Graeco-Gothic synthesis had been anticipated in earlier treatises, by Michel de Frémin (*Mémoires critiques d'architecture*, 1702) and Jean-Louis Cordemoy (*Nouveau traité de toute l'architecture*, 1706), both of whom proposed an ideal church of free-standing columns and entablatures supporting vaulting above, all brought together with the structural precision of Gothic construction, which they heralded as supremely rational.

As Laugier was writing, these ideas were being explored by two architects, Jacques-Germain Soufflot (1713–80) and Pierre Contant d'Ivry (1698–1777), both of whom would be entrusted in the 1750s with major Parisian church commissions that offered a testing-ground for these theoretic propositions of uniting a monumental Classical revival with a progressive and experimental architecture. As early as 1741 Soufflot delivered an altogether surprising discourse on Gothic architecture before the Academy of Lyon. A decade later Contant d'Ivry began exploring the theme of a Graeco-Gothic synthesis in building with St-Vasnon at Condé-sur-l'Escaut (begun 1751) and St-Vaast at Arras (begun 1753),

both in French Flanders where the tradition of the hall church provided prototypes for these attempts to rival the openness of Gothic space with the forms and monumentality of Classical construction.

The theme of a possible synthesis of two architectures—styles long considered antithetical but now upheld as parallel rational structural models, one in Classical trabeation, the other in medieval arcuation—represented a notion ripe with significance for the revival of the progressive 'modern' position and would echo in historicist architectural thought for the next century. In *Observations on Architecture* (1765) Laugier pursued his ideas to even more radical conclusions, proposing that the emulation of branching trees could lead to an altogether novel architecture. This idea had only limited direct influence, most strikingly in the curiously beautiful and paradoxically Rococo rendering of Laugier's ideas in Johann Friedrich Dauthe's remodelling of St Nicholas, Leipzig [2] around 1784.

The rediscovery of Greece

'Architecture owes all that is perfect to the Greeks,'[4] Laugier asserted in 1753, echoing a growing French commonplace, although he had never seen a Greek temple at first hand. Neither for that matter had that German antiquarian and pioneering historian of art, Johann Joachim Winckelmann (1717–68), who extolled the 'quiet grandeur and noble simplicity' of Greek art as an unrivalled standard in his *Reflections on the Imitation of the Painting and Sculpture of the Greeks*, published in Dresden in 1755. Winckelmann's renowned but paradoxical assertion that 'there is but one way for the moderns to become great, even inimitable; I mean, by imitating the Greeks',[5] was an early tremor in one of the most sustained polemical exchanges of the century, the Greek vs Roman controversy. The epicentre remained Rome, to which a cosmopolitan world of antiquarians, touring aristocrats, and royalty, as well as architects of the most diverse nationalities, travelled. The debates, engaged on Classical ground and reinforced by archaeological pilgrimages to Paestum, Greece, Dalmatia, and even Syria, soon reverberated in the centres of architectural thought and practice in Paris, London, and Berlin, as well as in numerous smaller courts from Parma to Copenhagen where architects—especially those from the French Academy in Rome—were solicited by rulers on the Grand Tour to reform building and artistic training.

Archaeological research, travel, and publication in the 1750s and 1760s, much undertaken in fierce intellectual and personal competition, was driven as much by a concern to reform contemporary taste as to deepen knowledge of the Classical world. Discovery of the lost cities of Herculaneum (1739) and Pompeii (1748) revealed that antique culture had been but partially understood and recorded. The influence of these ancient cities lost to Vesuvius was principally to be felt in a taste

Piranesi and the Grand Tour

Giovanni Battista Piranesi (1720–78) was born near Venice, trained as an architect and absorbed the radical thought of Lodoli. In Rome after 1740 he began engraving views of the city and its ruins, capturing the imaginations and purses of artists and aristocrats on the Grand Tour.

The Grand Tour, an increasingly canonical tour of Mediterannean culture and antiquities, studded with the acquisition of both art treasures and social graces, was to serve also as one of the great motors of the dissemination of Neoclassical taste, particularly among the English. Piranesi's powerful pictorial style transformed perception of the ruined remains of the Roman, Etruscan, and eventually even Greek past for several generations of artists, architects, and clients. Inspired by Baroque stage-craft, particularly dramatic low and oblique viewpoints, Piranesi favoured dramatic chiaroscuro shading. He particularly influenced students at the French Academy, across from his shop in the Corso. As an architect he remodelled two churches in Rome, the eccentric church for the Order of Malta, Santa Maria del Priorato (1764) on the Aventine Hill, and St John the Lateran.

Selected books
Opere Varie (1750)
Antichità Romane (1756)
Delle Magnificenze ed Architettura de' Romani (1761)
Campo Marzio (1762), dedicated to Robert Adam
Diverse maniere d'adornare i cammini (1769)

for Pompeiian style in decorative arts and interior decoration. This began with Robert Wood and James Dawkins's publications of the ancient Roman cities of Palmyra and Balbec in the Levant (*The Ruins of Palmyra*, London, 1753 and *The Ruins of Balbec*, London, 1757). It continued with the quest to publish accurate measured drawings from the Greek mainland; a series of luxurious plate books made views of long-fabled monuments available both to form the taste of patrons and inform the compositions of architects. The superiority of Greek culture, and the exemplary beauty of the Athenian Parthenon in particular, were largely articles of faith, since few had made the difficult voyage to the Ottoman-ruled peninsula. As travellers to the ancient Greek colony of Paestum, south of Naples [3], and then to the Peloponnese returned with measured drawings, discrepancies between Greek and Roman monuments caused a major questioning of the creed of a unitary Classical ideal.

The rivalry of Stuart and Revett with Leroy

James Stuart (1713–88) and Nicholas Revett's (1720–1804) pioneering *Antiquities of Athens*, conceived as early as 1748, was overtaken by several parallel and rival undertakings by the time their first volume appeared in London in 1762 [4], notably, and much to Stuart's chagrin, by the Frenchman Julien David Leroy's *Ruins of the Most Beautiful Monuments of Greece*, rushed into publication in 1758. Each project was initially framed simply to expand the corpus of sources beyond Antoine Desgodet's *Antiquités de Rome* (1682), which had long been the unrivalled source for measured drawings of ancient monuments. However,

4

James Stuart sketching the Erechtheion on the Acropolis, 1751

Stuart and Revett's expedition to Ottoman-occupied Greece provided the first accurately measured engravings of Greek architecture. Stuart adopted local attire to ease his work. He was so determined to extract an unadulterated vision of antiquity that he paid the owner of a house abutting the famous Tower of the Winds for the cost of demolition and reconstruction that he might free the Hellenistic monument momentarily from later accretions.

in the end they highlighted important differences between Greek and Roman buildings, hitherto considered stages in the refinement of a single canon. Setting out to endow architecture with absolute authority, Stuart and Revettt and Leroy unwittingly introduced notions of variety and fostered a debate over the relative merits of models. This, in turn, cast into high relief conflicting notions of the roles of imitation and invention in architectural design, the relation of modern culture to tradition, the nature of architectural progress, and the very matter of taste. Within a few years nearly all the key figures articulating both the ideology and the imagery of a Classical revival in architecture were drawn into this debate, from the fiery Venetian architect/artist Giovanni Battista Piranesi (1720–78), already famous for his engravings of the remains of ancient Rome, to the German Winckelmann, now keeper of antiquities at the Villa Albani in Rome, and to the Scotsman Allan Ramsey (1713–84) who in 1755 published his 'Dialogue on Taste' anonymously in *The Investigator*, setting Greece over Rome as the source of excellence in the arts.

Personal rivalries between architectural travellers were soon coloured by nascent nationalism. The English Society of Dilettanti, founded in 1733–34 to promote foreign travel and 'Greek taste and Roman spirit' among gentlemen and artists alike, had provided a small subsidy to Stuart and Revett. The enterprise, they hoped, would turn a profit, reform taste, and even bring glory to England. Difficult work-

ing conditions led Stuart and Revett to abandon their plan of giving priority to the key Periclean monuments of the Acropolis, and scrupulous standards of accuracy kept them in Athens for 3 years. When their first volume at last appeared (the fourth and last was issued only in 1818), many, including Winckelmann, admitted disappointment in finding smaller monuments illustrated rather than the Parthenon, Erechtheion and Propylaeum, all of which might have substantiated Winckelmann's theory of direct causal relations between Greek artistic perfection and the social, political, and topographical context of the Periclean achievement. Historical analysis was not remotely part of Stuart and Revett's conception.

Leroy (1724–1803) from the first envisioned Greek monuments as existing in a larger context, even travelling to Constantinople during his 1754–5 tour to see at first hand a broad range of post-antique monuments. At the French Academy in Rome from 1751 to 1754 he formed contacts in the circle of the Comte de Caylus (1692–1765), a wealthy antiquarian and collector whose researches were lavishly published as *Recueil d'antiquités égyptiennes, etrusques, grecques, romaines et gaulloises* (1752–65), the first work to treat ancient monuments as historical testaments. With Caylus's support, Leroy enlisted some of the leading architects of the day to engrave his drawings and consulted the historian Abbé Bathélemey on his text. By the time it appeared in 1758, his book too had taken on the aura of a national project.

Stuart and Revett devoted most of their short introduction to lambasting Leroy for inaccuracies; Leroy retorted in a revised edition (1770) that 'The ruins of ancient buildings can be envisioned from very different perspectives ... to servilely provide measurements'[6] had never, he claimed, been his intent. Radically different notions about the value of archaeological knowledge for modern architecture were reflected in these disputes. Debate quickly focused on whether or not ancient monuments were to be studied in order to approach a greater fidelity in reproducing the different ornaments and parts of the Classical orders or to gain insight into how civilizations gave rise to architectural forms. This, in turn, should guide the quest for a modern architecture worthy of the same respect and authority as antique architecture.

Stuart demonstrated one use of his plates in his own designs, reproducing, for example, the baseless Doric order of the Parthenon and the Thesius in garden pavilions at Hagley Park in Worcestershire in 1758 [5] and creating, the following year, a stunning interior at Spencer House in London replete with reproductions of ancient Greek furniture designs. For Thomas Anson, a founding member of the Society of Dilettanti, Stuart created a nearly identical temple in the landscape garden at Shugborough in Staffordshire, where follies based on the Tower of the Winds and of the Arch of Hadrian in Athens soon fol-

5 James Stuart

Doric Temple at Hagley, Worcestershire, 1758

The reproduction of historical architecture found its easiest application in small garden pavilions where recollections of other times and places added a dimension of world travel and the universe of knowledge to the experience of nature in the evolving aesthetic of the English picturesque landscape style. With the almost precious scale of this building, architecture was essentially on display.

6 Julien David Leroy

View of the Propylaea, Athens, *Les ruines des plus beaux monuments de la Grèce*, Paris, 1758

The first to publish a survey of ancient Greek monuments, Leroy juxtaposed picturesque views of the ruins and detailed measured plates of the orders with a handful of reconstructions in which he unabashedly 'corrected' the monuments according to the modern vision of Classical antiquity as a model of symmetry, regularity, and imposing scale.

lowed. Juxtaposed with Shugborough's earlier pavilions evoking China and its newly created rustic ruins, Stuart's travel souvenirs entered a complex visual discourse of accurate but discrete historical images, evocations of distant times and places in which Greece was but one of a series of cultures identified with distinctive styles. For Anson's London residence, Litchfield House, St James's Square (1764), Stuart introduced a columnar front with pediment and the novel forms of the newly recorded Grecian Ionic order of the Erechtheion, an advertisement at once for Anson's refined taste and for Stuart's contributions to erudite aristocratic culture.

Leroy made clear from the outset that models of imitation were never his intent, although he provided measured drawings and picturesque views of Athenian monuments [6]. Proposing an intimate relationship between the evolution of society and architectural

elements—most particularly the Doric order for which he proposed three distinct phases—Leroy married the concerns of architectural aesthetics and standards with the new history of Voltaire and Turgot. Greek architecture is analysed as a piece with Greek society, Greek learning, even Greek science, suggesting a kind of coherence in cultural forms that was a more valuable lesson for modern cultural identity than the specific forms of the orders. But Leroy went further, situating progress in Greek culture within a larger panorama of architectural developments, offering the image of a historical chain in which the Greeks forged the key links between the Egyptians and the Phoenicians on the one hand and the temples of the Christians, reached via the Byzantine churches he had visited en route to Athens, on the other. Leroy's research reflected an awareness of the current debate on the ideal church, and suggested that the answer would come not from a new canon of forms but from the evolutionary history of architecture. The Greek temple was proposed not as an inviolate type of perfection, but rather as a moment of harmony and perfection on a longer developmental continuum. Leroy attributed the Greeks' artistic excellence to favourable climate and social and political systems, but unlike Winckelmann he did not endorse the notion that the Greeks were unsurpassable. A longer view of the evolution of their achievements gave insight into the complex dynamics of historical change. By the time of his second edition in 1770, Leroy's theory of architecture was fully grounded in a theory of history. He sought, in the spirit of Montesquieu, to distinguish between that which was specific to a given societal configuration and that which was incontrovertibly universal. For the latter he drew on the latest elaboration of John Locke's theory of human sensations to argue for universal laws of human response to the environment as a constant in a world of continual historical evolution. The new history of artistic styles and the quest for absolute laws of architecture were momentarily allied; Leroy shared Laugier's quest for laws but he focused architects' attention on the study of real rather than mythic artefacts.

The battle of the Greeks vs the Romans and Piranesi

Stuart's anger paled in comparison to the ire Leroy's promotion of Greek excellence drew from the famous print-maker and *cicerone* Piranesi. Having based his fortune on promoting Roman antiquities, Piranesi viewed Winckelmann's claims, followed by Leroy's illustrations, as a threat to both his national pride and his personal livelihood. It spurred him to new artistic and polemical brilliance in 38 plates gathered together in 1761 under the polemical title *Of the Magnificence and the Architecture of Rome*, powerfully recording the sublime scale and power of Roman architecture. In a lengthy text, the first of a series of bombastic polemical writings that became increasingly shrill, even

paranoid, in tone through the decade, he sought, largely in an instinctive and reactive way, to define a theory of architecture. Piranesi argues that the Romans developed their architecture directly from the Etruscans, an older race than the Greeks, who brought the arts to a state of impressive perfection when Greek civilization was still in its infancy. He celebrated Etruscan skill in construction, claiming that such great works of infrastructure as the Cloaca Maxima, the aqueducts, circuses, and roads were all foundations upon which the Roman Empire later built its engineering prowess. The Etruscans, he asserted with little concern for historical documentation, learned the art of monumental building in stone directly from the Egyptians. Next to this rugged tradition, the Greeks offered an almost effete concern with beauty. Their architecture was concerned more with ornaments than the essence of architecture as a structure, echoing perhaps something of the rigorist thinking developed in Venice by Lodoli and his followers in the 1740s. Carried away by the strength of his own rhetoric, Piranesi even asserted that Greek influence was a principal factor in Roman architecture's decline from reason to caprice in the late empire, when Greek workmen and fashion permeated Italian culture [**7**]. Piranesi's nascent nationalism, over a century before Italian unification, was soon echoed in Etruscan academies that sprang up in Latium

8 Piranesi

Preparatory study for *Parere su l'architettura*, (Kunstbibliothek, Berlin), *c.*1765

With a brash and impassioned plea for originality in architecture, Piranesi imagined an architectural language drawn from a wide variety of architectural sources all governed by the compositional imagination of the individual designer.

and Tuscany as local antiquarians began to reconstruct a nativist genealogy for culture on Italian soil.

Imitation vs invention

As the polemic gained adherents, Piranesi was led to issue one of the most impassioned and ultimately moving pleas for the primacy of artistic genius and invention over rigid rules of imitation. The idiosyncratic *Parere su l'architettura* (*Views on Architecture*) (1765) offers for the first time a series of his own architectural compositions [**8**] in which he reveals an imagination unfettered by archaeological precedent, a position advanced with a brilliant sense of irony on the frontispiece, which cites without acknowledgement a quip from Leroy's own polemical exchanges with Stuart and Revett: 'In order not to make of the sublime art

Planche XI

Temple de Neptune à Pesto, vu de côté, et dessiné plus en grand, qu'on ne le voit dans la premiere planche

9 Piranesi

Temple of Neptune as illustrated in *Différentes vues de quelques restes … de l'ancienne ville de Pesto*, 1778

When he visited the ancient Greek colony at Paestum, south of Naples, near the end of his life, Piranesi was so moved that he created some of his most deeply felt and richly evocative engravings, capturing a sense of looming monumentality and powerful play of light and shadow on these stout and rugged Doric columns.

of architecture a vile trade in which one simply copies without discretion'. Four years later in a portfolio of his own fantastic designs for fireplaces, *Different Manners for Decorating Fireplaces and all other Parts of Buildings* (1769), Piranesi summarized his position: 'After having used Etruscan architecture through several centuries the Romans also had recourse to the Greek manner and united both. Similarly the modern architect must not be satisfied with being a faithful copyist of the ancients, but based on the study of their works must display an inventive and—I am tempted to say—creative genius; and by wisely combining the Greek, Etruscan, and Egyptian styles, one must give rise to the discovery of new decorations and new manners.'[7] Perhaps the ultimate irony is that the forceful proportions and volumetric presence of the Greek Doric were to have their greatest influence only a decade after the battle of the Greeks and Romans had subsided, inspired less by the lengthy arguments of Leroy's second edition than by Piranesi's brilliant engravings of the Greek temples of Paestum, first issued in 1778 [**9**].

Philosophy of history and the new church of Ste-Geneviève

Leroy's progressive vision of history and Piranesi's brilliant visualization of the power of ancient architecture came together in the church of Ste-Geneviève, whose design and construction remained at the centre of French architectural debate for over 30 years, even as its monumental Corinthian portico and tall dome dominated the skyline of

10 J.-G. Soufflot

Perspective view of the projected church of Ste-Geneviève, Paris, 1757, engraved by J. C. Bellicard

Soufflot's design would evolve over the next 20 years, most particularly in the design of the dome; but from the first the idea of combining a Classical temple portico with the dome characteristic of the greatest churches of Christianity reflected his notion that a modern architecture would evolve from a synthetic use of major themes from historic architecture.

Paris. The choice of Soufflot as architect, over the royal architect Ange-Jacques Gabriel (1698–1782), was a linchpin of the architectural politics of the Marquis de Vandières, the future Marquis de Marigny, who since his appointment in 1751 as Director of Royal Buildings, had sought to realign taste to a purer vision of the antique. With this appointment Marigny married the revolution in taste with the politics of royal architecture, since the project of rebuilding the ancient and venerated church of Paris's patron saint was a key element in Louis xv's quest to hone his image as a king of peace and beneficence for a troubled realm as well as to assert the independence of the Gallican church from Rome. Soufflot was not only well placed as Marigny's former tutor, but had distinguished himself with a series of distinctive public buildings in Lyon, including a new hospital, the Hôtel-Dieu (1741), the Commercial Exchange (1747–50), and most recently the Grand Théâtre (1754), the first of the series of free-standing theatres that were to reshape urban centres and sociability in the mid-eighteenth century.

Soufflot's project was continually revised and refined over the long years of construction, marking it as the foremost of a number of experimental buildings where the aesthetic and structural limits of architecture were tested and debated. In the design published in 1757 [10] the monumental free-standing temple front juxtaposed with a dome over a Greek-cross plan and the marriage of colonnades with a series of domical vaults on the interior marks this building as a milestone in the re-

11 Soufflot

Church of Ste-Geneviève (now Panthéon), Paris, 1757–89 interior

turn to antique purity and a new refinement of the Graeco-Gothic synthesis. The columns are not only modelled on the most recent archaeological discoveries—the baseless Doric of Paestum somewhat hesitatingly evoked in the crypt and the richly decorative Corinthian of Balbec carefully reproduced in the nave and portico—but deployed innovatively as point supports to carry vaults reduced to their minimum shape and mass. Years later one of Soufflot's collaborators, Maximilien

12 Soufflot

Section of the 1764 project for the church of Ste-Geneviève, Paris

A true modern, Soufflot continued to rework and refine his project, seeking ever greater effects of a light-filled cage of minimized structure and spatial transparency. The whole was to be pierced with large-scale windows which would silhouette the free-standing columns.

Brébion, summed up the architect's intent: 'to unite under one of the most beautiful forms the purity and magnificence of Greek architecture with the lightness and audacity of gothic construction'.[8] Greek architecture was capable of further perfection; Gothic offered lessons to construction but was not yet honoured itself as architecture [11].

Interpreting his brief to create a monument for the popular cult of Ste Geneviève to replace the dilapidated medieval church contained within the abbey complex, Soufflot imagined his building framed on three sides by an ample public space like an antique temple protruding into its forum, where several new streets might be made to converge. This dramatic staging in urban space was to be continued within where the open spaciousness of the structural frame would be emphasized by a flood of clear light from tall windows ringing the building. Laugier's call a few years earlier for an architecture in which every element had a structural rationale was given monumental expression. Soufflot set out to avoid the use of pilasters on both the interior and exterior façades, using only a series of projections to articulate the transitions of volumes in the massing of his cross-shaped plan. Construction began in 1758 on the crypt but progressed slowly as building throughout the French capital was all but halted during the Seven Years' War. By the time Louis xv laid the cornerstone on 6 September 1764, Soufflot had revised his project substantially [12], underscoring the role of the building as an urban-scaled reliquary for the remains of Geneviève, the fifth-century saint whose role in the conversion of the French monarchy to Christianity and in deflecting Attila the Hun's invading forces from

As they would be hidden from view in the completed building, Soufflot was able to experiment with a complex system of iron tie rods to reinforce the carefully calculated arcuated and vaulted structure of his building. He took direct inspiration from the earlier work of Claude Perrault in the colonnade (east front) of the Louvre Palace, which Soufflot was restoring during the same years he was designing the new church.

the capital took on new political resonance in Louis XV's determination to assert the primacy of the Gallican church and the glory of his own most Christian reign, even as France saw many of her overseas colonies, notably Canada, transferred to Great Britain by the Treaty of Paris (1763).

An experimental design and construction site

Determined to elevate further the dome, crowned by a statue to mark the saint's reign over her city, Soufflot raised both the profile and the stakes of his daring design. For the rest of the decade he experimented ceaselessly and relentlessly, modifying his project even as doubts were voiced that this pursuit of perfection was leading the architect beyond the limits of empirical reason. He invented machines to test the strength of materials and consulted his friend Jean-Rodolphe Perronet (1708–94), the leading engineer of the day, famous for innovative bridge designs and as the founder of the first professional training for engineers at the École des Ponts-et-Chaussées in 1747. With Perronet's pupil É.-M. Gauthey he studied different stones, and continued to examine French Gothic buildings for historical lessons. Finally a system of iron-reinforced masonry was devised to serve as an armature for lightweight spatial and structural effects [**13**]. In short, Soufflot turned the design process and the building site into a quasi-scientific labora-

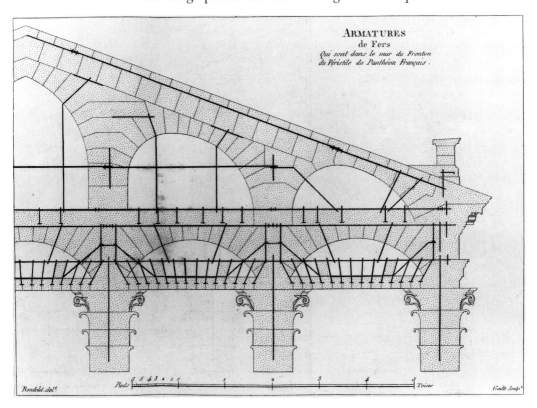

ARMATURES
de Fers
Qui sont dans le mur du Fronton
du Péristile du Panthéon Français.

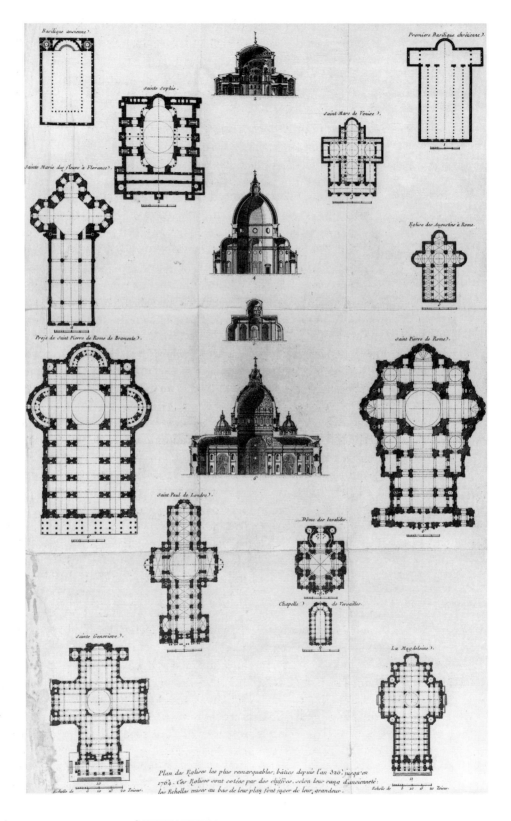

Baaislique ancienne.

Sainte Sophie.

Premiere Basilique chrétienne.

Saint Marc de Venise.

Sainte Marie des fleurs à Florence.

Eglise des Augustins à Rome.

Projet de saint Pierre de Rome de Bramante.

Saint Pierre de Rome.

Saint Paul de Londre.

Dôme des Invalides.

Chapelle de Versailles.

Sainte Geneviève.

La Magdeleine.

Plan des Eglises les plus remarquables, bâties depuis l'an 320, jusqu'en 1764. Ces Eglises sont cotées par des chiffres, selon leur rang d'ancienneté. les Echelles mises au bas de leur plan font juger de leur grandeur.

Echelle de   Toises.

Echelle de   Toises.

14 Julien David Leroy

Engraved plate illustrating the development of the Christian church type, Paris, 1764

Leroy's small book was dedicated to Marigny, whose reign Leroy hoped would bring a new historical flourishing to the art of architecture. Its only illustration was this genealogy of the Christian church type, culminating in the plans of the two great enterprises of Louis XV's religious politics: Ste-Geneviève (*bottom left*) and the Madeleine church (*bottom right*).

tory which confirmed his belief that even a building designed to embody the mysteries of Christian faith could be perfected by the application of human reason.

The effort to perfect the very type of the Christian church building went beyond a mastery of the laws of construction and the natural laws of architectural form; Soufflot, supported by his friend Leroy, sought to master the laws of history as well. For the inauguration Leroy returned to historical arguments he had developed in his publication of ancient Greek architecture and extended them to a developmental history of the Christian church type. This was summed up in a single image in which Leroy arranged the floor plans, and selected sections of Christianity's principal monuments [**14**]. With this, a historical mission was supplied to the two great enterprises launched simultaneously by Louis XV: Ste-Geneviève and the new church of the Madeleine, inaugurated a few months later and designed by Contant d'Ivry. Leroy offered a veritable genealogical tree of the Christian temple, beginning with the first adaptation of the Roman basilican plan to Christian worship and proceeding through a series of churches, each a refinement of its ancestors. The central problem, worked out over centuries, was how to marry the image of the Christian cross inscribed in the Latin-cross floor plan with a grand cupola which could represent the cosmos on earth and make the Christian temple an experience of the infiniteness of creation in the perfect space contained within a dome. Leroy's 'family tree' showed the progressive refinement of this form by technical experimentation as domes ever taller and more complex in section were carried on crossings ever more reduced in material structure and ever more conducive to open vistas within the church interior. The principal monuments of the great Christian capitals, including Hagia Sophia in Constantinople, the cathedral of Florence, St Peter's in Rome, and St Paul's in London, which Soufflot had asked his colleague Pierre Patte (1732–1814) to measure up, were all descendants of the first experiment. In the seventeenth century the historic mission passed to France, taken up in Louis XIV's church of the Invalides and royal chapel at Versailles, a pioneer of the free-standing, colonnade-carrying vaults. The challenge for Soufflot was to discern the developmental law inscribed in the church type's own history and to carry it to a new level of perfection.

The two agendas, architectural and political, met in one of the most extravagant public pageants of the century, when Louis XV laid the cornerstone before a full-scale mock-up of Soufflot's temple front on a quickly cleared public *place*, now treated as an amphitheatre to be formed by the concave façades of the future faculties of law and theology proposed to complete this Gallican complex. The cornerstone contained a copy of Leroy's *History of the Form and the Layout which Christians have given their Temples from Constantine to our own Time.*

An Enlightenment philosophy of history literally became the cornerstone of the new building. In the same year, Winckelmann published his *History of Ancient Art* in both French and German, in which a system of cultural evolution rather than individual genius was portrayed as the motor of stylistic progression. Not surprisingly, the seeds of modern art history and of historical philosophy in architecture were planted at the same time.

Leroy also explained that Soufflot's attempt to open his building to a maximum of light was calculated not simply for an aesthetics of luminosity but to give him the raw material to instil specific experiences. Ste-Geneviève was a great forest of columns, lifted above the ground since the side aisles were raised several steps, creating simultaneously a continuous plinth for the columns and a stage for the processions that would weave behind them. Leroy extols the ways in which, from this rational grid of structure, the richest effects could be achieved from the interplay of solid form, changing light, and a processing pilgrim. Looking through two rows of columns silhouetted against a wall pierced with large windows, as 'the spectator [moves he] will be presented with a succession of the most varied and changing views which result from the infinite combination of these simple objects—column and wall'.[9] Continually shifting diagonal views open and close in this orthogonal space, making the whole into a theatre in which light is manipulated and the building dramatizes the experience of nature and human movement, to awe and provoke the mind through the sensations of the eye and the body—to stimulate in short a contemplation of the divine. Soufflot drew not only on the science of construction and the newly discovered historical laws, but also on new theories of human perception and experience.

By 1770 Soufflot had developed a remarkable system of three superimposed masonry domes [**15**], creating at once a high exterior profile and, on an intermediary dome, a mysteriously lit surface viewed through the oculus of the innermost dome. Here was a great fresco of the apotheosis of Sainte Geneviève. This final effect even relied upon Gothic buttresses, carefully hidden from view behind the parapets of the perimeter walls, in the quest to direct structural loads efficiently. But before construction had begun on the dome Soufflot's project was again at the heart of a controversy, this time launched by his former ally Patte, who published a pamphlet questioning the stability of the dome, the first in a number of attacks, all of which wounded Soufflot's pride but spurred him none the less to continue his experiments. The controversy continued long after Soufflot's death in 1780, plaguing also his former assistants Brébion and Rondelet, who completed the dome around 1789. Contemporaries saw in it a stand-off between a new conception of architecture in which calculation and reason could lead to architecture's ultimate perfection versus a more traditionalist view of

the discipline of architecture which accorded a greater value to empirical knowledge acquired through experience. Subsequent historians have seen here a seminal rift between architect and engineer, one that would continue to grow through the nineteenth century, but Soufflot made no such distinction between the aesthetic and structural experiments married in his grand bid to bring architecture into line with the emerging Enlightenment faith in the progressive perfecting of humanity. As the building rose, debate took place as much over aesthetic preferences as intellectual adherence; many, including Blondel, objected that Soufflot's daring structure ran the risk of being more astonishing than pleasing.

The influence of Soufflot's church design

Soufflot's experiment was scarcely isolated. Not only did it continue a trajectory of exploration of a synthesis of both styles and structural techniques pursued by several of his contemporaries, but it was also to serve as a major impetus for that quest for perfecting French architecture which was the credo of the royal schools of architecture and of engineering. Elements of Soufflot's pursuit of open trabeation carrying cut-away vaults were echoed notably in the work of Gabriel, whose colonnades on the Place de la Concorde (1758–75) [**19**] pay homage to Perrault's Louvre and incorporate a series of pointed arched vaults behind, the columns thereby acting as buttresses. A series of parish churches begun in and around Paris after 1764, the year of the cornerstone of Ste-Geneviève, married the Graeco-Gothic analogy with a new archaeological interest in the Early Christian basilica, promoted by Leroy's studies. These include N.-M. Potain's design for St-Louis at St-Germain-en-Laye (1764), L.-F. Trouard's St-Symporien, Montreuil, near Versailles (1764–70), and most prominently J.-F.-T. Chalgrin's church of St-Philippe-du-Roule (approved 1768, built 1772–84) in Paris. French architects took something of this abroad—in these years French expertise was in high demand throughout continental Europe—notably Pierre Michel d'Ixnard in his curious reinterpretation of the Roman Pantheon in Graeco-Gothic terms for the abbey church of St Blasien in the German Black Forest (1768–80).

The lasting influence of Soufflot's design, completed finally in the 1780s and 1790s by his most loyal assistant at Ste-Geneviève, Jean-Baptiste Rondelet, was to be felt through the training of the Académie Royale d'Architecture, which since its founding under Louis XIV had seen considerable success in forging links between a corporate definition of architectural standards and the design of the most prestigious royal and public buildings. Since the 1720s—inspired by a practice already established in the Roman Accademia di San Luca—annual competitions had been a key component of the training of young architects, but after 1763 these were supplemented by monthly competitive exercises (*concours d'émulation*) requiring the students, frequently, to project a major public building in a matter of hours, thus honing their skills not only of rendering but of reasoning among the criteria of design. As the name implies, these competitions focused attention on the emulation of great models and instituted a type of thinking in composition that closely parallels Leroy's understanding of architectural programmes. In 1764 Leroy was appointed as Blondel's teaching assistant, remaining a leading force in the Academy for the rest of the century. Marie-Joseph Peyre (1730–85), who had won the *Grand Prix* in 1751, also contributed much to this thinking, publishing his own projects in the highly influential folio *Works in Architecture* (Paris, 1765). Among the exemplary designs was a project for a cathedral, originally submitted to a competition of the Accademia di San Luca, which was at once a purification of Bernini's St Peter's and Soufflot's Ste-Geneviève [see **23**] in light of Laugier's ideals and a purer geometric expression in planning. This vision of correcting history is a logical corollary of Leroy's emerging notion that St Peter's was but a link in a chain that future generations must continue to forge. The competition system in eighteenth-century academies had at its core the notion that history and architectural progress would be linked through the repeated design, comparison, and discussion of solutions to typological problems.

British architects in Rome: Chambers and Adam

The British Royal Academy in London was founded only in 1768, and could not until many years later even aspire to command a national discourse on architecture in a country where artistic culture was far less dependent on royal taste and patronage. Jockeying for private and royal clients and prestige, British architects were more zealous than their French counterparts in publishing luxurious volumes on antiquities because in a competitive market of reputations archaeological erudition was a credential suggesting that the most up-to-date and cosmopolitan antiquarianism could be offered for the interiors of London mansions and country houses.

Robert Adam (1728–92) determined after several years of practice in his native Scotland to try his prospects in London, but before he did he felt that an architectural Grand Tour was vital. He left for Rome in autumn 1754, 'convinced that my whole conception of architecture will become much more noble that I could ever have attained by staying in Britain'.[10] Three years in Rome was a calculated outlay shouldered by the whole Adam clan back in Edinburgh, and Adam set himself up grandly, as he would once again in London, so that he could bid for admission to Roman society and impress future clients. Keenly aware of the competition of British compatriots, including William Chambers (1723–96), already in Rome when Adam arrived, and fellow Scotsman Robert Mylne, who arrived shortly afterwards, Adam set about a feverish study of the antiquities. He took on the French architect and specialist in views of ruins, Charles-Louis Clérisseau, as drawing master, befriended Piranesi, and hired several young architects to help him in making moulds and drawings after antiquity on every scale from the Roman baths to fragments. In 1757 he travelled to the Dalmatian coast

Robert Adam (1728–92)

Trained in Scotland, where his father William Adam was leading architect until his death in 1748, Robert and his brother James opened an office in London after 1758 which became one of the most influential and innovative practices of the century. Their output was prodigious, including major country houses with their parks (e.g. Harewood House, 1759–71, Osterley Park, 1765–80, Newby Hall, 1767–80), castellated houses in Scotland (Culzean, 1777–92), city houses on all scales from mansions (Derby House, London, 1773–74) to terrace-house developments (Portland Place), churches (Mistley, Essex, 1776), and town planning (Pulteney Bridge, Bath, 1769–74, Charlotte Square, Edinburgh, 1791–1807).

Their greatest influence was in interiors, both for innovative planning techniques and delicate and colourful decorative vocabulary synthesized from an eclectic range of Classical sources and used to create a harmony of surfaces from wall paintings and stuccoing to ceilings, carpets, and furnishings. Their style was widely emulated on both sides of the Atlantic. Nearly 9,600 drawings by the Adam brothers were acquired by John Soane, who counted them among the great figures of an emerging modern British tradition.

so that he might return to London with a lavish folio publication on Diocletian's palace (*Ruins of the Palace of the Emperor Diocletian at Spalatro*, London, 1764), which he felt offered valuable lessons for a new monumental approach to grand domestic planning.

Although he styled himself 'Bob the Roman' in letters to his brother and future business partner James (1730–94), and remained loyal to Piranesi as the controversy over Greek architecture broke, Adam was no doctrinaire Roman. It was Chambers who would take up that cause with ardour, especially after the Society of Dilettanti financed additional voyages to Greece and the Levant in the 1760s. Chambers, educated in Blondel's school in Paris, feared that Stuart's promotion of a style of Grecian details might become the fashion, prompting English architects even further towards what he considered superficial obsession with details and decoration rather than mastery of the great principles of composition, harmony, and balance that a study of the Roman tradition could achieve. Like his teacher, Chambers sought to create a means of practice that partook of both the grandeur of the Romans and pragmatic common sense in his *Treatise on Civil Architecture* (London, 1759), one of the rare attempts in eighteenth-century England to offer a coherent body of architectural theory, rather than a manual, to guide practice.

Adam was equally determined to diminish the appeal of 'Athenian' Stuart's style, even managing within months of his own arrival in London to persuade the young patron Sir Nathaniel Curzon to prefer his designs for interior decoration to those already drawn up by Stuart for Curzon's country seat at Kedleston in Derbyshire. Yet in these very same years Adam was encouraging his brother James to extend his own Roman sojourn (1760–63) to include a trip to the Greek islands so that they could publish plates of a wide range of Greek architecture that could beat Stuart at his own game. Adam swore allegiance to no specific style. More than anyone, he took Piranesi's call for unshackled genius to heart; Piranesi in return dedicated one of his own most inventive exercises in archaeology, the recreation of the Roman Campus Martius, to Adam. When the Adam brothers announced in the first volume of their *Works in Architecture* in 1773 that they had created something of 'a Revolution' in architecture, it was not a style of universal truth that was proclaimed, but the signature Adam style, one of the most influential creations of eighteenth-century Britain in interior design and decorative arts. The Adam brothers proudly explained that in handling the orders they responded to individual circumstances as well as to personal taste. From his earliest designs Robert Adam devised a distinctive handling of the Ionic order, for instance, seeking 'a mean' between what he viewed as the heaviness of the Greek Ionic volume and the 'other extreme' of the much smaller Roman version. We might speak of a synthesis, but unlike the French there was no intellectualization or theory of history to back up the decision, endorsed only by the confident eye of the artist unabashedly expressing a personal taste. It was this celebration of savant empiricism which was the very essence of the philosophy of the picturesque, one of the most distinctive of British contributions to the experimental architecture of the second half of the eighteenth century. No less than the French, Adam brought an existing sensibility to the discovery of the antiquities of which he was to make such personal use in his long and protean career back in Britain. But over the years the picturesque, a term Adam used frequently himself, was to take on a more articulate intellectual clarity as he became versed in the thought of the Scottish aesthetician Lord Kames. Already under the tutelage of his father, William Adam, in an extensive Scottish country-house practice, Adam had developed a personal approach to the fashion for evocative garden 'follies', particularly in the Gothic style. On trips south he had discovered the pioneering picturesque architecture of Sir John Vanbrugh, one of the first to employ medievalizing style not only for its associations and evocations, but to liberate the composition of a building from the autonomous symmetries of Classical design in favour of an adjustment to the changing views of a moving spectator and to the landscape setting.

Robert Adam's early country-house designs

Within months of setting up in London, Adam had established himself as the most promising of young talents and attracted a roster of important clients, many sold on the Adam style to the detriment of established architects already at work on their estates. Edwin Lascelles of Harewood in Yorkshire, who had passed over Chambers in favour of the local architect John Carr, proved open in turn to Adam's helpful suggestions of improvements to Carr's design. In December 1758 Adam offered a critique of Matthew Brettingham and James Paine's Palladian design for Curzon at Kedleston and parlayed his portfolio of designs for garden structures into a commission for the 'management of his grounds'—providing designs for a lodge, bridge, cascade, and fishing pavilion in the guise of a hermit's hut. From the grounds Adam mounted his successful campaign to eliminate his competition, beginning with 'Athenian' Stuart. By 1759 Adam was fully in charge of the great house and estate, having also eliminated Paine, as he would do again later at Syon House, Middlesex (1760–69), Nostell Priory, Yorkshire (1765–80), and Alnwick Castle, Northumberland (c.1770–80).

Kedleston was Adam's manifesto of a fashionable new Classicism, evident in his reworking of Brettingham and Paine's façades as well as in his adaptation of the spaces and types of antique architecture to create astonishing settings for the social rituals and personal claims of his clients [16a, b]. If Adam was versed in history, it was not to unearth its

16 Robert Adam

Kedleston Hall

a) South (garden) elevation

The evocation of a Roman
triumphal arch brought a
whole new range of
associations to the country
estate of the landed
aristocracy at the same time
as it served as a
demonstration of those
staccato rhythms Adam called
'movement' in architecture.

b) Plan

Like his French
contemporaries Peyre and De
Wailly, Adam studied the
sequence of lobbied and
colonnaded spaces in ancient
Roman bath complexes as
sources for a new spatial
richness in grand domestic
interiors. At Kedleston the
sequence of rooms bears a
close relationship to Adam's
study of the layout of
Diocletian's palace at Spalato.

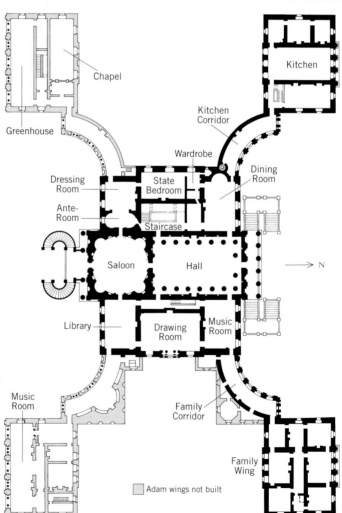

Chapel

Kitchen

Greenhouse

Kitchen
Corridor

Wardrobe

Dressing
Room

State
Bedroom

Dining
Room

Ante-
Room

Staircase

N

Saloon

Hall

Library

Drawing
Room

Music
Room

Music
Room

Family
Corridor

Family
Wing

Adam wings not built

underlying laws but to interpret, with great personal freedom, associations between the grandeur of the ancients and the quest for ascendancy and legitimacy, as well as fashion, among the English aristocracy, particularly the Whig aristocracy who cultivated the picturesque for its suggestions of natural law and liberty and the antique for its associations with their own political creed of democracy. At Kedleston, the application of a temple portico to the north or entrance front is still within the Palladian tradition of Lord Burlington. Adam was at greater liberty to make changes to the south front, where he juxtaposed the profile of a low saucer dome with a syncopated rhythm of free-standing columns crowned by statues evocative of a Roman triumphal arch. The house became at once a monument to its owner and his family and a demonstration of Adam's conception of 'movement', 'by which we mean the rise and fall, the advance and recess, with other diversity of form, in the different parts of a building, so as to add greatly to the picturesque of the composition'.[11] Movement applied not only to the path of the eye across a façade's surface but also to the sequence of spaces and experiences staged within. Drawing on the lessons of the Roman baths and of Diocletian's palace—as well as William Kent's earlier work at Holkham Hall, Norfolk—Adam created a central axis that leads from colonnaded hall to domed salon, a creative reinterpretation of the atrium–vestibule sequence in the ancient Roman house rendered here on a scale worthy of an emperor. Entirely top-lit, these central spaces provided an intense environment in which Adam calculated every detail and surface. He explored for the first time his favourite theme of relating ornamented treatments of the floors, here realized in inlaid marbles, to the rich stucco decoration of the ceilings. The design drew on an extraordinary range of antique sources from the grottoes of the Imperial Palace on the Roman Palatine Hill to the rich late-imperial motifs at Balbec and Palmyra. Work was entrusted to a team of artisans with whom Adam worked again and again, reminding us that Adam's signature pastel-colour palette and increasingly delicate ornamental line were in fact a corporate creation.

Few of Adam's great house commissions of the 1760s were realized *ex novo*, but it became increasingly a fundamental aspect of the picturesque philosophy that a designer should enter into a dialogue with the environment and the pre-existing, not only to find brilliant compositional solutions but even to play consciously with the overlay of meanings and associations in such interventions. At Syon House, outside London, Adam was almost entirely confined to the interior of a castellated Jacobean house [**17a, b, c**]. He was thwarted in his scheme to fill the courtyard of the building with a great rotunda—modelled like the salon at Kedleston on the Roman Pantheon—which could serve as the spatial focus. None the less he created in the four wings of

Syon House, Middlesex, 1760–69 **a)** View of the entrance hall

Screen walls and stairs not only add spatial richness but disguise asymmetries and changes of level that Adam encountered as he sought to endow an existing plan with grandeur and spatial coherence. This accepting attitude towards existing accidents and irregularities was a feature of the picturesque attitude in design.

b) The ante-chamber

The rich explosion of colours here is all the more effective as part of a chromatic sequence from the cool, stone-like tones of the entrance vestibule to the more delicate palette of the dining room. Adam's control of details was always intimately related to the social rituals of the house and the appropriate mood or demeanour for each of the great public rooms of the country house.

c) Plan

Adam's dream of a grand domed space at the centre of the plan to create cross-axes and a variety of paths in the existing courtyard layout of the Jacobean house was never realized. None the less he was able, by the use of screened niches and various surface treatments, to orchestrate a picturesque architectural and social circuit through the principal public rooms.

the house a picturesque circuit in which changes in floor levels and axes were brilliantly nuanced by the use of columnar screens and domed half-apses and in which the sense of sequence and the character of each space was carefully adjusted in the palette of both colours and materials. From the almost chilly whites, blacks and greys of the entrance hall, the eye is led, using carefully placed Roman statuary, much as Kent had earlier done in laying out a series of sequential viewpoints in picturesque garden design, towards the next space. The ante-room is an explosion of rich colours and reflections, from the high gloss of the scagliola columns to the gilt of a series of military trophies drawn from Piranesi's illustrations. The Ionic order here, which brilliantly creates

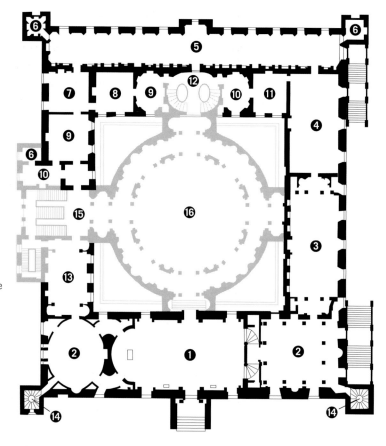

Key

1. Entrance Hall
2. Ante-room
3. Dining room
4. Drawing room
5. The Long Gallery
6. Closet
7. Ante-chamber
8. Bed-chamber
9. Dressing room
10. Powdering room
11. Writing room
12. Staircase to mezzanine
13. Private dining room
14. Ante-room
15. Grand Stair
16. Proposed rotunda

Not built

the illusion of a symmetrical square in an irregularly dimensioned room, is made of a combination of elements drawn from Leroy's illustrations of the Erechtheion in Athens and the Roman order familiar from the baths, which a follower of Adam, Charles Cameron, would not only record in his *Description of the Baths of the Romans* (1772), but export to St Petersburg to ornament the summer palaces of Catherine the Great. Evocation was the order of the day, as the house seemed to conflate a history as much fanciful as archaeological, for Adam asserted a theory, much explored by subsequent historians, that the lost vestiges of the villas the Romans built in Britain with their four corner towers were echoed in the form of such great Jacobean houses as Syon. Family history, national history, and the history of architecture were all intermingled.

The Adam style in the city: new challenges to classical norms

As early as 1759 Adam realized a small but prominent public commission, a new entrance to the Admiralty in London, defined by a screen in Whitehall that added not only Classical demeanour but a rich play of filtered views to what was emerging as the representative centre of national government and of Britain's overseas empire. In the 1770s he created a number of London houses where his ornamental style and his development of antique spaces into picturesque itineraries achieved ever greater sophistication, notably in the extraordinary diagonal views created at Derby House, 23 Grosvenor Square (1773–74; demolished 1862). But without a doubt Adam's most extraordinary interpretation of his knowledge and experience of antique architecture was his daring speculative real-estate venture, the Adelphi, between the Strand and the Thames in the centre of London, where work began in 1768. Here the first impression of Diocletian's palace as seen from the Dalmatian coastline was interpreted in a huge cryptoporticus which was also an area intended for shipping in a project that sought to balance, in both design and financing, commercial, residential, and public functions. Adam showed himself not only the master of interiors, but a master of architectural massing in an urban landscape. Effects came more from massing, rhythm, and 'movement', giving some sense of the extent to which the 'Grand' and the 'True', imbibed by this intense involvement with antique culture, was now detached from any slavish reliance on the orders. He even went so far as to omit the frieze on the Ionic order of the façade of the Royal Society of Arts, a charged gesture if ever there was one, explaining that he had adjusted his composition to the perspective view and to his own sense of refinement.

Adam's views were by no means universal. In his *Treatise on Civil Architecture* (1759), Chambers, who had served as tutor to the future George III, set forth once again a flexible code for use of the orders, informed by the most up-to-date French debate over their rhetorical capacity to respond to the hierarchies of use and social class and the expressive demands of the unprecedented building programmes of modern society. Although the Adelphi project ended in disaster, as the Adam brothers bailed themselves out of bankruptcy, it brought an urban scale to London rivalled only by Chambers' nearby Somerset House (see chapter 2) and reminds us that antiquity would also play a role, on both sides of the Channel, in new discourses on the city. Ultimately it was with these unexpected challenges that the debates over imitation and invention, the ancients versus the moderns, and universal norms versus relative circumstances would be put to the greatest test in the final decades of the eighteenth century.

What is Enlightenment? The City and the Public, 1750–89

The conviction that monumental public buildings and urban spaces might sponsor a renewal of civic life is one of the most lasting legacies of the intense involvement of Enlightenment thought with architecture, that most public of art forms. Turning their attention with equal vigour to theories of how governments might become agents of reason and guarantors of individual liberties and to pragmatic debates over reforming the city, philosophers contemplated a range of new building types and endowed them with an ethical charge. Monumental theatres, marketplaces, schools and academies, buildings for administration, and grand city squares were to provide the stage for a new public life, one in which citizens, or at the very least a burgeoning administrative class and urban bourgeoisie, might assume roles rivalling the aristocracy, clergy, and royalty who had traditionally made the city in their own image. Such buildings would not be merely symbols but veritable instruments for crafting an engaged citizenry by which the royal capitals of London, Paris, and Berlin, as well as numerous 'enlightened' princely and ducal seats in Central Europe and Italy, set out to modernize by recapturing an imagined flourishing public life and architectural grandeur of the Athenian agora or Roman forum.

Even one of the century's most influential books on domestic design pays homage to this renewed faith that architecture's highest calling was public building. In 1737 Blondel—teacher of many of the architects we will encounter in this chapter—turned his attention momentarily from the questions of planning private apartments in mansions, lamenting in *On the Layout of Maisons de Plaisance and on the Decoration of Buildings in General* the lack of public commissions in Regency France: 'It would seem that it is the scarcity of opportunities to erect great monuments which accustoms young architects to lose sight of the fundamental precepts of their art.'[1] After 1750, attacks on Rococo fashion were launched not only in the name of reason, but in defence of the public realm. Some of the finest Neoclassical design is to be found in private interiors and furnishing, but the ethos of Neoclassicism was born of the conviction that architecture might engender a renewal of civic life, even a revival of that strong moral fibre of society Winckelmann admired in ancient Greece. Literal imitation of ancient buildings was not possible, for the rise of an increasingly vibrant commercial society in Europe's cities lengthened enormously the roster of buildings in which public life could be enacted. By the 1770s British architects such as Robert Adam or Henry Holland could make bids alternately for grand public buildings and for commissions for up-to-date coffee houses, gentlemen's clubs, even taverns, all of which demanded that the architect explore the language of antiquity to craft settings for what Jürgen Habermas has called the emerging public sphere, 'a sphere between civil society and the state, in which critical public discussion of matters of general interest was institutionally guaranteed'.[2]

Modern architectural criticism, with its implicit notion that architectural taste can be formed by a dialogue between an informed public and professional designers, has its roots in the heated exchanges of London's coffee houses and liberalized press. In the early 1740s George Dance the Elder's Mansion House, the first of many administrative buildings to transform the landscape of the capital as the apparatus of state grew increasingly independent of the court, elicited impassioned public debate and scrutiny. At issue were principally financial mismanagement, expense, and corruption. Aesthetics were raised for the first time by James Ralph, whose *Critical Review of the Publick Buildings ... In and About London* appeared in 1733–34 in instalments in the *Weekly Register*, before being published as a book. Ralph aimed to reform his fellow citizens' taste by analysing the qualities and faults of public buildings and sculpture, much as Blondel later sought to do for students through on-site visits, a key feature of his innovative private school of architecture in Paris (founded 1743). The salon in France and exhibitions of the Royal Academy and the Royal Society of Arts in England had made works of art issues of public debate. Increasingly architecture, where issues of aesthetics and the body politic met, also became a preoccupation of reformist discourse.

The royal square in Enlightenment Paris
The Place Louis xv in Paris (today's Place de la Concorde), one of the most important undertakings of Louis xv's reign, was born of an act of courtly diplomacy but rapidly catalysed a public debate opening new ways of discussing the city. On 27 June 1748, as the Treaty of Aix-la-Chapelle ended the War of Austrian Succession, the city council of Paris, deliberating on a way to affirm its attachment to the monarch, determined to erect a statue of Louis xv, to be entrusted to the great sculptor Edmé Bouchardon 'for a site which His Majesty will deem

appropriate'. The king's director of buildings approached the Royal Academy of Architecture, whose members frequently acted as a royal architectural advisory board 'for plans for a public square to house the statue'. The *place royale,* or royal square, had been established over a century and a half earlier as an instrument of urban design and royal representation, initiated by Henri IV at the Place des Vosges (1610) and continued by Louis XIV, who promoted projects throughout France for harmonious architectural frames for the public display of the royal portrait. But neither established designs nor traditional procedures for choosing them were respected in 1748. The academicians looked to a number of provincial cities—notably Rennes and the thriving port of Bordeaux—where new commercial and public functions had been integrated with the representational function of royal squares, a shift ideally suited to Louis XV's ambitions to project a new ethos of public beneficence. Discussion of a site for a new royal square in Paris quickly escaped the closed debate of the academy as scores of unsolicited proposals poured in from non-members and even from *amateurs* whom the academicians were loath to recognize as architects. Sites throughout the capital were proposed, and many designers were not content to provide a simple frame for a royal portrait, seeking to seize the occasion to address pressing needs of the city, from traffic circulation to rationalizing markets and opening up space in front of monuments encumbered by houses.

Germain Boffrand (1667–1754), an elder statesman among architects, presented four separate projects, including an ambitious design to reorganize the central markets with a trio of colonnaded and arcaded fora, where Louis XV's quest for an image of beneficent provider would be daily verified in an abundance of foodstuffs and textiles, all rationally laid out and organized. In another project Boffrand—like several other participants in this unofficial competition—proposed to carve a square out of the mass of buildings which had grown up in between the Louvre and Tuileries palaces, at once liberating these buildings from parasitic buildings 'of no value' and creating a monumental pair of public buildings in the vast space created. These would house two novel cultural institutions which in future decades would play a key role in defining, first in theory and later in stone, a new space of sociability and cultivation, namely the Opéra and a public art gallery— something that had not existed since antiquity—including 'paintings and other precious works which are now simply piled up in the King's warehouses'.[3] From Lyon, Soufflot proposed nothing less than linking the two islands in the Seine, the Ile de la Cité and the Ile St-Louis, to form a grand public square on landfill. This daring and expensive project would have numerous advantages, from improving navigation on the Seine to rationalizing spaces and functions at the very heart of the capital. He proposed to relocate the central hospital from its site next

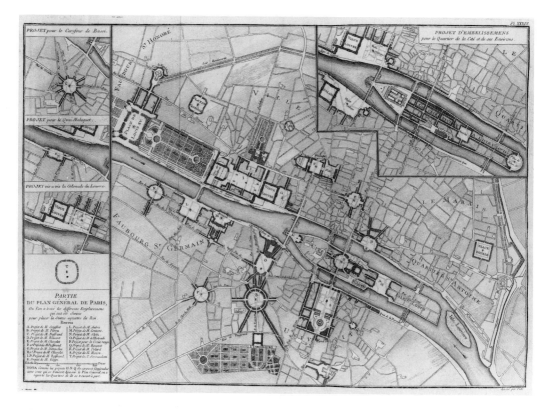

Pl. XXXIX

18 Pierre Patte

Composite map of Paris with rival plans submitted in the 1748 competition for siting and designing a Place Louis XV, 1765

Together the proposals by some of the day's leading architects offered a vision of a city reformed, with open spaces, broadened traffic arteries and new public buildings—a vision in which movement and exchange structured urban space and health and hygiene were goals of reforming the urban fabric. Patte's own comprehensive suggestion is presented in an inset at the upper right.

to Notre-Dame cathedral, which in turn would be given a dignified frame of open space, to demolish the houses that lined the bridges connecting the islands to the right and left banks, and to create new quays. A *pensionnaire* at the French Academy in Rome, the young Michel Barthélemy Hazon, excited by the recently rediscovered ancient city of Herculaneum, submitted an ambitious project to rebuild a huge sector of Paris's Latin Quarter in a form reminiscent of the ancient forum, the whole to serve as a triumphal setting for the royal statue in the foreground of a great Temple of Glory. Hazon attracted the attention of that taste-maker Madame de Pompadour and in 1751 was appointed site architect for Gabriel's École Militaire (1750–68), one of the grandest of Louis xv's Parisian undertakings.

Nearly every architect whose project was recorded on a composite map published in 1765 [**18**] by Pierre Patte demonstrated how designing a *place royale* required thinking about the overall structure of the city, or as the increasingly popular surgical metaphor of the day would have it, how any incision in the urban organism would have ramifications on its larger systems. Patte's map was emblematic of this emerging view of the city as a place of circulation, of traffic, of goods, of money, and of ideas, in short an efficient machine. His new perspective was combined with the more traditional values of a rhetorical hierarchy, one in which the public good would emerge clearly from the private realm of the city.

The map itself was transformed from a mere topographic record into a planning instrument, something happening those same years in the new French École des Ponts-et-Chaussées, founded in 1747 to train the state corps of engineers who would restructure the national territory with roads and canals and who began their training with exercises in map-making. Patte's map was not a record of the city as it existed but a project for a city in process, one in which enlightened intervention would progressively move towards a rationally ordered urban space.

As realized, the Place Louis XV [19] was far less forward-looking than Patte's utopian vision, for in 1753 Louis XV foreclosed debate by offering land on the edge of the city, just outside the Tuileries gardens. A competition to design a square at this vital hinge, where the boulevards laid out under Louis XIV on the old city walls met the Seine, was limited to academicians. Nineteen of the 40 architect members submitted designs, including Boffrand, who proposed that building be limited to the northern edge of the site to create a great landscape pulling together the gardens of the Tuileries and the Champs-Elysées and the panorama of the Seine. Although he had not submitted a design, the king's chief architect Gabriel was entrusted in 1755 with the commission as well as with a portfolio of proposed solutions. Gabriel proposed a solution which drew both on Boffrand's suggestion and on his own

19 G. L. Le Rouge

Engraving of the Place Louis XV (today de la Concorde) as inaugurated in 1763 to the designs of the royal architect Anges-Jacques Gabriel

In addition to its harmonious relation of building façades to a grand open space, Gabriel's plan created axial links to existing and planned monuments and created model façades for the houses lining the rue Royale, the prototype for later planned streets [**61**, **63**, **64b**].

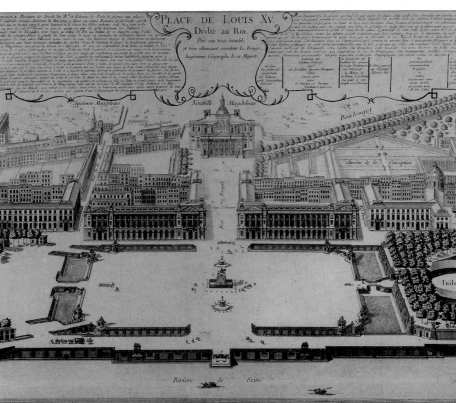

earlier royal square at Bordeaux, a great crescent open to the Garonne river. As at Bordeaux the statue was placed scenographically so that it might be viewed against the backdrop of the two monumental façades screening the new square from the varied city fabric and be the focal point of a series of streets and garden *allées*. For the first time since the statue of Henry IV on the Pont Neuf, erected in 1604, the king's statue would organize an entire landscape rather than simply a closed urban space. The two grand civic palaces—which ultimately housed the Naval Ministry and a warehouse of the royal household—established an all but unprecedented grandeur of composition and elegance of detail for the administrative buildings of the state. Unlike earlier such buildings, which were subordinated to the larger composition of a palace—such as at Versailles—these are urban monuments in their own right, reflecting the rise of an administrative state parallel to the monarchy. The desire for order and harmony was not confined to the setting for the statue, for the façades frame a view of the projected royal church of the Madeleine (Contant d'Ivry, 1764), closing the axis of the future rue Royale. While this new street was to be developed by private builders, all had to conform to Gabriel's contract design, an early example of a composition for an overall street frontage by which city reformers sought to invent prototypes for a regularized and harmonious urban fabric, at once dignified but subordinated to the grand monuments of the state.

Urban theory in Paris

Between the first proposals for the future *place* in 1748 and the final approval of Gabriel's design in 1755, an explosion of polemical tracts marked the birth of city planning debate in France. In the 1730s Voltaire had defended the rights and duties of a free-thinking critic/citizen to address himself directly to the king. By the time of the Place Louis XV 'competition' Voltaire's was but one voice openly criticizing the crown for its failure to initiate public works, and thereby elevate taste, improve the quality of life in towns, and stimulate the economy. 'It is time for those who rule the most opulent capital in Europe to make of it the most comfortable and the most magnificent of cities. There must be public markets, fountains which actually provide water and regular pavements. The narrow and infected streets must be widened, monuments that cannot be seen must be revealed and new ones built for all to see,' Voltaire insisted in a polemical essay on 'The Embellishments of Paris' in 1749.[4] In the same years, La Font de Saint-Yenne, often considered the first art critic, decried the fact that Louis XIV's great east façade of the Louvre, the famous colonnade of Perrault and Le Vau, was all but hidden from view by a dense quarter of modest houses.[5] Voltaire quipped that in order to make of Paris a city that could rival ancient Rome it was necessary to demolish more than it was to build. La Font de Saint-Yenne spelled out one of the key doctrines of Enlightenment urban theory, *dégagement*. To 'disengage' a building was to detach it from surrounding urban fabric, provide it with a frame of open space and designate it a work of architectural art to be admired separately. *Dégagement* would thus create a hierarchy between the monuments of the crown, state, and church and the background urban fabric of private citizens. One consequence would be to lay bare the history of a particular civilization, a prospect that corresponded to Voltaire's vision of history as an edifying practice and that Soufflot would soon interpret in architectural practice as he began the work of completing the Louvre colonnade by demolishing a row of houses that obstructed views of the monument. In these same years Soufflot designed a public plaza in front of his church of Ste-Geneviève in the form of the ancient Greek amphitheatre to allow his building to be viewed from the day it was inaugurated as a monument.[6]

'Our towns are still what they were, a mass of houses crowded together haphazardly without system, planning or design,' Laugier complained in 1753. 'Nowhere is this disorder more noticeable and more shocking than in Paris. The center of this capital has hardly changed for three hundred years; there are still the same number of little, narrow and tortuous streets, smelling of dirt and filth where the encounter of carriages causes constant obstruction.'[7] Echoing his Jesuit training in rhetoric, Laugier called for a city that was visually ordered and legible, and divided his analysis into three categories: entries, streets, and buildings. Grand free-standing entrances, like the introduction to a speech, should announce the size and importance of the city at the same time as clearly delimit country from town. Laugier proposed that they be treated as triumphal arches with statues of great men or bas reliefs of significant events so that the cityscape would become both a memorial and a didactic lesson.[8] Streets, straight and regular, should radiate from central plazas, offering a proper balance between order and variety. Like his contemporary Blondel, who set down in his highly influential *Cours d'architecture* the hierarchies of building types and degrees of decoration according to the academic notions of *convenance* or appropriateness and *caractère*, thus relating issues of social and aesthetic decorum, Laugier sought variety and regularity in an overall urban order.

Writing a decade later, Patte promoted an urban reform in quest of health, social order, and security, launching at the same time a medical or organic metaphor which compared the operations of urban design to those of the surgeons, who in these very years were asserting the scientific bases of their practice. Like the human body described in La Mettrie's *Man the Machine* of 1747, Patte saw the city as a place of circulation and continual exchange. With bad air and lack of fresh water its current state was pathological, Patte asserted, calling for more foun-

20 Pierre Patte

Project for an ideal street, 1769

Patte imagined the houses and the street as interlocking elements in a system, one which would process waste, move traffic, and provide light and air to render house and town commodious. His obsession with drainage epitomizes the growing belief that reform of the city 'body' was a step to promoting public health. Regulated ratios of building height to street width became common only in the nineteenth century.

tains to be placed at principal intersections and markets. Squares are recommended to promote the circulation of air, and for the same reason houses on the city's bridges should be demolished, a recommendation taken up in an edict of 1786. Patte criticized the location of hospitals next to markets and protested continued burials in overcrowded city churchyards, thus helping to launch the movement for cemeteries outside the city walls. This was endorsed by an Act of 1765 outlawing new burials and realized with the spectacular removal of 1.6 million cadavers from central Paris burial grounds to the catacombs in 1786–87.

This vision of the city as a machine promoting health by careful spatial articulation of functions is best embodied in Patte's project for a model street [20], in which a legislated proportion of the width of the street to the height of the building was to ensure plentiful air and light and create an almost unprecedented separation of pedestrians and vehicles. By vesting the power to legislate the dimensions of streets and building alignments in royal authority, and making all new construction conform to new standards, Patte formulated the Enlightenment dream of the city progressively renewing itself. In 1769, as he expanded his thoughts into a book on urban reform, the city of Paris appointed its first municipal architect, Pierre Moreau-Desproux, responsible not only for reforming the public thoroughfare but for policing private development.

London

In these same years John Gwynn launched a similar campaign in his *London and Westminster Improved ... to which is prefixed a Discourse on Public Magnificence* (1766). Gwynn lamented that Sir Christopher Wren's ambitious plan for rebuilding the British capital after the Great Fire of 1666 was 'totally disregarded and sacrificed to mean, interested and selfish views of private property'.[9] He rebuked his contemporaries who insisted that Paris's great buildings reflected the will of an autocrat, totally unsuitable for Britain where power was shared with Parliament and trade had established an active marketplace for goods and ideas. 'Public works of real magnificence, taste, elegance and utility, in a commercial city, are of the utmost consequence; they are not only of real use in point of splendour and convenience, but as necessary to the community as health and clothing to the human body ...'[10] Gwynn insisted in detailing his vision of a London of regularly planned wide streets and ample squares ornamented with worthy public buildings, including a vast new royal palace which he proposed to build atop a 25-foot (7.6m)-high terrace in the centre of Hyde Park, the whole surrounded by an iron fence rather than a brick wall to allow the public to take visual advantage of London's great royal green spaces.

Gwynn longed for a native school of architecture which could give visual expression to Britain's grandeur on the world stage, as he fought for both an academy and for monumental public architecture that could rival that sponsored by Louis xv. And he expressed an anxiety

The London square

Until the formation of the Metropolitan Board of Works (1855), landed estates controlled by a handful of aristocrat families stamped the development of London with characteristic rows of terrace houses and verdant squares. Bedford Square on the Bedford Estates (1776) is an early instance of an entire square being designed as a unified composition, but the handling of multiple houses as one grand unified composition originated with the Bedford Estate's Covent Garden in the 1630s. It was given spectacular impetus by the Wood family in Bath in the mid-eighteenth century. A resilient and flexible form of housing as commodity had been developed as terrace houses, of varied size and embellishment, housed a broad span of classes. A harmonious urban fabric was produced by the private market, with only occasional governmental intervention, such as the Dublin Wide Streets Commission of 1756 which made the Irish capital the envy of Europe for its broad, commodious streets. With English upper-class life centred a part of the year in country houses, even the aristocracy was often content with a broad terrace house in town, sharing both the honorific appliqué of a pediment and pilasters with adjacent houses and access to a locked garden at the centre of the square. The pattern of English town building, quite distinct from that of France, was set for over a century.

shared by others that the free market's role in the recent explosion in manufactured goods—what historians have called the Commercial Revolution—would lead to a decline of taste without state support for the arts: 'How much more valuable a manufactory would Birmingham be to this nation, if it was in the hands of people of taste,'[11] he quipped, referring to the explosion of new industry in the commercial capital of the Midlands. While London had fragments of planning on the estates developed by aristocratic landlords around its famous private squares, there was no comprehensive order that reflected the glory of the nation and the reign of reason. He encouraged the government to take a strong hand in 'disencumbering' existing monuments from parasitic fabric to create processional routes for the monarch and Parliament, at the same time as he recommended legislation to control London's burgeoning sprawl, the earliest recognition that the speculative growth of modern cities was eroding just that visual order and hierarchy so valued by Enlightenment urban theorists.

The reconstruction of Lisbon

Its ancient centre destroyed by a violent earthquake and tidal wave on All Saints' Day 1755, Lisbon became overnight the focus of European intellectuals' attention, as the city's reconstruction over the next decades under the enlightened despotic reign of the Marquis de Pombal was accompanied by a concerted effort to reform and rationalize one of Europe's most traditional and pious monarchies. At the centre of the new masterplan, drawn up by the engineer Eugénio dos Santos and approved in June 1758, just months before the Jesuits were expelled from Portugal, was a great urban square opening directly onto the broad wash of the Tagus river. Baptized 'Praça do Commercio' [21], it replaced the Rossio, the former main open space of the Baixa, or lower town, seat of municipal power and stage for the horrifying spectacles of the Inquisition. By 1785, even before the great triumphal arch which connects the square to the grid of streets behind, with their carefully legislated house façades, pavements, and sewers, was completed, a Scottish officer in service in Lisbon could note that this square was 'the grand theatre of Commerce of Portugal … as well as the place where all cases of civil and criminal justice are tried at the highest level'.[12] A royal statue commands the centre of this great urban forum, but it is significant that the palace was not rebuilt on this site, bordered now by customs services for the great symbolic centre of Portugal's far-flung maritime empire, by administrative buildings, and by open arcades for cafés and shops. The plan for reconstruction and guidelines for rebuilding throughout the city in terms of materials, earthquake resistance construction techniques, and height limits to retain air and light in the streets were all made force of law, an act that many viewed as the birth of an enlightened administration of both the townscape

21

Aerial view of the centre of Lisbon

The rebuilding of Lisbon's Baixa quarter after the devastating earthquake of 1755 provided the image of an entire city brought under control of geometry and rational planning. The Praça do Commercio occupied the site of the former palace, not only creating a new stage for public life but embracing the view of the Tagus River's broad channel into the cityscape.

and its civic life. Its fame spread as much by literature and philosophy as by actual visitors' impressions. Lisbon became the veritable symbol of the triumph of reason over the savage forces of nature—even if Voltaire's Candide seemed to have his confidence shaken arriving in the aftermath of the quake.

Even capitals that were not reduced to rubble by acts of nature began to look to the role of urban planning to create a newly ordered society, and to craft new alliances between enlightened power and its subjects, from Catherine the Great's St Petersburg, where an international competition for embellishments was announced in journals throughout Europe in 1765, to Turin, where the Dukes of Savoy set about expanding their capital by regulation, requiring all new streets to continue the famous ground-floor pedestrian arcades that had already made the Piedmontese capital a model of order and public well-being.

Monuments and speculative real estate: the Parisian model

The 1750s and 1760s saw a proliferation of urban proposals, designed and literary, pragmatic and utopian; but increasingly economic arguments came to the fore in which English mercantilism and the contemporary debate among the French physiocrats over the role of cities in the production and circulation of wealth were joined. Dussausoy, author of a widely circulated tract, *The Objective Citizen or various pa-*

Halle au Blé

Site plan as engraved in the architect's folio presentation of the design, with partial elevation and section

Design of a new grain market and the speculative development of a dense residential neighbourhood around it were inextricably linked financially and aesthetically. The new quarter was a microcosm of new demands for easy circulation of vehicles as well as light and air. To the north the architect studied connections with a projected square for the church of St-Eustache.

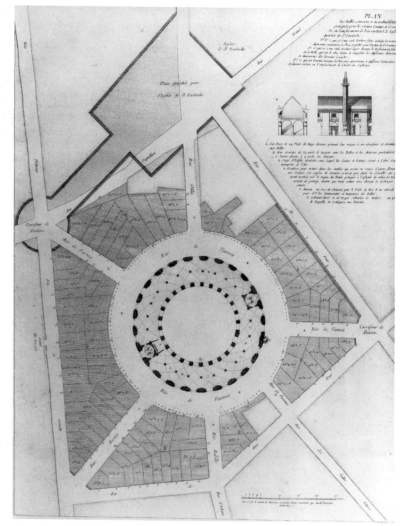

triotic ideas concerning useful embellishments for the city of Paris (1767), maintained that urban improvements have long-term benefits for the national economy and pointed for proof to an entire urban quarter of Paris then under construction in the shadow of a monumental new grain market, the Halle au Blé [**22**], both the work of his friend Nicolas Le Camus de Mézières (1721–c.1793). Begun within weeks of the signing of the Treaty of Paris (1763), this new market was the first of a series of major public buildings in Louis xv's reign to be financed principally from revenues of a speculative real-estate operation that also laid out a harmoniously designed urban frame for the monument.

At the Halle au Blé, as in most cases, the property belonged to an aristocrat eager to realize a quick profit, in this case the heavily indebted Prince de Carignan whose Hôtel de Soissons, once demolished, would offer a rare open space in one of the city's most densely built areas, on the edge of the market quarter. Le Camus de Mézières placed his building at the centre of the roughly hexagonal site, with a series of radial roads which not only made the ring-shaped market the focal point but multiplied the number of access roads to facilitate movement of horses and carts for deliveries and to maximize street frontage for speculative apartment houses, themselves a relatively new type of building. The market was at once a public monument to abundance and a solution to the functional requirements, achieved with stunning economy of means. Although contemporaries celebrated it as a modern coliseum, Le Camus stripped his cylinder of conventional architectural orders, honouring the period's notion of proper decorum (*convenance*) by which a utilitarian structure respected its place in the hierarchy of building types and demonstrating his own theory that simple geometric forms impressed most immediately and dramatically. Everything was studied to maximize space and circulation, be it of ventilation, goods, or traffic. Contemporaries marvelled at the light-weight brick vaults and at the double-helix staircases which allowed goods and administrative personnel to circulate completely independently in the same stairwell. For the first time in centuries a public market was raised to the level of a civic monument; the emerging discourses of functionality of design and the aesthetic of pure geometric forms were brilliantly merged.

Peyre and De Wailly and the new field of public architecture

Few careers encapsulate the increasing attention to public buildings in France after the Peace of 1763 than those of Marie-Joseph Peyre and Charles De Wailly (1730–98). Winners of the *Grand Prix* of the Academy in 1751 and in 1752 respectively, these architects followed Leroy to the French Academy in Rome and shared his determination to effect a renewal of French architecture. They also shared Leroy's passion for archaeology and were soon to echo Laugier's interest in structural purity. Together they explored an entirely new aspect of ancient Roman architecture, the drama of its spatial planning and manipulation of top and side lighting still visible in the ruined remains of the great thermal bath complexes of Diocletian and Constantine. Peyre sought to exploit these lessons, along with the lighting effects he admired in the works of Roman Baroque architects, in a series of ideal projects [23a, b] and, once he returned to Paris, in designs for aristocratic mansions, experiments that paralleled those of Robert Adam in England in these same years. But from the first he and De Wailly also sought to revive the great public rituals that centred around the Roman baths. Through his highly influential book of designs (*Works in Architecture*, 1765), these experiments sponsored a new approach to public architecture throughout Europe. De Wailly's atelier, opened in 1759, became almost overnight a magnet for foreign students, notably

23 M.-J. Peyre

Project for a cathedral and two palaces **a)** Perspective view **b)** (*far right*) Plan

Peyre's entry in the 1753 competition of the Roman Academy is a striking example of his quest to correct historical models by pure geometry and by the Neoclassical ideal of multiplying free-standing columns for sublime effects. Published in 1765, this and other designs were to have an enormous influence on design throughout Europe. Montferrand's St Isaac's Cathedral in St Petersburg is one famous descendant.

Basile Ivanovitch Bajenov and Ivan Egorovitch Starov who, after stints in De Wailly's atelier, would build some of the most impressive public buildings in St Petersburg and Moscow.

The theatre and the public

A lively debate over the role of theatre in social and political life engaged the passions of philosophers, playwrights, clergy, politicians, and competing troupes of actors from the 1740s until the end of the century. For Voltaire English freedom of thought and the liveliness of the English stage tradition went hand in hand, although architecturally the theatres of London enjoyed little advance over those of Paris. Both as playwright and polemicist Voltaire advanced the notion that, as in antiquity, theatrical productions provided images of moral rectitude for the public, a position that only deepened his growing rift with the church, which continued to view theatre as an agent of moral corruption.

Diderot touted the pedagogic and social benefits of drama, to be achieved not only in new techniques of staging but by an architectural reform. Drama and its public were to be transformed. In both plays and theoretical essays he defined a new kind of play, characterized by a realism of characters and situations resonant with contemporary bourgeois life, in sharp contrast with the grand classical dramas of Racine or Corneille. In keeping with the period's fascination with the origins of nearly all social institutions—including architecture—as a corrective for modern uses, Diderot advanced the theory[13] that theatre was born of a crowd gathering to watch a single actor in pantomime. This view was taken up by others, including Lessing and Goethe, and revived a century later by Charles Garnier (see chapter 8). Goethe maintained that as the crowd struggled to gain a view, the form of the ancient amphitheatre had been traced automatically in the earth. Diderot was as

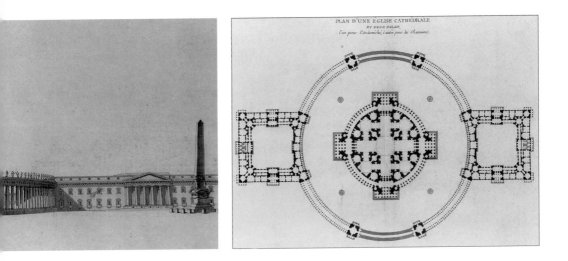

eager to recapture the natural gestures and unaffected mores of these first performances as he was to return to the first audiences' enraptured attention. Between the standing public in the parterre or 'pit' of the theatre, notoriously raucous and disrespectful, and the upper ranks of society seated in boxes, as interested in viewing one another as the stage, the drama on stage had substantial competition. It was common, moreover, to provide additional seating on stage. This blurring of the spectacle of everyday life and the work of art came to a dramatic end on 23 April 1759, when the Duc de Laurages paid the actors of the Théâtre-Français to remove these extra seats, enforcing a complete split between audience and actors. Historians have viewed this as the veritable threshold of a modern notion of aesthetic attentiveness, a prelude to the new ethical status of the work of art or architecture in bourgeois civic society.

The discovery of an ancient amphitheatre at Herculaneum beneath the solidifed lava of Vesuvius was to stimulate a rising generation of French architects to explore the paradigm of the ancient stage to meet the literary demand for new spaces of illusion and a new equality of the audience. In the decades preceding the Revolution, more than 20 free-standing theatre buildings, led by Soufflot's new theatre for Lyon (1753–56, demolished 1826), transformed the urban space and public life of French towns. Called upon to replace the existing theatre, housed, like many, in a remodelled tennis court, Soufflot compromised between existing social hierarchies and the new ideal of the amphitheatre with its equality of sight lines and sense of communal gathering. He was critical of recent Italian theatres such as Turin's royal theatre (Castellamonte and Alfieri, 1738–40)—he compared its superimposed galleries carried on glittering piers to a gilt chicken coop—and reserved praise for the sober design and amphitheatrical seating of Palladio's famous Teatro Olimpico at Vicenza and Serlio's Teatro Farnese at Parma. Neither of these was a free-standing building; and designing the exterior of a theatre remained a challenge, for few models existed. At Lyon, Soufflot retained balconies for social differentiation and seating capacity but staggered them and recessed the vertical supports so that the auditorium evoked the curved banks of the ancient amphitheatre. Like his later church design in Paris [10–13, 15], Soufflot's theatre, which Diderot singled out as a model, served as an experimental prototype worked and reworked by younger architects for the next 30 years. Not the least of its innovations was its integration into a residential quarter, Lyon's quartier Ste-Claire, in which Soufflot was involved as both architect and investor, making the theatre a centrepiece of a commercial and residential neighbourhood of carefully aligned streets.

The Comédie-Française (Théâtre de l'Odéon) in Paris (1767–82)

By the time De Wailly presented a view of the staircase of the projected Comédie-Française at the Paris Salon in 1771, he had been at work with Peyre for over 4 years, designing this new theatre for the royal troupe. They had worked through numerous variations of the design to accommodate different interests, fight off rival projects, and find the optimum aesthetic and financial harmony between Paris's first free-standing theatre and the layout of a new residential quarter which could underwrite the cost of a new civic monument. What De Wailly laid before the public in his theatrical salon presentation, and then in engravings illustrating Diderot's article 'Théâtre' in the *Encyclopédie*, was his vision of the theatre as a temple to the arts and a great salon of sociability in the modern city [24].

From the first, Peyre and De Wailly were committed to a circular auditorium in the antique spirit and they proposed a series of staggered balconies all set before a monumental ring of free-standing Ionic column/piers which they hoped to continue right onto the stage to form a permanent architectural proscenium (an innovation vetoed by the actors). The parterre was to be seated, and extra seating would be obtained above the cornice line of the great auditorium in the spaces opened in the vaults. These elements had been introduced by Soufflot, but the real innovation lay in the enormous attention paid to circulation. For the first time the public ritual of theatre-going was as much a part of the architectural programme as the sight lines, acoustics, and decoration of the auditorium.

Palace theatres, such as Gabriel's splendid Opera House at Versailles (1758–70), were connected to the ceremonial spaces of the palace itself and the existing theatres of Paris were modest and their difficult and cramped entrances notorious. Peyre and De Wailly treated the theatre as a public monument, indeed a monument to the public. With the exception of Antoine's recently completed building for the

INTÉRIEUR DE LA NOUVELLE SALLE DE COMÉDIE FRANÇAISE DE L'ANCIEN PROJET.

24 Charles De Wailly

Section of the Comédie-Française, Paris, 1776

This dramatic vision of an architectural design, which pays as much attention to spaces for public promenading and display as to those for staging a play, was first presented at the Salon. De Wailly was proud to be a member of both the academies of painting and architecture, using dramatic perspectives to portray an architecture staged within a city of new spaces for public interaction.

Mint, a short distance away, nothing like the grandeur of the new theatre's twin flights of stairs leading from the colonnaded entrance vestibule had been seen outside a palace. Laugier and Soufflot's aesthetic of a structural *dégagement* was exploited for its full potential to dramatize a series of architectural tableaux to be revealed as the theatre-goer progressed from the grand two-storey Tuscan portico via spaces of the most varied dimensions, heights, and lighting, echoing qualities De Wailly and Peyre had admired in the Roman baths, themselves places of public assembly and interchange in the ancient city. De Wailly's watercolours were peopled with a cross-section of Parisian society to reveal the extent to which his building was rich in vantage points for seeing and being seen, not only within, but also as the building was dramatically inserted into the city.

The architects developed a remarkable setting for the building, which extended experiments in theatrical vision and sociability to the very fabric of the city [**25**]. The colonnaded façade faces a public space shaped like a grand amphitheatre, its edges defined by an arc of apartment buildings designed in a deliberately sober style so as not to upstage the temple of the arts. This theatrical presentation of the porticoed façade was further enriched by a reciprocal view from the portico of glimpses of the city framed by the views down a series of radiating streets. It was almost as though Peyre and De Wailly had been able to remodel the real fabric of this quarter of Paris in the image of the famous permanent cityscape on the stage of Palladio's Teatro Olimpico. Cafés in the lower floors of the two apartment buildings

25 Charles De Wailly and M.-J. Peyre

Aerial view of Paris showing the Comédie-Française and its quarter

Inspired no doubt by Soufflot's semicircular *place* in front of Ste-Geneviève, Peyre and de Wailly orchestrated an entire urban spectacle. De Wailly designed the façades on the *place* and a number of those in the rue de l'Odéon leading up to the new building, the first street in Paris to be equipped with pavements. The Odéon quarter is in the lower right of the photograph, just above the Luxembourg palace and garden.

flanking the theatre's main façade were connected to it by bridges, thus extending the promenading during the intermission. The streets flanking the theatre, where carriages could wait during the performance, their drivers and footmen sheltered under the theatre's open arcades, were like theatrical slips when seen from the outdoor 'theatre' of the public square. It seemed almost predestined when, during the Revolution, De Wailly was called back to build a series of raked seats on the *place* for outdoor festivals in which the theatre served as the permanent stage set!

Marthurin Crucy, a student at the Academy as the Odéon was under construction, took inspiration from the entire urban setting of the new building when he was commissioned in 1783 to design a new theatre in his native Nantes as the centrepiece of the quartier de Graslin, a speculative development of an urban quarter named after the financier who orchestrated this complex, but increasingly typical, urban operation. The most spectacular of all French theatres of the period was the Grand Théâtre at Bordeaux, Nantes's rival in the booming Atlantic trade. Here it was the king's provincial intendant, the Duc de Richelieu, who was the motor behind the project, beginning with the selection of the Parisian architect Victor Louis, who shepherded the project through local opposition and financial difficulties between 1773

and 1780. Louis created the consummate framework for the theatre as a public place in eighteenth-century architecture. His stairway takes over all the apparatus of regal posturing and adapts it to create a setting for public interaction and spectacle [**26**]. Nowhere is the idea of the theatre as a grand domestic interior for an expanding public more vividly expressed, and this was reinforced by the complex programme for the theatre, which included cafés and shops in the arcades that line its principal and side façades. A few years later Adam would propose an elaborate scheme for a new Opera House in the Haymarket in London where a tavern, ballroom, and assembly rooms were all connected to the theatre by bridges crossing the public streets.

A remarkable transformation of Bordeaux's theatre-going public was already noted on opening night: 'before our theatre was one of the noisiest in the provinces; but without doubt the majesty of the setting made a stronger impression than police orders. A calmness and air of good demeanour reigned not only during the play but during the intermission, an atmosphere never before seen here.'[14] Diderot's request for a studied attention that could make theatre a public school of ethics had found a worthy collaborator in Victor Louis's architecture.

The Paris Mint and School of Surgery

With discussion under way in London of grouping government offices dispersed throughout the capital into a single great building, Chambers, angling for the commission, travelled to Paris in 1774 to study the public buildings erected since his student days there a quarter-century earlier. In addition to the work of his old friends Peyre and De Wailly, he stud-

27 William Chambers

River façade of the new Mint (Hôtel des Monnaies), Paris, 1774

Paris was a veritable school of public architecture when Chambers sketched Jacques-Denis Antoine's Mint, the façade of which was completed in 1773. Although the heavily rusticated embankment of the Seine was never completed, contemporaries admired the contrast between the prestigious river façade and the more utilitarian rear façade of the working mint, a study in contrasting 'characters' of architectural expression.

ied the new Mint (1771–75) [27] by Jacques-Denis Antoine and the School of Surgery (1769–74) by Jacques Gondoin, as well as Gabriel's Place Louis xv [19] and the École Militaire. All of these were examples of advanced Neoclassical taste, with their preference for purer and simpler geometric expression, adherence to the expression of the free-standing column, and restrained use of sculptural ornamentation and mouldings, and they attested to a desire to endow each building with individual and appropriate form, a physiognomy even, directly linked to its use. Since such programmes as a mint or surgery school had few precedents in either ancient or modern architecture, these new building types challenged architects to contemplate how architecture could communicate both new functions and new ideals with the inherited elements of the classical language of architecture.

This was to lead to two parallel lines of research in eighteenth-century architecture, one of which looked increasingly at a full range of values in composition—geometric forms, light and shade, proportions—which might be said to both precede and be more universal than the specific syntax of the classical language of architecture inherited from Greece and Rome. At the same time architects began to use traditional forms from Classical architecture in new contexts to build meaning through the association of ideas—the use of a triumphal arch not as a gateway celebrating a Roman army's glorious entry into a city, for instance, but rather to suggest honorific entry into any exalted domain. Both of these strategies are at play in the School of Surgery, where the courtyard plan of the period's grand urban residences was adapted to the practical needs and the professional aspirations of the surgeons. Gondoin's mastery was to incorporate a series of images from and associations with Roman building types into a scenographic

28 Jacques Gondoin

School of Surgery, Paris

a) Street view

Gondoin explained that the building 'should have a character of magnificence relative to its function; a school whose fame attracts a great concourse of pupils from all nations should appear open and easy of access'. The visual appropriation of private space by the passer-by had been proposed by the Abbé de Cordemoy in his 1702 treatise as a way of creating new public urban spaces.

b) Plan

Transforming the traditional type of the Parisian urban *hôtel* into a modern school of medicine, Gondoin's plan incorporates forms and images from antiquity, including a columnar screen reminiscent of the Propylaeum entrance to the Acropolis and the perfect semicircle of the Greek amphitheatre.

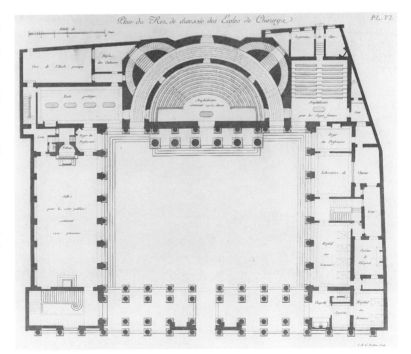

The steeply raked
amphitheatre provides each
student with an unobstructed
view and fosters excellent
acoustics throughout the room
at the same time as the
associations with the ancient
Greek theatre and its social
role reinforce the notion that
the spectacle of dissection is
at the heart of the community
of surgeons and their
commitment to progress of
medical understanding.

progression. The free-standing Ionic colonnade of the street front's
ground floor [28a] allows ample views of the courtyard, echoing a demand made decades earlier by J.-L. de Cordemoy that the courtyards
of buildings be treated as public spaces by creating spaces open to all
eyes.[15] At its centre the colonnade is closed by recessed panels which
evoke an ancient triumphal arch. Above, a large bas-relief panel depicts the king, accompanied by Minerva and surrounded by the sick,
ordering the construction of the building. The architectural plan inscribed on a scroll is presented by the Muse of Architecture, thus
putting on public display the very principle of organization of this temple to the surgeon's profession, so frequently dismissed as a cousin of
bloodletting or barbers, now affirmed as one of the age's progressive
sciences [28b]. In the courtyard the one-storey colonnade of the entrance is carried round the other three sides, interweaving at the rear,
on axis with the entrance, with a two-storey Corinthian temple front.
The forecourt of the Parisian hôtel type has been transformed into the
forum of a modern secular temple of medicine. Between the columns
portrait medallions of great surgeons recall Laugier's suggestion that
the city's principal public monuments become temples to the memory
of great men, a theme soon taken up when Louis XVI's director of
buildings d'Angiviller began to commission portraits of 'Grands
Hommes' for the Grande Galerie of the Louvre. In the pediment
above, a sculptural group depicts *Theory and Practice swearing on the
altar of Union*, this centred not only over the entrance reserved for the
faculty and honoured guests but also above the dissection table, which
stands just behind the threshold at the centre of the amphitheatre's
stage [28c].

The amphitheatre is Gondoin's most extraordinary translation of
antique architectural types for modern uses, since it combines the
purest of the period's homages to the Greek amphitheatre with a coffered half-dome reminiscent of the Roman Pantheon. Like Soufflot,
Gondoin was eager to learn from the progressive history of Classical
architecture rather than to imitate specific monuments, or arrest architecture in some golden moment. The School of Surgery is no mere collage of fragments of ancient buildings but rather a subtle use of each
element, both pragmatically and symbolically.

Somerset House

Somerset House in London is at once the masterpiece of the new
school of public architecture emerging in these years in Britain and a
direct response to developments in Paris. Chambers had proposed a
magnificent building for the Society of Arts, Manufactures and
Commerce as early as 1757, discussed the importance of buildings of refinement and luxury in the cityscape of a great commercial nation in
his *Treatise of Civil Architecture* of 1759, and had served since 1761 in the

government's Office of Works. But the opportunity to design a major public building came only in 1776 with Somerset House, a vast complex to house the offices of the Navy and the Tax Administration as well as quarters for the Royal Academy (of which Chambers was a founding member) and the Society of Antiquaries. That these administrations should be grouped conspicuously and efficiently, rather than dispersed throughout London, represented itself a threshold in British thinking about the public role of government and of architecture. As a 1781 guide to the recently completed building recalled, 'the buildings were to be erected in the plain manner, rather with a view to convenience than ornament. But Mr. Burke, and various other Men of taste in Parliament, having suggested the propriety of making so vast and expensive a Design at once an object of national splendour as well as convenience, it was resolved, not only to execute the Work with the strictest attention to the business of Public Offices but likewise with an eye to the Ornament of the Metropolis; and as a monument to the taste and elegance of His Majesty's Reign.'[16] A political and aesthetic programme seems to have been at stake as Edmund Burke quickly took up the question of the building in Parliament and portrayed it as key to advancing his notions of the role of Parliament and its members as representative of the common good, and of his commitment to the modernization of government finances, as well as his aesthetic theories advanced in his influential *A Philosophical Enquiry into the Origin of Our Ideas of the Sublime and Beautiful* (1757).

On the site of an old Tudor palace with only a narrow frontage on the Strand, the principal thoroughfare between the commercial City of London and the administrative City of Westminster, but with ample frontage on the banks of the Thames, Chambers imagined a veritable

city quarter, composed of a harmonious series of buildings arranged around a courtyard to which access is gained either through the great ceremonial head building on the Strand or via subsidiary service roads. That Chambers was inspired by Piranesi and that his client was eager for a public building that might take up something of the contemporary rhetoric of the rivalry of the British Empire with ancient Rome—even in the year when its American colonies began to fight for independence—is apparent in the way Chambers set his building in the landscape of the Thames [29], rivalling the dome of Wren's St Paul's Cathedral and Mylne's Blackfriars Bridge (1760–69), considered by many a monumental work of British civic improvement and engineering prowess. Seen obliquely from Westminster Bridge, the sweeping horizontals of the great podium of warehouses upon which Chambers placed his building, of the cornice line, and of the series of heavily rusticated arches stretching to the horizon seem to embody the principal characteristics identified by Burke as sublime: infinite extent and a feeling of massive weight and scale. Combined with Piranesi's lessons of the ways in which the Romans manipulated light and shade to provoke awe and to trigger the imagination, Chambers strove to explore new aesthetic registers to find the most effective set of images for a building which would raise the most mundane of government functions to veritable symbols of the grandeur of the state and exploit the aesthetics of awe towards the ethics of citizenship.

Chambers' use of the whole range of the classical orders, from the Tuscan in the massive working parts of the undercroft to the Corinthian which graces the façades at the entrances to each of its principal public institutions, creates a legible hierarchy for this complex as well as a coherent composition which maintains the unity of a

30

The courtyard of Somerset
House, London, 1776–96
A series of balustraded
parapets surrounded the
square, as indeed they did on
the Place Louis XV, but in
London they served to hide
from view lightwells for
additional offices below the
raised and levelled grade of
the great courtyard.

work of art, even one which must be experienced sequentially. But the orders are not used simply as a universal vocabulary, for, as John Newman has shown, by reference to well-known English classical monuments from Inigo Jones's original Somerset House to William Kent's Treasury and Horse Guards Building, Chambers 'adopted what he must have considered a "national style"'.[17]

On the exterior Chambers created a veritable mountain of stone which could awe visitors arriving in London by river and provide a vast terrace for taking in the view. Within he laid out a grand courtyard cum public square on the model of the Georgian residential square, with uniform façade treatments familiar from London real estate but now reinterpreted to create the city's first great *public* square [30]. Offices were organized on a system of independent staircases, each with its own doorway, but Chambers was thinking too of the Place Louis xv. As in Paris, a royal statue ornaments the square, but tellingly George iii is set not in the centre of the square but at the edge, himself a spectator of this great public space.

Even before the Royal Academy opened its first public exhibition in the Great Room in the Strand range, Somerset House was subject to public examination and critique. Scaffolding came down in 1778 on the street façade and within a matter of months critiques, many of them quite harsh, appeared. The architect had anticipated these, however, for no sooner had the façade been revealed than an anonymous 'puff'— a form already perfected in the burgeoning world of commercial advertising—appeared in a London newspaper explaining the aesthetic intentions of the building. 'The parts are few, large, and distinct, the transitions sudden and strongly marked; no breaks in the general course of the plan, and little movement in the outline of the elevation, whence the whole structure has, we think, acquired an air of consequence', the article, with little doubt penned by Chambers himself, explained. Chambers evoked those characteristics identified by Burke as the most potent for impressing viewers' minds and he clearly differentiated his own architecture from that of Adam, who boasted in his *Works in Architecture* of having introduced something entirely new—'movement'—into architectural design.[18]

Somerset House was still incomplete when Chambers died in 1796, but its influence on public architecture was already manifest in the 1780s when Chambers' most talented pupil James Gandon (1743–1823) emerged onto centre stage from a rather lacklustre career in England with victories in two open competitions for public buildings in Dublin. The Custom House (1781–91), the Four Courts (1786–1802), and the renovations for the Parliament House (1785–89; now the Bank of Ireland) were evidence of what contemporaries celebrated as a 'public spirit that has lately begun to display itself in the Nation'.[19] Ironically enough, it was left to this English architect, whose homage to Wren is evident in numerous details, to create symbols of Ireland's new importance in the British Empire after the loss of the American colonies.

The Greek ideal and Frederick the Great's image of Prussia

Nowhere were such images pursued more avidly in the closing years of the century than in the German courts, where the ideals of French Enlightenment philosophy and the political and economic liberties of British life were celebrated in a range of ambitious architectural commissions, many by émigré architects trained in Paris and Rome. Whereas the public buildings of Paris and London were often marked by a transfer of power and cultural participation from the world of the court to the urban stage, both in terms of public opinion and private speculative investment, the Neoclassical forums of the various German *Residenzen*—the word itself designating the capital as the residence of the prince—were held within the protective gaze of the ruler. Restyled as an enlightened cultural patron—a stance perhaps best outlined in Frederick the Great's *The Anti-Machiavelli* (Berlin, 1739)—the prince none the less remained the centre of a courtly cultural life increasingly staged in urban space rather than limited to the palace grounds. It is this that explains the precocious creation in Germany of one of the first free-standing theatre buildings, the Opera House in Berlin designed by Georg Wenceslaus von Knobelsdorff (1699–1753), ennobled for his efforts in 1740, and a pioneering public museum, the Museum Fridericianum built after 1769 by Simon Du Ry at Kassel, seat of the Landgraves of Hesse-Kassel. Both were remarkable in using a Classical portico to advertise the range of new values which accompanied the rediscovery of the Classical world at mid-century and by

31

View of the Forum
Fredricianum, Berlin

The work of different
architects devising images for
building functions previously
held within the spaces of the
palace, this public square was
a monument of Frederick the
Great's vision of an
enlightened absolutism. The
king himself suggested the
Roman Pantheon as the
model for Jean-Laurent
Legeay's St Hedwig's (1747), a
Catholic cathedral intended as
a sophisticated architectural
gesture towards the recently
conquered Catholic territories
of Silesia.

the way in which that portico anchored the creation of a grand new
square at the heart of a city dominated by the court and military. But
one should also recall that the frieze on the entablature of Berlin's
Opera House read: 'Dedicated by Frederick who protects the muses',
and that Kassel's museum contained, in addition to publicly accessible
collections, a private study and astronomical observatory for

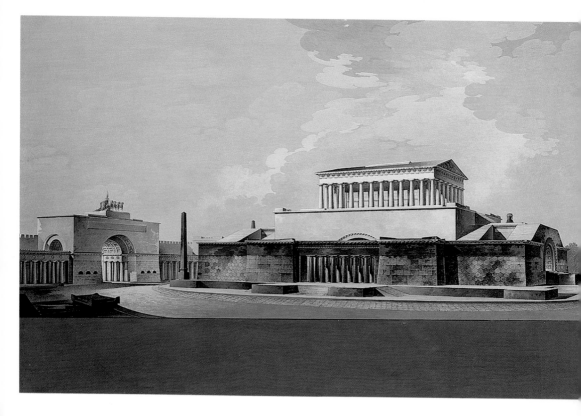

Landgrave Friedrich I. The Berlin Opera House, whose doors were open only to the nobility until 1789, when seats were first made available to a broader public, was the first of three buildings that were to form the image of a perfect public square, the Forum Fridericianum, forming an urban forecourt to one of the royal palaces on Unter den Linden, Berlin's great royal axis [**31**].

In a public competition opened in 1796, a decade after Frederick the Great's death, the young architect Friedrich Gilly (1772–1800) proposed transforming the entrance to Berlin at Leipziger Platz into a grand monument dominated by an exquisitely rendered acropolis [**32**]. Once again a public square was to be centred on a portrait of the king, but this was only to be discovered through a dramatically staged itinerary that took visitors entering the city through a powerful new city gate, through darkened tunnels, and up broad staircases towards the open sky, a process of individual enlightenment which also reinforced a sense of citizenship, for the final ascent to the cella of the Doric temple, raised high above the surroundings, offered a discovery of one's place in the larger landscape of Prussia's capital. Even as in Paris citizens were storming the palace, Berlin's architects were contemplating a future in which an enlightened citizenry would render homage to the monarch as a *grand homme*.

Experimental Architecture: Landscape Gardens and Reform Institutions

3

We must allow our minds to travel in time and space, as did many of the period's artists, intellectuals, and landed aristocracy. Not simply on the Grand Tour to the classical ground of the Roman campagna or the newly discovered ancient Pompeii, but also to the new worlds that patrons and architects sought to create back at home. These were often filled with souvenirs of antiquity, in the verdant settings of the landscape garden and the imaginary futures of utopian blueprints. Even as cities boasted new public settings for collective rituals in the 1760s and 1770s, architects were exploring the interaction between *individual* consciousness and architecture in places removed from the constraints of governments and social traditions. Since the Renaissance, gardens and utopias allowed a freedom from conventions, fostered a sense of a return to origins, and hosted startlingly original architectural design. In the late eighteenth century they were exploited as territory for the practical exploration of Enlightenment theories not only of nature, but more fundamentally of *human* nature. Aesthetics emerged as a distinct philosophical concern, although as it did it began to chart some of the territory that would later be claimed by psychology. Some of the most aesthetically daring experiments would be essayed in the controlled environment of the garden, where the period's taste for exoticism, from Chinese pagodas and Turkish tents to primitive cabins, would find free expression. Not only did these encourage playful reflection on the place of western culture in larger historical and geographic spectra, but architecture's own nature could be tested in these 'laboratories' and the findings rapidly introduced into the realm of civic architecture, striving to keep pace with the accelerating pace of political, economic, and social change.

Detail of 34b

The new philosophy of sensation

Few philosophical movements had such a sustained impact on architecture as did the epistemology of sensation in the wake of John Locke's epoch-making *Essay Concerning Human Understanding* (1689). Sensationalism, or the doctrine that all knowledge is derived from experience through sensations, was to have profound effects on aesthetic theory because it sought to elucidate the direct and immediate relationship between physical objects and mental states. It opened new horizons for thinking about how architecture conveyed meaning and how those meanings could in turn be manipulated. Having rejected the existence of innate ideas, Locke posited that all thoughts derive from experiences, some direct and repetitive, others developed over time through chains of associated ideas building one upon another. Cumulative experiences gradually constructed the human subject and its all-important capacity of memory. Locke's ideas were expanded and revised by Shaftesbury, Addison, and other British empiricist philosophers, and served as the basis for the writings of Condorcet and Helvétius in France, Charles Bonnet in Switzerland, and many others, so that by the mid-eighteenth century sensationalism sought to rival in the human realm the precision that Newton had brought to experimental exploration of the natural realm. Even as Laugier was seeking a natural model for structural expression, the philosophy of sensation opened the way for exploring the hypothesis that architectural meaning had a basis in nature and was embodied in a range of forms and configurations prior to, even outside of, the canon of the inherited classical language of architecture. It became possible even to argue that architecture had an equal, if not superior, effect on emotions, thoughts, and ultimately morals to the representational arts of literature, painting, and sculpture. After 1750 the spectrum of aesthetic categories was broadened and the precision with which aesthetic responses could be gauged and in turn exploited was honed as never before. The sublime, first posited as a literary category, and the picturesque, pioneered in garden design, came to rival the beautiful as architectural values.

Grounded in explorations of the interactions between the natural realm and inner mental states, it is hardly surprising that sensationalist ideas rapidly entered the complex nexus of ideas that sustained the fashion for the irregular or 'natural' garden in the eighteenth century. A whole new appreciation of the relationship of architecture to its environment was fostered, one in which buildings were composed in harmony rather than in counterpoint to their landscape setting, challenging thereby *a priori* canons of symmetry, frontality, and unity. In England, for instance, neo-medieval houses, from Vanbrugh's house at Greenwich (1718–21) to Payne Knight's Downton Castle in Herefordshire (1772–78), were valued for their asymmetrical integration with their natural settings as well as the contrived sense that this irregularity was the result of changes over time rather than a unitary design conceit. Along with the capacity of architecture to evoke historical or literary associations, the very mechanisms by which forms and compositional arrangements affected the emotions, and thus the soul, of viewers were tested in landscape design.

The picturesque and the landscape garden

The English natural landscape movement underwent significant change in the decades between 1719, when the poet Alexander Pope and the architect John Vanbrugh both employed 'picturesque' to advocate creating landscapes like paintings, thus substituting pictorial for architectural criteria in laying out gardens, and 1794, when Richard Payne Knight (1750–1824) and Uvedale Price (1747–1829) argued that the 'picturesque' was a distinct category of aesthetic experience with its own formal laws and emotive effects. From the first, this embracing of simple or 'natural' nature over the highly formal and geometric 'artifice' of the gardens of Versailles—which enjoyed Europe-wide prestige for over a century—was celebrated as a distinctly English invention, one which paralleled, endorsed even, the quest for a society founded on natural law, liberty, and tolerance. Shaftesbury, who, like Locke before him, argued that given freedom man would seek the good, used the wilderness as a symbol of nature in its primitive state and thus a symbol of universal order. The landscape garden became something of a utopia, a place where humanity's own natural morality rejoined the natural realm of which it was a part. Indeed, many of the most spectacular English picturesque gardens were created by and for members of the Whig aristocracy, whose political position was built on this philosophical foundation. Most notable of these were the famous gardens at Stowe in Buckinghamshire where, for the leading Whig Sir Richard Temple, Charles Bridgeman's grand formal layout of 1719–20 was deliberately eroded over the 1730s and 1740s as a programme of garden pavilions and natural tableaux was created by William Kent and, later, James Gibbs. A pointed commentary on British political liberties and artistic achievement was achieved by the introduction of garden buildings which carried a range of emblematic and associative meanings. By the time Rousseau visited Stowe in the 1750s it included some 38 miniature monuments—a veritable museum of architecture to complement the full palette of natural effects in settings such as Kent's 'Grecian vale', meant to transpose the visitor to the purity of an ancient Arcadia. 'All times as well as places have been united in this superb solitude with a magnificence that transcends the human,' Rousseau noted in admiration of Stowe in *La Nouvelle Héloïse*. Rousseau's own concepts of nature and natural sensibility were to be a powerful ingredient in the enthusiasm on the Continent for *le jardin anglais*.

The pioneer of the new fashion was the painter-turned-architect

33

Plan of the gardens at Rousham

Sequence, juxtaposition, contrasts of forms, lighting effects and colours became in the landscape palette the representational tools by which designers could become choreographers of emotions and thoughts.

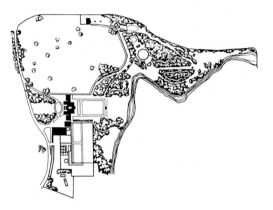

William Kent (1685–1748), whose beliefs in the simple and the natural were first honed under the tutelage of his friend and patron Lord Burlington, tireless promoter of English Neo-Palladianism and sponsor, in his garden at Chiswick, near London, of a new approach to garden design. At Stowe (*c.*1735), and then at Rousham (*c.*1737) near Oxford [**33**], Kent codified the syntax of the picturesque landscape subsequently developed and critiqued by others. The key features of this approach were asymmetric composition, winding paths, reciprocal vistas, and techniques for encompassing 'real' landscape beyond the garden's actual limits, thus blurring distinctions between the composed and the natural, between art and nature. These new techniques replaced the strong geometric frameworks of the French classical garden with an infrastructure emphasizing experience over intellect and instilling a sense of time itself, one of the preoccupations of the age. Not only did the new taste for fake ruins pictorialize the passage of time, enhanced by plantings which revealed the changing seasons, but passage through the garden was contrived to foster precisely those types of experience that sensationalists were analysing in aesthetic and physiological theory. The winding path, which Hogarth would celebrate as the line of beauty,[1] introduced sequence and thus delay, expectation, and revelation, enhancing not only the narrative qualities that had been explored in such literary gardens and houses as Pope's at Twickenham (1719–20) and Walpole's at Strawberry Hill (1749) nearby [**67**], but also a process of self-discovery which was to have potent implications for the garden as a realm of self-realization. Reciprocal views allowed a structure to appear from different positions in the garden and to be juxtaposed with new objects and settings, thus allowing meanings to accrue over time. With a growing spectrum of historical styles in pavilions, or follies, the garden became a place where the period's intellectual fascination with the relation between cultural relativism and universal truths of nature could be explored, even depicted. With it was set in motion the process by which simple experiences were built through complex chains of association, a process debated by Locke's followers and tested in scientific terms by the doctor David Hartley in his *Observations on Man, His Frame, His Duty, and His Expectations* (1749). Hartley proposed a neural basis for sensationalism by demonstrating the origins of all mental occurrences in sensations caused by vibrations of minute particles of the brain stimulated by external objects.

Three of the most famous and best-preserved landscape gardens, Stourhead in England (1744–56), Ermenonville in France (1766–70), and Wörlitz in Germany (1764–94), were composed around a great artificial lake. This surpassed the obvious advantage of planes of water for reflecting the carefully composed tableaux conceived by landscape designers. For Jean-Marie Morel (1728–1810), who worked at Ermenonville, 'Water is to the landscape as the soul is to the body.'[2] Morel went on to delineate with great precision, in his *Theory of Gardens* of 1776, the many characters of water, still and moving, limpid and frothing, and to suggest its power for affecting human sensibility. It was but one of the nuanced materials in the sensualist palette—including light, colour, and textures—with which landscape designers staged both nature and human experience. Its implications for architecture were enormous and immediate.

English garden design: the example of Stourhead

Stourhead [**34a, b**], developed on the Wiltshire estate of banker Henry Hoare, is perhaps the classic statement of the English picturesque garden. A winding path follows the banks of an artificially created lake, forming an itinerary that grows in accumulated experiences and images, an evocation even of one of the most famous literary journeys of self-discovery, Aeneas's descent into the underworld. Intertwined with this classical story is Hoare's devotion to laying bare what Pope had called the 'genius of the place', which extended to the natural history of the Stour valley, evoked in the statue of the river god marking the supposed source of the river's waters in an artificial grotto on the lake's distant shore. It also related to architectural monuments evoking and commemorating incidents in national and family history, most importantly King Alfred's stand against the Danes in the ninth century, which took place nearby and was commemorated by a 160-foot (48.7 m)-high tower, built to Henry Flitcroft's designs in 1762–72 and intended to expand the experience to a sense of the larger landscape and region. Hoare's art collection included by the 1750s Nicolas Poussin's *Aeneas at Delos*, the composition of which is emulated in the pictorial design of Stourhead, and echoes of which can be found in an inscription from the sixth book of the *Aenead* set over an altar in Flitcroft's Temple of Ceres or Flora: 'Begone all you who are uninitiated'. Other meanings are more

34

The gardens at Stourhead
a) Plan b) Coplestone Warre Bampfylde, 'Stourhead Pleasure Grounds, view to the Pantheon', watercolour, *c.*1775

The landscape is organized around an expansive, irregularly shaped lake created by damming up the river Stour near the village of Stourton a few hundred feet from Stourhead House, a neo-Palladian design by Colen Campbell of 1718. Drawn by numerous foreign visitors, its influence spread as far as Sweden and Russia.

readily accessible. Delightful and unexpected reciprocal vistas appear, as monuments frame views of one another across the lake. For instance, the view of Flitcroft's Pantheon, first glimpsed as one descends into the valley from the house, beckons the visitor to the garden journey. But once the opposite shore is reached, controlled views across the water take in the parish church and modest houses of the village. By the ingenious use of a sunken path—a variant on the 'ha-ha' ditches which had first made it possible to incorporate a broad panorama of nature into the landscape surrounding a country house and thereby confound the composed and the natural, the owned and the visually appropriated—the vernacular landscape itself is drawn into the visual realm of the garden and offered for contemplation. The everyday is seen in a new light as an object of aesthetic experience.

While the styles and iconography of architecture appeal to the initiated, Hoare also cultivated a purer realm of meanings and sensations in plantings. Directing his gardeners, he wrote, 'the greens should be ranged in large masses as the shades are in painting, to contrast the *dark* masses with the *light* ones, and to relieve each dark mass itself with little sprinklings of light and green'.[3] The garden would not only denote meanings but evoke moods, thus directing visitors to realms of thought. In the 1760s and 1770s these two registers of meanings, complementary in most landscape gardens, were to be cast as conflicting styles and philosophies of landscape as the first of a long series of doctrinal conflicts accompanied the growth of a gardening literature informed by sensationalist theory. In England the most famous controversy pitted the architect Chambers, who rode to fame with his collection of exotic buildings, including a Chinese pagoda at the royal gardens at Kew, against Lancelot 'Capability' Brown (1716–83), the first person ever to style himself as a professional landscape architect. Brown owed his nickname to his talents for seeing the potential of any landscape and enhancing its inherent qualities for effect; he emerged as a sharp critic of the proliferation of architectural structures in 'natural' landscape parks. Convinced that visual and emotional variety could be achieved exclusively through the manipulation of plantings and terrain, he championed abstract emotive capacities of colours, density of plantings, and the careful arrangement of his famous asymmetrical clumps of different tree species to create a landscape of moods of universal appeal in which nature spoke directly to the eye and thus to the mind and soul without the distractions of a historical or literary narrative. But in his *Dissertation on Oriental Gardening* (1772), Chambers not only praised Chinese gardens for their varied effects and numerous structures asymmetrically disposed as images of nature in freedom, but attacked Brown's style as little different from banal or unimproved nature.

35

Ermenonville. View of the Island of Poplars with Rousseau's cenotaph and, on the left, the Temple of Philosophy, designed by Girardin, 1766–70

The famous ruins, atop a dramatic cliff, of the Temple of the Sibyl at Tivoli were the source of inspiration, but Girardin transformed its associations with inscriptions to the progress of philosophy. In the monument to Rousseau the nineteenth-century faith in the moral benefits of commemorating great men in park-like settings is foreshadowed.

French garden design: the case of Ermenonville

A similar conflict erupted on the grounds of Ermenonville between the patron, the Marquis de Girardin, and the landscape designer Morel, both of whom wrote influential treatises on gardening in the 1770s. Like many of his generation, Girardin was enamoured of both English political philosophy and irregular landscape parks. At Girardin's estate near Senlis, north of Paris, Morel, who would ultimately rival Brown for sheer acreage of land 'improved', proposed a nearly abstract vocabulary of nature, stressing compositions of solids and voids, open and enclosed, expansive and intimate, and describing the interactions of light not only with nature but with the human spirit. Nature and man were subject to constant changes, but these could be known, exploited even, as a mastery of processes and cycles. Inspired by the paintings of Hubert Robert, the great master of antique ruins set in verdant nature, Girardin sought to integrate reminiscences of Classical ruins with his lush collections of plants, a technique he described later in *The Composition of Landscapes* (1777). He corresponded with Rousseau and urged the great philosopher and novelist to take up residence in the hermitage, one of the garden's evocations of the simple life in nature such as Rousseau advocated in *La Nouvelle Héloïse*, which contained the philosopher's own critique of formal gardens. As in other French *jardins anglais*, Ermenonville's pavilions were rich in inscriptions, something which Morel considered superfluous once the raw material of nature had been carefully and knowingly manipulated. After Morel's departure from the job, Girardin continued, adding a hilltop Temple of Philosophy above the lake. Unlike the artificial ruins of so many other picturesque gardens, Girardin left open the possibility that his was in fact a temple in construction, left incomplete to 'reveal the imperfection of human understanding'.[4] Each of the columns was dedicated to a philosopher: Newton, Descartes, Voltaire, Montesquieu, William Penn, and Rousseau. An uninscribed column lay in the grass nearby, while the temple's frieze asks 'Who will finish it?' After Rousseau's death in 1778 Hubert Robert was commissioned to design a tomb for him in the middle of the lake on an island surrounded by 16 cypresses, the tree which since antiquity had been associated with death on account of its melancholy form [35].

German garden design: the case of Wörlitz

While Ermenonville is the ultimate philosophical garden, the contemporary development of the ducal estates of Wörlitz [36a, b] drew on evolving theories of the picturesque to form the core of an ambitious programme by which Duke Leopold III Friedrich Franz of Anhalt-Dessau hoped to turn his small duchy into a model state. His admiration for Rousseau, who claimed that small states such as his native Geneva were closer to nature and thus retained a relative simplicity and innocence as a bulwark against further corruption, was combined with enthusiasm for the political and economic advances of English society. In 1763–65 the duke and his architect Friedrich Wilhelm Erdmannsdorff (1726–1800) visited Rousham, Stowe, and Stourhead, which the duke described as emblems of constitutional freedom, admired Adam's work at Syon, and studied British advances in agricultural reform and manufacturing. From England they travelled to Italy and sought out Winckelmann and Clérisseau to guide them in studying and collecting antiquities, convinced that an art collection would be an integral part of cultivating the local populace.

The garden developed at Wörlitz over the next three decades was but part of a great chain of contrived landscapes stretching along the banks of the Elbe on either side of Dessau. The creation of picturesque vistas along winding paths and canals went hand in hand with the introduction of new methods of irrigation, flood control, and land cultivation. Imitations of landscape effects were conceived, with the dual aim of deepening knowledge of nature and human nature, as for instance in Der Stein, a miniature imitation of Mount Vesuvius which would both fill the spectator with awe and serve as a research tool in volcanology. Nearby, a copy of William Hamilton's villa in Naples was built both to commemorate the great collector and volcanologist and to provide a setting for the duke's collection of vases and antiquities.

36

Wörlitz, near Dessau,
Germany

a) Copy of the Coalbrookdale
cast-iron bridge **b)** Plan

From the laying of the
cornerstone of the Neo-
Palladian block of Schloss
Wörlitz, the duke revealed his
determination to emulate in
both artistic and personal style
the manners of an English
landed aristocrat, but one
informed by Voltaire's notion
of the Enlightened prince
which also had such
resonance in the court of
Frederick the Great in Berlin.

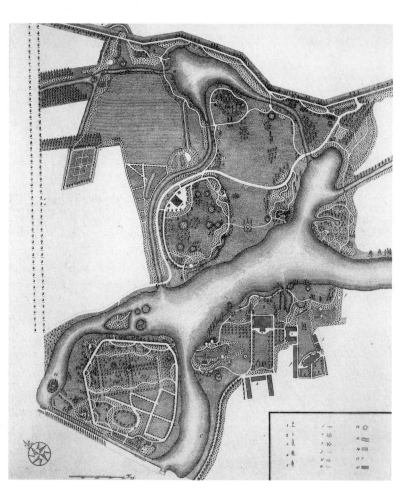

After 1773, national and family history were evoked and explored in the Gothic House, one of the very earliest Neo-Gothic structures in the German-speaking states, erected only a year after Goethe's panegyric on Strasbourg Cathedral as the embodiment of German identity (see chapter 5). For Anhalt-Dessau this identity was not confined to nostalgia, but remained cosmopolitan and contemporary. After Rousseau's death the duke commissioned a copy of the island at Erménonville for the lake at Wörlitz, and in 1791 the veritable museum of bridges which spanned the garden's canals was enhanced with a small-scale replica of the world's first cast-iron bridge at Coalbrookdale in the English West Midlands (1779) [36c]. Improvements were not confined to the estate; Erdmannsdorff's first commission had been for the 'Englischer Sitz' (1764), a covered bench in the form of a 'Palladian' arch, to serve as a prototype for the roadsides throughout the duchy, where a programme was also launched to rebuild parish church towers to serve as landmarks structuring the territory.

Many, including Goethe, remarked that it seemed the whole country was to be redeveloped as a garden, but a pedagogical garden in the spirit of the duke's heroes Rousseau and Lavater. Erdmannsdorff designed village schools, public housing, and a cemetery where distinctions of class and creed were abolished, all fulfilments of the ideals of the duke's 'Philanthropic Society'. Not only were engraved views of the grounds at Wörlitz studied in schools, but parts of the estate were regularly opened to the public. The pavilions flanking the entrance housed a small public library and a natural history and ethnographic gallery exhibiting the South Sea collection acquired from Georg Forster, who had accompanied James Cook on his second trip round

The sublime

Aesthetic philosophy flourished as never before in the eighteenth century. Its greatest impact on architecture was the introduction of whole new categories of aesthetic experience, broadening the register of emotional appeal and dethroning the beautiful as the unique category of judgement. The literary concept of the sublime, traceable to the ancient writings of Longinus, became a favourite topic and the most influential definition was offered by Edmund Burke in his 1757 *A Philosophical Enquiry into the Origin of our Ideas of the Sublime and the Beautiful*. For Burke, attributes of the sublime—obscurity, power, privation, vastness, and infinity—could readily be experienced in nature, but required artful deception in architecture so that they might have a stirring effect on the imagination. Like his French contemporary Condillac, who decomposed the five senses in order to recompose them in painstaking analysis in his *Treatise on Sensations* of 1754, Burke insisted that the imagination was an exact science: 'Natural objects affect us, by the laws of that connection which Providence has established between certain motions and configurations of bodies and certain consequent feelings in our minds ... architecture affects us by the laws of nature, and the laws of reason' (*Philosophical Enquiry*; here cited Oxford University Press edn, 1990, p. 149).

37

Entrance to the Désert de
Retz, in the Forest of Marly
near Chambourcy, c.1775

Artificial grottoes had been
features of landscape gardens
since the Renaissance to
evoke the raw power of nature,
but here the garden is entered
through a grotto calculated to
arouse the sensation of awe
and surprise meant to
heighten the emotions in
readiness for the experiences
of nature and architecture
awaiting along the garden's
sinewy paths.

the world. The Temple of Flora served for a while as a synagogue to substantiate the duke's commitment to religious tolerance. In the hands of Erdmannsdorff and Duke Leopold the English picturesque landscape assumed its most developed form as a project for bridging the realm of individual sensibility and collective reform; nature was the setting for a project of forming a cultivated citizenry.

The sublime

The most suggestive of the period's quests for 'an exact theory of our passions' was Burke's *A Philosophical Enquiry into the Origin of our Ideas of the Sublime and the Beautiful*, first published in 1757, which contained descriptions of the physical basis of emotion and the mechanics of the causal relations between natural objects and feelings, as well as concrete suggestions on how such knowledge could be deployed for aesthetic effect. It is hard, for instance, to look at the engraving of the entrance to the renowned Désert de Retz outside Paris [**37**], the pleasure-ground of the eccentric Nicolas-Henri Racine de Monville and one of the most fantastic of all landscape gardens, without thinking of Burke's description of how gloominess, roughness, and daunting scale are key spurs to sublime emotion. On special occasions fire-bearing satyrs lit the path and greeted party-goers, reminding us of the significant cross-overs between garden theory and the new rhetoric of the

38 Robert Adam

Culzean Castle, Scotland, 1777–90

Adam's building seems literally to grow from the cliffs of the Scottish west coast, suggesting that nature and medieval architecture shared the capacity for sublimity as it had been defined in the widely read texts of Edmund Burke. No less sublime is the view of the endless watery horizon from the salon's main windows.

theatre in this period. Like the literature of the period, which conducted its characters though a series of adventures, such gardens, with their carefully scripted itineraries, responded to the sensationalist notion of astonishment, which it was believed heightened the operations of the soul. In the naturally rugged landscape of Scotland, which was soon to emerge as a tourist destination for those eager to experience the sublime at its fullest, Robert Adam enhanced the register in works that at once take their cues from existing features and reveal the extent to which exaggerations of scale, jagged composition, and other architectural means could be used to provoke astonishment, as for instance in the over-scaled bridge at Dalkeith (1792) and Culzean Castle, which seems almost to grow from its cliff-like setting on the west coast of Scotland [**38**]. By the time this masterpiece of Adam's castle style was completed, the sublimity of the Gothic was confirmed both for its abstract embodiment of sublime qualities and for the power of its association with the dark and mysterious Middle Ages. The quest for a broadened array of emotive effects would go hand in hand with associationism's enlargement of the stylistic palette of historic references in design.

39 Étienne-Louis Boullée

Cenotaph for Newton, *c.*1784

a) Night view of exterior

For Boullée the sphere was both a natural form, and thus most immediately grasped by the mind and the soul, and a symbol of the scientific truths of the universe unveiled by Newton's genius. Although technologically infeasible, this essay on the ideal capacity of architecture to affect the emotions was widely emulated in the closing decades of the century.

b) Daytime view of interior

Boullée's claim that as an architect he set out simply to 'paint' using the effects of nature takes on a theatrical dimension in this startling premonition of the modern planetarium.

Boullée's cenotaph for Newton

After a successful career as a designer of country and city houses for wealthy clients in and around Paris, and a pioneering role in the now vanished picturesque garden at Chaville (*c.*1765), Étienne-Louis Boullée (1728–99) devoted much of his time in the 1780s to teaching and to the theory of architecture. Rather than writing a treatise like so many before him, Boullée produced pictorial studies of architectural monuments, buildings so vast in scale that they surpass the boundaries of both the page and the imagination. Years later he drafted explanatory texts in a manuscript, *Essay on Art* (*c.*1794), which sheds light on his intentions in this laboratory for a visionary architecture of the sensations. Boullée's most famous design is with good reason the cenotaph for Newton, in which he set out to honour the seventeenth-century scientist by imagining an architectural memorial that responded to the near hero-worship that had grown up in the half-century since Newton's death. At the same time he hoped to demonstrate that architectural art could rival science as a means of exploring the laws of nature. 'Sublime mind! Prodigious and profound genius … O Newton! With the range of your intelligence and the sublime nature of your Genius, you have defined the shape of the earth; I have conceived the idea of enveloping you in your discovery.'[5] In these words Boullée explains the novel idea for a vast spherical building which placed a symbol of our planet in the landscape and offered within an astronomical observatory for demonstrations of Newton's laws [**39a**]. With no little hubris, he claims this spherical building—a form emulated in the period by others such as C.-N. Ledoux and A.-L.-T. Vaudoyer, and perhaps inspired by the launching of the Montgolfier brothers' first hot-air balloon in Paris in 1783—as his own discovery of an architectural form perfectly suited to its purpose. He transcends the French academic ideal of 'character', or the appropriate physiognomy for different types or hierarchies of buildings, however, to propose a sensationalist machine for making ideas palpable to every visitor. The subject of this building is nothing short of the sublime itself, for, as Burke explained, the sublime was characterized by infinite extent, daunting obscurity, and overpowering scale, all qualities embodied in the sphere, a perfect form instantly perceived yet subject to infinite variety in lighting effects, which Boullée calls his only decorative accessories.

In this great hollow sphere, a space in which the hand cannot confirm what the eye sees, one is overcome with the palpable sense of infinity; by bodily sensation one understands the magnitude of Newton's discoveries. Light, the very essence of Newton's science, is also the medium of Boullée's experiment and one might imagine the experience of travelling from real daylight in the daytime view through the pitch-black tunnel which penetrates to the middle of the monument

only to emerge below the firmament [**39b**] as a realization of Burke's description of the sublime nature of light:

Mere light is too common a thing to make a strong impression on the mind, and without a strong impression nothing can be sublime ... A quick transition from light to darkness, or from darkness to light, has yet a greater effect ... all edifices calculated to produce an idea of the sublime, ought rather to be dark and gloomy ... to make an object very striking, we should make it as different as possible from the objects with which you are immediately conversant; when therefore you enter a building, you cannot pass into greater light than you had in open air ... At night the contrary rule will hold, but for the very same reason; and the more highly a room is then illuminated, the grander will the passion be.[6]

In both night and day views of the monument, Boullée demonstrates how his great sphere reverses the time of day as one passes to the interior: 'In order to obtain the natural tone and effect which are possible in this monument it was necessary to have recourse to the magic of art and to paint with nature, i.e. to put nature to work; and I can say that this discovery belongs to me,' Boullée boasts.

'Our buildings—and our public buildings in particular—should be to some extent poems. The impression they make on us should arouse in us sensations that correspond to the function of the building in question,' Boullée declares, explaining how he has converted the traditional concern for the appropriate character of a building into a science of using architecture to produce precise and knowable emotive effects. Academic tradition viewed character as a code for using the classical language of architecture to find the suitable and appropriate expression for every building type, a technique in short for making fine-tuned distinctions of visual rhetoric between different social classes. In his most challenging proposals, Boullée advocated that the natural law of architecture should have priority over antique precedent. His own library was as rich in scientific texts as architectural sources, including works by Copernicus, Bacon, Buffon, and Newton. His willingness to limit his vocabulary to spheres, cubes, and pyramids provided him with a test case for his 'theory of volumes'. In scores of imaginary projects he sought 'to discover the properties of volumes and their analogy with the human organism',[7] and thus to harness their power of the senses. In such designs as the Newton cenotaph, for the first time a monumental public building was proposed without recourse to the classical language of architecture, although in designs for a museum, a library and an opera house, columns proliferate to harness both the impact of the sublime and the aura of antiquity to the day's vision of new public institutions.

Funerary architecture and sentiment

Funerary and commemorative monuments, not surprisingly, outnumber all other buildings in Boullée's portfolios, since they were the least encumbered by practical requirements; indeed the necessity that they house human remains was overshadowed by the demands that they serve as markers of the longing for immortality and as instruments for evoking the sentiments of mourning, grief, and melancholy. Boullée's tomb designs were not only demonstrations of his self-proclaimed inventions—'buried architecture' and 'the architecture of shadows'—but contributions to the debate in the closing decades of the century over

the creation of public cemeteries on the outskirts of towns, both as a
hygienic measure to close overcrowded parish churchyards and to create moralizing landscapes where monuments could recall exemplary
public figures and the sentiments of remembering the dead could be
cultivated. A form partially buried in the ground appears heavy, because the mind restores the complete form in the imagination and by
association imagines the weight on one's own shoulders. A tomb designed as a low-slung pyramidal form conveys death through emotive
response—the darkness of the deep void, the heaviness of the overall
form, the close spacing of the weighty supports holding the over-
scaled lintel—and only secondarily by cultural association with the
pyramids of the ancient Egyptians.

If Soufflot had responded to Laugier's call for a natural architecture,
basing the design for Ste-Geneviève entirely on purely expressed
structural elements [11], Boullée offered a perfected vision of
Soufflot's design in which columns and domes are exploited as instruments of sublime emotion [40]. He blatantly plagiarizes in his text describing the 'Metropole' Leroy's earlier description of the effects of
walking through a colonnade, published in his 1764 essay on the history
of church design. But in the startlingly original perspective views of an
interior dominated by seemingly endless rows of columns spaced much
more closely than any Classical canon would condone and by penden-
tives so over-scaled that the dome seems almost to have come to earth,
Boullée created one of the century's most compelling demonstrations
of how a building dominated by a play of light, now entirely limited to

indirect top lighting, could create an overpowering sense of divine presence and mystery. Boullée drew greatly—particularly for ideas on light—on the theories expounded by Le Camus de Mézières in his *The Genius of Architecture, or the analogy of that art with our sensations* of 1780, dedicated significantly to the garden theorist Watelet.

Boullée's projects were born of his teaching in the Academy, and echo the increased concern for public building in a period when the monarchy was actively questioning its own role as a reformer, but above all they respond to the challenge of finding an appropriate form even for wholly unprecedented programmes, including a museum—the Louvre would not be opened as France's first public museum until 1793—a public library [**41**], and a legislative assembly. In each instance Boullée set out to reveal how precisely architecture could be used not only to evoke emotions but to form values, such as a reverence for the moral value of art in the museum, patriotism in an enormous stadium/coliseum he imagined for mass gatherings, even dignity and respect for the law in a Palace of Justice, which was to be reached by a seemingly endless staircase, the forerunner of the countless staircases which for the next century and a half would require that citizens ascend to the court chambers in judicial buildings throughout Europe and North America. The courtrooms were placed here over the prisons, whose windowless, battered walls evoke 'the shadowy lair of Crime', a potent use of the sublime not only to express function but to act as a vigilant deterrent.

The architecture of prison reform: Dance and Ledoux

In his influential *Cours d'architecture* (1771–77), Boullée's teacher Blondel advocated the use of *architecture terrible*, a terrifying architecture, for the exterior design of prisons. The expressive means of the Classical orders and their parts would be pushed to their limits by exaggeration of scale and mass to achieve a 'repulsive style' of heaviness that would 'declare to the spectators outside the confused lives of those detained inside, along with the force required for those in charge to hold them confined'.[8] This idea influenced countless projects for prisons as the movement for penal reform gained momentum, inspired first by the theories of the Italian Cesare Beccaria, whose *On Crimes and Punishments* had appeared in 1763, and then by the vigilance of John Howard, a humanitarian crusader, whose *The State of Prisons* (1777) served not only as a survey of prison architecture, but as an impetus for the passing of the British Penitentiary Act of 1779.

George Dance the Younger's (1741–1825) Newgate Prison in London [42], built 1768–75, gave compelling form to the notion of an architecture so terrifying that a mere glimpse could deter crime. In a period in which public spectacles of execution and flogging were to give way to solitary confinement, the urban presence of prisons was called in to fill the void left by the disappearance of punishment from the public arena. Dance used the heavy rustication introduced by such sixteenth-century Mannerist architects as Giulio Romano to create an impression of foreboding, reinforced by walls virtually unrelieved by windows, a deliberately inelegant articulation of the composition, and by such overt symbolism as the carved chains over the entrances. Dance had been in Rome in 1759–64, during the years when Piranesi

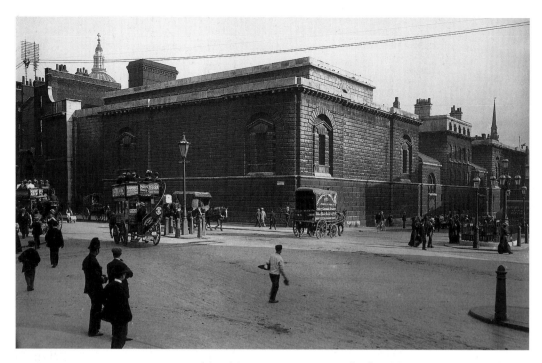

was reworking his *Carceri* engravings [**43**], adding new layers of violent dark-etched lines to these exercises in sublime spatial effects. Something of Piranesi's influence is perhaps to be detected in the way Dance carves out a triangular space before his building so that a dramatic angular view of it would have something of the impact on Londoners passing in nearby streets that Piranesi's prison views had on the eighteenth-century imagination.

But Piranesi and Dance's views were implicitly criticized in the work of prison reformers in the 1770s and 1780s who thought that space itself could be manipulated to condition human responses, even return criminals to civic society. A French advocate of this new strategic approach to punishment, de Mably, put it strikingly in his *On Legislation* (1776): 'Punishment, if I can speak so, should strike the soul rather than the body.'[9] Theories of sensation were now to be used to address personalities formed by malign rather than benevolent natural effects, turning the techniques of manipulating emotional response by the environment into a programme for reforming criminals, calming the mentally ill, and curing the sick. Burke had explained the aesthetics of the beautiful and the sublime in terms of sensations of pleasure and pain; now Jeremy Bentham (1748–1832) proposed that these sensations be exploited to gain access to the criminal soul and gradually reconstruct it, studying with almost mathematical precision what he called the 'felicific calculus'. But while earlier advocates limited their demands to solitary confinement in which the prisoner could commune with his wrongdoing, Bentham became increasingly

convinced that architectural design alone could solve the problem.
Like Boullée he boasted of an invention that would control vision and
sentiment. The 'Panopticon' [44], or all-seeing eye, called for an open
ring of individual cells all facing a central void dominated by a cylindrical central tower. As in Boullée's cenotaph, light was central to the
effect, for Bentham proposed that the cells be lit only by windows on
the exterior wall, providing ample light but also serving to silhouette
the prisoners for better observation. At the centre, the guards remained in darkness. Bentham even suggested that occasionally they
might absent themselves, for the prisoners would never know at what
precise moment they were under surveillance. In effect the spatial
configuration itself ensured the proper functioning of the prison, even
effecting a kind of self-surveillance, as Michel Foucault pointed out in
Discipline and Punish. For Foucault, Bentham's disciplinary apparatus
is a veritable metaphor for the economy and distribution of power and
surveillance in modern society.

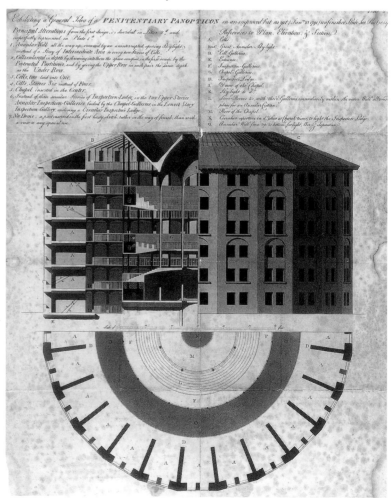

Hospital reform

'Whenever one gathers a group of people one alters their modes of behaviour, when one gathers them together in an enclosed space one alters at once their modes of behaviour and their health', Pierre Cabanis
wrote in 1790, in the culmination of his psycho-physiological research
into the mechanics of human behaviour and the design of institutions
by which societies dealt with deviance from norms.[10] When Paris's
Hôtel-Dieu burned in a spectacular fire in December 1772, it unleashed
a vibrant debate over the perfect form of a modern hospital. Whereas
the old central hospital in the shadow of Notre-Dame had housed a
haphazard medley of the sick, mad, criminal, and indigent in notoriously overcrowded buildings densely intertwined with the city fabric,
the proposed new buildings responded to that revolution in medical
thinking through careful classification, instruments at once of epistemology and political control. Two competing models were developed:
a radial system of wards sharing a common hub[**45**], similar in some
ways to Bentham's later 'Panopticon', and a pavilion type [**46**] where
the wards were arranged like the teeth on two parallel combs, connected by arcaded passages and subordinate to a head building housing
a chapel and common services. Both were grounded in the faith that
the hospital could be rendered a 'machine for curing', in the words of
physician Jean-Baptiste Leroy, brother of the architect (see chapter 1).
Leroy was convinced that hospital architecture could aspire to the
same degree of exactitude and certainty as the study of disease through
careful application of experimental observation, with consistent results. He proposed norms for the precise spacing of beds, the size and
dimensions of windows, and the overall size of wards so that hospital
buildings would become instruments for healthy circulation of air and
light, all of which would dispel the noxious vapours and humours.
With the installation of drains and metal beds it would even be possible regularly to cleanse and purify the wards with water and fire. If
properly distributed the design could, like Bentham's Panopticon,
achieve an optimally minimal staff for a maximum number of inmates
in identical sanitary and humane conditions. These French hospital
plans of the 1780s were enormously influential until the late nineteenth
century, when the germ theory of disease coupled with advances in mechanical systems and gas and electric lighting began to make the carefully calibrated spatial relations less essential. Even more important for
the evolving ideology of the social role of architecture was the belief
that architectural form and space could be made into precise instruments. Whether by enforcing the distribution of bodies in space, or the
visual stimulation of volumes in a visual field, in these model hospitals
and prisons the laws of architecture were being rewritten by the new
philosophy and science of human behaviour.

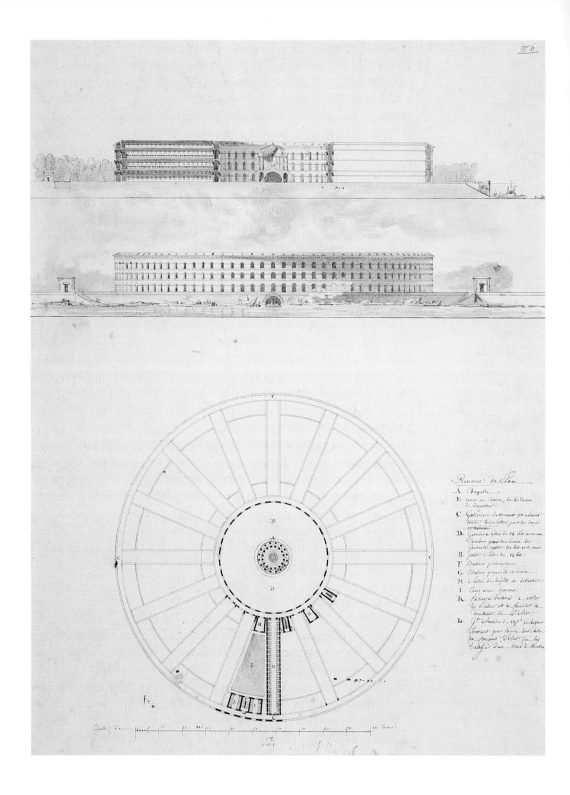

Ledoux and '*architecture parlante*'

Few careers were as marked by the debates over the ways in which architecture communicates meanings and affects behaviour as that of Claude-Nicolas Ledoux (1736–1806). His name, like those of Boullée and Jean-Jacques Lequeu, is so often equated with the concept of '*architecture parlante*', a term coined by his critics to deride his interest in an architecture in which the overall architectural form as well as the rhetorical power of ornamental elements was carefully calculated to speak overtly of the structure's purpose or function, that the subtleties of Ledoux's utopian quest for an architecture that might reform society through its rhetorical clarity across social registers has only recently been fully appreciated. More than anyone, Ledoux experimented tirelessly with the sensationalist proposition that architecture spoke directly to the emotions and the soul through the eyes. Like Boullée, Ledoux enjoyed a highly successful career as a designer of fashionable hôtels before devoting his energies to utopian projects for public architecture. Already in his residential designs Ledoux challenged the traditional understanding of architectural *caractère*, seeking to find means of expressing in hôtel design not simply the social status of the owner by the conventional hierarchies of the Classical orders, but more precisely the profession and individual identity of each owner through manipulation of architectural symbolism.

The grand entrance gate of the Hôtel d'Uzès of 1768 (now demolished) featured free-standing Doric columns crowned with antique torsos bearing shields, helmets and arms, and lion skins, honouring the

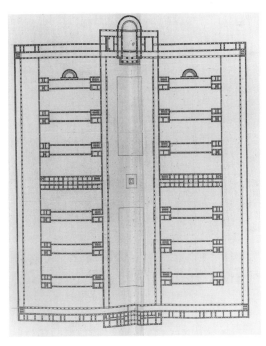

47 C.N. Ledoux

Hôtel Thélusson, Paris, 1778

The last and grandest of Ledoux's *hôtels* was theatrically staged at Paris's northern fringe, and adopted a novel reference to picturesque nature in the city. The garden is set before the house so that the public view, seen through a Classical proscenium, is evocative of its Classical source, the Temple of the Sibyl at Tivoli. Set above a grotto (compare **37**), the engaged rotunda houses the reception rooms of the house, which enjoy views of the city framed by the monumental portico. Tourists were admitted with tickets.

military exploits of the Duc d'Uzès. At the end of a long tree-lined *allée* the visitor reached the house itself, announced by a two-storey Corinthian portico of the type reserved up until then for public buildings. Ledoux's former teacher Blondel sharply criticized the house in remarks which reflect a generational shift in the understanding of the key concept of character. To Blondel the colossal order was a solecism, as shocking socially as it was architecturally: 'A giant order should only be applied to a sacred building or a public monument.'[11] Ledoux was indeed challenging both the social and the architectural status quo even while he explored the very essence of how architecture conveyed meaning. A decade later in the Hôtel Thélusson [**47**] Ledoux staged his building in the city with many of the devices that had been perfected in the landscape garden. The traditional entrance court of a city house was replaced by an irregular garden which would serve as the foreground view to the house. The entrance gate, sunken to achieve something of the sublimity Piranesi had revealed in the half-buried remains of Roman architecture, framed a view of the house whose main feature, a rotunda inspired by the Temple of the Sibyl at Tivoli, rose above a grotto.

From the beginning of his professional career Ledoux divided his time between the salons that made Parisian intellectual life the envy of Europe and the countryside, where he worked as an architect for the administration of roads and bridges. In his quest for an architecture that spoke directly to the eyes and thus to the soul, he was keenly aware that the syntax of the classical language was a learned rhetoric, whereas the formal components of architectural composition provided a more rudimentary vocabulary whose elemental forms were universally understood without reflection, as sensationalist aesthetics had underscored. Although Ledoux's design for a model hospital in the aftermath of the Hôtel-Dieu blaze was quickly passed over, a year later, in the rural Franche-Comté, he was given a utilitarian assignment—a new salt works in the remote village of Arc-et-Senans—which he rapidly turned into an intellectual laboratory every bit as potent as Boullée's paper museum of public buildings.

The salt works and the utopian city of Chaux

Salt was a precious commodity in the *ancien régime*, controlled by royal monopoly and subject early on to the emerging logic of industrial production. Despite great improvements in highways and canals in the reign of Louis xv, it was still more efficient to assemble labour at the remote rural sites near natural resources, such as the saline sources and great forests of the Franche-Comté. The development of these remote locations was to become policy once the economist Turgot took over the Ministry of Finance in 1774 and advocated a physiocratic exploitation of natural resources as a lever for progress. Ledoux's assignment was thus not only for a sort of model factory—one that might, like the designs for the Hôtel-Dieu, serve as a prototype—but also a self-contained town in which workers would be housed adjacent to their place of work. It is not surprising therefore that he began to conceive of the complex as something of an ideal town, nor that, with the enforced leisure the 1789 Revolution brought to former royal architects, Ledoux expanded both the design and its social programme. The semicircular core of the salt works, built between 1774 and 1778, was doubled in paper projects after 1790 to make a full elliptical hub as the centre of a utopian town called Chaux, for which Ledoux drew up designs for a full range of public buildings, exploiting the syntax of sensationalism and the association of ideas to imagine a precise physiognomy for the most diverse building programmes [48].

The architectural historian Anthony Vidler has described the salt works as a 'theatre of production' and analysed the specific links between Enlightenment debates on reforming theatrical space and the abrupt change in plan from a square cloister-like scheme to a great half-circular open space flanked by an arc of residential and service buildings facing the salt production sheds and the director's house along the diameter.[12] A medieval image of a working community was abandoned for the layout of the ancient amphitheatre. Ledoux explained that this new, more purely geometrical form was not only aesthetically superior but would maximize efficiency, productivity, and surveillance since it always drew the shortest line between any two

points. The director's house became the focus, the all-seeing eye of administration.

Mindful of Turgot's efforts to improve France's economic efficiency, Ledoux was careful to extrapolate the radial lines of his plan to remap and subordinate even the surrounding territory, not only creating a series of access points but placing his salt factory at the crossroads of the natural resources on which it depended. Ledoux seems from the first to have had two audiences in mind for his architecture. In addition to the illiterate local population who would experience the monumental buildings daily, he addressed a learned audience who could admire the careful coordination of parts of this complex project in the engravings of a book he planned for years before it was published in 1804 as *Architecture Considered in Relation to Art, Morals, and Legislation*. The title alone summarizes his novel aims for architecture.

The monumental gateway to the salt works featured colossal baseless Doric columns which the learned would at once recognize as the appropriate Classical order for utilitarian buildings, even though many would argue—as apparently the king himself did—that such a lavish architectural gesture was extravagant for a rural factory. But even those unversed in the conventional rhetoric of the classical language would be awed by the scale and simple forms, as well as the processional axial approach, which gave an overwhelming air of ceremonial dignity in the open plain of the landscape. And all could immediately read the purpose of this building, for great urns were carved at regular intervals along the convex outer façade, oozing saline water. Entry leads via the wider central interval of the colonnade—the learned might recognize the Athenian propylaea as published by Leroy and speculate on the factory as a modern acropolis—and then through a great apsidal void treated not as a Roman half-dome, as in so many Neoclassical projects, but as an imitation of a grotto from which more saline water is seen to emerge. Ledoux combines two orders of meaning—a daring pushing of the rhetorical codes of the Classical language to their extreme of expression with a pictorial realism—and explores the many ways in which the language of architectural form communicates both meaning and sentiment.

Taking his earlier design as the point of departure for a utopian town, Ledoux filled the woods surrounding the salt works with the institutions needed by a society more complex than a simple company town. Ledoux's buildings, both by the activities they housed and the messages they conveyed, serve as veritable lessons for a new society set amidst a Rousseauian nature. Functions that societies had traditionally relied upon for spiritual and material well-being would be retained, including market halls, a church, and multiple dwellings (although Ledoux proposed communal living with shared kitchens). New functions would occasion explorations of the capacity of architecture to give both form and purpose to unprecedented institutions. In a series of institutions, some prophetic, quixotic, even quirky, Ledoux—giving vent to his deep involvement, like so many late eighteenth-century architects, in freemasonry—imagined architecture as a foundation of social harmony. The Pacifière [**49**] was to be a tribunal for personal disputes—a sort of forerunner of a family court. The Oikema, or house of sexual education, would operate as a controlled brothel to channel the carnal passion of young men. Here a libertarian, if sexist, vision was glorified by a temple front, while only the twin apses at the end of the long corridor building hinted at the phallic floor plan revealed to the initiated and clearly visible to readers in the aerial perspective published in Ledoux's book.[13] In a series of highly individualized houses, sculptural form would literally pictorialize the inhabitant's profession:

49 C.-N. Ledoux

'Pacifière' for Chaux

For his expansion of the salt works into a model society Ledoux invented such novel institutions as a family tribunal. Messages of stability and perfect harmony conveyed by the elemental language of geometry would be fine-tuned for the literate—illiteracy would rapidly disappear in utopia—with texts from the laws inscribed in a series of tablets punctuated with bound fasces, the ancient Roman symbol of authority.

a great house made of rings for the coopers, a house in the form of a monumental cylindrical sluice for the keeper of the river dam who harnessed natural power for the good of the town and its industry. For the first time character would be used to establish identity through professional contributions—a vision of an emerging bourgeois mindset—rather than traditional hierarchies of the classes.

Ledoux was seeking a design syntax which challenged both the traditional orders of architecture as well as of society. Chaux was to be such a fine-tuned instrument, a city in nature, that it would call forth the highest capacities of human nature. In this Ledoux's work seems to sound in resonance with the ideals of the Marquis de Condorcet, who preached the perfectibility of the human species in his *Sketch for a Historical Picture of the Progress of the Human Mind*, published in 1795 even as Ledoux was putting the finishing touches on his vision of an ideal city. Ledoux himself had just successfully appealed his imprisonment during the Terror, and it is telling that for his ideal city set in nature he drew no prison, spoke of no police force, confident to the last that architecture could engender a better world. At Chaux the experiments of the eighteenth-century landscape garden and the new science of institutional planning were merged in a utopian alternative to the emerging industrial town.

Part II

Revolutions

VERTUS DU PEUP

Revolutionary Architecture

4

Architecture's capacity to carry messages, to shape and even reform behaviour, was harnessed as never before in the 1790s in the wake of political and economic revolutions which aimed at nothing less than changing fundamental values and daily environments. In the wake of the 1789 political revolution in France carefully designed monuments were needed to serve new institutions from the legislative assembly to festivals, but more importantly to help foster those very notions of nationhood and an engaged citizenry central to the Revolution's bid to 'regenerate' humanity. The Revolution swept away age-old privileges, opened markets, and, confiscating aristocratic and church land, led to a significant redistribution of ownership. Less dramatically, but perhaps of even greater consequence, in Great Britain the industrial and financial revolutions, under way for decades, were given a major stimulus at the turn of the century by the upheaval and then war on the continent. Neither the political nor the economic revolutions would be contained by national borders; both were to have enormous impact throughout Europe—especially in the wake of the Napoleonic Wars—exporting at the same time the new symbolic and spatial forms by which architecture became an integral part of bids to give birth to societies of enlarged political franchise and new economic and social relations.

Architecture as propaganda

Nothing confirmed the connotative and emotive powers of architecture more dramatically than the storming of the Bastille on 14 July 1789, a largely symbolic act heralded immediately as a threshold between revolt and revolution in which the king would be forced to acknowledge the claims of the sovereignty of the people. Quickly the fourteenth-century fortress prison, a symbol of royal tyranny already slated for demolition to create a 'Place Louis XVI', became part of the language of symbolic forms by which the revolutionaries sought to make art and architecture central to propagandizing the message of a new world order. As the Bastille was erased from the skyline, it was turned into a symbol not of oppression but of liberty, in an act of appropriation fundamental to creating a revolutionary visual vocabulary, a veritable republican iconography. The stones were sold to the builder with the

Detail of 54

50 Pierre-François Palloy

Monument to the Revolution to be erected on the site of the demolished prison of the Bastille, 1789

Partly reusing the stones of the Bastille, now converted into symbols of liberty and the dawn of a new era, Palloy's project was one of many during the 1790s to return to the theme of the ancient Roman triumphal column. At the same time he hoped to invent a new republican iconography.

highest bid for the contract to demolish, one Pierre-François Palloy, who proposed a monument of his own design to rise on the site [**50**] and withheld enough of the stones from sale as building material to create small models of the Bastille. Some were sold as souvenirs, others sent to the county seats of each of the newly created *départements* to foster national unity. Political allegories proliferated in the newly un-censored marketplace in engravings and pamphlets, and the image of the Bastille now circulated far from Paris as the attribute of the allegor-ical female figure of Liberty. Liberty held a small model of the fortress, one of many instances in which age-old techniques of religious art were appropriated to the programmes of secularization.

This act of semantic reversal, of imparting new meaning, runs throughout the cultural politics of the Revolution, which posited nothing short of transforming the subjects of the king into citizens, by changing their language, both spoken and visual. Overnight the daily environment began to change: streets were renamed, signs of 'feudal-ism' were scraped off buildings, and administrative space was redrawn. The *départements*—symbolically 89 at first—were created to rational-ize national administration and to wean people off allegiances and ha-bitual references. It was even thought to lay graph paper over the map of France, but eventually names evoking geographic features of the country were adopted. The French language itself was altered by de-cree, the polite form of 'vous' abolished in favour of the egalitarian 'tu', to be exchanged between all *citoyens*. The Abbé Grégoire, one of the most insightful cultural activists of the period, proposed that local dialects be abolished in favour of a universal French which he saw as an instrument of equality and liberty. Grégoire proposed that public monuments bear inscriptions in French rather than Latin, and that changing of street and place names be coordinated to create a grammar of place related to new values. 'When one reconstructs a government from scratch no single abuse should escape reform, everything must be republicanized,' he noted. 'The legislator who doesn't take account of the importance of signs will fail at his mission; he should not let escape any occasion for grabbing hold of the senses, for awakening republican ideas.'[1] The psychology of sensation and the language of signs, explored by philosophers from Burke to Condillac, had become a strategy of revolutionary consciousness. Perhaps Grégoire's most insightful and influential theories were those voiced in two impassioned essays on 'vandalism' (a word he coined, he said, in order to kill the thing), pleading for an end to revolutionary attack on works of art and architecture. Rather than signs of their royal, aristocratic, and ecclesiastical owners, these works were now to be relics of national heritage, an integral part of the shared experience of Frenchmen.

Accompanying this restructuring of the citizen's relationship to space through language was a new relationship to time, both lived and remembered. A new calendar was adopted, counting the year 1 with the passage of the constitution in 1793. The weeks and months were to be rationalized, stripped of superstitious references to mythology, and punctuated by new holidays celebrating benchmarks in the progress of the Revolution. Alexandre Lenoir proposed the first chronological display of works of art in his famous Musée des Monuments Français, opened in 1795 in the former monastery of the Petits Augustins. Works of sculpture salvaged from deconsecrated churches and abbeys as well as from aristocratic seats were to be cleansed of their old messages and given new patriotic and national significance in the didactic context of the newly emerging narrative of the history of art. The first tentative efforts to inventory historic buildings as national heritage were made. The ideology of the museum as a celebration of national identity and artistic achievement was soon to be given expression in the Louvre, a royal palace converted in 1794, the prototype of the great national art museum as a patriotic spectacle.

At the same time the system of measurement was to be a universal and rationalized instrument with the adoption of the metric system in 1795. Building design was to be affected at every level, from this new quantification of space to the symbolic charge of forming citizens. Stylistically the many projects of the Revolution did not differ radically from the progressive architecture of the preceding 20 years, but for the first time architectural design and research were seen as integral to the process of building the modern nation state divorced from royal patronage.

Architectural language and public building in France

Throughout the 1790s architectural ambitions were divided between ideal projects and the pressing need to house institutions for a rapidly changing society by adapting existing buildings. The Enlightenment ideal of a single perfect form for each function, one in which forms were so aptly chosen that the very functioning of an institution might be optimized, often fell victim to strapped resources and to rapidly shifting political alliances and ideas. The adaptive reuse of churches, monasteries, palaces, and mansions made available with the successive acts expropriating buildings and land as national property was not only pragmatic but symbolically charged. It was based on a ritual suppression of one reality by another, while it implied that architectural character could be used not only to create, but even to topple and alter a structure's message.

A democratic national assembly

The quest for the perfect place of national legislative assembly raised the question of how the latest theories of architectural space could be used to reform society as a whole. The States General had not met since 1614 when Louis XVI agreed in 1788 to call an assembly to consult on France's fiscal crisis and made available an outbuilding of Versailles for 1,200 delegates. Pierre-Adrien Pâris, the king's architect of festivals, was in the habit of channelling his knowledge of ancient architecture imbibed at the French Academy in Rome in the 1770s into artifice for royal representation. He adeptly converted the modest rectangular building into a dignified setting based on the civic basilica, the place of justice and public assembly in ancient Rome, crafting out of wood and plaster a great coffered vault carried aloft on baseless Doric columns modelled on Paestum. Platforms were built so that carefully segregated banks of seats for the three estates shared a view of the raised dais for the king at one end of the hall. In the early weeks the delegates were absorbed with procedural questions—heatedly debating whether to vote by individual delegates or by estate—and soon with the layout of the room itself. After the group declared itself a National Assembly on 17 July 1789, Pâris remodelled the room, shifting the focus to one of the long sides and arranging banked seats in a great elliptical double amphitheatre. Not only were acoustics and sight lines improved, but the hierarchical space was made more egalitarian and the distinctions between the three estates erased. The ancient amphitheatre as the spatial form for the modern legislative assembly was born, and its democratic associations grew with each new use as the form was replicated first at the Tuileries (1792–93) and then at the Palais Bourbon (1795–98) once the National Assembly moved to Paris. Eventually it would be used for the permanent chambers of the two houses of the French legislature, even as it was incorporated in the projects adopted in 1792 for the leg-

Project for a national palace to be erected over the incomplete foundations of the royal church of the Madeleine, 1792. Section and site plan

The great temple front would be visible from the Place Louis XV, renamed the Place de la Concorde [19]. Within, delegates would sit in an adapted Greek amphitheatre facing 10 tablets of the law, reminiscent of those proposed by Ledoux in his Pacifière [49].

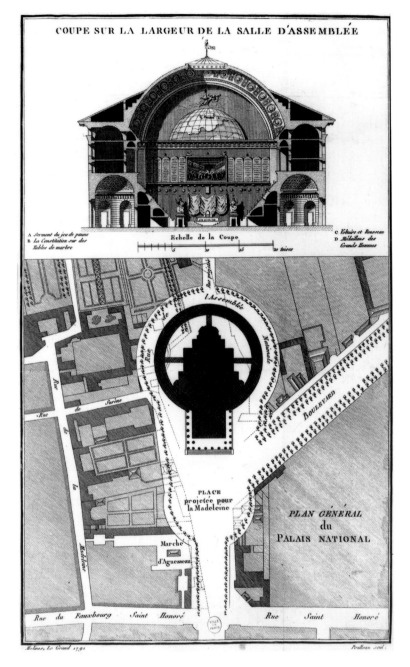

COUPE SUR LA LARGEUR DE LA SALLE D'ASSEMBLÉE

A *Serment du jeu de paume*
B *La Constitution sur des Tables de marbre*

Echelle de la Coupe

C *Voltaire et Rousseau*
D *Médaillons des Grands Hommes*

PLACE projetée pour la Madeleine

PLAN GÉNÉRAL du PALAIS NATIONAL

Marché d'Aguesseau

islative capital of the young American republic. The tendency of political blocs to sit in blocks of seats gave birth to the terminology of modern politics—left, right, and centre—as language confirmed the intimate relation of space and politics.

A national palace was the keystone of the architectural policy outlined by Armand-Guy Kersaint before the Paris city council in December 1791 and then published as a pamphlet with a series of architectural designs by Jacques-Guillaume Legrand and Jacques Molinos. Drawing on earlier theories of *architecture parlante*, Kersaint declared public monuments 'a voice which speaks to all nations, conquers space, and triumphs over time', and advocated that diverse cultural issues under debate be considered as elements of a unified programme to build reverence for the nation and its laws.[2] The National Assembly was to be a veritable cult site, a sanctuary for the laws and a temple of debate as a foundation of democratic government in which respect for the law by citizens was fundamental to the new social contract.

Kersaint proposed building the new national palace on the foundations of the Madeleine [**51**], the royal church whose construction had languished for decades, not simply to economize but to appropriate something of its aura and to reconfigure Paris's new royal centre so carefully laid out by Gabriel, Marigny, and Louis xv. An amphitheatre of seats would face a podium, flanked by statues of Voltaire and Rousseau, intellectual forefathers of the Revolution, while overhead Jacques-Louis David's painting *Oath of the Tennis Court*—recently commissioned—would place the Acts of the Assembly in line with the foundation moment of legislative sovereignty. For town squares throughout France Kersaint proposed small monuments, to be known as *prytaneum* after the public halls in ancient Athens where a sacred fire was kept burning; there laws would be posted and *grands hommes*, great exemplary public figures, honoured and remembered.

The Panthéon and the revolutionary festivals

Festivals, processions, and pageants had been used since antiquity to reinforce the power and aura of church and crown, but during the French Revolution new forms of public ritual were devised to foster patriotic attachment to the abstract concept of 'the nation' and to endow new monuments with symbolic meaning. None was more spectacular than the first revolutionary festival, the Festival of Federation, which called 14,000 delegates from the new municipal 'federations' to Paris on the first anniversary of the storming of the Bastille [**52**]. Staged on the Champ de Mars, the great royal military exercising terrain in front of the École Militaire, the centrepiece was an enormous national arena, designed by a group of architects led by Cellerier and modelled on ancient Roman circuses, in which patriotic rituals were performed at the central 'altar of the fatherland' with its 'Liberty tree', one of thousands planted throughout the nation. Rousseau's moral plea for festivals in *Letter to d'Alembert on the Theatre* (1758) was realized almost literally: 'Plant a post crowned with flowers in the centre of a site, assemble the people there and you will have a festival. Do even better: display the spectators as spectacle, make them actors themselves, make each of them see himself and love himself in the others, in order that all will be better united.'[3] Revolutionary festivals became

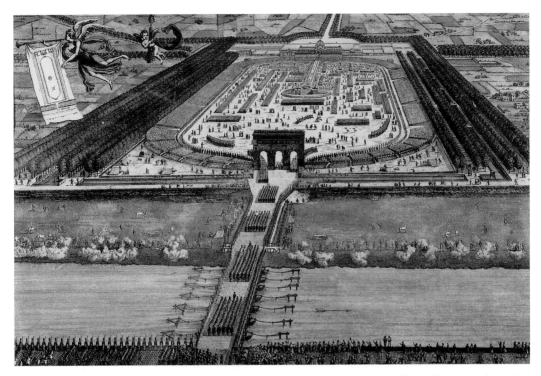

veritable barometers of political views and shifting alliances, changing subtly not only the content of the spectacle but also the itinerary of the parade through the city as the decade progressed.

Nowhere was this bid to edit the past more poignantly essayed than in the Panthéon, created by converting Soufflot's scarcely completed church of Ste-Geneviève [10] into a Temple to Great Men. Resonant as the building was with religious and royal associations, this was a controversial and fraught venture. The Panthéon was intended to foster a new civic religion of public hero-worship, beginning with Voltaire and Rousseau—the only 'precursors' admitted to the Revolution's honour roll—and with Mirabeau, whose death in April 1791 occasioned the first debate over public monuments in the legislative assembly. Kersaint's claim that monuments triumph over space and time was put to the test in highly charged circumstances with the decree to replace Louis xv's dedication to Ste-Geneviève on the frieze of Soufflot's great temple front with a new text: 'To Great Men from a Grateful Fatherland'. 'It is not enough to put a name on a monument to give it the desired character,'[4] the young architect A.-L.-T. Vaudoyer (1756–1846) protested, echoing the opinion of many that a building carefully studied to perfect the whole tradition of Christian church building could never be made to speak of a different purpose.

Even though he had been opposed to the idea, the sculptor and architectural theorist A.-C. Quatremère de Quincy (1755–1849) took up the challenge of directing the transformation and wrote a series of re-

VUE PERSPECTIVE DU PANTHEON.
Dédié aux Grands Hommes.

On a cherché, dans ce Projet, à donner le Caractère de la solidité que doit avoir ce Monument. La partie supérieure qui couronne cet Edifice peut être considérée comme le Temple de l'immortalité orné des Statues des Grands Hommes. On peut y arriver aussi bien par les Escaliers intérieurs que par ceux extérieurs pratiqués sur les Angles de la Pyramide qui est terminée par la Statue de l'Immortalité.

ports on the challenge of obtaining the suitable architectural character for the solemn revolutionary cult. 'The art of characterizing', he had stressed in his article 'Caractère' in his 1788 *Dictionnaire d'Architecture*, 'is of all the secrets of architecture, the most refined and the most difficult to develop as it is to grasp.'[5] It was, as he explained, the very key to

53 Charles De Wailly

Project to transform the
Panthéon, 1797

Perhaps inspired in part by the
Temple of Philosophy at
Ermenonville [35], it is
interesting to note that De
Wailly's proposal is
contemporary with Friedrich
Gilly's project for a monument
to Frederick the Great as a
monument to the Enlightened
Monarch as Great Man [32].
The dome is transformed from
a landscape marker to a
platform for observing the city,
remarkably the newly invented
Panorama.

the social role of architecture, for it was through precision in expression that architecture became an instrument of public instruction and moral elevation. 'Isn't it obvious', he asked, 'that a monument is nothing but a great thought, divisible if one so desires to analyse its parts, but indivisible as far as its soul is concerned on the principle which should unite it into a whole?'[6] The funerary and commemorative functions of the Panthéon should be severed since mourning and the reflection on exemplary lives gave rise to contradictory sentiments. The Panthéon was not to be the residence of death but of immortality; the bodies would be relegated to the crypt while the nave would be a carefully curated sequence of busts and statues, arguably the first of the didactic national museums proposed in these years.

Of all the changes made, none was more central than the decision to wall up the windows of the side aisles and apse. Quatremère de Quincy felt this to be the only way to defeat the 'lightness' and 'gaiety' of the architecture and instil the severe and sober character that would echo the moral fibre of the great figures to be honoured. Without windows the exterior would present those uninterrupted surfaces so admired by Boullée and which Quatremère de Quincy felt were key to distinguishing the building from surrounding houses and rendering the dome the all-important first impression. Within, the flickering light of Soufflot's conception would give way to a more carefully controlled top lighting. During the same years architects explored the possibility of skylighting for the Grande Galerie of the Louvre to create an overall museum light as well as an atmosphere of aesthetic reverence and detachment from real-life concerns before works of art, reflective of the notion of indifference in aesthetic experience theorized in these same years by Kant in his influential *Critique of Judgment* (1790).

Alternative propositions proliferated in the climate of debate which coloured the Revolution, perhaps none more daring and original than De Wailly's proposal [53] to solve with one grandiose gesture both the structural and the symbolic challenges of the Panthéon. Removing the dome while leaving intact its ring of columns, De Wailly would not only defeat the dome's religious connotations—literally decapitating the church—but transform the building into a base for what he called a 'Temple of Immortality ornamented with statues of Great Men'. Diagonal buttressing at the four corners would at once support a smaller dome over the crossing and give the impression on the exterior of an enormous pyramid around which the church had been constructed, as though this modern cult site were built on the site of an ancient pharaonic tomb, at once a symbol of burial and immortality. De Wailly was after elemental forms and universal symbols, but at the same time he conceived a building that appeared to have come into existence in stages; he sought to achieve in a monument both that unity of thought which Quatremère de Quincy and others described as central to architectural character and the capacity to evoke a narrative destined for a long life in the historically conscious nineteenth century. At the same time De Wailly's admittedly fantastic project was intended to alter the visitor's perception of the everyday environment. Monumental staircases conduct visitors to the very centre of the absent dome, where from a viewing platform they would witness the skyline of Paris rising beyond a foreground crown of great men in the portrait statues atop the colonnade remaining from Soufflot's dome. De Wailly was one of the most committed designers of transformations of the key institutions and spaces of Paris, and exhibited at the 1789 Salon a comprehensive plan of public works to make Paris a commodious capital which was largely taken up in the famous Plan des Artistes for Paris of 1793, created to take advantage of the sale of confiscated aristocratic and church property. De Wailly also drew up unsolicited projects for transforming the Louvre to house a universal museum of arts and sciences and made designs for outfitting his own amphitheatrical *place* before the Comédie-Française (today's Théâtre de l'Odéon) as an outdoor theatre for festivals.

The competitions of the Year II and the apotheosis of public architecture

No single event offers a greater cross-section of the Revolution's fundamental questioning of the very institution of architecture in society than the competitions of the Year II (1793–94), the progress of which paralleled that of the Revolution's most radical phase, the Jacobin Terror. These were the denouement of a series of challenges to the élite world of royal art and architecture, including the abolition of the Academy of Architecture and its scholastic competitions in August 1793. Public competitions for public buildings would emulate in architecture that ethos of public participation and debate in civic affairs evoked in the Constitutional Act and the Declaration of the Rights of Man and of the Citizen in June 1793. With the launching in spring 1794 of 25 artistic competitions, a procedure long used by the academies to discern an élite was recast as a referendum on an issue of general public concern. Thorny issues of artistic judgement and public taste in a democracy quickly came to the fore. A first jury appointed by the state included politicians and scientists but was ultimately rejected in favour of a jury of artists elected by the contestants, renewing the ideal of a Republic of the Arts as a meeting of artistic talents. Although the submission of nearly 200 projects made the event the largest public canvassing on architecture ever staged, many established architects shunned the procedure as a mere vying for political favour, particularly in an atmosphere where overt signs of patriotism and allegiance to the shifting ideals of the Revolution could be matters of life or death. None the less, fundamental questions about the architect's role in society were raised, if not resolved. The subjects, or programmes, of the competitions covered such a broad range that the cumulative exercise was nothing short of a bid to reinvent public architecture. In addition to overtly propagandistic symbols such as a monument to the Revolution to be erected in the Panthéon, contestants were invited to submit designs for everyday needs from tribunals to theatres, markets, slaughterhouses, and even a model farm. The net result—proposed briefly to be put on public display as a museum of modern architecture—was a vision of architects working for both the glory and the well-being of a new society, both as symbol givers and problem solvers.

The greatest number of prizes was awarded to a former pupil and a former assistant of Boullée, Jean-Nicolas-Louis Durand (1760–1834) and Jean-Thomas Thibault (1757–1826). Durand was later to become famous as a teacher at the École Polytechnique—set up in 1794 to provide engineers to meet the needs of the revolutionary armies as well as civilian public works in even the remotest corners of the Republic—and in particular for his textbooks which proposed a rationalized system of design based on gridded space and an architectural vocabulary reduced to its austere essence. Durand's pedagogical exercises were arranged by building type, making programme determinant. But although he was versed in the quest for architectural character, already in competition designs Durand suggested that the spatial disposition of the programme in a lucid plan must precede the quest for proper expression. In the spirit of classification of artefacts then being essayed in the newly founded museums of natural history and of technology in Paris, Durand and Thibault demonstrated how a single analysis might give rise to different but related solutions and expressions. At the same time they sought to demonstrate how architecture could face even unprecedented demands with the great variety possible in the manipulation of a limited formal and structural vocabulary. Influenced by the contemporary 'Idéologues' in philosophy, Durand and other contestants recognized that post-monarchical society would call upon architects to design humble and everyday buildings.

Durand and Thibault's prize-winning design for a temple to the revolutionary cult of equality received considerable attention, was widely circulated in engravings, and copied by Durand's students, including a number of young Germans, later to be influential architects [54]. Durand announced his life-long quest to hone the entire heritage of the classical language of architecture to an efficient and replicable system, one that could raise the level of the expedient architecture of military engineers and of rural construction, even as it answered to the austere budgets of France at war. As energies were focused on converting cathedrals into temples of reason, Durand and Thibault offered a model of a perfectly rationalized public monument, its classical columns replaced by a regular grid of square piers.

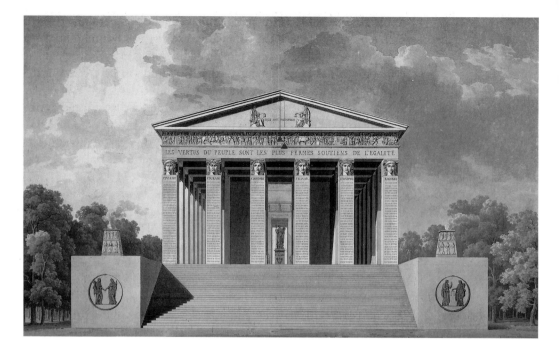

LES VERTUS DU PEUPLE SONT LES PLUS FERMES SOUTIENS DE L'EGALITÉ

Project for a Temple of Equality submitted in the Competitions of the Year II (1794)

Each pier represented a republican virtue—wisdom, economy, work, peace, courage, and prudence—and large murals depict principal events of the Revolution. As in ancient Athens, the temple was to make permanent the rituals of festivals and ceremonies. The drawing was copied by pupils, including, as here, Leo von Klenze, later crown architect in Bavaria.

The temple was dedicated to 'Public Well-Being', and Durand developed that theme as the very ethos of architecture in courses in architectural composition at the École Polytechnique, printed in his *Summary of Courses offered at the École Polytechnique* (1802–05), and destined, along with his great folio of comparative plates of historic and contemporary buildings, the *Portfolio and Parallel of Buildings of all Types Ancient and Modern* (1800), to be one of the most influential architectural books of the century. 'Whether one consults reason or examines the great monuments of the past,' Durand maintained, 'it is obvious that to please has never been the purpose of architecture. Public and private utility, the well-being and the maintenance of individuals and of society, that is the aim of architecture.'[7] The modulation of language, as well as concerns from revolutionary fervour to the utilitarian spirit of the Napoleonic period, is unmistakable, but already in 1795 the state Council on Public Architecture established a regular procedure for reviewing all public architecture against programmatic and budgetary standards. It was destined to play a major role in the shape of cities and architectural thinking, as well as in France's political consolidation and colonial ventures, for the next century.

In the end the Revolution stamped few landmarks with the stoic ethos it developed in debates, in pamphlets, and in competitions. Institutions more than buildings were its most lasting legacy, notably the four public museums opened in 1793–94 in former royal and monastic complexes. Pioneering public art museums, the Louvre and Lenoir's Musée des Monuments Français, presented art not as symbols

Gallery of Architecture opened in the rue de Seine, Paris, c.1806

Leroy's universal history of architecture [14] was challenged for the first time by a presentation in which the relativity of architectural forms to specific cultures was displayed. The stage was set for nineteenth-century debates over the lessons to be derived from the systematic study of architecture as a process of change rather than a codification of ideals. Cassas's models were later acquired by the École des Beaux-Arts.

of princely power but rather as stages in the development history of national genius. At the same time science museums offered spectacles of progress, institutions for public education, and settings for scholarly research, most notably the Natural History Museum formed of the old Royal Botanical Garden and the Conservatoire des Arts et Métiers, Europe's first museum of technology. Both opened in 1794. A museum of architecture was even proposed as part of the newly reorganized School of Architecture to include a gallery of models arranged in chronological order [55].

Britain's industrial and financial revolutions: new environments of work

While French revolutionaries trumpeted the heroic mission of forming citizens for a new polity, in Great Britain architecture served as a handmaiden to the equally radical, if slower, processes of economic change. By the 1790s factories, banks, and stock exchanges had entered daily life not only in London, but in many small towns where their impact on the landscape was particularly dramatic. Instruments and symbols of profound social as well as economic transformation, these buildings became focal points for public debates over the proper place, even the morality, of commerce and credit in society. Even before the Bastille was stormed, factories in the English Midlands had been attacked and machines vandalized as threats to artisanal livelihoods. In London the headquarters of the Bank of England, the veritable nerve centre of the symbiotic relationship of public borrowing and private

The grid of iron supports and spans set within an envelope of brick walls pierced with windows was a technical revolution in building with enormous consequences. Driven by the imperatives of production, the open spaces created were ideal for assembly-line production. Exterior walls had only to support themselves, a principle later elaborated in cast-iron construction in Britain and America after 1850.

credit, was targeted during the Gordon Riots of 1780, along with the nearby Newgate Prison [42].

Factories

The transformation of the textile industry, which can be traced as far back as Lombe's Silk Mill in Derby of 1717, depended as much upon the progressive mechanization of the processes of spinning and weaving and on the tapping of water, and later steam, power to drive the new inventions as it did on the development of factory buildings as efficient instruments of production [56]. The same business logic that assessed the potential economies of investing in the inventions that are milestones of industrializing textile manufacture—the flying shuttle (1733), the spinning jenny (1764–69), or the water frame (1769)—were applied to perfecting the structures that housed them. The factory building was an integral element in mechanization as it organized the distribution of both mechanical power to the machines and of a workforce whose efficiencies depended on rational spatial layout and easy surveillance. By the 1770s factory buildings assumed characteristic internal layouts which would be little affected by either dimensions or exterior expression, although occasionally historical references would be used to lend an air of dignity to these buildings of unprecedented scale. Although mills changed little in overall appearance or organizational logic for the next century, progress in modes and materials of construction was often breathtakingly rapid. It is no coincidence that in the 1790s Jeremy

Bentham, the father of utilitarianism, would propose that his own invention, the Panopticon, a building that could achieve maximum results with the minimum human workforce, be taken up as a model workhouse [**44**]. Bentham proposed that the building be constructed of iron and glass to allow for a completely fireproof structure with maximum daylight to enhance the working environment.

Bentham was no doubt influenced, like many factory builders in the 1790s, by a spectacular fire on 2 March 1791 in London's Albion Grain Mills, which unleashed public debate and resulted in attempts to reform factory buildings (much as 20 years earlier the Hôtel-Dieu fire in Paris had ignited a debate over hospital design in France). The Albion Mills had been completed only 5 years earlier and achieved instant renown not only for the quality of detailing by the architect Samuel Wyatt, but for efficiency, producing an unrivalled 150 bushels of flour an hour. The same engines drove machines for sifting, dressing, and ventilation so that the building, an innovative structure of timber framing and inverted brick-arch foundations, was itself an enormous and complex machine. The fire proved a spur to the development of structural iron and eventually skeletal frame buildings, forerunners of innovations that would be exploited in a wide range of building types for decades to come. The first step was taken by Jedadiah Strutt, who developed factories at Derby and Belper, initially in association with the inventor–manufacturer Richard Arkwright, inventor of spinning machinery. In 1792 Strutt's son William, an engineer, built the first fireproof mill at Derby with iron pillars and floors carried on shallow brick arches, the whole powered by a huge waterwheel and a Boulton and Watt engine. The following year he built an even larger factory with thinly dimensioned colonettes: the six-storey, 190-foot (58 m)-long structure, the West Mill at Belper of 1793–95, still standing. Strutt's mills demonstrated the extent to which the factory system of labour was destined to transform the physical and social landscape. Surrounding them were laid out the earliest versions of the factory-based community, with row upon row of brick housing for workers. Capital's conquest of space would not be confined to the factory.

The architecture of money

Industrialization's dependence on new technologies of space was apparent to contemporary observers, and many worried that utilitarian values threatened to erode cultural standards. New relations of credit linked distant points in Britain's global empire, as well as Lancashire's mills to London's banks and created a shifting network governed by ever more abstract forms of exchange—securities, bonds, notes of credit—as well as an ever more dispersed cadre of investors. For the first 40 years after it was chartered as a private company by Parliament (1694), the Bank of England made do in rented quarters. The marine insurance underwriting of Lloyd's was already a linchpin of the credit network long before it left the coffee houses of the City for purpose-built buildings. The second half of the century saw not only the creation of permanent quarters for these institutions, but the rapid specialization of the City as a financial district and the linked development of London's West End as a fashionable residential district dominated by the new class known as 'the financial interest'. London established the pattern of urban distinctions between work and residence as well as an increasingly distinct geography of class and wealth, which would soon be reproduced in most European cities. This, as much as new ideals of public culture, would drive the extraordinary specialization of building types in the coming century.

The influence of the Bank of England grew dramatically with the rapid emergence of what historian John Brewer has called 'the fiscal–military state'.[8] The Bank was the veritable fulcrum between the government's insatiable hunger for credit and the growing class who made their living investing. By the 1770s a market in financial abstractions had emerged in Britain—decades before it would mature anywhere else in Europe—and along with it a realm of life that rendered old divisions between public and private realms ambiguous. Political debate was coloured by the perceived conflict between the landed and financial interests, and 'commercial values' were alternately portrayed as a threat and a promise to Britain's political liberties and prosperity. Martin Daunton has argued that 'The sinews of power of the British Empire in its worldwide tussle with the French, which reached a triumphant conclusion at Waterloo, rested upon the ability of the government to raise finance to pay for the war, without provoking a serious political crisis such as drove France to revolution.'[9] This was one of the primary factors in the very different functions and ethos of public architecture and the debates surrounding it in the 1790s on either side of the Channel.

The Bank of England

The majestic quarters which the Bank's directors had commissioned from George Sampson in 1732–34 for the Bank's dual private–public functions as private bankers to the merchants of the City and official lender to the state rapidly proved inadequate in both scope and imagery. The elegant Neo-Palladian façade on Threadneedle Street echoed the current fashion and ideology of the English country house. Quotations of the English Renaissance master Inigo Jones were patriotic and underscored the Bank's determination to garner respect in the growing debate over the uneasy relation between England's commercial vocation and the ethos of civic virtue. Under the architectural surveyorship of Sir Robert Taylor (1714–88) between 1765 and 1788, the Bank expanded physically to become a veritable precinct within the City, even as its role in administering the soaring public debt assumed greater prominence.

By the 1760s some 60,000 Englishmen owned shares in the national debt and the Bank's trading halls hosted a daily influx of investors. As the Bank grew in scale and complexity, it also sponsored an architecture ever more innovative in its application of the latest perceptions of the effects of spaces and forms on the emotions and beliefs of its audience. These were not mere luxuries, for by the middle of the century the confidence of the public was vital to the smooth functioning and growth of the credit system. In his top-lit, Classically ornamented banking halls Taylor took inspiration from the church architecture of Gibbs and Wren and created a separate dignified universe of calm in counterpoint to the bustle of the City's streets and to the inherent risks of credit. Spaces such as the central rotunda, with its evocations of the Roman Pantheon, framed bureaucratic acts of transferring funds as private gestures in a space of public ritual. They provided spaces which maximized movement, visibility, and a sense of participation in an ordered market. And they served the goals of the Bank's directors to foster public faith in the reasoned and sober management of markets and to counteract frequent criticism that financial speculation was a spiralling corruption of moral values and of the larger public interest.

The most famous chapter in the Bank's architectural history, the 45-year-long tenure of John (later Sir John) Soane (1753–1837) as surveyor after 1788, also coincides with one of the most tumultuous periods in the real and psychological demands on Britain's evolving place as the centre of credit. Not only had the French Revolutionary Wars spurred a major exodus of capital to London, but the resulting crisis in government finance led, in 1797, to a suspension of the gold standard and the issue of small-denomination notes—£1, £2, and £5—all without immediate convertibility for gold or silver. While grain shortages and escalating prices erupted into occasional local food riots, and the Bank's bullion reserves slipped to an all-time low, London's bankers and politicians worked to bolster shaky public confidence. The financier Sir Francis Baring argued, calling for recognition of the Bank's notes as legal tender, that the Bank of England commanded 'from their central position … long experience and practice', necessary to administer the circulation of paper money, reiterating essentially Adam Smith's point in *The Wealth of Nations* (1776) that the 'stability of the Bank of England is equal to that of the British Government'.[10] During these very years Soane was entrusted with rebuilding the Bank, replacing Taylor's wooden and plaster interiors with an extraordinary series of domed and vaulted trading halls innovative in their use of brick arches and fireproof vaulting of hollowed clay pot construction.[11] Soane endowed with a sense of aura, even numinous presence, ephemeral transactions of stocks and notes of credit. He offered not simply a template for the modern banking hall, but his own distinctive commodity, a style so individual and so radical that, as Sir John Summerson asserted, 'there was not, anywhere in Europe, an architecture as unconstrained by classical loyalties, as free in the handling of proportion and as adventurous in structure and lighting'.[12] How did these two radical departures from accepted standards, the Bank's from the gold standard and its architects' from the canons of Classicism, come to coincide?

Soane and the ethos of public architecture

Despite or perhaps because of his determined pursuit of a personal style, Soane's career in the 1790s reflects contemporary debates over the public realm. Soane had been apprenticed in George Dance's office during the years Dance was at work on Newgate Prison [**42**]. This powerful example of a heightened emotional handling of the language of Classicism was complemented by attendance at Thomas Sanby's lectures at the Royal Academy. Sanby interpreted much recent aesthetic doctrine, and in particular theories of the sublime and of associationism elaborated by Burke, Kames, and others, in relation to a credo of public building as the highest calling for an architect. Even as Soane studied in Rome between 1778 and 1780 and imbibed the legacy of recent French Neoclassical theory, he continued to groom himself to fulfil his ambition of crafting a modern *British* architecture, one in keeping with the growing patriotic association of a recovering commercial empire with the glories of ancient Rome.

As national character was debated ever more vehemently in the face of political revolution across the Channel, Soane sought a professional foothold in two competing arenas of public representation. In 1788, having built little more than modest country houses and garden structures, he was selected, with the backing of William Pitt—former prime minister—to succeed Taylor at the Bank. This lucrative position would dominate Soane's career and, together with his wife's inheritance, allow him to establish himself among the professional classes in Lincoln's Inn Fields. Here, in a house that eventually extended across three brick fronts, Soane would continually, even obsessively, craft his own professional and artistic identity in dialogue with his public work. Soane took up a first post in the government Office of Works in 1791. By the time he was able in the 1820s to realize a portion of his dreams of transforming the Palace of Westminster into an appropriate setting for both parliamentary rule and royal display, Soane had all but completed work at the Bank of England, which might lay equal claim to being the power centre of the empire.

The Bank Stock Office of 1791–93 [**57**] was his earliest design for the Bank. Here Soane invented spatial solutions he would repeat as theme and variation in each of the subsequent banking halls and established themes that would be central to his powerful integration of space-making, lighting, and ornamental detail for the rest of his career. Reusing Taylor's foundations and emulating his layout of a central vault held aloft by free-standing supports, Soane distinguished a central area for

57 Joseph Gandy

Rendering of Soane's Bank
Stock Office

Roman baths and basilicas
had been preoccupations of
Neoclassical architects in
Rome, but Soane went even
further afield to contemplate
vaulted spaces and their
capacity to activate 'the
mysterious light' of poetry in
architecture. Through his
extensive library he may even
have explored the effects of
the sixth-century church of
Hagia Sophia in Istanbul,
whose great low dome
seemed to float over a collar of
light.

customers and a periphery for the clerical staff. During an intensive pe-riod of design study his mind and pencil retraced much of the history of domed and vaulted spaces, studying the ways in which they divided a space psychologically even while freeing the floor of partitions and mas-sive supports to maximize circulation. Soane's library contained no fewer than 11 editions of Laugier's *Essay on Architecture* [1], which helped inspire a strict, almost primitivist, return to fundamentals in order to build anew an architecture of rigorous structural logic. At the same time Soane was an avid reader of Le Camus de Mézières, whose *Genius of Architecture* is evoked in what Soane called 'the poetry of archi-tecture', explaining his belief that light and shadow as much as form and ornament were key to endowing buildings with emotive character.

Within a simple rectangular space, Soane set a complex tripartite canopy of vaults, the central vault treated as pendentive dome pierced by a broad lantern, and the hollowed-out piers creating a cruciform config-uration of the room. This resulted in a functional and efficient zoning of space and created a powerful experience for the customers, for whom simple paperwork was now instilled with an aura of mystery and won-der. Soane seems to have been attracted to the pendentive dome be-cause of the great continuity between support and span, between structure and surface. Abandoning any literal use of Classical orders—simple incised uprights to evoke pilasters rather than full-bodied sculpted Classical members—he emphasized surface, freed himself from time-honoured canons of proportions, and dimensioned his spaces for maximum emotive effect. As in the Piranesi engravings of half-buried ruins that Soane was collecting, these spaces are defined by low sprung vaults whose surfaces created a sense of enclosure, centring, and monumentality wholly unexpected in a relatively small room.

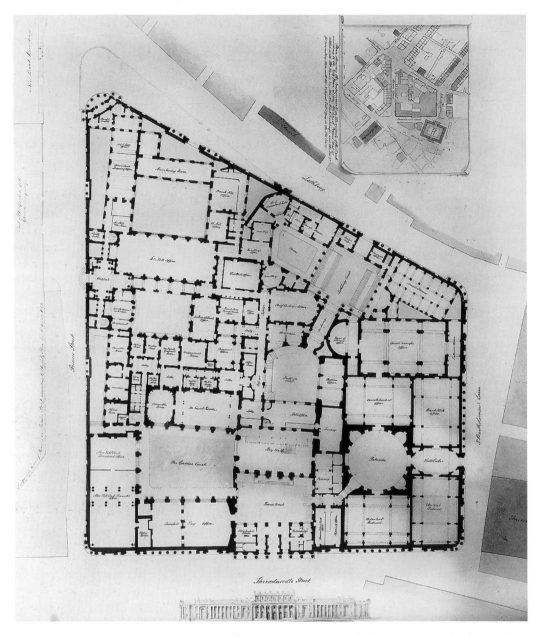

For the next 30 years Soane explored this theme, developing it alternately with greater archaeological reference or greater abstraction. The Consols Transfer Hall (1797–99) derives from the example of the Roman Basilica of Maxentius with its more massive piers exploited to control visually the largest of the public banking spaces, while the thinness of the fireproof terracotta vaults is dramatized, even exaggerated, in the attenuated lines and great vertical thrust of the Colonial and Four Per Cent Offices (1818–23), where the piers are reduced to an almost Gothic thinness and linearity even as they merge with the pendentive and dome.

58 Sir John Soane

Plan of the Bank of England, London, 1794–1810
Like Adam and De Wailly [see **17c**] before him, Soane was inspired by top-lit Roman thermal complexes, but the Bank's plan—which grew over time—has nothing of the symmetry or organizing axial matrix of contemporary French public buildings. Accommodating a difficult urban situation to great effect, and creating entirely independent entries and spatial sequences for the public, employees, and officials, Soane fragmented spaces in a purposefully picturesque manner.

Soane's willingness to exaggerate proportions, create abrupt transitions, and stage lighting for emotional effect reveals him to be a critical student of both the sublime and the recent debates over the elevation of the 'picturesque' to a category of aesthetic experience—one characterized by 'variety and intricacy' and set as a mediator between the beautiful and the sublime. Indeed, Soane set out to master the complex problem of creating a unified work of art on the irregular and successively enlarged site of the Bank at precisely the moment this concept was being debated by Uvedale Price, Payne Knight, and the landscape architect Humphry Repton in a series of publications.[13]

The Bank's perimeter wall—enclosing more than 3 acres by the 1820s—was particularly challenging since for security reasons it was to remain windowless, even while maximum lighting was needed in the great halls within. The complex functions of the Bank required separate entries for different private and public functions, including one for access to the bullion vaults which became something of a patriotic tourist

59 Soane

Tivoli Corner, Bank of England
Soane's brilliant adaptation of the Temple of the Sibyl at Tivoli to create a memorable corner for a complex urban building that could never be experienced as a whole is illustrative of his highly imaginative and idiosyncratic relationship to Classical models.

The picturesque

Over the course of the eighteenth century numerous attempts were made to turn the adjective picturesque into a rigorous aesthetic category that might take its place, as William Gilpin and Uvedale Price argued, as a mediating term between the beautiful and the sublime. By the time a heated debate emerged in the 1790s among the writers Price, Richard Payne Knight, and the garden designer Humphry Repton over the precise use of the term and its validity in landscape design, the picturesque as a sensibility had spread beyond the taste for making gardens in an informal, irregular, or 'natural' way that found inspiration in the pictures of Claude Lorrain or Salvator Rosa. In architecture it sanctioned asymmetry, jagged profiles, and contrasting scales and textures at the same time as it gave rise to a way of composing in harmony with nature and from multiple points of view, all of which made the picturesque a major factor in the dissolution of the Classical system of Renaissance and Baroque architecture. In his didactic poem *The Landscape* (1794), Knight argued for a more empirical, inherently eclectic approach:

> Nature in all rejects the pendant's chain
> Which binding beauty in its waving line
> Destroys the charm it vainly would define …

60 Gandy

The Bank of England imagined in ruins, 1830

In this highly evocative image, prepared for exhibition at the Royal Academy, Soane's favourite draughtsman imagines the Bank in ruins, at once a comparison of Soane's great building to the very antique complexes which had served as inspiration and a provocative challenge to the images of stability he and the bank officials were eager to conjure up in the architecture of the Bank!

site in these years. Soane's severing of the exterior wrapping of the building from its internal plan was perhaps the most radical of the challenges he posed to the tradition of Classical wholeness and the rationalist insistence that the exterior reflect the structural system and spatial divisions of the interior [**58**]. The most striking exterior feature, the Tivoli Corner, so called because its point of departure was the much-admired ruins of the round Temple of the Sibyl at Tivoli, responds to its urban context rather than the spaces behind [**59**]. Projecting almost like a ship's prow, it puts the Bank prominently in view along the picturesque winding streets at a key juncture between the financial district and the residential areas developing on the northern fringe of the City.

As early as 1796 Joseph Farrington criticized Soane's eccentricities, calling the Bank interiors 'affected and contemptible'. Another critic labelled Soane 'The Modern Goth', suggesting that departures from Classical canons were more likely to promote cultural decline than reinforce Britain's quest for cultural grandeur in the face of French claims of having regenerated mankind. After Waterloo a reaction set in, as strongly to the commercial and credit revolutions of the late eighteenth century as to non-canonic architectural expression. Soane became a favourite target, a common enemy shared by opposing ends of the spectrum of architectural positions emerging in the 1820s and 1830s. Both A. W. N. Pugin and C. R. Cockerell, young architects determined to establish ethics and stylistic consensus as professional goals, saw Soane's style as a restless quest for novelty and renown, at once the product and incentive of a commercial spirit in British life that threatened cultural degeneracy.

As Soane's successor both at the Bank, after 1833, and as professor at the Royal Academy after 1840, Charles Robert Cockerell (1788–1863) had numerous occasions to criticize the idiosyncrasies of Soane's style and its failure to establish worthy models. To the students he complained of the unclassical flat segmental vaulting of Soane's Bank Stock Office, explaining that only a truly hemispherical Roman vault could create a dignified *public* space. 'Such contrivances may be excused in domestic or industrial buildings … but never in … monumental architecture.'[14] In his more archaeologically inspired designs for a Royal Exchange (1839) and for provincial branches of the Bank of England, it was Cockerell who established much-imitated building types for nineteenth-century banks. Even Benjamin H. Latrobe (1766–1820), influenced by Soane in a handful of works in and around London in the early 1790s, gave an implicit critique of Soane's vision of banking space. Emigrating to America after the French Revolutionary Wars slowed commissions in London, Latrobe designed the first purpose-built bank in the New World, the Bank of Pennsylvania in Philadelphia (1798), exploiting Soane's top lighting and domed spaces but replacing his personal style with a clear evocation of the Roman Pantheon in the banking hall, a symbol immediately recognizable in its easy alliance of the young American republic with the virtues of ancient Rome.

Soane responded to these criticisms with the extraordinary perspective view rendered by Gandy of the Bank of England as a ruin [**60**], at once to lay before the eyes of the public the complexity of his achievement and to assimilate his great work with the noble ruins of the ancients which still spoke eloquently of the greatness of their culture even after the pettiness of daily life had long been extinguished and forgotten.

A new commercial and residential architecture

While debates over commerce coalesced around such symbols as the architecture of the Bank, European cities changed more rapidly and radically than ever before with the explosion of speculative housing development unleashed by new forms of credit and the increased volatility of capital. Historians long assumed that political unrest and war brought commercial and residential construction in France to a virtual halt during the 1790s, only to take off with Napoleon's coup d'état (1799) and military conquests, but recent research reveals that the revolutionary decade, especially the years of the Terror, 1793–95, witnessed a veritable building boom in Paris, stimulated as much by rampant inflation as by the auction sale of confiscated aristocratic and church property. Not only were real-estate markets liberalized, but the title 'architect' was for the first time all but unrestricted. New middle-class speculators took up the development of residential quarters that aristocrats had pioneered in the 1760s and 1770s, but these were no longer structured either formally or financially around a public monument.

Retail developments and arcades

The notion of a virile neo-antique vocabulary stripped of all but essential decorations met squarely with the demands of profitability in a venture such as that of the Parisian rue des Colonnes, designed as early as 1793 by the architect–speculator N.-J.-A. Vestier and built by Joseph Bénard, a disciple of Boullée, in 1797 [**61**]. Begun as a private street leading to Legrand and Molinos's recently completed Feydeau Theatre (1791) (censorship too had been eased), the layout embodied the spirit of the ideal street projected by Patte decades earlier [**20**]. The covered passages behind the primitively detailed columns and arches lend at once a civic character and a sense of place to the street and ensure the

61 Friedrich Gilly

View of the rue des Colonnes in Paris, 1798

The young Berlin architect [see **32**] recorded the remarkable transformation of the Parisian streetscape with new forms of speculative real estate, exaggerating the sublime effect of repetition in this austere composition so often compared to the stoic and virile character of the architectural setting in J.-L. David's famous painting *The Oath of the Horatii* (1785).

commercial success, and thus the rents commanded, for the shops on the ground floor. But the squat Doric order was used here neither to fulfil a canon of beauty nor to experiment with the emotive force of architectural form, but rather from a logic of economy, creating maximum rental space in a street whose dimensions and ratio of overall height to width correspond impeccably with the pioneering legislation controlling new streets adopted in Paris in 1783. The intersection of market and building code had generated a new building-block of the commercial city, the arcaded street allowing leisurely strolling past shop windows.

The 1790s witnessed the birth of an array of new forms and sites in which retail shopping and urban space were transformed in tandem. In addition to the explosion of new shop fronts, glass-roofed arcades proliferated. One of the very earliest, the Passage Feydeau, ran parallel to the rue des Colonnes. By the late 1820s the dense neighbourhoods surrounding the Parisian boulevards were permeated by passages, bringing both the emerging markets in fashion and luxury goods as well as shoppers deep into urban building plots too small for residential subdivision. Capital's conquest of urban space was rapidly generating new forms, although like all products of fashion the arcades were themselves ephemeral, each vying to be more up to date and novel in decor, all of them rapidly rendered obsolete with the appearance by mid-century of bazaars and then department stores (see chapter 7).

Housing

New experiments in housing types proliferated in the adventurous real-estate markets of the period on both sides of the Channel. In London the first districts of free-standing 'villas' [62], middle-class houses on the edges of cities, began to appear and the terraces pioneered by John Wood in Bath in the 1750s were taken up for a variety of urban situations. In Paris Ledoux—always an anglophile—was commissioned in 1792 by a rich sugar planter from Santo Domingo, Jean-Baptiste Hosten, to develop a site at the northern edge of the city with a group of 15 houses on the model of a London terrace. Facing a shared landscaped garden, their severe blocks formed a remarkable urban and collective interpretation of the principle of appropriated space first explored in the English picturesque garden.

With shopping arcades, street fronts built to an overall design, and new approaches to integrating the landscape into the city, speculative architecture for profit was changing the look and atmosphere of daily life equally in smaller European cities, where architectural fashions were almost as quick to be emulated as those in clothing and furnishings. New revolutions in printing led to a proliferation of model books and illustrations in magazines which spread images widely and quickly. While actual housing plans tended to develop a local charac-

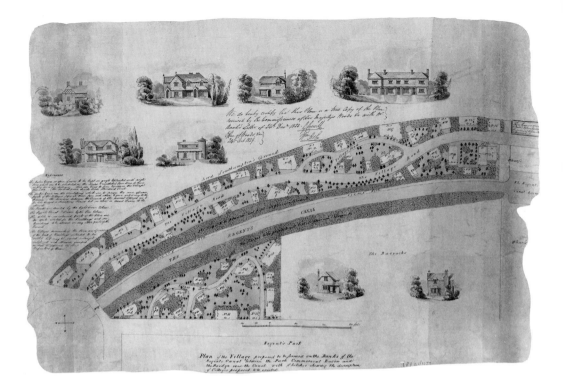

ter in relation to social norms and expectations, revolutions in fabrics
and wallpapers made it possible for the rapid dissemination and interpretation of such stylistic phenomena as the linear adaptation of
Pompeiian and Italian Renaissance decoration by Napoleon's architects Percier and Fontaine through both their own publications and
those of such commercial publishers as Krafft and Rainsonnette. The
'Empire style' was spread as much by images in the period's new journals of 'taste' to middle-class interiors throughout Europe as it was
through the work of Percier and Fontaine's countless pupils who
worked for aristocratic and royal families throughout the Napoleonic
Empire.

A series of new alliances between the state and the real estate market was of far greater consequence for the nineteenth-century city than
the political regimes celebrated in monumental rhetoric. Even as they
came into being, Paris's rue de Rivoli, begun in 1802, and London's
Regent Street, begun in 1811, were viewed as contrasting models of
urban improvement. Both exploited ground-floor shopping and residential development above. Historians have celebrated the rue de
Rivoli [63] as a product of imperial fiat, and for bringing light and air
into the heart of the historic fabric and fostering easy circulation of vehicles and pedestrians. Regent Street, on the other hand, has been upheld as the first large-scale urban design in which the principles of
picturesque landscape were applied to the city, empirically exploiting

63 Charles Percier and Pierre-Louis Fontaine

Rue de Rivoli, Paris, 1802–c.1825

Arcades stretched only along the north side of the rue de Rivoli to create a smart promenade along the Tuileries Gardens and a clear boundary for the Louvre–Tuileries palace complex. Designed by the Emperor Napoleon's favourite architects, the house fronts were produced slowly over the next decade, following the fortunes of the speculative real-estate market in these tumultuous years of warfare and social change.

each impediment posed by unobtainable building plots to create a street of studied irregularity, sequence, and even surprise. Parsimony and the picturesque formed a new alliance. Numerous architects were involved, but the whole was choreographed by John Nash (1752–1835), recently returned to London from the West Country, where he had worked closely with the landscape designer Humphry Repton (1752–1818) (notably at Blaise near Bristol) and come under the influence of picturesque theorists Knight and Price. The striking formal differences between the rue de Rivoli with its monumental regularity and Regent Street with its cultivated picturesque charm and incident have led many to overlook the underlying similarities in approach and aim, namely to use regulation and strategic incentive to channel market forces towards realizing a grand urban composition and a commodious public amenity.

In reality both streets developed in fits and starts, acquiring the image of a singular moment of design only after decades. The idea of a street parallel to the Tuileries Gardens had been floated repeatedly in the eighteenth century, but it was not until Napoleon's administration set up a novel framework for development that work actually began. The decree opening the street in 1801 contained an important condition: 'building lots will be sold with the stipulation that purchasers build according to plans and façades provided by the government's architect'.[15] As part of the grand assignment to Napoleon's favourite architects Percier and Fontaine to improve the immediate surroundings

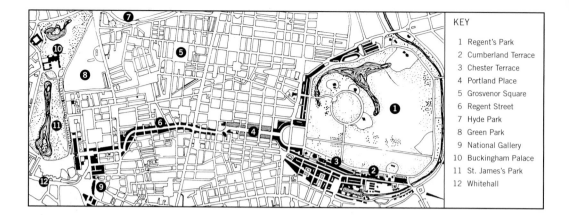

KEY

1 Regent's Park
2 Cumberland Terrace
3 Chester Terrace
4 Portland Place
5 Grosvenor Square
6 Regent Street
7 Hyde Park
8 Green Park
9 National Gallery
10 Buckingham Palace
11 St. James's Park
12 Whitehall

64

a) Map of Regent Street and Regent's Park complex

By 1820, as Regent Street was taking final form, George IV had ascended the throne and moved his residence to Buckingham Palace, where Nash would follow as his architect for important interior remodelling. Carlton House, the axial focus of Lower Regent Street, was demolished soon afterwards as the ceremonial processions intended for this street ceded the path definitively to the new art of fashionable promenading.

of the Louvre and Tuileries Palace—where they also undertook a major redecoration in the characteristic style soon to be known as 'Empire'—a template was created for the new street. The marketplace would be free to build the street, but the state's regulatory imprint was placed on the deeds of sale, which included prohibitions on use and activities—forerunners of modern zoning—with the aim of restricting the social class of future inhabitants. The houses, some divided from the start into apartments, would benefit from an expansive view, a principle of appropriated space derived from the picturesque and adapted to the marketplace, brilliantly exploited by Nash a few years later in the terraces ringing Regent's Park.

The development of Regent's Park and Regent Street to connect them with the centre of power and government at Westminster a mile away [**64a, b**] was, likewise, as much a product of market forces as original design intent. As Nash's vision of a dense development of terraces of houses arranged in a double circus at the heart of Regent's Park gave way to a handful of generously spaced villas, an important prototype for the modern urban park as a public amenity came into existence thanks more to a lacklustre housing market than to civic-mindedness. In turn this great open space proved a major financial and design asset for the dense ring of terrace housing Nash arranged around the park's perimeter. Nash designed scenographically, exploiting views of nature in the principal rooms and arranging the houses into grand compositions to serve as a backdrop for promenades in the park.

Regent Street, launched in 1812 as the Prince Regent declared his aim to eclipse Napoleon's Paris, had its origins in the 1790s when reforming civil servants transformed the administration of crown lands into a modern government department and set out to maximize revenues, using financial analyses more common in the banks of the City than in the royal household. Originally planned as a processional way from Carlton House to a royal summer pavilion planned for the park,

the sinewy line of the street was traced as a brilliant scheme of finding the meandering edge between the commercial and artisan Soho district and the smart Mayfair neighbourhood to the west. Buying cheap and selling dear, the very motto of any market, provided a veritable model for speculative development. It was also a line that targeted most of what Nash called 'the bad streets', and thus a prototype for nineteenth-century slum clearance with all its social ambiguities. While the street gained in dignity and poise as it approached its royal and residential extremities, the middle section was developed as a commercial thoroughfare. Not only would goods vie for attention in shop windows, but the commercial blocks were designed by different architects retained by each of the property-owners or speculators. Soane and Smirke's designs for similar blocks faced one another in the central stretch of the street, offering two competing visions of Classicism, one full-bodied and archaeological, the other quirky and individualistic, both evidence of the increased market pressures on the very notion of architectural style. Nash himself bought the plots that formed his famous colonnaded 'Quadrant', negotiating the difficult curve of the street north of Piccadilly Circus where Regent Street takes a sudden sweep westward before continuing north. As he explained, 'Being a peculiar sort of building, it could not be erected house by house, as in other parts of the street, it was obliged to be erected at once, and the speculation was too great for one person.'[16] The modern city demanded continued negotiations between the state and the market.

Weinbrenner's Karlsruhe and the legacy of metropolitan models

Countless other urban compositions of these years are ripe for reconsideration once the stylistic history of art and the history of real estate can be integrated. In Karlsruhe, where the Neoclassicist Friedrich Weinbrenner (1766–1826) left his imprint on both Baden's capital and its school of architecture throughout the first quarter of the nineteenth century, a new alliance of state regulation and speculation was pioneered for the German states. Here the French Revolution and new models of state-directed markets served as the basis for updating the model of the *Musterland*, or model state, pioneered in Dessau two generations earlier (see chapter 3). Karlsruhe had been laid out in 1715 as an idealized Versailles. The town plan was inscribed in a perfect circle with 32 avenues radiating from the royal palace at the centre, more than half of them *allées* in a hunting park, the others streets for the court and townspeople. Weinbrenner's first proposal of 1797 for a market square betrayed the joint influence of Winckelmann's idealized archaeology and the sensationist preference for pure forms; it also implied a seminal adjustment of power relations in the spatial planning of Baden's capital. Pendant porticoes of the town hall and state church would face one another across a square surrounded by arcades, the whole focused on a public monument celebrating the town's founder, Margrave Karl Wilhelm of Baden-Durlach. Weinbrenner referred to the space as an agora and saw it as fostering a new community life, one endorsed by Baden's adoption in 1806, under French influence, of the first constitution adopted in any German state. By then Weinbrenner had replaced his project for a portrait of the city founder as the square's central monument with a monumental sandstone pyramid [**65**], more universal and immediate in its impact, he explained. Weinbrenner drew up expansion plans in 1802 and 1815, both of which further eroded the singular focus on a princely centre in favour of spaces for civic life, but which also embraced the notion that the regularity and harmony of the town could evolve in cooperation with speculative development over time. Model façades and regulations that specified heights and widths and other aspects of design were laid down in such a way that individual designers and changing tastes would not compromise the geometry of either street plan or the overall profile of the town in the landscape. Weinbrenner's projects both for the town and for his textbook reveal an increasing willingness to reinvent a classical language of architectural expression according to new criteria, jettisoning canons of proportions for studies of optics and human perception, making composition thus subordinate to the wide range of emotions architecture could elicit and to the place of individual buildings in the larger urban landscape. Even in this provincial capital the stage was set for debates over style and the national and regional meanings of architectural form which animated the architectural profession throughout Europe in the second quarter of the nineteenth century.

Part III

Nationalism, Historicism, Technology

Nationalism and Stylistic Debates in Architecture

5

> The character of whole nations, cultures, and epochs speaks through the totality of their architecture, which is the outward shell of their being.
>
> Jacob Burckhardt, *Weltgeschichte Betrachtungen* (lectures given in 1868–71), translated as *Reflections on History*, London, 1943

The conviction that architecture might represent, even sustain, the glory of kingdoms can be traced to the dawn of civilization, but the notion that architecture can bear the stamp of national character is a modern one born of eighteenth-century historical thinking and given political currency in the wake of the French Revolution. Of all the new functions architecture was called upon to perform, few were so ideologically charged as building the identity and reinforcing the claims to naturalness of nation-states. As the map of Europe was repeatedly redrawn, architecture was called upon to rally and focus loyalties and to grant the aura of a glorious past to even the most recently contrived national boundaries.

The shift in meaning of the notion of architectural 'character' from its eighteenth-century sense of modes of expression within a universal vocabulary to the nineteenth-century concern with *national* styles did not occur without considerable resistance from those who believed that architectural ideals transcended vagaries of time and place. Proposals for 'national orders' of architecture were advanced episodically in the eighteenth century. But Sebastien Leclerc's 'French order' of 1714, with its fleur de lys, or James Adam's 'British Order' of 1764, with its St George's lions, were emendations to the Classical vocabulary, enhancements of the rhetorical capacity of the orders handed down from antiquity and codified by Renaissance treatises. The evolution of post-Classical antiquarian studies from curiosity with artefacts to the polemical position that such research provided models for specifically national architectures was one of the most potent of challenges posed to the transcendent validity of Classicism.

Johann Fischer von Erlach, whose 1721 *A Plan of Civil and Historical Architecture* included non-western architectural styles, noted that

Detail of 72

'Nations differ no less in their taste for architecture than in food and raiment ...'[1] Winckelmann, taking up Montesquieu's association of political and legal systems in different cultures with geography and climate, asserted that Greek excellence in the arts was a direct result of a felicitous climate, political system, and society. But neither Winckelmann nor his Neoclassical followers, including such powerful figures as Quatremère de Quincy of the French Academy, whose influence remained strong until the mid-nineteenth century, would embrace the relativist implications of their own historical explanations. The stage was set not only for a battle of styles, but for a tug-of-war between universal and relativist aesthetic models. Political as much as aesthetic convictions were at stake.

Inspired by Rousseau's pleas for love of homeland as a great civilizing virtue and by Herder's appeals to sustain the distinctiveness of national cultures as preserved in dialects, folk songs, and the like, the intellectual project of patriotic nationalism was initially staged as a progressive and liberating force compatible with the Enlightenment notions of progress and poised against received ideas. The Revolution gave a new impetus with its cult of 'the fatherland', and its investment of the rights and the identity of nationhood in citizens rather than subjects; nationalism would fill a void left by older allegiances to church, crown, and aristocratic privilege. But patriotism was one of the most contradictory exports of the Revolution. As French armies advanced through Europe, initial enthusiasm for new democratic ideals turned into a reaction against French imperialism, awakening a sense of national identity even in the fractured political landscape of Central Europe.

Pluralism and revivalism

In addition to the credo of universal Classicism, two new, and often contradictory, attitudes about historical style in architecture were discernible by the early nineteenth century. Both would be called into the service of forming symbols and building national identity. Pluralism advocated the simultaneous use of the expanded range of styles antiquarian study had made accessible. Revivalism held that a single historical model was appropriate for modern architecture. Each position had its roots in eighteenth-century explorations of the ways in which architecture conveys meaning. Pluralism, cultivated first in the quest for 'variety' and the evocation of different times and places in picturesque landscape gardens, had, by the early nineteenth century, found spokesmen who associated historical architectural styles with the various new buildings required by contemporary society. Thus the emotive arguments of the doctrine of association were joined with the ever-growing interest in the sequence and taxonomy of architectural styles to produce a veritable palette of historical building idioms usable towards new ends: Egyptian for prisons, Gothic for churches, or Italian Renaissance

66 John Foulston

View of Devonport, near Plymouth, 1820s, including an 'Egyptian' library, a 'Hindoo' nonconformist chapel, a 'primitive Doric' town hall, and a street of houses with a Roman Corinthian order

The goal of rendering new building types meaningful was little different from that essayed decades earlier by Ledoux [48], but the means changed radically as the quest for character shifted from a flexible Classical vocabulary to the deliberate juxtaposition of historical styles.

for banks and exchanges, for instance. These choices were meant to activate prevailing cultural associations: the pharaohs with death and eternity, the Middle Ages with Christianity, or the Medici with the rise of banking and modern commerce. Greek architecture was invested with the new ideals of liberty and thus all its links with antiquarianism were branded as progressive. Thus, for instance, in the early 1820s the leading Regency architect of the west of England, John Foulston, composed a townscape at Devonport [66] in which radical stylistic contrasts were intended to create a legible landscape.

Revivalists, despite frequent disagreements over issues of which historical style was appropriate, none the less shared the goal of a stylistic consensus. Whether their choice was Classical, medieval, or Renaissance, all revivalists shared the strategy of advocating a particular style with explanations drawn from *national* history, itself one of the great enterprises of historians in the early nineteenth century. A single historical period—increasingly specific in its definition—was claimed to be the only one capable of providing models grounded in national traditions, institutions, and values. Issues of style became matters of state. For several generations historical style loomed as one of the most pressing issues in architecture, each new debate viewed as another skirmish in an ongoing 'battle of styles'. Over time the battleground shifted as concern with asserting national identity spread from old continuous nation states seeking to rally their citizenry (Britain, France, Spain, and Portugal) to those seeking independence from a larger entity or foreign power (Belgium, Greece, Hungary, and the Czech lands of Bohemia) or unification of diverse smaller states which shared language and historical ties (Germany, Italy, and Romania).

The Gothic Revival

The Neo-Gothic revival of medieval forms, the most sustained of all revivalist positions, first found architectural expression in the mid-eighteenth century in the houses of a number of wealthy and politically influential antiquarians—nowhere more spectacularly than in England. Rapidly these private pleasures achieved a notoriety that made non-canonic choices of style resonate with larger significance, and none more famously than Horace Walpole's Strawberry Hill [**67a, b, c**]. Despite this romantic castellated house's seminal role in both the popularization of a sentimental fascination with 'Gothick' associations and in the establishment of more archaeologically accurate standards for 'Gothic' Revival, its creator admitted in a letter to a friend that Gothic's modern uses were limited. Grecian forms alone, he felt, were suitable for public buildings, while the charming irregularity of domestic architecture was best embodied in medieval styling. Indeed, a fine-grained understanding of the Gothic style, and in particular a taxonomic classification and periodization, would not be achieved before the nineteenth century. These would in part be the contribution of

67 Horace Walpole

Strawberry Hill, Twickenham, London, begun c.1750
a) Exterior view **b)** The Long Gallery

The son of the powerful Whig prime minister, whose country house, Houghton Hall, in Norfolk, was one of the benchmarks of English Palladianism, Walpole's Gothic fantasy could not fail to attract attention to the Gothic style and suggest powerful associations of it with Englishness. Open to a select public, it was as much a museum as a house.

c) Plan

Unlike the French, who preferred to subsume the national Gothic past into efforts to refine the classical language of architecture with new structural feats of lightness and openness [**15**], English Gothic Revivalists cultivated visual associations of Gothic pinnacles and ornaments. Asymmetry was actively cultivated in plan and massing to create a palpable sense of the passage of time, one of the fundamental preoccupations of the period's obsession with history.

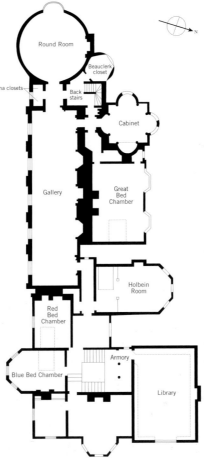

68

The collapse of Fonthill Abbey on Christmas Day, 1825

Historians have pegged the event as a threshold to a new sophistication in understanding Gothic as a system of structure and not simply a repertory of decorative motifs. Beckford—who had sold the house in 1822—lamented only that he had missed such a sublime and impressive event!

Horace Walpole's Strawberry Hill

Strawberry Hill, Twickenham, begun 1749, was not the earliest English house to adopt elements of the national medieval past, but it was the first to become a tourist attraction. With Walpole's passion for collecting medieval artefacts, collections and house grew in symbiosis. By 1784 he had printed a guidebook and issued tickets. Continually expanding and 'improving', Walpole employed architects as collaborators and consultants, including Adam. Fireplaces, plaster-vaulted ceilings, and other accoutrements were copied from medieval sources, and Walpole's spirited 'Committee of Taste' became a clearing-house for the study of English Gothic architecture and sculpture. Initially designs were drawn from plate books, but soon his architects went directly to buildings, in turn fuelling a new generation of antiquarian publications. It took a non-architect—a dilettante and man of letters—to conceive a building that would seem to have been designed not by a single intelligence but to have grown over time. This literary architecture included not only associations of Gothic with mystery and darkness—Walpole wrote an early 'Gothick novel', *The Castle of Otranto* (1764)—but the crafting of a building which itself narrated a story, a feature expanded by the aesthetics of the picturesque movement.

Thomas Rickman, whose *Attempt to Discriminate the Styles of English Architecture* (1817) established terminology still largely in use today. None the less the notion that Gothic was associated with England's glorious past and cherished institutions was established as early as 1741, as reflected in James Gibbs's sturdy brick Gothic Temple of Liberty at Stowe. In coming decades other antiquarians remodelled or conceived anew houses in this 'Gothick' fashion, including the ruins of Alnwick

Castle in Northumberland and the extravagant Fonthill in Wiltshire. Fonthill was designed by James Wyatt for the eccentric novelist William Beckford, whose involvement led to the combination of a new level of accuracy in archaeological details—inspiration came from as far away as Batalia in Portugal—with fantastic theatrical and emotive effects in the sequence of spaces. Centred on a 225-foot (68.6 m)-high tower, no building did more to reinforce the notion that Gothic was most conducive to the sublime in its scale and contrasts of volumes, wholly opposing the rules of Classical composition.

Fonthill's dramatic collapse on Christmas Day 1825, engraved as an unintended artificial ruin [68], was extolled by a younger generation of Gothic Revivalists as the death knell of a frivolously picturesque and eclectic interest in the national past. With a veritable explosion of anti-quarian publications by John Carter (*The Ancient Architecture of England*, first edition 1795), John Britton (*The Architectural Antiquities of Great Britain*, 1807–26), L. C. Cottingham, A.-C. Pugin, and others, England had by the early nineteenth century set standards for research into 'national antiquities' only later rivalled on the continent.

The invention of 'German' architecture

German Romantic writers and architects were the first to promote Gothic as a powerful expression of national genius and character and in turn to use it to foster a sense of national identity in territories still divided amidst countless princes, dukes, and local lords. A call came from the 22-year-old Goethe in a paean to Strasbourg Cathedral, 'On German Architecture', written in 1772 and published a year later by Herder in the programmatic collection *On German Character and Art*. Herder had already launched a major critique of Winckelmann's cultural position with the question 'Why should we always imitate foreigners, as if we were Greeks or Romans?'[2] Now Goethe's attack on the hegemony of French aesthetics, and on Laugier's rationalism, framed for the first time German aesthetics in counterpoint to France, and indeed to the whole Enlightenment project of love of reason. For Goethe, the ability to appreciate Gothic architecture with its appeal to sensibility rather than rules, to individual genius rather than abstract systems, was key both to intellectual independence for Germany as a 'cultural nation'—as Schiller would soon define it in his appeal for a German-language 'national theatre'—and to new criteria for aesthetic experience.

Soon the role of iconic symbol of German Gothic would be taken over from Strasbourg—which passed into French hands with revolutionary expansion—by the great unfinished Gothic cathedral of Cologne [69a]. Georg Forster, a pioneer in publishing books on German medieval architecture, extolled Gothic's aesthetic power as early as 1790: 'Whenever I am in Cologne, I visit this splendid temple,

to feel the thrill of the sublime. In the face of such bold masterpieces, the spirit prostrates itself, full of amazement and admiration; then it rises again, and soars upwards beyond these works … It is greatly to be regretted that such a magnificent building must remain unfinished. If the mere design, when completed in the mind's eye, can move us so mightily, how overpowering might not the actual structure have been!'[3]

a) Cologne Cathedral as it appeared in the early nineteenth century

Construction on the great Gothic cathedral had been halted since the late Middle Ages, but in the wake of the Napoleonic occupation of the Rhineland the building was taken up as a nationalist cause and its completion promoted as an instrument for rallying the population as well as exploring the principles of a native national architectural style.

b) Tony Avenarius (artist) Ceremony for Dedication of Cologne Cathedral, 1880, with model of building and allegorical figure of Germania

By the time the cathedral was finished with a neo-Gothic nave and west front, Germany had been unified by Bismarck. But the unique validity of Gothic to represent German national identity was still contested as new national buildings were erected, such as the Reichstag in Berlin. This was completed in a grandiose Classic style, much to the chagrin of such Gothic advocates as August Riechensperger, who had sustained the Cologne effort for decades.

It was an argument that would recur in proposals for using a Gothic style for buildings meant to transport the mind to a transcendent realm, notably in Karl Friedrich Schinkel's (1781–1841) renowned defence of his Gothic design for a mausoleum for Queen Luise of Prussia in 1810 over the crown's stated preference for a Greek temple design.

Apart from a fashion for Gothic garden pavilions, Goethe's appeal had little immediate impact on German architectural practice. He himself would soon abandon this youthful passion after an overwhelming encounter with the temples at Paestum during his 1786–88 trip to Italy. They spurred him to define a Romantic vision of Classical culture, one he actively cultivated in Weimar where he became court adviser, notably on the construction of the Roman House in the ducal gardens. None the less 'On German Architecture' helped set the stage for one of the preoccupations of antiquarian research increasingly tinged with national competition, namely the efforts by intellectuals, architects, and even political figures in England, France, and Germany to claim Gothic as peculiarly their own. In 1798 the Romantic poet Ludwig Tieck noted, 'perhaps we shall discover one day that all the splendid buildings of this kind in England, Spain, and France were created by German masters',[4] and in 1804 Friedrich Schlegel asked 'what can be more out of place than … Grecian or Italian columns in a strange land or climate? Gothic architecture is the style of building best adapted to a northern climate and a colder zone.'[5]

Georg Forster's *Views along the Lower Rhine* of 1791 helped establish the jagged profiles of the castles and cathedrals of the Rhine valley— the disputed political border with France—as German cultural icons. Eighteenth-century intellectuals had been content to seek cultural unity through the art forms that could reach a literate public, the theatre and literature, but the French occupation of the Rhineland in 1794 opened a new epoch in which unity became a political issue and national architectural symbols were regarded as held captive. Cologne Cathedral became a veritable metaphor for the unfulfilled aspirations of German unity. For almost a century, the project to complete it played out in close parallel to the evolution of the politics of German unity, evolving from impassioned pleas during the Wars of Liberation against France and a touchstone of the politics of Protestant Prussia in its Catholic Rhineland provinces after 1815, to the great neo-medieval dedication pageant in 1880, which celebrated and consolidated Germany's recent unification [**69b**].

The Napoleonic Wars and the patriotic Gothic Revival in Germany

German liberals initially greeted the French Revolution as the dawn of a new age in human history, heralding ideals of the rights of man and of liberty as solvents for the entrenched privileges and traditions of Germany's micro-principalities and rigid class structures. But

70 Karl Friedrich Schinkel

Project for a cathedral to the Wars of Liberation, 1814

For Berlin's Leipziger Platz, the very site for which Gilly had proposed a monument [**32**], Schinkel proposed a building that could represent the nation and serve as an instrument for national reconstruction and renewal. It would be of exposed brick, celebrated as a national material, and erected with the help of the entire population carrying bricks to the site.

French troops on German soil set in motion a violent reaction, in which intellectuals took the forward charge even before the Battle of Leipzig reversed Napoleon's fortunes. In occupied Berlin in the winter of 1807–08, the philosopher Johann Gottlieb Fichte delivered his *Speeches to the German Nation*, aimed to fire up not only Prussians, but citizens of other German-speaking states, to a patriotic and cultural self-awareness. 'The fight with arms is over, and now will begin the combat of principles, mores, and characters,' Fichte declared.[6] His words found resonance in a series of projects conceived by architects and displaced rulers, beginning with plans to rebuild Berlin's Petrikirche in its original Gothic style after a fire in 1809 and culminating in Schinkel's grandiose scheme for a commemorative cathedral for the Wars of Liberation, designed in the heat of the culminating battles leading to Napoleon's final defeat in 1815. Unlike Goethe, who devoted himself to resurrecting the originating genius of Erwin von Steinbach, architect of Strasbourg Cathedral, that Gothic might rival Classical art as the creation of a great artist, Schinkel saw the Gothic cathedral as the product of the labours and talents of an entire civilization, one which again, in the hour of Germany's need, could serve as beacon and communal focus [**70**]. A vast Gothic arcade would form a huge public square dominated by the domed cathedral. The church would literally be raised by citizens carrying bricks, the native material of Prussia long hidden under stucco, to the site. For Schinkel this was a patriotic revival of the *Bauhütte*, or medieval building workshops, which had served as a centre of crafts and trades at the heart of the medieval city. For Fichte the German medieval city embodied 'the nation's youthful dream of its future deeds … the prophecy of what it would be once it had perfected its strength'.[7]

Schinkel explained, 'To erect a large sacred monument to this remarkable period in the soul-stirring style of ancient German architecture, an architecture whose ultimate perfection is to be achieved in the immediate future, since its development was broken off in its prime by a marvellous and beneficial reversion to Antiquity, with the result that the world is apparently now destined to perfect this art form by introducing an element that has been missing so far.'[8] Gothic was thus ripe for development, the first inkling that a revivalist position would ultimately merge with theories equating national and biological evolution as a new conception of style and the role of the artist in preparing the future. A hint of a new element came when in 1818 Schinkel was able to realize a much-reduced monument to the Wars of Liberation on the heights of Kreuzberg, an enormous cast-iron pinnacle. Iron was not only that new element that suggested a future for Gothic, it was also charged with patriotic significance by the campaign encouraging citizens to turn in their jewellery for the production of weapons, giving rise to the slogan 'I gave my gold for iron'. Like the project for the cathedral, the monument atop Kreuzberg was crowned by the Iron Cross, Prussia's highest military honour, also designed by Schinkel.

Greek and Gothic in Bavarian nationalism

The rivalry between Bavaria and Prussia to act as midwife to German unification was in part played out in rival projects for a 'national monument'. In Bavaria Ludwig I, who developed a passion for architecture as statecraft even before ascending the throne, restructured the urban space of Munich, transforming the *Residenz* of the Wittelsbach dynasty into a modern European capital with public buildings and monuments. Inspired by Fichte's call to oppose the pro-French policies of his father's reign, Ludwig branded Napoleon the 'Archenemy of the German nation', referring to the abolition of the Holy Roman Empire and its replacement by modern bureaucratic vassal states. Ludwig began working with a small group of architects, who became his close friends, to craft a series of Romantic landscapes throughout Bavaria, intended as sites for patriotic pilgrimage. Already as crown prince he had projected two institutions which were to remain linchpins of his programme of projecting Munich as the cultural capital for a future Germany: a memorial hall on the model of the Parisian Panthéon and a public sculpture gallery to display antiquities, including the statuary from the Greek Temple of Aegenia acquired in 1811. Here were paired the programmes of public museum and national memorial which were to colour the creation of museums in nearly every European capital for the rest of the century, culminating in the creation of the Swiss National Museum in Bern in 1897 with its hall of murals depicting scenes from the 'national' history of the confederation of Swiss cantons.

In 1813, a year after Napoleon's defeat at Leipzig, a competition was opened for a 'Walhalla', a term borrowed from Ancient Nordic mythology to designate a hall for slain warriors, even though Ludwig

71 Leo von Klenze

Painting showing Walhalla
(near Regensburg)

Construction began in 1830
on the anniversary of the
Battle of Leipzig and the
dedication took place on the
same anniversary 12 years
later. The Walhalla is a Grecian
pendant on the Danube to the
equally nationalist pilgrimage
site of Cologne Cathedral on
the Rhine, to which both the
Prussian and Bavarian
monarchs pledged support.

72 Leo von Klenze

Königsplatz, Munich with
Glyptothek (1816–34) and
Propylaeum (1843)

In contrast to Schinkel's
projection of a great Gothic
forum as the entrance to
Berlin [70], the Bavarian
capital would recast its
principal western entrance as
a great neo-antique forum
complete with a novel public
art gallery devoted to a
historical panorama of ancient
and modern Classical
sculpture.

intended it for pan-Germanic cultural heroes. Despite the Nordic reference, Ludwig stipulated the use of Greek forms, arguing that the Athenian Parthenon was not only a model of perfection, but closely linked to the Greek victory over the Persians which had fostered ancient Greek unity. From Berlin, Schinkel submitted a Gothic counter-proposal, opening the debate over the appropriate stylistic image for 'Germanness' which would continue to agitate architects and public monumental design even after unification in 1870. The Prussian's design was quickly passed over in favour of an ancient Greek-style design submitted by Carl Haller von Hallerstein of Nuremberg, then studying monuments in Athens. Greek Revival design, stripped of all later Roman and Renaissance accretions, was launched on its course of representing modern myths of national purity and grandeur.

Even once the Walhalla and Glyptothek [71, 72] had been uncoupled as buildings, the first to be located on the banks of the Danube, the other in the recently laid-out quarters on the edge of Munich's medieval core, the Bavarian marriage between antiquity and nationalism was not to be dissolved. The Glyptothek, as designed by Leo von Klenze (1784–1864), was developed as a key element of the new urbanism of Bavaria's capital. Klenze was an adamant promoter of the Greek Revival. 'There was and is only one architecture and there will only ever be one architecture, namely that which realized its perfection in the formative years of Greek civilization,' he wrote. 'That it should be the Greeks who discovered this perfected architecture was merely coincidence, or even more divine destiny, it belongs as much to Germany as to Greece.'[9] While not the first museum opened to the public in Germany—the Fridericianum in Kassel (1769) holds this honour—it was the first to develop a programme of display in which a public initiation to art was considered key to fostering a cultivated citizenry.

Many of the sculptors admitted to the Glyptothek's only modern gallery also contributed to the great programme of busts of famous Germans admitted to the Walhalla, including artistic and intellectual heroes from all German states, including Austria. The Walhalla is set in a landscape resplendent in its natural purity of woodlands from which the monument rises above a great series of pedestals with processional switch-back stairs for modern pilgrims arriving by boat and ascending to this secular cult site. The spot is a key juncture in the new networks of roadways and canals by which Ludwig set out to underscore Bavaria's modernity and its role as a crossroads of a future united Germany. Ludwig also played a major role in the struggle for Greek independence from Ottoman rule, and his architects would later be called into service by his brother Otto von Wittelsbach, placed on the throne of Greece in 1830. Ironically enough the Greek Revival adopted for most new public buildings designed for Athens in the mid-nineteenth century was almost exclusively a product of German, Danish, and French architects,

all of whom sought to superimpose an image of Greece as a cradle of the modern Enlightened nation-state on the Byzantine street plan and architectural vernacular of the new capital of modern Greece.

British nationalism

From 1796 to 1815 Britain was in a nearly permanent state of war with France. The war slowed all but private construction, and had a direct and lasting cultural impact. 'There is no more effective way of bonding together the disparate sections of restless peoples, than to unite them against outsiders', Eric Hobsbawm has observed,[10] to which we might add that nothing is more effective in the bid to perpetuate such sentiments than highly visible public monuments. Much as Napoleon's campaigns gave the fragmented German lands a sense of common purpose, battle and economic rivalry with the French served as a self-defining mirror for Britain. As Linda Colley has demonstrated, this new sense of Britishness and patriotism overshadowed for a time the discordant cultural longings of Scots and Welsh and 'transcended the boundaries of class, ethnicity, occupation, sex, and age'.[11] Such sentiments could not but bolster the sense of importance surrounding that boom in construction, fed by the gains of war, which rapidly altered the face of British cities after Waterloo. As regent and later as king, George IV spent unprecedented amounts on both royal palaces and metropolitan improvements in London. Regent Street, Trafalgar Square, and other new urban 'improvements' were to serve as backdrops for a new cultivation of ceremonial, a key instrument in crafting a more populist image of the monarchy, especially in light of events in France. Projects for monuments to war heroes—the Nelson Column in Trafalgar Square, the monument to the Duke of York overlooking Pall Mall, the transformation of Apsley House into a state residence for the Duke of Wellington, and an English Valhalla for Regent's Park—proliferated, each one strategically placed in conjunction with newly planned avenues, squares, and parks that would transform London with symbolic itineraries of national symbols. Architecture helped sustain the analogy of Britain, modern saviour of Europe, with freedom-loving Athens in the Periclean age after the Persian Wars.

The Scottish national monument

A high point of George IV's great state visit to Edinburgh in 1822—the first by a reigning monarch since the Union of Scotland and England in 1707—was the cornerstone ceremony of the Scottish National Monument atop Calton Hill, a 'facsimile of the Parthenon', designed by Cockerell [73]. Stage-managed by Sir Walter Scott, whose enormously popular novels were set in the medieval past, the event drew on long-forgotten Scottish Highland traditions even in this urban setting. Paradoxically enough, to launch this Doric enterprise George IV

73

Aerial view of Edinburgh showing Calton Hill with the incomplete colonnade of the projected Scottish National Monument

Few nations were able to agree unilaterally on a single stylistic image for the construction of both a national past and future. The incomplete National Monument, a modern Greek temple, never captured the popular imagination in Scotland like the gothic Scott Monument in Prince's Gardens, a beloved and perennial icon in a city otherwise dominated by Classical public buildings and rows of porticoed houses.

donned a tartan kilt![12] A lively discussion ensued over whether the honours of Scotland's Parthenon should be limited to those fallen in war or extended to all Scotsmen who had gained fame in culture, politics, and science. But the project soon foundered in the changing tides of public enthusiasm; after only three years construction was halted for insufficient subscriptions. Yet when Scott died later that year, contributions arrived in a torrent to answer an appeal for a public memorial to the 'nation's' novelist. George Kemp's Scott Monument, a soaring 200-foot (61 m) Gothic spire with arched diagonal buttresses, was submitted in an 1836 competition under the pseudonym 'John Morow', the medieval master mason of Melrose Abbey. Melrose's Romantic ruins featured prominently in Scott's novels and had become—along with Scott's extraordinary Gothic Revival showplace house at nearby Abbotsford—a popular tourist attraction. The choice of Gothic was a tribute to Scott's project of fostering profound and emotional attachments between England and Scotland, based on a shared medieval heritage, rather than the simple legalities of political union. Kemp's monument drew as much on English and continental models as on Scotland's own medieval heritage.

The vicissitudes of Greek and Gothic in the skyline of the Scottish capital [73] underscore the fact that throughout the century ideological associations of Revival styles were continually shifting and realigning, an occurrence that gained in frequency and complexity with the growth of modern party politics, and even international diplomacy. Any study of the period's debates over historical style divorced from attention to the configuration of political, social, and cultural stakes at a precise moment falls short of understanding the meanings attached to stylistic choice. It also explains why some of the most contested and protracted building enterprises of the day lost much of the original potency of their stylistic rhetoric even before they were finished, as the coalition of forces that found expression in the first presentation drawing often dissolved long before the monument was finally unveiled.

The English Greek Revival

In the 1810s and 1820s, intent on surpassing Napoleon's legacy of Roman imperial grandeur, a generation of English architects turned their attention to careers in public architecture, devoting themselves with fervour to the project of reviving purer Grecian models. With the purchase in 1816 for the new *British* Museum of the Parthenon marbles from Lord Elgin, the associational link of modern Britain with ancient Athens was transformed from an antiquarian conceit into a national cause. But this purification of taste had been anticipated by a virulent debate over a private building endeavour a decade earlier, when the connoisseur Thomas Hope counselled the Masters and Fellows of a recently endowed college at Cambridge to adopt a monumental Grecian image for their planned

74

Aerial view of Whitehall with Houses of Parliament and the National Gallery on Trafalgar Square

By the 1830s one of London's major arteries and processional axes, Whitehall not only passed the ministries but connected two competing images of an appropriate national style, William Wilkins's temple-fronted art museum and the Gothic Revival Houses of Parliament with their picturesque skyline.

buildings. In 1804 Hope published a pamphlet attacking the Franco-Italian academic Classicism of James Wyatt's design for Downing College as a 'degraded' Roman Classicism, thus self-consciously restyling a debate over taste among intellectuals into a matter of public concern and record.[13] Promoting the talents of the young architect William Wilkins, a Cambridge classicist just returned from a 3-year tour of Greece and Asia Minor, Hope not only praised Wilkins's proposal to reinterpret the traditional quadrangle of the Cambridge college with a baseless Doric Propylaeum gate and peripheral ranges punctuated by monumental porticoes; he also set a pattern for public building for years to come. Grecian architecture was quickly taken up in country houses, notably Wilkins's own Grange Park of 1804–09. But only after Britain emerged as the premier power in Europe at the Congress of Vienna did the Greek portico, set either firmly on the ground or atop a flight of stairs, become the veritable sine qua non of public building, used prominently for the British Museum (1823–46) and the General Post Office (1824–29), both designed by Sir Robert Smirke. Since 1813 one of three architects attached to the Board of Works, along with

Soane and Nash, Smirke raised Grecian Classicism to the stature of an official style. In 1826 Wilkins was selected to design London's first university, launched by a group of social reformers eager for a progressive scientific institution to rival the traditionalism and churchly associations of Oxford and Cambridge. Work began in 1827 on the main wing, which combined a Corinthian portico modelled on the Temple of the Olympian Zeus at Athens and a grand dome, an eclectic mixture for the new temple of progressive secular culture.

While these highly visible London buildings upheld 'Greek' ideals, their architects were in reality no more exclusive in their tastes than their eighteenth-century predecessors. Smirke's numerous castellated country-house designs helped address the concern among the aristocracy in the aftermath of the French Revolution to assert ancestral roots. Wilkins provided Gothic designs for King's, Trinity, and Corpus Christi colleges in Cambridge, setting precedents which were to have an enormous and lasting legacy in forming the popular image of college life not only in Britain but throughout her colonial empire and in the United States well into the twentieth century. And Wilkins was equally at ease, and arguably more skilled, in providing a highly detailed, if always emphatically symmetrical, Gothic design replete with a rich roof line of gables and pinnacles to underscore the longevity and tradition of ancient colleges as he was in detailing lofty stairs and stately porticoes for public buildings, including the classical National Gallery, begun in 1834 to complement the triumphal imagery of Trafalgar Square. By the time it was completed the museum marked one pole of an axis drawn by Whitehall, the other marked by the Houses of Parliament rising on the horizon and postulating a medieval past for Britain [74]. In the 1830s, style became a matter of national debate rather than personal or local preference.

The Gothic Revival in Britain

Gothic first began to appear in public in the opening decades of the nineteenth century in church design, as it became associated with concerted efforts towards renewal within the Anglican church, long complacent in its position as Britain's established church. The rapid growth of urban populations—the population of England alone grew by 7 million in these decades—and the accompanying growing popularity of nonconforming sects gradually sounded alarms with the church episcopate, who set out in the years after the defeat of Napoleon to reconquer the souls of Britain's swelling cities. Given the extent to which patriotism was intermixed with the ethos of Britain as the great upholder of Protestantism, the politics of church building was from the first an issue of national consciousness. In 1818 Parliament approved one million pounds to fund 600 new parish churches. Only 214 were built in the end, but the act made the necessity for both standardization and economy

75 A. W. N. Pugin

75 A. W. N. Pugin

'Contrasted chapels', a plate from *Contrasts*, 1836

In this satirical comparison, the spindly modern Gothic building (upper image) would be recognized by readers as the recently completed St Mary's Chapel, Somers Town, celebrated as an act of charity in a working-class neighbourhood. Pugin was more critical of non-archaeological Gothic than of Classical design, fearing that it belittled his cause and diminished his hope that the revival of Gothic would instigate a national moral renewal.

more than the choice of style a key issue in selecting designs. Often Gothic won approval over Classical since it was held to be less costly. The vast variety of executed designs reveals marked regional preferences, notably in the north where such inventive designs as those by Thomas Rickman in Manchester, Liverpool, and Birmingham—several employing cast-iron elements—are markedly in contrast with the thin Gothic appliqué on otherwise plain stock-brick preaching boxes of the capital, such as the Inwoods' St Mary's Chapel, Somers Town [75].

Their architectural quality aside, the construction of these churches in working-class neighbourhoods did as much, if not more, to establish Neo-Gothic in the national consciousness as did the same sum spent by George IV—one million pounds—on expanding and decorating Windsor Castle in the Gothic taste. This highly publicized project was supervised by Sir Jeffry Wyatville, whose numerous cathedral restorations would soon be lambasted for their freedom of interpretation by a rising generation of archaeologically correct Gothic Revivalists. Not the least of his critics was the young Pugin, who began his career designing furniture for the Windsor project. By the 1830s Pugin's sense of a personal calling to Gothic would convert him not only from a lax Protestant to a fervent Catholic but from a skilled practitioner of one of the modes of Regency architectural pluralism into the self-appointed prophet of a universal Gothic Revival.

Pugin and the Houses of Parliament

The emergence of the Gothic Revival as the credo of a substantial portion of the English architectural profession can be attributed to two crucial events of the mid-1830s. The first was the decision in 1835 by a parliamentary committee to require either Gothic or Elizabethan style for rebuilding the Palace of Westminster after a devastating fire; the second was Pugin's fiery campaign for the Gothic Revival as a means not simply of reforming taste but of restoring the social fabric and even the moral fibre of industrializing England. An open architectural competition, wrested from the administration through public opinion's harsh critique of the excessive spending and jobbery of the established architects of the Office of Works, was viewed as proof of political progress through evolution rather than revolution. (Across the Channel the 1830 Revolution had led to another violent change of regime in France.) Opening artistic decisions to democratic procedure and to a free market of younger talent was celebrated as fulfilment of the promises of the expanded parliamentary representation of the 1832 Reform Bill. The public exhibition of entries, an unprecedented display of modern Gothic design, occasioned a lively discussion. Advocates of Gothic argued for pious contextualism—respecting the medieval St Stephen's Chapel and Westminster Hall which had survived the fire—and cited Parliament's 'Gothic' or 'Saxon' origins. The aesthetic opposition was organized by W. R. Hamilton, a scholar of antiquity, who asserted that, as the noblest achievements of humanity, Greek and Roman temples were peculiarly appropriate for embodying the lofty ideals of British parliamentary rule.

No-one addressed this issue with more fervour than Augustus Welby Northmore Pugin (1812–52) in his satiric *Contrasts; or a parallel between the noble edifices of the Middle Ages and Corresponding Buildings of the Present Day; shewing the Present Decay of Taste*, finished in 1836 only months after he had completed work on the Gothic detailing of two of

Contrasted towns in 1440 and 1840. Plate added to the second edition of *Contrasts* in 1840

In the contemporary town, the spires and battlements of churches and protective town walls have been allowed to decay, their dominance replaced by factory smokestacks and a radial-plan prison. Pugin added his voice to a rising litany of critics of the early nineteenth-century industrial town culminating in Friedrich Engels's 1844 *Report on the Conditions of the Working Classes*.

THE SAME TOWN IN 1840.

1. St Michaels Tower, rebuilt in 1750. 2. New Parsonage House & Pleasure Grounds. 3. The New Jail. 4. Gas Works. 5. Lunatic Asylum. 6. Iron Works & Ruins of St Maries Abbey. 7. St Evans Chapel. 8. Baptist Chapel. 9. Unitarian Chapel. 10. New Church. 11. New Town Hall & Concert Room. 12. Wesleyan Centenary Chapel. 13. New Christian Society. 14. Quakers Meeting. 15. Socialist Hall of Science.

Catholic town in 1440.

1. St Michaels on the Hill. 2. Queens Cross. 3. St Thomas's Chapel. 4. St Maries Abbey. 5. All Saints. 6. St Johns. 7. St Peters. 8. St Alkmunds. 9. St Maries. 10. St Edmunds. 11. Grey Friars. 12. St Cuthberts. 13. Guild hall. 14. Trinity. 15. St Olaves. 16. St Botolphs.

the most admired entries in the Parliament competition, those of the Scottish architect James Gillespie Graham and the winning entry by Charles Barry (1795–1860). Borrowing techniques from the political cartoons and the popular press of the day, Pugin conceived an entirely novel architectural book. Page after page offered vivid contrasts between the architectural splendour and social harmony of medieval England and scenes of contemporary social ills staged frequently in modern Greek Revival streetscapes [76]. In a lengthy historical text Pugin argued for a causal relationship between the decline of Gothic architecture and the rise of Protestantism, and related the revival of Classicism to a progressive erosion of ethical values which had culminated in modern laissez-faire commercialism. *Contrasts* was the first publication to abandon the antiquarian project of providing designers with historical sources in favour of the polemical use of historical argument to justify the integral revival of a past style of building for a modern national architecture.

Pugin was thus a pioneer in the Revivalist logic which argued for a universal national style suitable for the full range of building types, including those required by modern industry and commerce, ironically the very forces he sought to temper in his barbed critique of the nineteenth century's moral shortcomings. In the heavily reworked 1841 edition, Pugin extended his argument that the state of architecture and the state of society are inextricably linked, with two additional plates, most famously in contrasted views of the same urban scene in 1440 and 1840 [76]. Against industrializing Britain's faith in progress, Pugin offered a pessimistic vision of modernity as a decline from a medieval golden age, a conservative social discourse of such Tory writers as Scott, Disraeli, and especially Carlyle, as well as the nostalgia for Christian art as a golden age preached by such continental Romantic Catholics as Rio and Montalembert. A return to Gothic would assert not only Christian and English values, but moral truth. Architecture was to be converted from mirror of society to opening wedge in a massive social reform, in which Pugin, like many of his Anglican contemporaries in the Oxford Movement, saw the church as taking a leading role.

The Houses of Parliament

The new Houses of Parliament stood on the cusp between a long standing British interest in the associational value of Gothic and the project of Pugin and his followers to derive a design method from the study of medieval construction and ornamentation. It was an ideal which Pugin, like the whole generation of Gothic Revival architects who expressed their views in the reformist Anglican journal *The Ecclesiologist,* would articulate both in words and in bricks and mortar. In 1836, while Barry's design was being publicly debated, Pugin lambasted the entire architectural profession in a plate in *Contrasts* which parodied architectural competitions as reflections of the lax attitude towards style which had accompanied the commercialization of architecture [77]. Although only a few years earlier Pugin had made his living by supplying Gothic ornaments to Nash, Wyatville, and others, he was now eager for an artistic conversion every bit as complete as his religious awakening. Using Catholic connections in the wake of the Emancipation Act of 1829, he launched himself as an architect. By the time he published his second tract, *True Principles of Pointed or Christian Architecture*, in 1841, Pugin could offer a self-portrait as an architect monk, conflating his faith and profession into a vision of architecture as a system of ethics. The frontispiece of his 1843 *Apology for the Revival of Christian Architecture* illustrates some 20 church designs, many under construction. St Giles, Cheadle, Staffordshire (1839–44) alone fulfilled Pugin's vision of a renewal of the liturgical arts and of polychromatic splendour [78].

77 Pugin

77 Pugin

'Poster advertising an architectural competition' from *Contrasts*, 1836

'Gothic or Elisabethan' were clearly interchangeable when the practice of architecture had been reduced to a mere trade 'on new improved and cheap principles'. Pugin played on the broadsheets of the day to create a damning appraisal of architectural practice in a competitive marketplace and a clear satire on the Houses of Parliament competition in which he himself had taken part.

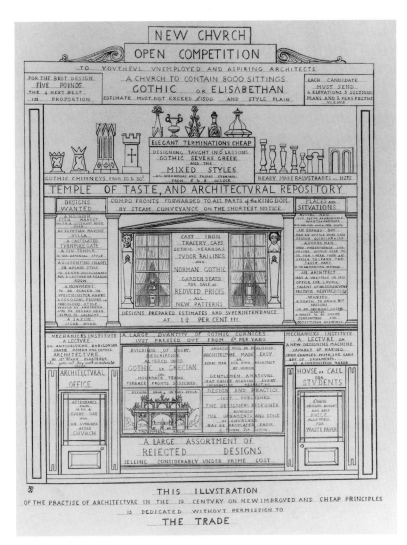

78 Pugin (page 162)

St Giles, Cheadle, interior, 1839–44

Of the numerous Neo-Gothic churches Pugin was able to realize in his short career, only Cheadle and his own private chapel at Ramsgate fulfilled his dream of an interior in which Gothic style and his principles of truthful design permeated every form from the architectural frame to the liturgical equipment of the high altar. Here, too, Pugin demonstrated his ideas for a polychromatic decorative vocabulary to complement the architecture.

By the time Pugin was able to bask in the international recognition of Cheadle—both Montalembert and Reichensperger, leading forces in the French and German Gothic Revivals, attended the dedication—he had also returned to the Houses of Parliament, where construction began in 1840. In addition to furniture and woodwork, ceramic tiles, wallpapers, and stained glass—all of which would have tremendous influence on the revival of craft industries—Pugin designed every detail down to the inkwells. With the contributions of painters and sculptors the building became the framework for a complex pedagogy in British history. Yet, as brilliantly as Pugin and Barry collaborated on creating a setting which cemented anew the associations of Gothic style and the British legislative tradition with every royal opening of Parliament, the two architects' views on Gothic and its modern relevance diverged rapidly in the 1840s.

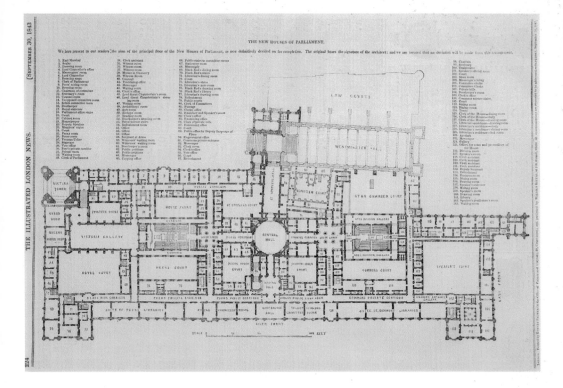

79 Charles Barry

Plan of the Houses of
Parliament

Realizing that the Thames
façade would mainly be
viewed obliquely, Barry dared
to defy the logic of academic
composition by refusing
emphasis on the centre and
offering only the most minimal
projection of the corners. The
overall masses are regular and
simple, but Barry plays off the
existing towers of Westminster
Abbey and calculates from the
viewpoints of a moving
pedestrian, the whole in the
best tradition of picturesque
composition.

Few could deny the brilliant clarity of Barry's plan, with its lucid hierarchies between public and private areas, grandeur of approach to the great octagonal hall at the centre of four radiating corridors, and accommodation of several score of offices for the two houses [**79**]. What might easily have been one of the most monotonous compositions ever conceived, with its endless repetition of the same narrow-bay module for the full 800-foot (244 m) length of its river front, is transformed into a brilliantly picturesque urban set piece through a few simple but masterful gestures, notably the asymmetrical placement of three great vertical elements, the stalwart Victoria Tower, the open lantern over the vestibule at the heart of the building, and Big Ben, Parliament's trademark clock tower.

'All Grecian, Sir; Tudor details on a classic body', Pugin is said to have quipped to a friend.[14] This testifies both to Pugin's changing views about historical models and his increased conviction that Gothic was a paradigm, not an image to be reproduced. Repudiating his earlier work, Pugin had come to view Perpendicular architecture as a decadent finale to Gothic's long development. Only at its purest, he now felt, had Gothic achieved subordination of ornament to structure. Pugin provided his own commandments in the opening paragraph of *True Principles*: 'The two great rules for design are these: 1st, that there should be no features about a building which are not necessary for convenience, construction, or propriety; 2nd, that all ornament should consist of enrichment of the essential construction of the building.'[15] Despite the fact that these principles are framed with no reference to a particular style—they bear witness to Pugin's familiarity with Laugier—few contemporaries found contradictory Pugin's assertion that 'in pointed architecture alone ... these great principles have been carried out'.[16] The Ecclesiologists, who prided themselves on turning matters of aesthetic and historical judgement into infallible scientific laws, went further in dogmatic insistence on specific models. In addition to meeting a rigid list of liturgical requirements, new churches should take as their stylistic point of departure what the historian E. A. Freeman called 'the early late middle pointed'.[17] By the mid-century this prelapsarian argument was echoed in manifestos for any number of revivals, from the French Gothic Revivalists who proposed the twelfth-century Gothic of the Ile-de-France as purest alloy to Heinrich Hübsch in Karlsruhe who proposed to begin anew with the German Romanesque.

In 1836 Pugin had designed little apart from his own house, St Marie's Grange, near Salisbury [**80**], where he printed *Contrasts*. Like so many architects' houses it was brimming with ideas and determination, not the least the declaration that brick itself should be expressed rather than covered with stucco as it had been in miles upon miles of recent London terrace housing. As contrived as it might seem to compare this little house in the country with the Houses of Parliament, the contrast highlights Barry and Pugin's divergence of creed. As much as Barry sought to accommodate the complexity of his programme within a simple form that could send a unified and powerful message, Pugin was concerned to dramatize the different spaces and functions required even in the simplest domestic programme. Barry carefully moved the eccentric elements of his programme to the centre, stacking the repetitious offices to the façades to create a uniformity that yields an almost sublime cliff of masonry along the Thames; Pugin pulled stairs, chimneys, and other services to the periphery so that they might transform this simple building into a highly articulated architectural sculpture. With his concept of 'picturesque utility' Pugin insisted that the architect's aesthetic palette comprise uniquely the necessities of the programme and structure rather than rhetorical signs of style. In church design this taste for articulation was defended vigorously in the name of liturgical requirements and traditions. No less than in architecture where 'the smallest detail should have a meaning or serve a purpose',[18] in religion every form and usage should be justified by the restoration of ancient Catholic practice with its rich symbolic and ritual significance. Pugin made it as much a principle of liturgical expression as of architectural honesty that the separate articulation of nave, chancel, side aisles, steeple, and entrance porch allowed a clear reading of the plan and the different functions of the building from the exte-

Pugin's own house, St Marie's Grange, near Salisbury, 1835
The variety of masses, window types, and terminations allow one to read the placement of individual rooms, staircases, and even Pugin's private chapel, on the exterior of the building. This transparency of the building's programme was one aspect of Pugin's notion of architectural honesty, complemented by the exposed brick construction, eschewing decorative stucco for truth to materials.

rior. Pugin added to the dictates of convenience and construction, which suggested a kind of structural and programmatic determinism, a third factor, propriety. 'Propriety' required not only that a church and a house look different but that a clear hierarchy of richness in materials, elaboration, and ornamentation be respected. Pugin's moral criterion for judging every detail of architectural design was to shift fundamentally the discourse on architecture in Britain. One of the most prolific of the Victorian period's Gothic Revivalists, George Gilbert Scott, proudly proclaimed that he had been 'morally awakened' by Pugin's writings, abandoning a career of stylistic indifference.[19]

France: architectural restoration and national style
The campaign for the Gothic as a model for modern building gained force in France only in the 1840s, by which time even the most patriotic

antiquarians in Germany and England had admitted that the Ile-de-France was the cradle of the Gothic, as much as it was of the French monarchy. Despite this association of Gothic with 'la France ancienne' and with France's Christian tradition—asserted as early as 1802 when Chateaubriand published his *Genius of Christianity* four days before the celebration of the Concordat between Napoleon and Pope Pius VII—French Gothic Revivalists would never have the chance to build a secular building of national prominence comparable to the Houses of Parliament in London, or even to initiate a national debate over style such as accompanied the design of the Reichstag in Berlin after German unification in 1870.

During the first half of the century, as regime succeeded regime, Gothic was occasionally called upon to assert legitimacy and continuity, even as a whole new structure of power and rule was put in place. Such were the colourful medieval decorations created by Percier and Fontaine for Napoleon's coronation in Notre-Dame in 1804 or the grand Gothic family burial chapel for the Orléans branch of the royal family, erected in the 1840s at Dreux by Louis-Philippe, 'King of the French'. Gradually the Gothic found sporadic support within the clergy and the 1830s to 1850s were rocked by battles to force the state's architectural review boards to accept Gothic Revival designs, notably in the battle over the church of St–Nicolas in Nantes.

Born on the barricades of the July 1830 Revolution, Louis-Philippe's constitutional monarchy was nervously in search of legitimacy and identity. Within a few years, largely through the efforts of the historian-turned-minister of state François Guizot, a series of projects for recording and preserving national history was launched under the auspices of the Ministry of Education and Worship. The raw materials of Guizot's own craft as a historian, such as medieval charters granting freedoms and privileges to city fathers, forerunners of the newly enlarged bourgeois voting franchise, were to be preserved and recorded in government-sponsored publications. Even more innovative was Guizot's response to the Romantic notion that the soul of the nation was embodied in France's great architectural monuments. Victor Hugo had sounded the alarm, declaring battle on 'Demolishers', hoping to reverse the tide of neglect and active vandalism of medieval buildings. He captured the public imagination with his novel *Notre Dame de Paris* (1830), in which the cathedral took on the role of a major character, as the veritable embodiment of the nation. In 1830 Ludovic Vitet was appointed to travel the countryside to identify buildings worthy of preservation and attention, and in 1837 Guizot created a state office, now under the direction of Prosper Mérimée, charged with the actual restoration of buildings in danger. By 1840 the first restorations were under way, beginning with the medieval church of the Madeleine at Vézélay, which the young Eugène-

Emmanuel Viollet-le-Duc (1814–79) saved from imminent collapse.

Such recording and classification of architecture by period and style had forerunners in Lenoir's museum, the volumes of lithographs in Baron Taylor and Charles Nodier's *Voyages pittoresques et romantiques dans l'ancienne France* (1820–78), and the efforts of Arcise de Caumont, founder of the Society of Antiquaries of Normandy, to apply the techniques of botanical classification to the diversity of medieval architecture. But for the first time this recording was tied to direct intervention to save individual buildings as *national* monuments. 'To restore an edifice means neither to maintain it, nor to repair it, nor to rebuild; it means to reestablish it in a finished state, which may in fact never have actually existed in any given time,' Viollet-le-Duc explained with great candour in the article on restoration in his *Dictionnaire raisonné* (1854–68); 'both the word and the thing are modern'.[20] Medieval buildings were to be carefully pruned of later additions so that they might more clearly speak of their place in the evolution of French artistic and national genius. Gothic cathedrals, which Hugo celebrated as the work of civilization rather than individual artists, architects, or stone masons, began a career they enjoy to this day as secular pilgrimage sites of French history. The first great national effort was the restoration of Paris's Sainte-Chapelle, begun in 1836 under the direction of Félix Duban. He was assisted by two younger architects, J.-B.-A. Lassus and Viollet-le-Duc, who rose to national fame in the new speciality of architectural restoration when their project to restore Notre-Dame Cathedral was approved in 1843. They proposed not only to repair the damage of the Revolution and earlier restorations but to add elements that had never existed historically but which they considered indispensable for a complete cathedral, notably spires crowning the twin towers of the west front. During the same years Baron Haussmann's plans for modernizing Paris (chapter 8) created a frame of empty space around the building, freeing, ironically enough, the historical monument from the accretions of time. In the same years Duban pursued a different restoration philosophy at the royal château at Blois, making sure that each wing—construction spanned the eleventh to the seventeenth centuries—reflected its own historical moment. The whole would become 'a veritable summary of our national architecture', and modern architects could witness an architecture in progress rather than a crystalline ideal. Revivalism versus pluralism was to be debated as much in restoring historic architecture as in creating new national monuments.

Gothic and the rise of nationalism in Central Europe

Nowhere was national identity a more complex issue than in the Habsburg Empire. While Austria fought on the real and symbolic battlefield with Prussia to assert leadership in any future united Germany, its own empire was a patchwork of the most diverse ethnicities, languages, and traditions. Spreading from Lombardy and Croatia in the south to Poland in the north, the Habsburg lands were held together through centralized bureaucracy rather than blood, history, and culture, increasingly the criteria of modern nationalism. Local historical buildings as well as new public buildings thus occasioned a self-consciousness about the messages and uses of style in architecture as new forms of local rule and cultural expression were negotiated in the wake of the 1848 revolutions, the springtime of nations which pushed the frontiers of national consciousness far to the east. It is no coincidence that a year later one of the great advocates of maintaining national differences in architecture, John Ruskin, noted that architectural style 'half constitutes the identity, as it concentrates the sympathy, of nations'.[21] Already in the 1840s the aristocratic fashion of building modern Gothic castles took hold among Bohemian nobles as a protest against the official Classicism of Metternich's Vienna; indeed the rare use of the Gothic in Vienna for the emperor's Votivkirche [**130b**] may be directly related to the appointment after 1848 of the Bohemian nationalist Leo Graf von Thun-Hohenstein as Minister of Education and Religion. After the Austro-Hungarian Compromise of 1867, which granted Hungary self-determination in its internal affairs, the need for a Hungarian past became a pressing necessity. Ironically enough, this was to be crafted largely by the Hungarian pupils of the great German architect Friedrich von Schmidt (1825–91). Schmidt trained as a master mason under Ernst Zwirner at Cologne before setting up an independent practice in Vienna in 1857 after taking first prize in the town hall competition with a Gothic design [**130b**]. In these same years Scott sought to export the

Gothic abroad, in parallel with his efforts to enrich his own Gothic with continental elements, notably in competition designs for St Nicholas (1844) and the Town Hall in Hamburg (1855), proof of the extent to which nationality was an ideological construct of intellectuals.

The nationalism of the Hungarian Gothic Revival was especially stamped by the theories of Imre Henszlmann, who first became interested in the 'Old German' churches of Hungary in the 1840s, but soon developed notions that would lead him to envision Gothic as a way of differentiating Magyar Hungary from Germanic Austria. He spent the 1850s abroad in England and France, where, under the influence of Pugin and Viollet-le-Duc, he developed a theory of Gothic proportions. In 1861 he collaborated on an entry in the competition for a new headquarters for the Hungarian Academy, a highly charged undertaking in Hungary's attempt to craft an identity within the empire. Associations with the great monuments crowning old Buda on the left bank of the Danube were of importance, but his stylistic choice had more to do with Viollet-le-Duc's compelling theories of the Gothic as the style of freedom in contrast to Romanesque monastic architecture. Henszlmann celebrated Gothic's origins in France, playing now on the unpopularity of all things German in the wake of the defeat of the Hungarians at the hands of the Austrians in the war of independence. In the heat of the moment, Gothic, which no-one considered indigenous to Hungary, had the great advantage of not following Austrian norms. Although the competition was won by the Berlin architect August Stüler, who submitted a neo-Renaissance design, the Gothic ultimately triumphed as the symbol of Hungarian national freedom with Imre Steindl's designs for the great Gothic Revival Parliament, submitted in the competition of 1883. Rising on a dramatic site on the Danube, the Hungarian Parliament transformed the waterfront of Budapest with a new national symbol [**81**]. Completed in 1904, little more than a decade before the dissolution of the Habsburg Empire, it was a swan song of the use of the great historic styles as dramatically pure and clear signs of identity. By the time it was inaugurated a number of Hungarian architects had turned to studying the vernacular of the countryside in search of a 'truly national' style that would also demand a great deal of personal interpretation, at once freeing national character from the diplomacy of the great European styles and opening a new chapter in the use of architecture to craft identity through nostalgia for a lost 'natural' community. This was to manifest itself in that national Romanticism of the closing decades of the nineteenth century that was to touch nearly every European country from the neo-Manueline style in Portugal and the neo-Romanian of Bucharest's northern suburbs in the 1890s to the imaginative and colourful exploration of the rustic vernacular in Sweden and Finland around 1900.

Historicism and New Building Types

6

Art, the expression of society, manifests, in its highest soaring, the most advanced social tendencies: it is the forerunner and the revealer. Therefore, to know whether art worthily fulfils its proper mission as initiation, whether the artist is truly of the avant-garde, one must know where Humanity is going, know what the destiny of the human race is.

Gabriel-Désiré Laverdant,
De la mission de l'art et du rôle des artistes, 1845

Utopian socialism and architecture

Less than a decade after Napoleon's defeat at Waterloo, 'avant-garde' began its migration from the terminology of warfare to the ethos of artistic practice. A theory of the artist as a visionary, critical of the status quo and preparing a better future, formulated by Claude Henri de Saint-Simon before his death in 1825 and refined in the writings of such disciples as Émile Barrault and Gabriel Laverdant, sponsored a number of utopian blueprints. A handful of architects participated in these short-lived communal experiments, including those of rival utopian socialists Charles Fourier in France and Robert Owen in Britain, both of whom imagined self-sufficient communes—veritable anti-cities—that challenged class structures and the separation of labour from the land [83]. But it was Saint-Simonianism's challenge to artists to join with the new elite of industrialists and scientists—masters of the challenges and resources of an emerging industrial order—that had the most lasting influence on the generation of French architects who came to maturity in the intellectual and political ferment of the 1820s and 1830s, determined to reform architecture and its institutions from within.

As the liberal opposition to the Bourbon Restoration was sustained by theories of the national past as a record of struggles between races, classes, and nations, history was advanced as the study of the process of change and evolution rather than a glorious chronicle of kings and battles. Historians engaged as never before with the nascent system of party politics and with public debates on the social and economic

82 Sir George Gilbert Scott
Midland Grand Hotel, St Pancras Station, London 1868–74
Scott brilliantly masked the great shed by the engineers W. H. Barlow and R. Ordish with the grand sweep of the terminus hotel, which exploits the oblique relationship between the Midland Railway tracks and the great east–west corridor of Euston Road. Borrowing freely from the pinnacled and gabled skylines of north German civic Gothic, the hotel declares modern railway travel and its new spaces as the civic arena of the industrial present, and bristles in its rich colour palette of materials.

83

Victor Considerant's
Phalanstery, published in
1834

Considerant adopted the
palace of Versailles as the
framework for creating a
perfect and self-contained
society based on Charles
Fourier's theories of
harmonizing the diversity of
human types and talents. An
attempt near Rambouillet
failed within a year, but
Fourierist communities
sprang up in the US, two
dozen by 1846, and even in
Tsarist Russia. The interior
was to include glass-covered
'streets', adapted from the
period's shopping arcades.

order. The Saint-Simonian theory of history as a progression of 'critical' and 'organic' periods was but one attempt to uncover the dynamic
at the very heart of historical change and variety, in short to propose
that human history obeyed laws as verifiable as those that scientists
were testing in the natural realm. In the 1820s the philosophical and
historical lectures of Victor Cousin and François Guizot and the writings of Augustin Thierry in Paris, and the stirring public lectures of
Hegel on history and aesthetics in Berlin all contributed to an interest
in history as a new science of society and a vital framework for debating
issues of the day.

For architects, these theories challenged the doctrine of the imitation of ideal models which was the bedrock of the academic system.
Between 1828 and 1830 the Paris Academy of Fine Arts, dominated by
the idealist aesthetic doctrines of its secretary Quatremère de
Quincy—who held a tight rein over the promotion of École des
Beaux-Arts students to posts as architects of major public buildings—
was rocked by provocative interpretations of antiquity sent back by
young architects resident at the French Academy of Rome. 'Why
shouldn't architecture have its own little revolution?', asked Léon
Vaudoyer (1803–72), the youngest of this group who styled themselves
'Romantics' in homage to current debates in painting and literature.
'It's entirely natural, it's the force of circumstances that drives us. A culture's architecture should take its character firstly from its institutions,
second from its mores, thirdly from the climate, and fourthly from the
nature of materials etc. ... Therefore the architecture of 1830 cannot be
that of 1680 when Versailles was built, allowing the people to die of
hunger and misery.'[1] Months later, revolution brought down King
Charles x, seeming to confirm that architecture might be as much an
annunciation as a reflection of a social order. Not coincidentally, one of
the first preoccupations of the new constitutional monarch, Louis-
Philippe, was the transformation of Versailles from a palace into a national history museum.

Henri Labrouste's restoration of Paestum

'Quite simply a revolution on a few sheets of elephant folio paper' is how Viollet-le-Duc later characterized the study of Greek monuments at Paestum. Henri Labrouste (1801–75) was sent to Paris in 1828 [**84**] to fulfil the fourth-year requirement of Fellows of the French Academy in Rome for a graphic restoration of a building from the Classical canon. Part of a staged sequence, this assignment was intended to hone the skills of a privileged élite of the profession, laureates of the Rome Prize. As Quatremère de Quincy explained in *On Imitation*—written in 1823 to stem the growing enthusiasm for Romanticism and its emphasis on individuality and cultural relativity—Classicism 'is quite simply the taste which has reigned for two or three thousand years and which has served as a model for all the cultures of modern Europe, the taste which informs all the works which have been admired down to our own time'.[2]

Labrouste's choice was scarcely novel; the storm over the discrepancies between the colonial temples and the canons of Roman temple design had been weathered 70 years earlier [**3, 9**]. But his claims about the evolution of architectural form in relation to society challenged academic notions of timeless standards. He disputed the dating of the temples, proposing to replace traditional assumptions of progressive formal refinement with a chronology documenting the gradual adaptation of imported Athenian models to the material and cultural realities of a new social and physical setting. Echoing contemporary historians' fascination with the process by which modern European states emerged as distinctive cultures from their Roman imperial background, Labrouste turned the study of colonialism into a challenge to Neoclassical aesthetic doctrine. Much of his demonstration centred on the unusual Temple of Hera, with its broader span, squatter proportions, and unusual two-storey columnar spine bisecting the interior. Following Piranesi, he insisted that the building was not a temple at all but rather an assembly hall, a non-hierarchical space for secular rituals. Restoring even trophies and festoons for which there was no material evidence, Labrouste suggested ways the ancient colony might have

84 Henri Labrouste,
Temple of Hera I at Paestum, 1828–29

Labrouste imagined the surfaces of the building enlivened by colour, festooned with shields and garlands left over from a celebration, and marked by graffiti and inscriptions to underscore his view of the intimate relationship between a society and the forms of its architecture, a challenge to academic notions of ageless aesthetic ideals.

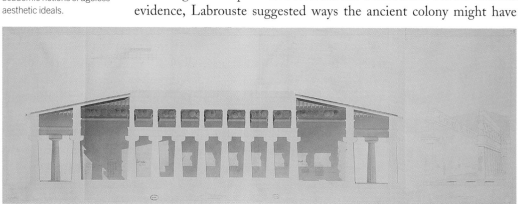

used the space, and implied that only when a building began to bear the imprint of social use did it acquire its full meaning.

In the same year Félix Duban (1797–1870), completing his Roman sojourn, submitted an equally provocative exercise. The *pensionnaire's* final duty was to conceive a building 'in keeping with French uses', paving the way to a successful career as a government architect. Academic design worked by analogy; a design for a law court, for instance—such as Labrouste had prepared in the 1824 Rome Prize competition—would look to the basilicas in which law had been administered in ancient Rome. But Duban deliberately chose a building type for which there was no ancient precedent, a Protestant church, and thereby raised the question of the relationship of archaeological study to modern design. The choice was doubly provocative. The government in Paris had recently veered sharply to the right, towards an ultra-Catholic position and, in 1828, the first lectures of the Saint-Simonians described Protestantism as the spearhead of the critical phase of historical development that established the problematic of modern society.

The 'Romantics'—Abel Blouet (1795–1853), Émile-Jacques Gilbert (1793–1874), and Louis Duc (1802–79), in addition to Duban, Labrouste, and Vaudoyer—greeted the July Revolution euphorically, embracing it not merely as political change but seeing there evidence of that pattern of evolution they were eager to master in guiding architecture to new forms in harmony with large social developments. Labrouste was paraded through the streets of Paris by students who beseeched him to open a studio to teach the new approach. Labrouste's portfolio of drawings, filled with studies of diverse historical styles, including the Etruscan—notably newly discovered tombs—and the Moorish-tinged Romanesque of Sicily, circulated widely in copies. Such styles were more than fodder for an increasingly competitive market in novel decor; they offered evidence of transitional moments in architecture, analogous to the dilemma of the present on the brink of modernity. In these same years the German émigré architect Jacques Ignace Hittorff (1792–1867), who would emerge as one of the most successful and original architects in Paris in the 1830s, published studies of Sicilian architecture, documenting extensive evidence of colour, notably in the temples upheld since Winckelmann as embodiments of a pristine white abstraction. The 'polychromy controversy' raged for over a decade and proved a challenge to Neoclassical doctrine throughout Europe [85].

The Romantics' first chance to give permanent expression to their point of view came in 1832 when a reorganization of architectural posts intended to open careers to new talent resulted in Duban's appointment to succeed François Debret on the ambitious project of crafting a modern École des Beaux-Arts out of the buildings of the disaffected

monastery of the Petits Augustins. The seventeenth-century monastic buildings, as well as medieval and Renaissance fragments left behind in 1816 when Alexander Lenoir's revolutionary Museum of French Monuments was disbanded on Quatremère de Quincy's insistence, proved an embarrassment to Debret. Duban embraced them as an opportunity to compose an object lesson for students and visitors alike of the threads that tied the diverse forms of French architecture together across the ages.

There was little latitude to change the footprint of Debret's new 'Palace of Studies', a great neo-Renaissance palazzo in homage to Vignola, whom Debret upheld as the 'legislator' of modern design. But Duban recast the design so dramatically that it was recognized immediately as a manifesto of youthful romanticism. Duban's friends Hippolyte Fortoul, Léonce Reynaud, and Vaudoyer had turned to the

86 Prosper Morey, after Duban

Drawing of the École des Beaux-Arts, Paris

Like contemporary historians, Duban was determined to find an essential plot in the history of architecture. In the school's forecourt he was eager to underscore that the Renaissance had not been a negation of the architecture of the Middle Ages, indeed to demonstrate that modernity had its origins in the selective reflection and learning from the past.

period's liberalized press to promote a theory of the history of architecture as a dialectical progression, variously labelling the terms 'tradition' and 'innovation', or even 'art' and 'science', to describe the interaction between technological progress and artistic imagination in the lawful progress of civilization. Duban went so far as to suggest, in design rather than words, that his own building—a richer Renaissance variant of Debret's unfinished project—had a family relationship to the entrance porticoes of the late Gothic and Renaissance châteaux of Gaillon and Anet exhibited in the forecourt. The so-called 'Arch of Gaillon', a hybrid design which featured elements of Renaissance style mixed with Gothic mouldings and details, stood at the cusp between two stylistic periods, at the precise threshold between the Middle Ages and the Renaissance which the young Romantics saw as the onset of the critical period to which the nineteenth century would be the denouement. Duban positioned it accordingly on the main axis of entry so that its lacy screen-like composition intervened between the viewer and his own building, almost like the flaps architects used to show design changes on a drawing [**86**]. As students and visitors entered the school they would traverse a carefully curated 'summary of our national architecture', although this vision was somewhat compromised as Duban never found the High Gothic pendant he hoped to juxtapose with the Renaissance portico of Anet. Yet it would be hard to imagine a more compelling demonstration that architectural types were subject to historical evolution, a theory that echoed new theories of biological evolution animated by the famous debates between Geoffrey St-Hilaire and Georges Cuvier. The academy was not after new species, and it was precisely Duban's use of historical fragments that caused the greatest stir in the review of his design by the government agency on public architecture whose members were nervous about the message that might be sent to students by Duban's attitudes towards the non-canonic past.

The Bibliothèque Sainte-Geneviève

Commissioned to design a fireproof, free-standing home for the books and manuscripts of the former abbey of Ste-Geneviève, Labrouste was the first of the group to take on an entirely new building and to confront the issue of what a synthetic modern architecture might be. He set out to solve the logistics of book storage and delivery straightforwardly, and, at the same time, to develop the symbolism of this all but unprecedented assignment of a *public* library. The Saint-Simonians believed that great phases of human civilization could be associated with a single building which embodied a culture's highest spiritual aspirations and served as a focal point of its social and intellectual life. This was the temple in the ancient world, the cathedral in the Middle Ages, a point rendered vividly in Hugo's immensely popular *Notre Dame de Paris* (1832), for which Labrouste served as architectural adviser. As Neil Levine has revealed, the architect was responding to the novelist's assertion—in the famous chapter 'This Will Kill That'—that with the invention of the printing press in the fifteenth century, on the brink of the Protestant Reformation, the handwriting of history passed from monumental architecture to printed books.[3] Whereas time continually eroded the historical memories embodied in even the most monumental piles of stone, such as Paris's great cathedral—restoration began in 1844 on Notre-Dame in response to Hugo's appeals—printing meant that literature's diffusion would be universal and eternal. Designing a monument for books, Labrouste could not help but wonder if architecture could be made to speak once again, to live up to the motto coined by the critic Fortoul: 'architecture is the veritable handwriting of civilizations'.[4]

The new library would form part of the urban space still only partially carved out as a frame for Ste-Geneviève [see **10**] and was thus integral to King Louis-Philippe's most fraught forays into artistic politics. After 1830 the new regime 'restored' Soufflot's building—which had been triumphantly given back to the church under the Bourbon Restoration—to its role as a secular pantheon and set about drawing up a new roster of 'great men'. Labrouste's library, on its narrow site on the square's north edge [**87**], would not only need to fit into a larger urban compositon but to participate in a complex architectural

87 Henri Labrouste

Bibliothèque Ste-Geneviève, 1838–50 **a)** Exterior view

Something of the austerity of Labrouste's façade was conditioned by its role as backdrop to Soufflot's Panthéon, given renewed prominence in the July Monarchy's artistic politics. The library's arcades capitalized on the fact that the building could only be viewed obliquely, even though academic doctrine generally considered public building as framed in open space and approached axially.

b) Reading Room on the second floor

In celebrating iron as the material of the new age of positivist inquiry Labrouste was no doubt aware that less than a century earlier Soufflot had embedded iron within masonry [**13**]. The temple of positivist knowledge was also a temple of progress, and Labrouste set out to demonstrate the capacities and natures of the full palette of building materials of the industrial age.

c) Plan of the second floor

A master of academic composition, Labrouste believed that a building's plan should feature a clear hierarchy and progression in relation to its purpose and, in turn, generate its exterior forms as a legible expression of that spatial clarity.

landscape, both deferring to Soufflot's architecture and responding to its philosophy of history.

The entire upper floor was given over to a lofty reading room, not only because this culminated the procession through the building, but because the space here could be opened up fully [**87a, b**]. Loftiness and an extensive use of iron would create a luminous space, ideal for reading and study. New systems of ventilation, heating, and gas lighting would make the space a magnet for readers, even in the evening. Through months of designing Labrouste consciously negotiated the demands of an unprecedented programme, the possibilities of new materials, and the conviction that architectural forms, to be legible, must derive from historical evolution. He turned to iron not only for pragmatic reasons— to maximize space on a narrow site and minimize interior divisions— but also for symbolic reasons. Early sketches reveal that Labrouste might have spanned the reading room with a single truss, since the building's stone envelope would protect it from the wind forces which had felled the first fully metal train shed at Paris's Gare St-Lazare in 1840! But Labrouste rejected a unitary span; he explored the richer spatial articulation offered by a double-barrelled solution, not coincidentally a spatial configuration which Romantic architectural history was tracing as an evolutionary line of great secular spaces [**87c**]. The Greek colonists of Paestum created a civic space with such a central colonnade. And in 1836 Labrouste's pupil J.-B.-A. Lassus—soon a leading missionary for the Gothic Revival—exhibited drawings of the thirteenth-century refectory of St-Martin-des-Champs, a marvel of the poised economy and airiness of medieval vaulted construction. Refectories were the secular space of monasteries, used for reading aloud during communal dining. (Vaudoyer was just then converting the St-Martin refectory into a library for Paris's science museum.) For Labrouste a modern public library, a space for the scientific research that Saint-Simonians celebrated as characteristic of the modern epoch, would take its place in this chain of communal spaces. Tensile and tall to express the ductility of iron, the cast-iron columns have volutes turned 45 degrees to receive the membrane-like iron arches and trusses, synthesizing Greek and Gothic structural systems, the joint rejoicing in the dematerialized potential of building in iron.

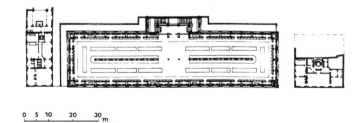

0 5 10   20   30 m.

Apart from the display of books along the outer walls, the reading room was decorated primarily by the ornamental treatment of the curved iron trusses, echoed in stencilling on the terracotta panels, luminous reflectors for the readers below, as well as on the intrados of the stone arcades lining the space, their thickness in deliberate counterpoint to the spidery fineness of the iron. Like Pugin, Labrouste taught that ornament must derive from construction, but he went further and took up the challenge of giving an aesthetic as well as a structural role to iron. Saint-Simonian theorists of art echoed Labrouste's gesture, advocating iron and glass architecture with its dematerialized luminous effects as symbolic of the new industrial era.

In initial designs, exterior and interior alike reflected Labrouste's extensive study of precedents and his respect for the increasingly codified norms of the State Council of Civic Buildings which would review his project. Sansovino's Library of Saint Mark's in Venice (1536–60), Wren's Trinity College Library, Cambridge (1676–84), and Boullée's fantastic vision of the royal library as a vault rising above walls of books [41] are among the great buildings recalled, but Labrouste takes over basic configurations rather than details. His façade, with its abstract severity and repetitive rhythm of arches carried on rudimentary flat piers above an austere planar basement, is conditioned less by historical models than by respect for its place within the accepted hierarchy of buildings, deferring to the grandeur of the Panthéon. As Labrouste's design evolved he relentlessly studied every detail, making adjustments in line with his conviction that architecture's forms must derive from both the nature of construction and the social meanings of its functional programme. Every detail was calculated to lay bare the fundamental facts of the building's construction. The thinness of the

Iron in French architecture

Iron, pioneered in bridge design as early as the 1770s, began to appear in public buildings and spaces in Paris in the 1830s and 1840s. The iron and glass greenhouses by Charles Rohault de Fleury at the Jardin des Plantes opened in 1833, and on the Place de la Concorde and along the Champs-Elysées the metal lamp standards, music kiosks, and shelters were key features of J. I. Hittorff's redesign of parks and promenades. In 1840 a massive strike of carpenters spurred the introduction of iron floor members in Parisian housing construction. Iron's spanning capacities were exploited in spectacular train sheds that accompanied the railway's phenomenal growth in London and Paris in the 1840s and on much of the continent by mid-century, notably in Léonce Reynaud's Gare du Nord, Paris, much admired for its hollow columns which doubled as a drainage system. This was built in 1842–46, just as Labrouste was refining the design for his library, the first major public building in which exposed iron played a prominent aesthetic role. In 1847 Blouet updated the great classic work on structures, Rondelet's *Theoretic and Practical Treatise on the Art of Building* (1805), to include new chapters on iron, bringing industrial materials into the academic curriculum.

masonry infill below the great windows of the reading room on the upper storey is all the more telling in contrast to the heaviness created by the progressive stepping back of large-scale masonry courses at the building's base, a recollection of the studies of archaic stonework the Romantics had undertaken in Italy. The iron framework within is announced in the metal ornaments between the arches which proclaim the simple anchoring of the metal assembly within the masonry perimeter.

The Romantics maintained that the ornaments of ancient architecture derived from ritualistic practices such as adorning buildings with trophies and garlands during celebrations. Rather than blindly applying these Classical forms—as had become convention—Labrouste sought to reinvigorate them. He expanded the repertoire by making the library's carved surfaces speak directly of interior functions. As the exterior was nearing completion, he eliminated a fairly conventional engaged portico framing his understated entrance in favour of an arch of over-scaled voussoirs flanked by low-relief carvings of oil-burning lanterns. The motifs derived from Etruscan tomb architecture, but the use was contemporary: the voussoirs dramatize the play of forces in the masonry wall, while the lanterns announce the library's novel gas lighting. When it was necessary to raise the height of the stacks, and thus the extent of blank wall between the storeys, Labrouste added festooned swags, which lend a sense of movement to the façade and a visual connection to the two buildings he built flanking the library—the library administration building and the Collège Sainte-Barbe. These refer both to the ancient practice of decorating temples with swags on important occasions and to the oak and laurel swags on Soufflot's Panthéon.

From 1830 to 1837 the sculptor P.-J. David d'Angers designed the Panthéon's new pediment. The figures he chose represented the political and intellectual forces which had shaped France since the Revolution; at the same time they reflected his republican beliefs so vividly that they were dedicated only after considerable hesitation by a regime that had become rapidly more conservative and fearful of social unrest. A decade later, as the library was nearing completion, Paris was again engulfed in upheaval, as the July Monarchy was brought to an end by the Revolution of February 1848. Under the short-lived Second Republic the painter Paul Chenavard began work on a series of didactic murals to turn the Panthéon into a Temple of Humanity, and the public flocked to witness the first large-scale demonstration of Léon Foucault's pendulum, which gave visual proof of the earth's rotation on its axis, under the dome of the Panthéon. At that moment, Labrouste struck upon a way of inscribing his library into this new acropolis of the century's belief in its own revolutionary change as a new high point in an inevitable progress. As the scaffolding was to come down in August

1848, he ordered the workmen to carve the names of authors whose works were contained in the library onto the panels under the reading-room windows. It was as though the library catalogue itself generated a new form of architectural ornament. Names were not to be arranged alphabetically but rather chronologically to illustrate the progress of humanity from monotheism to scientism, from the writings of Moses to those of the Swedish chemist Berzelius. This new litany derived directly from Auguste Comte's recently published philosophy of Positivism, which predicted not only the apotheosis of rational scientific explanation as the mode of modern intellectual endeavour but offered a rigorous organization of all preceding systems of knowledge according to a 'calendar' of great thinkers.

Labrouste was not alone. Other monumental buildings of these years took up the challenge of deriving legible forms from historical laws and the particular history of their sites. Vaudoyer's great Romano-Byzantine cathedral at Marseille (1852–93) was poised at the entrance to 'the port of the Orient' and sought to render visible in its rich mixture of stylistic references both the universal history of the Christian church type and the local stories thought to lie buried on this coastline just then being celebrated as the disembarkation point of both Greek culture and Christianity on French shores [112]. Louis Duc's remodelling of France's central courts, the Palais de Justice, would over the course of two decades recast the profile of the western half of Paris's Ile de la Cité as a panorama of the evolution of modern French architectural styles.

The *Rundbogenstil* in Germany

In 1828, the year of Labrouste's Paestum studies, a parallel debate was launched in Germany by a small pamphlet whose provocative title resounded for decades: *In what style should we build?* The Saint-Simonians postulated that the press would be 'the public square of the nineteenth century', and in Germany, still fractured into myriad states and principalities, the young Heinrich Hübsch (1795–1863) gave focus to issues which were just emerging in the designs and teaching of the leading architects of Bavaria, Prussia, and Austria as well as such smaller states as Hamburg and Hübsch's native Baden. Two decades after its publication Hübsch's manifesto was still actively debated in the burgeoning architectural press.

As early as 1811 Schinkel had proposed—in a memorandum on rebuilding Berlin's Petrikirche—a possible synthesis of the Greek and Gothic styles described as opposing principles by such Romantic writers as Augustus Wilhelm Schlegel. After Ludwig I ascended the Bavarian throne in 1825, he fuelled style debates with his ambition to make his capital 'a city such that no one can say they have visited Germany if they have not visited Munich'.[5] Along with a new

Renaissance-style wing of his palace, closely modelled on the Florentine Pitti Palace, and a copy of Rome's Arch of Constantine to close the new boulevard bearing his name, the Ludwigstrasse, the king commissioned five new churches, each to adopt a different historical style. In 1826 Georg Friedrich Ziebland was given a travel stipend to Ravenna and Rome to study Early Christian basilicas as models for a church dedicated St Bonifacius, the evangelizer of Germany. Ziebland's building and Joseph Daniel Ohlmüller's Neo-Gothic St Marie (Mariahilfkirche in der Au) would be easily recognizable additions to what French critic Fortoul lambasted as an urban museum.[6] By contrast Friedrich von Gärtner grafted Byzantine, German Romanesque, and even early Florentine elements into his evolving design for St Ludwig, a complexly composed and theoretically reasoned example of stylistic synthesis which quickly made Gärtner's office one of the cradles of progressive historicism in Germany. Leo von Klenze, at work for a decade developing a universal Grecian Classicism—'a firm principle for all time' [71, 72]—admitted that a new relationship with models was inevitable.[7] 'We no longer live in a period of an unconscious natural artistic creation such as gave birth to earlier architectural dictates, but rather in an era of thought, of research, and of self-conscious reflection.'[8] His response, both in Bavaria and in Russia, where he was called to extend the Hermitage Museum in 1837, was that Classicism was flexible enough to absorb both later discoveries and modern requirements.

Before turning to architecture, Hübsch studied mathematics and philosophy at Heidelberg and frequented the Boisserée brothers just then rediscovering the medieval art and architecture of the Rhineland. In 1815 he enrolled in the Karlsruhe *Bauakademie* where Weinbrenner taught his pupils to view Classical architecture as a continuous negotiation between transcendental ideals of the beautiful, reflecting Kant's aesthetics, and materials and structural forces, a view influenced by the utilitarian teachings of Durand and Rondelet in Paris. By the time Hübsch returned from three years of touring Italy, Greece, and Constantinople in 1820, he had determined to submit the very underpinnings of Neoclassical theory to scrutiny. Taking as his target the archaeological manual of the Berlin academy, Alois Hirt's *Architecture According to the Principles of the Ancients* (1809), Hübsch attacked the very issue of imitation, soon to be central to French debates as well. He rejected the theory that the forms of Greek temples derived from wooden models, a notion first advanced by the ancient Roman architectural writer Vitruvius, given new currency by Laugier [1], and the subject of countless recent archaeological studies, notably by Klenze and Weinbrenner. Hübsch mustered considerable evidence from onsite observations to argue that the Greeks created an architecture the forms of which gave vivid expression to the demands of monumental stone construction; but more than archaeology was at stake. Whether or not architectural models were primarily ideas that transcended materials and structural laws as well as cultures and epochs was both a historical question and an issue of burning actuality.

If we admire what the Greeks achieved and uphold them as exemplary rational builders, Hübsch maintained, it is illogical to imitate their buildings far from the sunny shores of the Aegean and after centuries of technical and social progress. Style for Hübsch signified an organically developed and complete structural system. Of these there were as yet but two: the trabeated or post-and-lintel system perfected by the Greeks, with its monumental repose; and the arcuated or arched and vaulted architecture first explored by the Romans but only fully developed in diverse, locally appropriate ways by the Byzantines in the east and medieval masters in the west. The genealogical relations of these styles were hotly debated in antiquarian circles in both France and Germany in these years. History for Hübsch was a critical and philosophical enterprise, not a neutral taxonomy of styles. He took the Romans to task for the discrepancy between the technical achievements of their buildings—accomplished with new systems of vaulting—and the borrowing of Greek architectural motifs as applied decoration. Pilasters, engaged columns, and entablatures for him were not the embodiment of a transcendent beauty and expressive of ideal proportions, but the 'first great conventional lie in architecture'.[9] Laugier had said as much, but Hübsch's argument was of a different nature, the forerunner of the historicist arguments to be employed a few years later by the French Romantics, by Viollet-le-Duc and many others at mid-century who called specific phases of historical development into the court of historical justice not to judge them by an absolute standard but against the laws of progress discerned by the new philosophies of history. For Hübsch the Romans had failed to find a language of forms derived from the technical possibilities of arches and vaults. This task was left to the post-Classical world and made all the more challenging in medieval Germany where architects worked with the small quarried stones available in Germany rather than monolithic marble. These materialist attacks were also launched against the Neoclassical establishment by fighters for the Gothic Revivalists rallying around the project to complete Cologne Cathedral [**69a, b**], but Hübsch argued for a third, mediating position. Rather than replacing one perfected model with another, he proposed that the earlier Middle Ages had untapped potential for flexible adaptation to such modern needs as large spaces, broad roof spans, and generously sized openings.

This notion of a vibrant historical moment cut short, capable of further development, derived from the Pre-Raphaelite position of Hübsch's Nazarene painter friends, but it was not the notion of a limited brotherhood. It was shared by diverse theories of progressive revivalism articulated between the 1830s and the 1850s which linked architectural judgement to the dynamic models emerging in historical studies and in the natural sciences. By 1840 Fortoul and Vaudoyer in France had developed a similar argument around the early Renaissance, while Gothic Revivalists placed the fall from historical grace in the Renaissance. Battles over style were promoted from the realm of taste to the arena of historical explanation and nationalist politics.

Hübsch's architecture in Baden

Hübsch's numerous buildings in Karlsruhe, where he served for more than three decades as state architect, gave concrete form to the *Rundbogenstil* credo that architecture must remain a process of technical and historical experimentation. The new buildings for Baden's Polytechnic, the result of an administrative reform absorbing architectural education into a modern scientific and engineering faculty, were designed in 1831. The sandstone-fronted building, with its exposition of a range of colourful building materials and textures, stood in deliberate counterpoint to the monochromatic, stuccoed Classicism that dominated the streets of Weinbrenner's Karlsruhe [**65**]. The flexible and flowing spaces of the floor plan were responses to the challenges of public architecture in a period of palpable change.

Unlike his many contemporaries and followers who studied the Rhenish Romanesque to create an architecture expressive of a distinctive local heritage, Hübsch, like his contemporary J. C. Lassaulx in Koblenz, continually integrated new forms into the matrix of style inherited from the past. The segmental arch became a veritable signature of Hübsch's architecture—most famously in the new pump room for the spa at Baden-Baden [**88**]—favoured not only for its broad span but because Hübsch considered that it derived logically from the history of forms, an ideal synthesis of the Greek lintel and the medieval

88 Heinrich Hübsch

Pump Room, Baden-Baden 1837–40

The segmental arch was a trademark of Hübsch's quest for an architecture which developed new forms from the trajectory of technical progress. This form was also favoured by such French Romantics as Vaudoyer, Duc, and Labrouste, who used segmental vaults in the lower level of his library, and César Daly, who developed a theory of formal development based on the elliptical line.

89 Hübsch

St Cyriakus, Bulach, near Karlsruhe, 1828–37. View of exterior and interior as published in the architect's own *Bauwerke*

Hübsch departed from the stucco rendering of his master Weinbrenner's buildings [65] in forging a vocabulary in which each material was given its own expression. In many of his buildings a frame of stone, infill of brick, and vaults of terracotta also provide a rich colour palette.

pointed arch. In church design, beginning with St Cyriakus, Bulach [**89**], he explored a range of new vault types, explored the use of a mixed terracotta infill and masonry diaphragm construction, and even contemplated developing new vaulting types from models of catenary

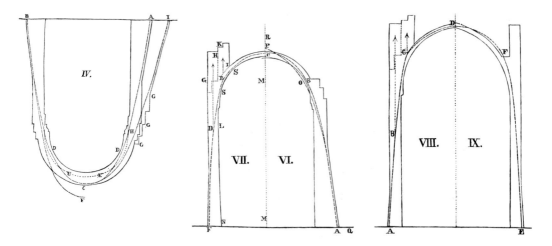

90 Hübsch

Experiments with vaulting
forms derived from the use of
hanging models, c.1838

In his quest for a vault which
could provide a new spatial
framework Hübsch used
weighted chains to derive the
most structurally efficient
profile. His advocacy of the
catenary arch derived from
scientific experiment rather
than artistic imitation, but
would not be seriously
pursued until the end of the
century in the independent
experiments of the Catalan
architect Antonio Gaudí.

arches, expressing his conviction that the most recent developments
in mathematics could be incorporated into the further development of
architecture on its historic trajectory [**90**].

Karl Friedrich Schinkel's natural history of architecture

'Every great period of civilization has left behind its own style of architecture, why shouldn't we attempt to find a style of our own time?',
Schinkel mused in notes for an architectural textbook which record a
lifelong quest to discover universal laws of form. Schinkel rose to the
pinnacle of the Prussian architectural bureaucracy in the excited years
of the Reform movement, when a constellation of intellectuals undertook a fundamental examination of the country's political, economic,
and cultural institutions. His sense of the architect's mission as 'the en-
nobler of all human relations' took shape in a heroic series of public

Karl Friedrich Schinkel (1781–1841)

The pre-eminent German architect of the nineteenth century, Schinkel came of age in
the period of the Napoleonic Wars and defined his role in architecture as a public
mission to form not only a national architectural vocabulary but also the engaged
citizens of a reformed monarchy. In Berlin and Potsdam Schinkel defined the modes
and landscapes of both public and private architecture more definitively than any other
architect of the century. His Berlin public buildings include: the Royal Guard House,
Unter den Linden (1816), the New Theatre (Schauspielhaus) (1819), the Museum
(1824), and the Architecture School (1835).

In a series of churches he defined an austere rational approach to medieval brick
construction widely emulated in northern Germany, notably in the Friedrich
Werdesche Church (1824), and the estates he created with the landscape designer Peter
Joseph Lenné established a series of Classical and Italian rustic vernacular models,
influenced by English plate books, which continued to serve Berlin house architects
for much of the rest of the century. Of these the most famous are the Charlottenhof at
Sanssouci (1824) and its picturesque Court Gardener's House (1829), which served as
the point of departure for Schinkel's pupils, notably Ludwig Persius.

buildings which transformed Berlin in the decade following Napoleon's defeat at Leipzig. Beginning with the guardhouse on Unter den Linden (1816–18), a monument to the sweeping reorganization of Prussia's military from mercenary service to citizens' army, and culminating in the great colonnaded front of the art museum, opened in 1830, Schinkel honed the vocabulary of a modernized Classicism that might partake of education minister Wilhelm von Humboldt's conviction that Greek models could stimulate individual development and national renewal.

The Schauspielhaus (1818–21), which Schinkel designed to replace the burned national theatre on Berlin's Gendarmenmarkt, was emblematic of this vision [91]. A grand Ionic portico survived the fire, but Schinkel gave it a new role, elevating it atop a steep flight of stairs that made attending the theatre into a veritable journey to Mount Olympus (Apollo and his chariot preside over the central pediment), one which also took in sweeping views of the city, recalling Schinkel's involvement with painted panoramas. The portico was set before harmoniously interlocking masses, the simplicity of which belies the complexity of interior functions—stage, auditorium, small concert hall, rehearsal rooms, offices—all contained behind a grid of pilasters and entablatures. Here was an abstracted system of trabeation that confirmed Schinkel's belief that the essential lessons of antiquity lie in harmonic and constructive relationships rather than in precise copying of mouldings and ornaments. He would exploit this system in the most diverse buildings, including the remodelling of a sixteenth-century farmhouse as a reverie on the antique villa for the Humboldt family at Tegel (1820–24); a villa for the crown prince at Charlottenhof (1825) in the domain of Sanssouci, and the new Berlin Museum (1823–30). In all these designs banal Prussian brick construction, clad in stone, was elevated to the level of architectonic expression, just as individual Prussian citizens were elevated to the level of full participants in novel cultural activities.

It was precisely this dual interest in the visual expression of architecture's own language and the fulfilment of a social mission—Schinkel referred to the architect's duty to the 'progressive development of the human race'—that is easily discerned in the debate between Schinkel and Hirt over museum design. Eager to meet royally imposed budget restrictions, Hirt attacked prominent features of Schinkel's project for a new building facing the palace; the colonnaded stoa front, central rotunda reminiscent of the Roman Pantheon, and exterior stairhall were but extravagances. Schinkel's response was as firm as it was pointed. The design was an organically conceived whole from which no single element could be removed without rendering the overall form unintelligible. The impressive spaces through which the public would be conducted on a journey through the history of architectural form, from Greek trabeation to the great domes which lay at the origins of all

vaulted forms, were essential to the 'higher purpose' of a museum in society rather than simply the 'trivial purpose' of the brief.

The very language of this exchange—with its references to organic wholeness and communication—points to the route Schinkel himself travelled as he took inspiration from the most varied disciplines which shared his quest to link clear taxonomies of form with laws of historical change. As he designed their country retreat at Tegel—which would include a gallery of Classical sculpture—Schinkel came into frequent contact with the researches of the Humboldt brothers. Both Wilhelm von Humboldt in work on comparative linguistics and Alexander von Humboldt in natural history studies aimed to unveil fundamental structures underlying the great diversity of forms assumed by both divine and human creations. Architecture, arguably, lay at the point of intersection between the laws of nature and the patterns of human expression, governed at once by irrefutable laws of statics and materials yet capable of embodying mankind's highest aspirations. In 1828, as Schinkel's museum was nearing completion, educated Berliners flocked to Hegel's lectures on aesthetics and to Alexander von Humboldt's stirring account of the earth's surface and its plant life, lectures later published as *Cosmos: A Sketch of the Physical Description of the Universe* (1844), one of the most widely read books of the century. Schinkel, in those years, was developing economical church designs for Berlin's rapidly growing suburbs. He proposed a related series of five variant plan types, each of which was developed in elevation to reveal the possibilities inherent in one of the diverse structural languages from rectilinear Greek trabeation to soaring skeletal vaulting. During these years he also reconceived his projected textbook as a comparative morphology of building [**92**], and sought to instil these principles even in the most diverse building types in the corrections he imposed on designs submitted for his review from Prussia's expansive territories, spreading from Aachen in the west to Königsberg (Kaliningrad) in the east. All this research came together in the crowning building of Schinkel's short but tremendously influential career, the Berlin Bauakademie [**93**]. The great four-square brick and terracotta building, built between 1832 and 1835 to house the School of Architecture and the state architectural administration, puzzled even its earliest admirers. Was it a variant on an Italian Renaissance palazzo or did the exposed brick piers tie it to the north German Gothic tradition, which Conrad Hase in Hanover and Alexis de Chateauneuf in Hamburg were promoting as the starting-point for a modern German architecture? The English architect and historian James Fergusson singled it out in his *History of the Modern Styles of Architecture* as a way out of the quagmire of Revivalism: 'The ornamentation depends wholly on the construction … nothing can be more truthful or appropriate … it marks an epoch in the art, when a man in Schinkel's position dared to erect anything so original and set free from Classical or Gothic feeling as this design'.[10] The site architect Emil Flaminius (who took the building as a point of departure for his own later work in Zurich) explained that the entire repertoire of forms, including the use of segmental arches and vaults, emanates from the nature of brick construction; everything can be related to this single generative principle.

The Bauakademie was the first true masonry-frame building in Prussia, where half-timber had long been a vernacular tradition; it was

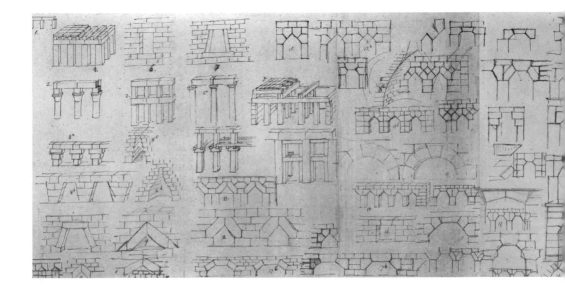

also the first literally built as frame and infill. In the first year the piers were built on individual foundations. Once the entire frame was up and the vaults constructed, the masons began to fill in the walls and hoist the terracotta window frames into place. An important catalyst was Schinkel's study of textile mills during an 1826 tour to Britain with Peter Beuth, head of the Prussian Ministry of Trade and Commerce. They were both searching for inspiration to accelerate Prussia's modernization and make its manufactured goods—including terracotta building elements—competitive. But they returned determined to avoid some of the aesthetic and social ills they had observed in the English Midlands, where Schinkel was alarmed by the living conditions of factory workers. In Britain Schinkel saw one possible future for Prussia and he was determined that it was not inevitable. By offering models of form, in both architecture and product design, Prussia could be the handmaiden for a new synthesis of the laws of harmony inherited from the great periods of civilization with the new facts of an industrial economy. New buildings for the customs administration and the Bauakademie were to bring exposed brick to the banks of the Spree, but Schinkel was eager to demonstrate to Berlin's citizens that even unprecedented forms could be cultivated as products of both economy and art.

The Bauakademie derives its vocabulary from the history of its own construction. Colourful patterns etched on its surfaces by deep purplish-blue and saturated red bricks emphasize its novel structural system as well as underlying harmonic proportions, echoed by terracotta representations of Amphion, the mythological figure whose lyre inspired harmonic construction of ancient city walls. Other histories are detailed didactically in panels set below the windows and round the

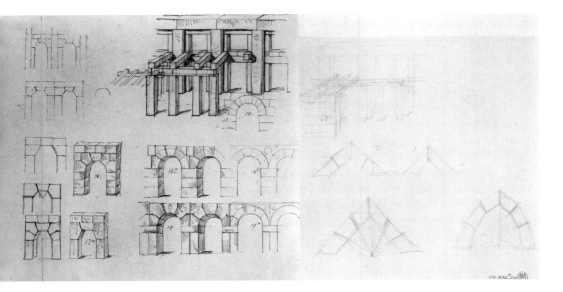

door, histories which, as in Duban's École des Beaux-Arts, were directed to future generations of architects. The window sills form a frieze which, in Schinkel's words, 'represent various moments in the history of the development of the art of building',[11] tracing the cycles of the rise and fall of the genius of architecture. In the terracotta door frames two narratives are intertwined: a human and a natural history. While the framing panels depict the traditional stories of the discovery of the forms and orders of architecture, including the famous story of Callimachus literally calling forth the Corinthian from the forms of nature, the reveals of the doors point to research into the ordering systems of the natural world. The plant forms do not repeat as in conventional ornament, but rather sprout, grow, and flower. Represented is nothing less than Goethe's famous theory of the primordial plant as the kernel for understanding the diversity of form in botanical species. As Goethe explained, 'Eternally nature creates new forms. What now is, never was in time past; what has been cometh not again—all is new, and yet always it is old.'[12]

During construction Schinkel corresponded with the Bavarian crown, troubled in particular with the vexing question of what sort of style should be adopted for the new public buildings of Athens, where the throne of a newly independent Greece had been assumed by Otto, King Ludwig's second son. Maximilian, the Bavarian crown prince, posed the same question to Klenze and Schinkel: 'Whether or not there is an ideal in architecture, whether or not there is one for Greece, and if so which one it would be?' Schinkel's reply went to the heart of the problem of universal and relative standards, evoked just a few years earlier by Hübsch, replying that 'the ideal in architecture is only fully attained when a building completely expresses its purpose in both spiritual and physical respects in both overall form and its every part ... We might draw nearer to it if we could remain true to ancient Greek architecture in its intellectual principle all the while expanding it to accommodate the conditions of our own new epoch and undertake the harmonic admixture of the best of all in between periods.'[13] His sketchbooks of the 1830s are filled with ideas for new hybrid constructions, including iron trusses carried on classical columns, façades of a skeletal openness that exploited segmental arches for great breadth, and a revival of late medieval fan vaulting to generate newly spacious interiors. He penned a new preface for his textbook, still incomplete when he took to his bed with an illness that would cut short his career in 1841: 'History has never copied earlier history and if it ever had done so the art produced would not matter in history; in a certain sense history would come to a halt in that art. The only art that qualifies as historical is that which in some way introduces something additional—a new element—in the world, from which a new story can be generated and the thread taken up anew.'[14]

Something of that spirit pervaded an event which raised eyebrows even in its own time, the public competition for a new style of architecture opened by Maximilian shortly after he assumed the Bavarian throne in the wake of his father's abdication during the 1848 revolutions. The laureate 'Maximilianstil'—the name is testimony to the tense mixture between a signature for the new reign and the period's philosophy of history—was a Gothic-inflected variant on the *Rundbogenstil*, a stylistic matrix that integrated a family of styles at the same time as it developed a brick vocabulary celebrated for its flexibility to accommodate the range of new buildings required by the rapidly expanding Bavarian capital. In 1842, a year after Schinkel's death, the Prussian crown passed to Friedrich Wilhelm IV, whose fascination with archaeology, particularly his zealous exploration of Early Christian architecture in a paradoxical search for an appropriate expression for Protestantism, tied official architecture much more literally to historical research than to that line of organic research opened up by Schinkel.

High Victorian Gothic in England and the theory of 'development'

The battle lines defined by Pugin's *Contrasts* continued to shape debates over building designs in Britain for decades, but by the late 1840s both the Gothic and Classical parties were engaged in soul-searching over the relation of modern creation to antiquarianism. Even as Pugin set forth a vision of a perfected Gothic to be adapted for the burgeoning parishes of Britain's industrial cities, a position was elaborated in brick and mortar which challenged the very notion of literal historical models. Towering over one of the main approaches to London from the rapidly growing southern suburbs, James Wild's Christ Church Streatham [**94**] was difficult to classify stylistically even for the most avid and erudite reader of the new books bringing images of the Byzantine and Islamic worlds to western drawing boards. 'We must study from all sources and adapt our knowledge with invention, as our forefathers did, or we can but produce caricatures of their works',[15] Wild offered as elucidation of the range of transitional styles 'only half developed' he put forth as sources of design method rather than templates for imitation. Wild was appraised of the archaeological and historical researches in Andalusia of Owen Jones, who celebrated the Moorish Alhambra as an architecture born of cultural cross-currents and took it as the starting-point for a growing conviction that the geometric inventiveness of ornament in the Islamic tradition could guide modern architects out of the impasse of revivalism. Wild's curiosity soon took him to the Near East to witness at first hand how styles developed, adapted, and changed. For the expatriate community in Egypt he designed St Mark's, Alexandria, by grafting Islamic elements onto an Early Christian basilican framework, seeking at once to create a modern building that bore the traces of cultures that had intermingled in

94 James Wild

Christ Church, Streatham, 1839–41

On an Early Christian basilican plan Wild grafted stylistic echoes of diverse later moments in the evolution of both Christian and Islamic architecture, including the Italian Romanesque profile and free-standing campanile, as well as various Ottoman and Islamic decorative details. This synthetic eclecticism was related to Thomas Hope's recent historical research and anticipated the stylistic experiments a few years later of Léon Vaudoyer at Marseille [**112**].

this Mediterranean crossroads and to foster a fusion of styles which could negotiate the delicate diplomacy of English Protestants in the Islamic world.

Britain's commercial and colonial empire invaded consciousness more and more; as it did it began to challenge the underlying logic of archaeological revivalism. At the outset the Ecclesiological Society—High Church advocates for Gothic Revivalism whose approval was eagerly sought by a whole generation of Anglican architects—was ardently doctrinaire. 'We would suggest ... that instead of new designs, or "original conceptions," ... *real ancient designs* ... of acknowledged beauty of detail should be selected for exact imitation,' they inveighed in 1842. But the challenge of supplying a universally valid prototype to a far-flung empire soon softened such rigidity. In 1841 the Society proposed that for New Zealand, where European settlement had only recently begun, Romanesque would be the appropriate model. Its simpler forms were suited to native skills and the imagined ruggedness of life in the South Pacific. As colonial society matured, they offered, it could advance towards the perfected forms of Gothic. But this notion of recapitulation soon yielded to a more complex theory of historical progress and more inventive responses to local conditions. In 1861 Scott designed an innovative hybrid for Christchurch Cathedral, New Zealand, combining a stone exterior with an independent wooden interior, at once expression of the primitive ruggedness of what he imagined to be the Maori wood tradition and an experimental response for this earthquake-prone colony.

Study of the Gothic's diversity on the European continent reflected the more international outlook in the pages of *The Ecclesiologist* in the 1850s paralleling experimental new designs testing the adaptability of Gothic to tropical climates and even to industrial prefabrication, making it possible to ship out entire buildings along with colonists, goods, and bibles. R. C. Carpenter (1812–55), the Ecclesiologists' house architect, designed a brick cathedral surrounded by open verandahs for Colombo (Sri Lanka) in 1846, and worked in tandem with William Butterfield (1814–1900) to devise wooden Gothic church designs for Canada, Australia, India, and South Africa.

The population surge in London and the industrial Midlands presented equally unprecedented conditions and new audiences for architecture at home. Urban minsters, as the Ecclesiologists called the new large-scale parish churches required for working-class districts, were intended as beacons in the city. They made a bid through universally understood values of scale, strong form, and ornamentation rather than through erudite historical references to compete with the appeal of prospering 'dissenting' religious sects. The overarching concept put forth to equip architects to confront these new challenges without abandoning their faith in Gothic was 'development', or the slow and accretive adap-

tation of historical models, evolutionary rather than revolutionary. Inspiration came from natural history, in particular Charles Lyell's widely read *Principles of Geology* (1830–33), rich in parallels with theories of architectural monuments as bearing the traces of the progressive development of the races and civilizations that peopled the earth. But the direct source for the term and much of the architectural theory elaborated around it was John Henry Newman's 'development theology', avidly debated in High Church circles in Oxford in the mid-1840s and

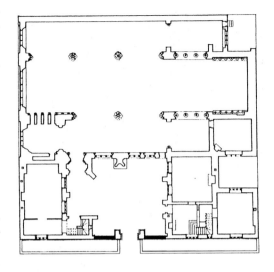

adapted to historical studies by Edward A. Freeman. Freeman's views paralleled the vision of contemporary French and German writers that architecture was a veritable mirror of its age, but most importantly he described a history of formal change as one of continuous—almost geo-logical—evolution. 'The years … are like a stream winding gradually away from its source, changing, developing, or corrupting, but all gently and gradually without any sudden perceptible break or jar,'[16] he wrote in a brochure on church restoration, arguing at once for the careful preser-vation of the diversity of stylistic traces in ancient buildings and provid-ing the springboard for the theory of development elaborated in Scott's writings and designs and those of his former assistants G. E. Street, William White, and G. F. Bodley. 'Let us retain every beauty which Christian art has produced, from its birth to its decay, hoping that each will take its place in future and more comprehensive developments,'[17] Scott wrote in 1850. High Victorian Gothic style was characterized by a rich palette of colouristic and material effects, a highly sculptural ap-proach to composition, as well as a taste for the expressive and massive forms of an early phase of Gothic which gave 'developed' buildings a ro-bust quality contemporaries often described as 'vigorous' or even 'mus-cular'. During a period of intense experimentation in the 1850s and 1860s, Gothic Revivalists set out to develop a flexible vocabulary for the range of building types required in England's burgeoning cities.

In a position paper entitled 'The True Principles of Architecture, and the Possibility of Development' (1852), which was published in *The Ecclesiologist* just months after Pugin's death, Street attacked antiquari-anism and called for a style that could continue to grow and change. He singled out one building for praise, William Butterfield's All Saints, Margaret Street [**95a**], then under construction under the sponsorship of the Ecclesiological Society's new president, A. S. Beresford Hope, son of the man who had led the defence decades earlier of Wilkins's Grecian design at Cambridge (see chapter 5). With its startling juxtapositions of bold forms, streamlined profiles derived from an integral facing in brick, and replacement of complex carved mouldings with a rich range of patterns and colours in stripes and diapering of different colours and materials, Butterfield's building offered a startling and original interpretation of Gothic. Yet many elements can be traced to specific continental examples of medieval brick design, notably the tower based on the thirteenth-century church of St Mary at Lübeck, and a close look at its plan [95b] reveals scrupulous adherence to the rules of liturgical layout laid down by ecclesiology. For Street the building was more a manifesto of development than a model church in any conventional sense; it 'must be looked at as the first only of a long series in which more and more improvement may be looked for', he concluded, taking much from it for his own St James the Less, Westminster, begun in 1859. There Street replaced Butterfield's jagged picturesqueness with a new sense of sculptural repose he felt more appropriate to the urban landscape. James Brooks simplified both the forms and the colouristic effects of the model in the great 'slum minsters' he built in London's East End in the 1860s, responding more perhaps to the revival of the British tradition of the sublime than the specific historical models suggested to church designers in such influential texts as Street's *Brick and Marble in the Middle Ages* (1855) or John Ruskin's *Stones of Venice* (1851–53). By then the doctrine of 'development' seemed to many to respond to Ruskin's enjoinder that 'the architecture of a nation is great only when it is as universal and as established as its language'.[18]

The battle of the styles in mid-century British public buildings

By the late 1850s the greatest challenge facing advocates of the Gothic was to conquer the burgeoning field of public and commercial buildings required by the daunting expansion of industry, trade, and government bureaucracy. Ruskin had sounded the battle-cry in his *Seven Lamps of Architecture* in 1849, praising the Lombard and Venetian Gothic for their adaptability to the full range of medieval society's needs, religious and civic. In *Remarks on Secular and Domestic Architecture, Present and Future* (1857), Scott made an impassioned appeal for modern or 'developed' Gothic as 'free, comprehensive and practical, ready to adapt itself to every change in the habits of society, to embrace every material or system of construction, and to adopt implicitly and naturally, and with hearty good will, every invention and improvement'.[19] Progress in winning over the clergy was great, and commissions began to come in for Gothic Revival city and country houses. But public architecture remained hotly contested.

The tug-of-war in 1857–58 between the anti-Gothic Prime Minister Lord Palmerston and Scott over designs for new government offices—

one of the most protracted and farcically conducted design competitions of the Victorian period—belatedly gave the name 'battle of the styles' to debates already decades old. In 1861 *The Building News* recommended that architects cease quibbling over the relative merits of different phases of Gothic and 'render the Gothic of the present as great, by rendering it as definite, as the Gothic of any one of the great eras of the past'.[20] In the dispute over buildings for the Foreign and War Offices, the theory of 'development' was stretched almost to breaking point. To keep the commission, awarded through High Tory support, Scott was forced to accommodate Palmerston's demand for a Classical design. Scott first responded with a Byzantine essay, thinking to return to the historical moment when the dichotomy between Gothic and Classical had yet to gel. But Palmerston, not prepared to tolerate even a hint of High Church medievalism, dismissed it as a 'regular mongrel-affair' and Scott was forced, in collaboration with Matthew Digby Wyatt, to redesign in the language of Palladio and Vignola. Together they produced, at least in the façades facing St James's Park, a remarkably confident Classical exercise whose picturesque massing is worthy of Nash, for whom issues of style had always been subordinate to visual effect. Despite this momentary setback, the exhibition of competition schemes and the publicity given the Gothic designs—a small minority—in the architectural press yielded a tremendous progeny. For the next 15 years the Gothic town hall, based often on Flemish models, successfully unseated the Classical temple as the preferred model for town halls as Britain's cities asserted a new autonomy in the wake of the Municipal Corporations Act (1835). Scott's unbuilt competition designs of the 1850s for town halls in Hamburg, Halifax, and Bradford were widely imitated, but some of the most original designs came from younger architects: Alfred Waterhouse, only 29, won the competition in 1859 for Manchester's Assize Courts and went on to build the Town Hall there in 1868; E. W. Godwin launched his career with town halls at Northampton (1860) and Congleton, Cheshire (1865). The most magisterial of all was Fuller and Jones's Canadian Parliament (1859), which emerges from the cliffs over the Ottawa River with all of the ruggedness and power which Ruskin argued were the foundations of Gothic in nature.

It was only in 1866 when Scott won the limited competition organized by the Midland Railway for a new London terminus, St Pancras (1868–74), that the period's most prolific Goth was able to demonstrate that a picturesque urban profile of Gothic details was fully compatible with modern requirements. Scott used the asymmetrical massing of his building to orchestrate the efficient arrival and departure of both the horse-drawn carriages and the steam-driven engines that met momentarily under the engineer Barlow's iron shed, at 240

96 G. G. Scott

A view of the grand staircase,
Midland Grand Hotel, St
Pancras Station

A true disciple of Pugin, Scott
took over the polychromatic
richness Pugin had pioneered
in church design [see **78**] to
the realm of public
architecture. At the same time
he unabashedly introduced
exposed structural iron,
submitting it to the same
scheme of rational two-
dimensional ornamental
treatment. This grand
staircase is as modern and
daring as the iron train shed
behind the hotel.

feet (73 m) briefly the greatest arched span in the world, efficiently
jointed to form a slightly pointed profile. But iron was not limited to
the shed, for Scott used iron beams to cantilever the great ceremonial
staircase of the hotel, brightly painted and ornamented with the latest
motifs of reformed Gothic ornament [**96**]. Despite the romance of its
dormers, pinnacles, and carved bosses, the hotel was a veritable machine, with ventilation, heating, and dust-removal systems surpassing
any. In 1866 Scott and Street competed to prove, in designs for the
limited contest for the new Law Courts in the Strand (built to Street's
designs, 1874–82), that picturesque urban composition and Gothic variety were fully compatible with the rational organization of the com-

plex spatial programme of overlapping but mutually exclusive circulation for convicts, lawyers, and the public. Political wrangling led to the competition's requirement of Gothic, but ironically this grand achievement of Gothic Revival public architecture was essentially to be the last. Street's brilliant demonstration that institutional planning and stylistic image were not indelibly related gave way to an ever greater progressive eclecticism in the flurry of public buildings which transformed the centre of London in the century's closing decades.

Classical eclecticism

Scott came to blows over the issue of style again in a shrill exchange with the classicist Alexander Thomson (1817–75) over the new building of Glasgow University, completed to Scott's designs in 1871. Despite his nickname, 'Greek' Thomson was no archaeologist. He left behind in three United Presbyterian churches for his native city some of the most startling original Classical buildings of the century. His use of a Greek temple set atop a high pedestal—a notoriously difficult mould for a Christian church—allowed him to create arresting urban images, to develop brilliantly top-lit interiors rarely seen since Soane [see **57**], and even to provide a matrix for development in which Greek tectonic expression was flexible enough to accommodate inspiration from Egyptian and even Indian architecture in a highly personal mix controlled more by the eye than an underlying text [**97**]. Similar challenging

97 Alexander Thomson

St Vincent Street Church, Glasgow

In Glasgow 'Greek' Thomson formed a highly personal idiom which, as much as it merited his sobriquet, was controlled as much by the legacy of the sublime and the picturesque in its combination of long passages of repetition with exuberantly detailed asymmetrical accents.

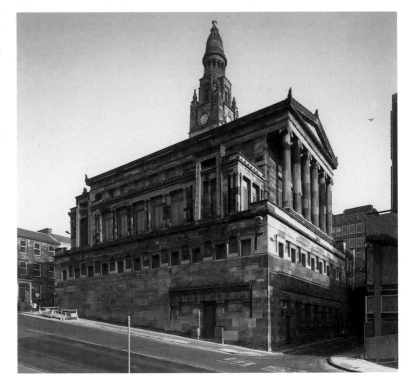

expansions of the Classical vocabulary were developed notably by the Dane M. G. B. Bindesbøll (1800–56) in his vividly polychromatic Thorvaldsen Museum (1839–48) in Copenhagen [98], the end product of a design process which took the architect through nearly the entire history of architecture, and by Joseph Poelaert in his Palace of Justice in Brussels (1862–83).

The mutual admiration between the young Irish architects Thomas Deane and Benjamin Woodward and the critic Ruskin, whose stylistic latitudinarianism in advocating medieval models contrasted markedly with the sectarian Ecclesiologists, produced one of the most stunningly original historicist designs of the 1850s, Trinity College Museum in Dublin. While critics debated the stylistic category of the great palazzo exterior with its richly clad, domed courtyard/staircase [99], Deane and Woodward basked in the recognition of the critic whose writings had provided them with a philosophy of design as well as historical models for details and effects. As they were honing designs for a four-square palazzo-type building centred on a courtyard, the first volume of *The Stones of Venice* was published. Ruskin counselled readers to reflect, as he had, on a wide range of Italian medieval styles as examples of an architecture based in its place and culture, but also as evidence of the great variety of form possible from respecting fundamental architectural principles. Four possible stylistic matrices, ranging from the Pisan Romanesque and the Venetian Gothic to the

English Early Decorated, were described, obliging those who might follow Ruskin's sermon to formulate a method rather than simply a repertoire of forms. In each, Ruskin praised a combination of a largeness of scale, overall clarity of form, and infinite variety of surface detail revealing the hands of those who had made the building. Ruskin was delighted to learn that at Trinity College Deane and Woodward had left the specific ornamentation of window frames and column capitals to the talents of the O'Shea brothers, master carvers from Cork who represented for Ruskin rare historical survivals of a vanishing crafts culture that industrialization had all but eradicated in England. 'I believe the right question to ask, respecting all ornaments,' Ruskin wrote in the 'Lamp of Life' in the *Seven Lamps of Architecture*, 'is simply this: Was it done with enjoyment—was the carver happy while he was about it?' With Deane and Woodward he had found modern architects who substantiated his belief that architecture could take a critical, avant-garde position towards the challenges modernization posed both to art and society without negating the lessons of history.

New Technology and Architectural Form, 1851–90

7

The iron 'problem'

By 1850 iron was interwoven in the fabric of daily life at every scale, from mass-produced decorative embellishments of apartment houses and commercial buildings to train sheds that welcomed the 'iron horse' to the gates of the city [**100**]. Yet Queen Victoria's opening on 1 May 1851 of the glass and iron hall hosting the 'Great Exhibition of the Works of Industry of All Nations'—the first of some 40 'Universal Exhibitions' in the second half of the century by which the competitors in global industrialization sought to contain an expanding world of both knowledge and trade under a single roof—also inaugurated debates over the 'new' material and over relations of art to industry. Technologically Joseph Paxton's (1803–65) 'Crystal Palace' [**101**]—as the satirical *Punch* dubbed it—offered little more than refinements of technology developed in greenhouses, including those designed in the preceding decade by Decimus Burton at Kew and Paxton himself at Chatsworth, and in the youngest generation of railway sheds, notably London's King's Cross Station (Lewis Cubitt, 1851–52), Paris's Gare de l'Est (Duquesny, 1847–52) [see **121**], and Munich's Hauptbahnhof (Bürklein, 1849). Iron had not been confined to gardens or the working edge of cities. Already in 1829 Percier and Fontaine, style-makers in Parisian architecture for over two decades, introduced iron skylights into the Palais Royal with their Galerie d'Orléans, a late addition to those shopping arcades by which light, pedestrian shoppers, and commercial capital penetrated the dense heart of cities.

The Crystal Palace

But the Crystal Palace demanded attention in a new way. Its scale was daunting. At a symbolic 1,851 feet (564 m) long it enclosed an unprecedented 18 acres—and even mature trees—in an enclosure free of internal walls. The breathtaking speed of its assembly—in a mere 9 months 6,024 cast-iron columns and 1,245 wrought-iron girders were manufactured, delivered, and assembled—was spectacular even for Victorians

Detail of 116b

207

100

Aerial view of King's Cross and St Pancras stations, London

Unprecedented as building types, train stations challenged architects aiming to design buildings that could communicate function and fulfil monumental expectations even for utilitarian programmes. Conceived as new city gates, stations were given every conceivable form from Cubitt's frank expression of the shed itself as a monumental triumphal arch to Scott's use of north German Gothic, borrowed from medieval town halls, for the hotel which fronts St Pancras Station **[82]**.

regularly appraised of the country's new engineering feats in the pages of the illustrated press. Yet it was less the record-breaking statistics than the pretensions of this unadorned building to the status of a representational monument which made it the object of vociferous debate. Set amidst greenery in Hyde Park, within view of royal residences and London's smartest districts, the prefabricated building, the largest to date, was a monument on display. Even while the architectural profession on both sides of the Channel debated how the laws of history or of nature might serve as guides to the vexing dilemma of how the nineteenth century could invent a style indelibly its own, unprecedented crowds were flocking to what *The Times* of London heralded as the embodiment of 'an entirely novel order of architecture, producing, by means of unrivalled mechanical ingenuity, the most marvellous and beautiful effects'.[1] No less compelling than questions of whether the Crystal Palace deserved a place in the architectural canon was the spectacle of the globe's production: over 100,000 objects from Britain and rival industrialized nations of Europe as well as from the vast 'new' world that colonization and trade had opened up, from China and India to the Caribbean, filled the nave and transepts of Paxton's show-

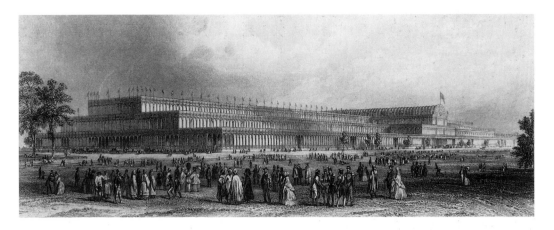

case, destined to have an impact not only on exhibition buildings but on an emergent mass consumer culture. In the wake of Chartism, economic depression, and public anxiety over the 'Condition of Britain', which had rocked the country in the 1840s, and with fresh memories of revolutions that had swept the continent in 1848–49, Victoria and Albert presided over a dazzling demonstration of Britain's place as standard bearer of the march of industry and prosperity.

An eyewitness, Lothar Bucher, Prussian newspaper correspondent, summed up just what it was that gave pause to architects grappling with issues of architectural form and values in modern society: 'In contemplating the first great building which was not of solid masonry spectators were not slow to realize that here the standards by which architecture had hitherto been judged no longer held good.' Because of the relatively narrow structural module adopted—a mere 8 feet (2.4 m)—and the extraordinary thinness of the members, the interior offered 'a delicate network of lines without any clue by means of which we might judge their distance from the eye or the real size … Instead of moving from one wall at one end to that of the other, the eye sweeps along an unending perspective which fades into the horizon. We cannot tell if this structure towers a hundred or a thousand feet above us, or whether the roof is a flat platform or built of ridges, for there is no play of shadows to enable our optic nerves to gauge the measurements … all materiality is blended into the atmosphere'.[2]

Boullée [**39b**] could only dream of simulating nature's atmosphere and stimulating emotions through kinaesthetic experience, but Paxton created unprecedented visual effects even while his attention was focused elsewhere, on honing his extraordinary supple kit of parts to meet a tight budget and schedule. With a last-minute sketch Paxton eliminated not only the 245 designs entered earlier in competition—including that of French architect Hector Horeau [**102**]—but the selected project by the engineer I. K. Brunel with its great dome of sheet iron. Now he worked furiously to craft a complete architectural system.

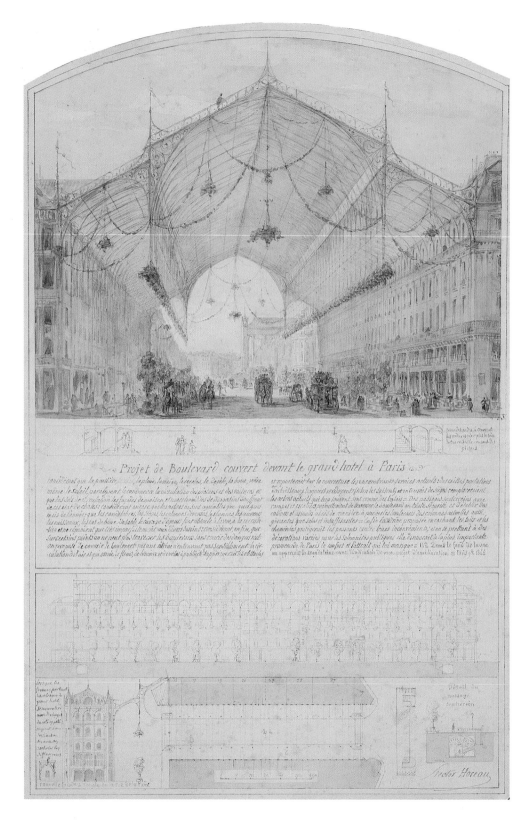

102 Hector Horeau

Proposal for covering the projected Avenue de l'Opéra, c.1862

A fervent advocate of vast covered spaces of iron and glass as remedies for the ills of the modern city, Horeau took up the prophetic role of glass and iron architecture first advanced by Saint-Simonians. The technology of the Crystal Palace, for which he had bid unsuccessfully, could foster a whole new vision of urban space, such as this proposal for the boulevard projected to terminate in the new Opéra [see **127**].

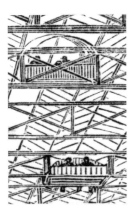

103

Glaziers' wagons at the Crystal Palace

Paxton masterminded both the design of the Crystal Palace and its assembly-line production, including adaptations of narrow-gauge railways used in mines to run along the metal members of his famous ridge and furrow roof design installing the pre-cut glass panes (*see detail above*). For the first time the spectacle of building as a factory system rather than a craft-bound skill was available prominently in the national capital.

Hollow cast-iron members served not only as structural uprights but as a drainage system, while the much-vaunted ridge and furrow roof design channelled water at the same time as it created tracks for small iron carts used by the roof glaziers to insert thousands of glass panes into the iron frame [**103**]. The Crystal Palace was at once assembly line and finished product; not surprisingly Paxton's profits derived both from his fees and from the new patents registered for his design.

Yet the visual effects were not entirely an unconscious byproduct of Benthamite utilitarianism, for the fitting-out of the interior was entrusted to Henry Cole, who for 15 years had been formulating strategies to forge new alliances between art, commerce, and industry through periodicals, associations, and a series of tuition-free schools of design in Britain's manufacturing cities. Cole turned to fellow explorers of fundamental laws of forms to make the Crystal Palace a veritable ad-

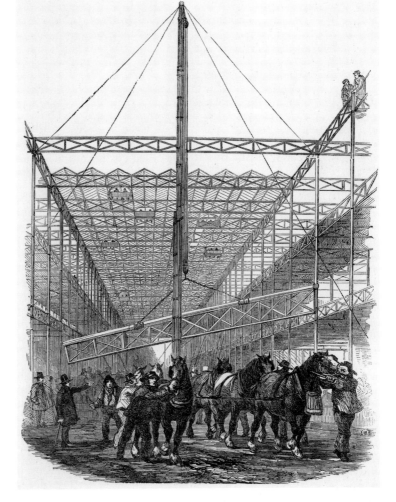

vertisement for the quest for a new industrial art. Painting the girders in turn with the three primary colours alternating with white, the Welsh architect Owen Jones explored the scientific chromatics of Michel-Eugène Chevreul's *Of the Law of Simultaneous Contrasts of Colours* (1839) to enhance the atmospheric haze, an effect contemporaries associated with the paintings of J. M. W. Turner, himself an advocate of simulating optical effects rather than imitating natural appearances. The whole was treated with that abstraction and flatness subscribed to by nearly all mid-century design reformers, those apprenticed in Gothic Revival architectural offices and those tutored in the government's schools of design.

Truthful to materials, honestly expressive of its structural principles, and—with the exception of difficulties in controlling interior temperature—admirably suited to its purpose, the Crystal Palace seemed the fulfilment of those ethical laws of architecture Pugin sought to extract from the Gothic and which the Ecclesiologists and Ruskin, in his *Seven Lamps of Architecture*, had also preached. Yet the Gothic Revivalists were in resounding agreement that Paxton's building set a dangerous precedent. 'Crystal Humbug' and the 'most monstrous thing ever imagined' exclaimed Pugin. Yet Pugin himself gave vivid demonstration of the potential of machine production harnessed to principles of historical form in the 'Medieval Court', an influential display of his own designs for ecclesiastical metalwork manufactured by Hardman of Birmingham, the very city that supplied Paxton's iron girders. Although 'lost in admiration at the unprecedented internal effects of such a structure', *The Ecclesiologist* felt compelled to draw a line in the sand: 'the conviction ... has grown upon us, that it is not architecture; it is engineering of the highest merit—but it is not architecture'.[3] Ruskin agreed: 'mechanical ingenuity is *not* the essence of either painting or architecture, and largeness of dimension does not necessarily involve nobleness of design. There is assuredly as much ingenuity required to build a screw frigate, or a tubular bridge as a hall of glass;— all these are works characteristic of the age; and all, in their several ways, deserve our highest admiration; but not admiration of the kind that is rendered to poetry or art.'[4] In 'The Nature of Gothic', the central chapter of his influential *Stones of Venice*, Ruskin formulated his compelling critique of industrial and commercial capitalism in the afterglow of the Crystal Palace, taking as his theme the rise and fall of the mercantile Venetian Republic.

Paxton is never mentioned in 'The Nature of Gothic', but Ruskin drew a vivid portrait of the dangers of the factory system to the dignity and freedom of individuals which he took as the most pertinent lesson to be drawn from the prefabricated palace. He advanced his arguments in appreciation of a different 'central building of the world', the fourteenth century Doge's Palace in Venice, celebrating not only the way an

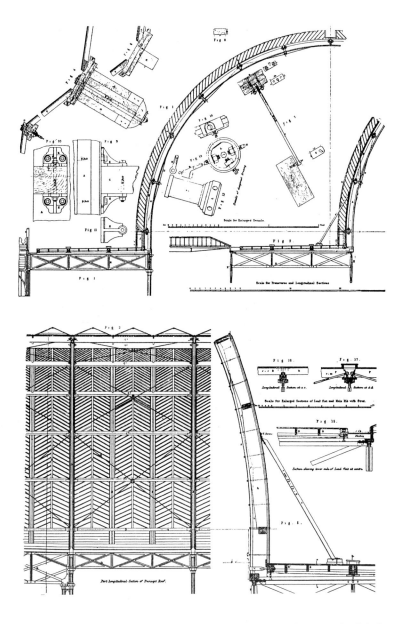

amalgam of Roman, Lombard, and Byzantine influences had left a
legible portrait of Venetian civilization at its apogee, but the fact that
the variously designed column capitals bore testimony to the diversity
of nature and the multitude of individual workmen pursuing their
craft. Every stone confirmed the central mantra of Ruskin's 'political
economy of art', namely 'the value of the appearance of labour upon architecture'.[5] The Doge's Palace not only encapsulated the seven ethical
lamps of architecture that Ruskin had defined, including the capacity
to serve as the repository of civilization's memory and thus be a school
of morals and culture; it served as the springboard for an impassioned

105 Ruskin

Fondaco dei Turchi, Venice, 1853

In exquisite watercolours the author of *The Stones of Venice* captured not only the passage of light over a building's surface but celebrated the visible traces of human and natural history. The encrustation of different styles bore witness to the march of human time even as the weathering and decay provided a rich patina on the palette of materials, a vibrant example of Ruskin's call for architecture as a repository or lamp of memory.

condemnation of the modern factory system which had transformed the English landscape in less than two generations [**76**]:

We have much studied and much perfected, of late, the great civilized invention of the division of labour; only we give it a false name. It is not, truly speaking, the labour that is divided; but the men:—Divided into mere segments of men—broke into small fragments and crumbs of life … And the great cry that rises from all our manufacturing cities, louder than the furnace blast, is all in very deed for this,—that we manufacture everything there except men; we blanch cotton, and strengthen steel, and refine sugar, and shape pottery; but to brighten, to strengthen, to refine, or to form a single living spirit, never enters into our estimate of advantages.[6]

In place of the system of working drawings [**104**] by which Paxton assured virtually flawless manufacture and assembly, Ruskin advocated roughness and imperfection—not simply as elements of the Burkean sublime but as voices for the labouring hand and individual mind 'which it must be the first aim of all Europe at this day to regain for her children'.[7] 'All cast and machine work is bad, as work … it is dishonest',[8] he inveighed in 'The Lamp of Truth'. The architect should 'work in the mason's yard with the men'.[9] Stone alone he felt could develop the patina of history and take its place in the legible landscape [**105**].

Deane and Woodward's Oxford Museum

Even as Ruskin was putting the finishing touches to *The Stones of Venice*, plans were afoot for a building he hoped would be the apotheosis of his conviction that architecture should elevate and educate both its makers and its public. In 1853 Oxford University announced a competition for designs for a new museum building to accommodate the great expansion in scientific teaching; research rather than tutorials would be central to 'new' branches of learning. The selection of Deane and Woodward as architects [**99**] meant that Ruskin's influence would permeate the building, which rose over the next 7 years in counterpoint to the project entrusted to the Cole circle to re-equip the Crystal Palace in its new location at Sydenham as a museum of civilization. The symmetrical Venetian Gothic façade with its stout central tower was a veritable billboard for the suitability of Gothic for secular design, but the demonstration went beyond exterior image as the museum's chief promoter and Ruskin's friend, Henry Acland, Regis Professor of Medicine, set out to craft a museum whose didactic mission was contained as much in its building fabric as in its collections. In the years before Darwin published *On the Origin of Species* (1859)—one of the first public debates over Darwin's theories would take place in the museum's lecture hall—the Oxford Museum simultaneously celebrated God's presence in all things and mankind's capacity to order and penetrate nature's abundant diversity. Under the chisels of the O'Shea brothers, brought over by Woodward from Ireland, the window and door frames were to be rich in naturalistic ornament, a modern evocation of the medieval cathedral façades Ruskin celebrated as stone bibles [**106**].

106

James O'Shea carving a jamb of a first-floor window of the University Museum, Oxford, *c.*1860

Using leaves as ornamental models, the O'Shea brothers realized the didactic realism that Ruskin advocated as a vital role of public architecture. In contrast to the mechanization of construction [cf. **103**] these Irish workmen were rare survivors of a disappearing craft, expressing their own identity in the framework of another's design. Tellingly, the work was never completed.

107

Central Court of Oxford Museum

The museum's façade would bristle with carvings of the flora and fauna of the earth, even as the polychromatic façades and interior arcades comprised a built-in collection of geological specimens. These were arranged to help the student remember the latest systems of classification—the stone piers, for instance, classed by mineral type with igneous rocks on the ground floor and sedimentary specimens above. Here was a demonstration not only of Ruskin's principle 'that all art employed in decoration should be informative, conveying truthful statements about natural facts',[10] but of his conviction that 'all architectural ornamentation should be executed by the men who design, and should be of various degrees of excellence, admitting and therefore exciting the intelligent cooperation of various classes of workmen'.[11] Even today much of the exterior ornamentation remains uncarved, a poignant reminder of the struggle facing the pre-industrial crafts in the capitalist world of survival of the fittest.

107

Central Court of Oxford Museum

The great glass and iron shed of the Oxford Museum provided a flexible exhibition space and was deliberately left open at the rear for future expansion, acknowledgment that the systematic classification of the world's natural history was an open-ended research. Few spaces speak more compellingly of the emergence of organic analogies between the structure of nature and the quest for architectural style than this great hall of skeletons.

In the astonishing glass and iron courtyard [**107**]—required by the competition brief—the Oxford Museum took up the challenge of the industrial age most clearly. Here was proof, in the words of *The Building News*, of the 'applicability of Crystal Palace architecture Gothicised'.[12] The design and manufacture were contracted to F. A. Skidmore of Coventry, an ironmaster in the circle of the Ecclesiologists. In an 1854 lecture, 'On the Use of Metals in Church Building and Decoration', Skidmore critiqued Paxton's mute utilitarianism, arguing that iron could be hammered and worked into a formal language at once its own, finer and more delicate than stone, and capable of imitating the natural forms Ruskin upheld as guarantors of truth in art. Ruskin remained sceptical; like others he doubted if the frailty of iron construction had the makings of monumental architecture with a public presence and a moral aura. Woodward and Skidmore created an ogival arched skeleton that at once echoes in architectural terms the anatomical specimen collections and, in the spandrels, literally bursts into leaf and flower to add native and exotic trees to the building's visual encyclopaedia, while vines of all sorts ornament the trefoils of the girders. Even iron, they demonstrated, had the potential for higher expression in the aesthetic of realism preached by Ruskin and the Pre-Raphaelite painters just getting their start in Oxford in these years.

Both nature and the nature of materials were open to interpretation. Even before it was completed the glazed roof had to be dismantled and redesigned as Skidmore had underestimated the sheer weight of even its thin members; the whole had begun to buckle under its own weight. Paxton, for all his critics accused him of reducing architecture to calculation, proudly maintained that nature had been his guide for finding efficient forms of broad-span iron and glass structure. The hollow ribs and thin leaf membranes of the Duke of Devonshire's exotic giant water-lilies—the famous *Victoria Regia* for which Paxton had designed

108 Paxton

a) Lily house at Chatsworth
b) Botanical diagram of structure of leaf and stem of the *Victoria Regis* water-lily

Paxton built a special glass house to display the Duke of Devonshire's prize specimens, the great *Victoria Regis* water-lily. To demonstrate the strength of its rib and infill leaf structure Paxton had his daughter walk across one of the great circular leaves and claimed it a moment of revelation for his own inventions. In contrast to Ruskin, Paxton maintained that nature provided structural lessons rather than forms.

a special greenhouse (1849–50)—had provided the first inspiration for his innovative architecture of frame and infill, as much a product of the intellect as the factory [**108a, b**]. Structure rather than ornament, he claimed, was the true lesson of nature. By the time of Paxton's writing, the circle around Cole was formulating a theory of ornament and form in opposition both to Ruskin's vision of didactic naturalism and his fear of the machine.

Art and industry: Henry Cole and William Morris

Despite resounding popular success, the manufactured goods displayed in the Crystal Palace signalled to many, including the design theorists Cole had gathered to work on the installation, a veritable crisis in art's relationship to industry. 'The absence of any fixed principles in ornamental design is apparent,' Cole concluded reluctantly. Finding 'the art manufacturers of Europe ... thoroughly demoralized',[13] he was not alone in admiring the originality and integrity of the hand-crafted objects sent by Asian and Islamic countries. Seeking explanations and correctives, architectural theorists in the 1850s addressed the whole range of everyday objects, redefining the relationship between the decorative arts and the fine arts, and postulating comprehensive theories of architectural form—most influentially in the seminal writings of Ruskin, Viollet-le-Duc, and Semper—which were to be the foundation for European architectural debate and practice for the rest of the century. Responding to official reports, such as those drawn up by the Comte de Laborde in France in 1856, governments promoted design reform as a strategy of commercial competitiveness as never before.

The greatest impact came from Cole's renewed efforts to educate designers, manufacturers, and consumers. After 1852 the vortex was the Department of Science and Art within the government Board of Trade, which took up quarters at Marlborough House while plans were studied for a permanent home at South Kensington. Inspired by Pugin, whose Medieval Court Cole thought one of the few successful marriages of good design and quality manufacture, Cole set up a museum of prototypes which included examples from all historical periods as well as a 'Gallery of False Principles in Decoration', best known today through Charles Dickens's parody of this pious effort at reforming public taste in *Hard Times*. What had captured the public's fancy in the Crystal Palace was now to be the object of scorn, as visitors learned to reject products that defied the nature of materials and to disdain illusionistic 'direct imitation of nature', particularly in fabric and wallpaper design. While the gallery was short-lived, the influence of the museum—today's Victoria and Albert—was enormous; by the end of the century it had spawned numerous imitators in the Arts and Crafts museum movement in German-speaking countries. Despite the emphasis on models, the mission shared by Cole's circle was to combat illusionistic imitation, be it expressed in the 'vulgar' products of the marketplace or in the naturalistic approach to ornament championed by Ruskin. In his widely consulted *Grammar of Ornament* (1856) Owen Jones juxtaposed ornamental motifs culled from the most diverse cultures, with unprecedented attention to Islamic, Chinese, and even Maori ornamental forms. But unlike contemporary historicists who argued for inalienable links between individual forms and their cultures, Jones derived universal principles of good design—37 in all—

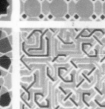

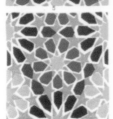

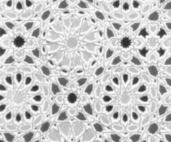

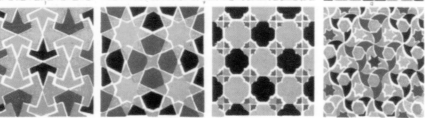

'Moresque Ornament', details of mosaics from the Alhambra Palace, lithographic plate (no. 153) from *The Grammar of Ornament* (London, 1856) In his great compendium of decorative systems, Jones paid particular attention to the building he had first studied in the 1830s, the Alhambra in Spain, 'the very summit of perfection of Moorish art, as is the Parthenon of Greek Art ... every principle which we can derive from the study of ornamental art of every people is ... present here.' He was not alone in proposing that the underlying geometries of such abstract systems, as nature itself, could liberate architecture from historicism; similar proposals were made in France in the 1860s by V.-M. Ruprich-Robert.

from his folio museum. The richly coloured lithographic plates could easily be misused as templates to be copied, but careful study brought the student to a series of plates—drawn by a pupil of the school, Christopher Dresser—demonstrating how original designs could be derived by abstracting the underlying patterns of leaves and plants [109].

In the 1850s Dresser pursued these new interests in both nature and the art of the east as paths away from what Jones condemned as the 'fashion of copying'. As a student of the Schools of Design in the late 1840s, he attended Richard Redgrave's lectures on 'The Importance of the Study of Botany to the Ornamentist'. A decade later he enrolled at the University of Jena to write a dissertation on Goethe's theory of metamorphosis in relationship to plant morphology, the doctrine celebrated three decades earlier by Schinkel in his Bauakademie [93]. By the 1860s Dresser was teaching that conventionalization of natural forms was a stage rather than a goal in the artistic manipulation of geometric principles of order observable in nature. In *The Art of Decorative Design* (1862) he laid out a veritable set of spiritual exercises by which the designer progressed from 'natural adaptations ... the lowest form of ornament' to 'purely ideal ornament'. 'The designer's mind must be like the vital force of the plant, ever developing itself into forms of beauty, yet while thus free to produce, still in all cases governed by unaltered laws,'[14] Dresser concluded, in lines that recall the German Romantic theory of the free genius in rapture before nature as much as they anticipate the growing impact of the young science of experimental psychology on theories of abstract form in the 1880s and 1890s. Yet for all his celebration of inspiration, Dresser also embraced the rationality of machine production, which he thought had unlimited potential and provided the only means by which the artisan could assert his place in society on an equal footing with industrial producers.

William Morris, Philip Webb, and the quest for an earthly paradise

William Morris (1834–96), Ruskin's most avid disciple, reached this same conclusion only with great reluctance at the end of a lifelong quest to revive endangered handicrafts as the basis for a renewal of both architecture and society. The legendary Red House [110], designed by Philip Webb (1831–1915), a fellow member of the 'Crusade and Holy War against the age', was a microcosmic utopia of Morris and Webb's rearguard action to restore the ethics of both design and labour they admired in the thirteenth century in defiance of industrial capitalism. 'The beauty of the handicrafts of the Middle Ages came from this, that the workman had control over his materials, tools, and time,' Morris explained years later in a lecture to a socialist group.[15] With his private fortune it was possible to create a house, much in-

Red House stairhall, near
Bexleyheath, Kent, 1860s

To the ongoing cultivation of
the small free-standing house
as an architectural and social
type for British middle-class
society, Webb added the
philosophy of Morris and his
friends that all aspects of the
interior should be designed in
harmony. The Red House
announces the theme of the
private interior as a
psychological retreat from
urban realities that would
make the house increasingly a
site of architectural
experimentation.

William Morris

The son of wealthy parents, William Morris (1834–96) was educated at Oxford, where he imbibed antipathy to commercial values by reading Carlyle and Ruskin, took up painting under the influence of Rossetti and Burne-Jones, and learned architecture in the office of G. E. Street, where he met Philip Webb. Together with Webb he designed the Red House, a manifesto for a reunion of architecture with handicraft, which he considered the greatest legacy of the Middle Ages. The notion of the collaborative effort of decorative arts and architecture, a joint set of principles of honesty, handwork, truth to materials, and non-illusionistic pattern, derived largely from Ruskin and Pugin but was now applied to the domestic realm. Morris & Co., with its wallpapers, textiles, and stained glass, was to be the cradle of the Arts and Crafts movement. In 1877 Morris and Webb founded the Society for the Protection of Ancient Buildings. 'Anti-Scrape' was their critique of prevalent practices of restoration which sought minimal intervention in historic buildings, for fear that the loss of original fabric and handwork, precious vessels of genuine and tactile historical records, would extinguish historic architecture's 'lamp of memory' (Ruskin).

spired in its honest brick and asymmetrical expression in massing and fenestration of different functions by the contemporary parsonages of Butterfield and Street, and to design and craft by hand all its furniture—much of it built-in—panelling, wallpaper, and textiles. Not a single thing was to be purchased from the marketplace. Pugin had done as much in his own house at Ramsgate a decade earlier, but Morris and Webb were determined to work with minimal recourse to machines, launching a philosophy that laid the foundations for the British and American Arts and Crafts movements at the end of the century.

For the next 30 years 'the firm'—reorganized in 1875 as 'Morris and Co.' under Morris's sole control—took on numerous commissions, many of them to decorate the country houses designed by Webb—and later William Lethaby, Ernest Newton, and others—for a close-knit clientele of artists and others who shared their disdain for ascendant bourgeois conventions. Increasingly Morris's designs and Webb's architecture drifted from the pronounced medievalism of the Red House towards a self-consciously modest astylar expression which drew considerable inspiration from rural vernacular buildings—notably those of the seventeenth century misleadingly called by Richard Norman Shaw and others 'Queen Anne'—and from the austere utilitarian aesthetic of such Cistercian buildings as the barn at Great Coxwell, 'unapproachable in its dignity, as beautiful as a cathedral', Morris said.[16] In their commitment to honest expression of materials, quest for simplicity, and preference for abstracted natural patterns in decoration, Morris and Webb organized their lives and work in defiance of 'the present system of commercialism and profit-mongering'.[17] Morris had given up architecture when he realized that he could not control the entire design process, although he continued to preach that architecture was

the master art, even expanding the word's definition to embrace every-thing from teacups to town planning. He defined architecture alter-nately as 'the turning of necessary articles of daily use into works of art' and as 'the moulding and altering to human needs of the very face of the earth itself'.[18] Along with Dresser, he was one of the first to iden-tify himself professionally as a 'designer', but he refused to conceive of this as part of a chain of command. Morris mastered every step and technique of the successive crafts he took up, from mural decoration and wallpaper to embroidery, dying and the weaving of carpets, tapes-tries, and textiles, book design, stained glass, and ceramics.

Webb likewise refused to take on more commissions than he could personally supervise, controlling every element of design and con-struction, and increasingly striving to conceive his buildings from ma-terials found locally—at Smeaton Manor, Yorkshire (1876) the bricks were made from clay on a nearby site—and taking cues both for design and construction from local vernaculars. Like Morris, Webb never re-laxed his standards or convictions. Both admitted, in turning to active engagement in socialist politics in the 1880s with hope that some chal-lenge to 'the cash nexus' might be on the horizon, that their practices were fraught with paradox. 'Our architects are constantly trying to find workmen who can use materials with the simplicity and directness of those of earlier times, so that the workmen themselves should be able to ease the *designer* of the unbearable burden of directing the manipu-lation of all trades from his office,'[19] Webb wrote, even as he main-tained an office that never exceeded three employees and continued to provide full-scale drawings and detailed instructions not to leave any element of his designs to chance in a capitalist labour market. Morris lamented that he was never able to produce his designs cheaply enough to reach more than a rarefied market of consumers; indeed they risked becoming precisely the type of commodity he struggled to resist through a painstaking study of Marx and Engels's writings in the 1880s. Gradually Morris came to admit that machines might be used to pro-duce designs provided they remain firmly under the control of the de-signer: 'It is not this or that steel and brass machine which we want to get rid of, but the great intangible machine of commercial tyranny, which oppresses the lives of all of us.'[20]

Industry and style: Viollet-le-Duc and Gottfried Semper

The burning issues that moved Morris and his followers, symbolized by the Crystal Palace, were to spark two other great undertakings in architectural theory in the 1850s. No less than Ruskin, Eugène-Emmanuel Viollet-le-Duc in France, and the German Gottfried Semper formulated comprehensive theories to guide the search for ar-chitectural form in light at once of the historical evolution of society and the challenges of industrial materials and methods. But unlike

Ruskin, whose understanding of architecture remained grounded in his literary métier, Viollet-le-Duc and Semper were practising architects whose quest for universal theories of form—typical of the mid-century's quest for systems of knowledge—was tempered by the realities of construction even as they drew fresh inspiration from developments in the most diverse disciplines, from biology and physiology to anthropology. A theory of style, and of the mechanism which explained the interrelationship of physical, cultural, and aesthetic determinants in its formation, was the keystone of their respective overarching explanatory systems. Jointly their legacy was as important for the subsequent development of art history as a discipline as it was for architects' continued anxiety over the question Viollet-le-Duc put so succinctly: 'Is the nineteenth century condemned to come to an end without having found a style of its own?'[21]

By the time he conceived the project of a 10-volume dictionary of medieval architecture (*Dictionnaire raisonné de l'architecture française du XIe au XVIe siècle* (1854–68))—the format alone betrayed his quest for an objective and systematic theory—Viollet-le-Duc had emerged not only as an adamant combatant for the Gothic Revival but as the leading exponent of structural rationalism. In a serialized history of medieval architecture in the pages of the *Annales Archéologiques*, the organ of the Gothic party of the Catholic Revival, he laid down clearly the foundations of his later work in the 1840s. There he advanced the historical hypothesis that was his most lasting legacy: that in less than a century the architects of the medieval cathedrals of the Ile-de-France had perfected a structural system in which every element contributed to the dynamic equilibrium of the whole, and in which material was reduced to a daring, but reasoned, minimum. The resulting architecture possessed what he called, in his definition of 'style', 'the perfect harmony between the results obtained and the means employed to achieve them';[22] form and structure, in short, were identical. Unlike elements of Classicism learned by rote at the École des Beaux-Arts—in this Viollet-le-Duc paralleled Ruskin's belief that Classical architecture was a form of slavery of the human spirit—Gothic offered flexible lessons of materiality, rationality, and economy as relevant in the nineteenth century as in the thirteenth. 'Cathedrals represent the first and greatest application of the modern spirit to architecture, emerging from the midst of an order of ideas quite opposite to those of antiquity,' he proclaimed.[23] Fiercely nationalist, he believed this rationality to be the genius of the nation that had produced Descartes, the scientific discoveries of the early nineteenth century, particularly the biological work of Cuvier and St-Hilaire, and several generations of engineers whose bridges and roads were the envy of Europe. In the same years that the Comte Léon de Laborde drew up conclusions from his observations on the Crystal Palace jury, proclaiming that it fell to France to prove that art and industry could be brought into a fruitful alliance, Viollet-le-Duc began to recast himself less the prophet of the Gothic Revival and more the suffragette for the place of French architects in giving form to 'the abundance of means and materials' presented by industrial and engineering advances.[24]

In the 1840s Viollet-le-Duc fought in the trenches with a group of young architects—most notably Labrouste's pupil Lassus—for opportunities to demonstrate that the style of the French thirteenth century was the only conceivable starting-point for a new national architecture and a way of breaching what they considered the fortress of the Academy and the centralized architectural administration, bastions of Classical doctrine. Each new Gothic Revival church was a momentous political battle, from Lassus's design of St-Nicolas at Nantes (1843) to the Parisian church of Ste-Clotilde (1846–57), begun by F. C. Gau and completed by Théodore Ballu, the Gothic spires of which rose defiantly over the Classical portico of the French National Assembly.

In the wake of Guizot's organization of the State Commission on Historic Monuments in 1834, Viollet-le-Duc not only crafted the fabric and the reputation of France's medieval monuments as embodiments of the national spirit, but formulated an influential theory of restoration as an idealist construction of perfect monument 'which may in fact never have actually existed at any given time'.[25] As a historian he considered the cathedral building yards of the Middle Ages crucibles of the national school of rational architecture. As an architect and reformer, he used his restoration projects at Notre-Dame in Paris, Amiens, Carcassonne, and countless other sites to forge a new union of building technique and architectural design and to foster nothing less than a counter-culture to the academic routines of the École des Beaux-Arts. A whole coterie was formed, some of whom worked in the French provinces, notably Eugène Millet, Émile Boeswillwald, Paul Abadie, and Edmond Duthoit, others carrying the doctrines abroad, notably Viollet-le-Duc's son-in-law Maurice Ouradou, who worked in Cracow, and Suréda, who helped set up the Historical Monuments Commission in Spain. In the mid-1840s he prided himself on designing with Lassus a new sacristy and vestry for Notre-Dame Cathedral that could be easily mistaken for medieval work; by the 1850s this life-long atheist was losing faith in the literal imitation of Gothic forms in favour of a position which paralleled the theory of 'development' explored by the English followers of Pugin. As in England an important catalyst was to be the use of iron in architecture.

Fewer than 4 years separate London's Crystal Palace from France's response, the Palace of Industry on the Champs-Elysées to house the Universal Exhibition of 1855, by which France determined to rival England not only in the marketplace but in the showcases of industrial progress. But in those years debate over iron came to the fore, first with the insistence of Emperor Napoleon III in 1853 that Victor Baltard halt construction of new stone buildings for Paris's central markets [124] and replace them with a building in 'iron, iron, nothing but iron',[26] then with the controversy unleashed in the press in 1855 over Louis-Auguste Boileau's (1812–96) St-Eugène–Ste-Cécile, Paris's first cast-iron church. Whereas both of those buildings were predominantly conceived in iron, at the Palace of Industry conception was divided between an architect, Jean-Marie Viel, who styled the Renaissance masonry façades, and an engineer, Alexis Barrault, who was able to exploit this rigid envelope to create a glass and iron vault held aloft with no intermediate supports to subdivide the interior space. The great triumphal arch entry flanked by caryatids symbolizing 'Science' and 'Art' expressed ambitions long at the heart of Saint-Simonian theory—former Saint-Simonians dominated the team entrusted with staging France's 1855 and 1867 exhibitions—and most recently recommended as national policy by de Laborde, namely that it was the destiny of France to effect new alliances between the material and the spiritual, between art and industry. In the heat of these controversies Viollet-le-Duc formulated a challenging theory of contemporary architecture, one in which advances in iron technology would be assimilated to the lessons of rational structure and the principle of dynamic structural equilibrium which were the legacies of French Gothic.

Boileau took up the challenge. In large part prefabricated, St-Eugène [111] exploited the lightness of cast iron and sheet metal to create an open cage of structure filled with light. Flying buttresses, which Viollet-le-Duc's academician critics had repeatedly derided as the weak point of Gothic architecture, were rendered unnecessary by light infill walls of stucco over brick, gaining thereby the maximum amount of interior space in a structure built to fill its cramped corner site. A restrained exterior gave way to an interior of iron painted in brilliant colours, emulating the system of abstracted Gothic ornament that Duban, Viollet-le-Duc, and Lassus had pioneered in their restoration of the Sainte-Chapelle a decade earlier. The church was dedicated by the Empress Eugénie, and celebrated in an article by Michel Chevalier, a former Saint-Simonian and economic adviser to the state. Chevalier asked why the system Boileau had already proposed to patent and generalize—Boileau's pamphlet *The New Architectural Form* describing the so-called 'synthetic cathedral' appeared in 1854—had not been adopted for the expensive new churches then under construction by the state.

Above the new steamship ports at Marseille, Vaudoyer was supervising the foundations for a new cathedral which embodied the notion of historical accretion through the chain of continuous progress and the vital lessons to be learned from moments of cultural transition and intermingling, a theory he and his friends Léonce Reynaud and Albert Lenoir had formulated alongside Romantic historians and artists in the

The first of a series of all-iron
Gothic Revival churches
designed by Boileau, this
Parisian church catalysed a
lively debate over the use of
new industrial materials in
public architecture. Later
examples were constructed at
Montluçon and in the suburb
of Le Vésinet [134]. In
subsequent decades iron
buildings were exported to
France's colonies, notably in
the Caribbean.

1830s. In an eclectic but purposeful amalgam Vaudoyer sought to create
a building which pictorialized, even as it found its logic in, the role of
Marseille as the historical crucible between the east and the west, the
place where French culture had continually been provoked to stylistic
experiment and advance by contact with eastern Mediterranean cultures from the Greeks to the Byzantines to the Arabs [112].

Both the literal imitation of Gothic forms in new materials and the
vision of history as a process of eclectic cultural intermingling were
concepts Viollet-le-Duc was determined to combat; he lashed out
against both Boileau's cast-iron church and Vaudoyer's historicist
cathedral. Boileau modelled his cast-iron uprights on the svelte stone
columns of the twelfth-century refectory of St-Martin-des-Champs,
a building Viollet-le-Duc praised and which Labrouste had taken as a

point of departure. But whereas Viollet-le-Duc admired Labrouste's Bibliothèque Ste-Geneviève enormously [**87**], he dismissed Boileau's view of both architecture and history as vulgarly mechanistic. Adopting a line of attack Hübsch had advanced in refuting the notion of the transposition of archaic wooden forms into the stone syntax of the Greek temple, Viollet-le-Duc bemoaned that the rational spirit of Gothic should be defamed by a crude notion of imitation that defied the nature of materials. In a stunning exploded perspective drawing [**113**] for his *Dictionnaire* he demonstrated that Gothic was an organic system in which every component had a structural role and form that was reasoned in relationship to its place in a perfectly functioning whole. In this architecture were paralleled the creative potential and laws of nature, 'her deductions follow one upon the other according to the order of an invariable logic'.[27] Using his pencil as a scalpel to uncover nature's laws he took inspiration from the displays of articulated skeletons by which Cuvier had made visible his 'law of correlation' at the Museum of Natural History and from the stunning sectional dissections in the illustrations of Marc-Jean Bourgery's (1797–1849) seminal *Complete Treatise of Human Anatomy* (1831–54). Rather than copying, architects should imagine what the consummately rational medieval builders would have done if blessed with large sections of iron. Baltard's central markets [**124**], with their frank expression of programme and materials, were more suggestive of a starting-point for finding a modern architectural language.[28] Viollet-le-Duc recommended studying them as a tonic to avoid the pitfall of those

Springing point of the arch
from the article 'Construction'
of the *Dictionnaire raisonné de
l'Architecture*, 1858

Taking inspiration from both
the method and the drawings
of contemporary treatises of
comparative anatomy, Viollet-
le-Duc's exploded perspective
technique conveys instantly
his theory that in architecture
as in nature every part was a
uniquely functioning element
of a larger organic order. Here
he analyses the complex
stereotomy of ribbed vaulting
at its key structural joint.

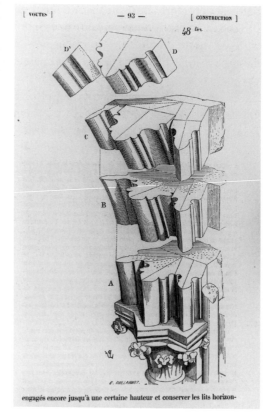

[VOUTES]   — 93 —   [CONSTRUCTION]

48 *ter*

engagés encore jusqu'à une certaine hauteur et conserver les lits horizon-

Revivalists 'who make one think of those people who believe they are
performing their religious duty in reciting Latin prayers of which they
don't understand a word'.[29]

Language remained an important metaphor to Viollet-le-Duc as
he continued to puzzle over the problem of finding an appropriate formal system for modern architecture. Here his quest for a universal law
of form met with his belief in the importance of historical guidance.
Although he agreed with Labrouste's generation that architectural
forms must change and evolve with society, he rejected their vision of
historical hybridization as a motor of progress. 'Why seek to compose
a macaronic language when one has at hand a beautiful and simple language all our own?'[30] he remarked, in reviewing Vaudoyer's plans for a
Romano-Byzantine-style cathedral at Marseille [112]. Taken with the
racist theories of the Comte Arthur Gobineau, who preached that
racial mixture was the source of cultural decline, Viollet-le-Duc argued increasingly for the national specificity of architecture. As he
moved on in the 1860s and 1870s to studies of both the geology and the
vernacular architecture of the Alps, he sought to understand the com-
monality between the evolution of forms and types and the principles
that could be extrapolated for the future of architecture. He was fasci-

nated by the coexistence of a limited number of laws in nature and her dizzying diversity of forms, notably in crystals. The capacity of mankind to create, the very nature of art, was to be revealed by the simultaneous study of the science of history and the history of nature. 'Any school that has studied natural flora minutely, and natural fauna as well, and that has succeeded by the application of logical method in creating out of stone an organism with its own laws similar to those of a living organicism'—and by this point Viollet-le-Duc did not even need to identify the Gothic by name—'does not have to be preoccupied with style; these methods, then as always, constituted the very essence of style. The day when artists go out looking for style, that is when art no longer has style.'[31] He disbanded his atelier when his students thought to please him by creating French Gothic designs when asked to imagine a building for North Africa. Solicited for advice on a future Russian architecture, Viollet-le-Duc demonstrated in *L'Art Russe* (1877) how a rational framework of structure had been found in the brick architecture of seventeenth-century Moscow which might serve as a point of departure for integrating the new resources of iron. Universal laws of form and the relativism of culture were, he maintained, not incompatible.

114 Viollet-le-Duc

Concert Hall, *c.*1866

An iron armature resting on eight cast-iron columns is at once independent of, and interacts with, a thin masonry shell in this imaginary building published in Viollet-le-Duc's *Lectures on Architecture*. He was at pains to show that universal principles of form, evident in the equilateral triangles that form the web of ribs over the vaults, could raise iron construction to the highest ideal of architecture.

Viollet-le-Duc's most sustained and influential reflection on the future of architecture came in the wake of student protests which aborted his lecturing career at the École des Beaux-Arts, whose curriculum he had been instrumental in reforming in 1863. In the second volume of his *Discourses on Architecture,* he painted an alarming portrait of a profession rapidly losing ground, not only to engineers but to the larger cultural antagonism between the arts and science and technical knowledge. Was the architect to be reduced to a fashionable decorator? Was the modern city to be composed of nothing but, as he put it, hangars and hypogea, the utilitarian iron and glass markets of the engineers and the public architecture of the academicians nostalgically enslaved to the period of Louis xiv? Modern buildings, like modern societies, were complex organisms, but their envelopes were no more in harmony with the sophisticated systems of heating, ventilation, and gas lighting recently developed than they were with the structural capacities of iron. The cultural spirit of rational inquiry that was the motor of unprecedented progress in science, philosophy, history, even archaeology, was absent in architecture alone, Viollet-le-Duc complained, echoing the Saint-Simonian dream of an organic society. Also Saint-Simonian was his choice of a great hall of secular assembly, a concert hall, as the building to encapsulate suggestions for what forms might result from a modern fusion of architecture and engineering [114]. Calling for a mixed system of construction in which cast and wrought iron, brick and stone masonry, and even enamelled tile infill would all be developed to maximize their individual capacities in relation to one another, Viollet-le-Duc called his invention an 'organism' which took its place as the next link in a long chain of architectures for mass gatherings. The hall was a successor to the Roman baths and the Gothic cathedrals, just as nature 'neither forgets nor omits anything of her past ... From the polyps to mankind, she follows an interrupted path.'[32] He was at pains to argue that his organism was equally prepared to struggle for survival in the marketplace of construction bids and changing economics of materials.

Gottfried Semper and the problem of representation

'Let the discoveries, machines, and speculation work as hard as they can, so that the dough will be kneaded out of which interpretive science ... will be able to shape new form. In the meantime, however, architecture must step down from its throne and go into the marketplace, there to teach and there to learn,'[33] Gottfried Semper (1803–79) wrote in a perspicacious essay on the Crystal Palace. Exiled from Saxony for his part on the barricades of the failed bourgeois revolution of 1848, the former royal architect was keenly aware in London that economically the world was changing at an unprecedented rate, even if challenges to traditional forms of political power had been rebuffed. Even as fellow

Gottfried Semper (1803–79)

Born in Altona, and trained in Munich and Paris, Semper travelled in Sicily and Greece with Jules Goury, and participated in the period's debates over architectural polychromy. As a royal architect in Saxony after 1834 he grappled with stylistic and social ideals in seminal designs. Dresden's opera house and art gallery established the neo-Renaissance—recalling the city states of Italy—as a style for public buildings in modern middle-class urban society.

In the 1844 competition for rebuilding St Nicholas, Hamburg, Semper submitted a *Rundbogenstil* design, an explicit critique of what he viewed as the inherent neo-conservatism of the promoters of the Gothic Revival Cologne Cathedral. Like many Germans who saw career prospects dimmed by the uprisings of 1848–49, in which Semper and his friend Richard Wagner had taken part, he contemplated emigrating to the United States. But in 1849 he accepted an invitation to London, where he worked in the design reform movement led by Henry Cole. In 1855 Semper took up a teaching post in Zurich, and designed a number of important buildings there, including the railway station; and from 1869 he designed key structures for the Viennese Ringstrasse (chapter 8).

exiles Marx and Engels, whose *Communist Manifesto* had appeared in 1848, sought to formulate the historical laws that could master the sweeping changes under way in the social and economic relations of the factory system, Semper grappled with what he had witnessed in the hothouse of Paxton's 'world market', where both consumers and makers were confronted with a dizzying 'abundance of means ... the first great danger with which art has to struggle'.[34]

The Great Exhibition confirmed Semper's belief that the chaos of contemporary architecture resulted from the lack of an integrating 'world view', something earlier societies enjoyed unselfconsciously but which the modern world could only harness through the new science of history. For nearly a decade he had been developing an organizational schema for a comprehensive theory of architecture, one that could complete the work begun by Durand in his famous taxonomic plates of building types, but infuse it with something of the organic unity captured in the great synthetic systems advanced by Cuvier and by Humboldt. His great work, the never completed *Style in the Technical and Tectonic Arts or Practical Aesthetics* (1860–63), grew from this project for a 'Comparative Theory of Building'. Semper reflected continually on the parallels between the inner dynamics of the social art of architecture and the patterns of change in nature, revealing in an 1843 letter to his publisher that he had been drawn in Paris to Cuvier's display of skeletons and fossils 'as if by a magical force'. 'Just as everything there envelops and is explained by the simplest prototypical form, just as nature in her infinite variety is yet simple and sparse in basic ideas, just as she renews continually the same skeletons by modifying them a thousandfold according to the formative stages reached by living beings and the conditions of existence ... works of art are also

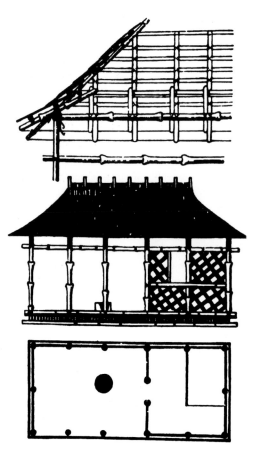

based on certain standard forms conditioned by primordial ideas, yet permit an infinite variety of phenomena according to the particular needs that affect them.'[35] Taken out of context one might imagine this a passage from Viollet-le-Duc, but while the French and German theorists were to develop in similar intellectual environments, they were to develop radically different notions of style and diametrically opposed prescriptions for the present.

Semper's great originality was the centrality of the symbolic or representational role of architectural forms and the belief that those forms, no matter how evolved, could be traced back to fundamental social practices. A history of becoming was fundamental to his unwavering aim to formulate 'an architectural theory of invention ... that teaches the way of nature and avoids characterless schematicism and thoughtless caprice',[36] evoking the dual spectres of academic convention and eclecticism. At the Great Exhibition Semper found a building that gave powerful visual form to his theory, not in Paxton's design, which broadcast only the contemporary 'devaluation of meaning', but in the exhibition of colonial Trinidad, one of those 'half-barbaric nations'[37] whose production yielded glimpses of 'earlier stages of cultural development', before industrial acceleration derailed the slow process by which artistic forms metamorphose. Unlike the novelties of the Crystal Palace produced by an emerging consumer market in anticipation of demand, the full-scale model of a wood and thatch hut [115] embodied Semper's conviction that architecture had evolved from handicrafts. Architecture had its origins in the choice of a site to erect a hearth, which as the nucleus for family and social assembly came to organize man's craft activities in the enterprise of shelter. Lifted off the humid ground by a substructure of masonry and shielded from the elements by a roof, the fire is both protected and consecrated in its own space. Finally the whole was hung with textiles to form walls. Both a symbol and a tool, the hearth was the origin of society and—transformed into the altar—of its religious beliefs, of ceramics, and thus of making in general. Architectural meaning and social meaning evolved in tandem: 'Around the hearth the first groups assembled; around it the first alliances formed, around it the first rude religious concepts were put into customs of a cult. Throughout all phases of society the hearth formed the sacred focus centre around which the whole took order and shape.'[38]

It is tempting to recall Laugier's primitive hut of a century earlier [see 1], and the whole tradition of structural rationalism in France which stemmed from it, but for Semper the hut had the status of a palaeontological artefact rather than an ideal standard. Nor was he willing to allow any single determinant of architectural form, be it laws of structure or materials, to predominate. In lectures at Cole's Department of Practical Art he went so far as to proffer a mathematical equation to symbolize the way in which materials, techniques, climate, society, politics, and even personal taste all acted upon a building's function and thus on the resulting style. On numerous occasions he derided any literal materialist view, even ridiculing Viollet-le-Duc's doctrine of material determinism in the pages of *Style*. Semper coined two terms to underscore the fact that an ongoing process of transformation, and thus representation, remained at the core of the art of architecture, and of its continued fulfilment of both the material and spiritual needs of society. The concept of *Bekleidung*, or dressing, derived from the earlier theories of the Berlin architect Karl Bötticher, who in his dense *The Tectonics of the Hellenics* of 1844 drew an influential distinction between the literal structure of a building, which he called its core form, and its visual expression, or art form. While the theory derived from long-running debates over the use of colour, particularly in Greek architecture, its most lasting legacy was to explain the conventionalized vocabularies of architectural ornament not as simple decoration but as a symbolic language embodying the very essence of architecture. To Bötticher's theory, grounded in the notion of discrete architectural cultures succeeding one another, Semper added a key operative concept, the *Stoffwechseltheorie*,

116 Alexandre Laplanche

Au Bon Marché, Paris, 1872
a) Exterior
Architect Laplanche's stone façades borrowed recognizable motifs freely from recent public architecture, deliberately blurring the boundaries between culture and commerce and pioneering the use of historical architectural forms in the new techniques of advertising and marketing developed by the nineteenth-century department store. The iron frame behind allowed a proliferation of display windows, giving tantalizing glimpses of the full splendour of goods arrayed within.

b) Interior
A veritable pendant to Charles Garnier's contemporary stair at the Opéra [**117**], Boileau's iron stair was likewise as much for seeing the latest in goods, especially new fabrics, as for being seen on. Department stores were among the rare spaces where single women could stroll acceptably in public. The Bon Marché encouraged them to linger by opening a reading room and a buffet with free cakes and refreshments, as the world of private commerce increasingly crafted spaces of public leisure.

or theory of the transformation of materials, by which he explained that even when the materials of construction changed, the chain of meaning in architecture remained unbroken. The hut again confirmed this notion, for the prime example of primordial motifs and their mutations for Semper was the origin of the wall in the symbolic patterns of the textile arts rather than in the constructive laws of masonry. Once these spatial dividers—and in this he referred also to the tents of the ancient near east—were replaced by more permanent materials, builders continued to recall the patterns of the original textile wall in decorative cladding, be it stucco, paint, or glazed bricks or tiles. In the exhibits of the British Museum and the Louvre Semper found confirmation, noticing that Assyrian glazed brick walls were often patterned on models of wicker mats, such as those used in the Caribbean hut. 'Although architecture produces original formations and is not an imitative art like painting and sculpture, it has over the centuries created its own store of forms from which it borrows the types for new creations; by using these types, architecture remains legible and comprehensible for everyone,'[39] Semper concluded in response to 'the Babylonian confusion of tongues' that he observed at the Crystal Palace. The marketplace was a school for the astute eye, armed with a knowledge of the genealogy or etymology of architectural language, but most makers and consumers would require a more orderly exposition. For this Semper proposed museums as schools of public taste, a project given its most concrete realization in the interpretation of his ideas in the formation of Vienna's Museum of Applied Arts and in Semper's own design for museums as the public forum of Vienna, where he would culminate his long and chequered career as a builder [**131**].

The first department stores

While Ruskin, Viollet-le-Duc, and Semper challenged architects to respond to industrialization and commercialization, the marketplace itself pioneered novel uses of iron and glass to create an architecture of display and consumption that made the ephemeral display of the world fairs a permanent feature of modern urban life. Just a year after the Crystal Palace was dismantled, Aristide Boucicaut opened what historians of mass consumption have labelled the first department store, Au Bon Marché on Paris's left bank [**116a, b**]. By 1874 the shop had grown to fill a city block, and architecture was added to the list of innovations such as fixed prices and no-obligation-to-buy which transformed shopping from a task of provisioning to a leisure spectacle, fuelled by the steady increase of middle-class purchasing power in the second half of the nineteenth century.[40]

As the store expanded, its exterior took on the form of a veritable public monument [**116a**], its main entrance picked out from the commonplace façades of the rue de Sèvres by an elaborately decorated piling

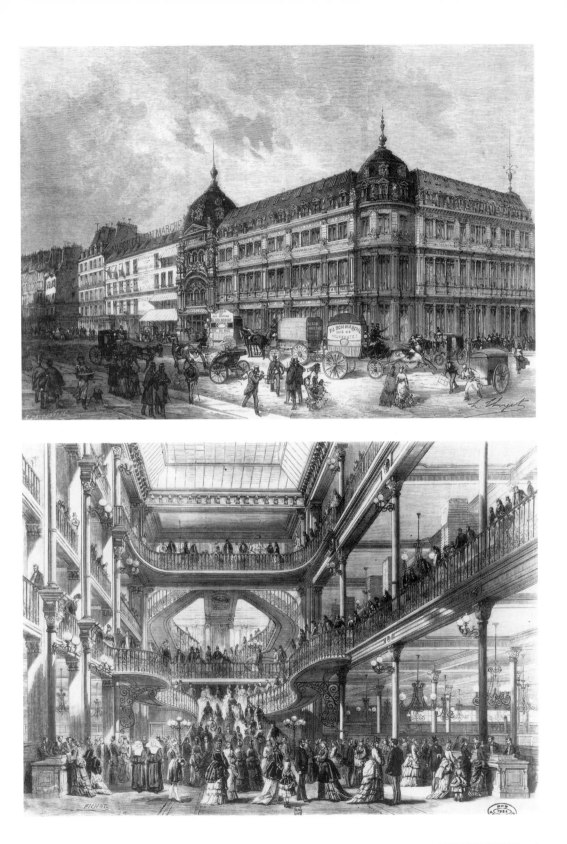

up of motifs borrowed from the French Renaissance Revival launched a decade earlier by Visconti and Lefuel at the Louvre [119] and its corner rotunda adapting a motif much admired in Labrouste's design for the National Library (1859–68) to the brief of attracting customers. The entrances advanced subtly onto the pavement, hoping to ensnare window shoppers attracted by the broad display windows where architecture and merchandise collaborated in making the building a veritable advertisement for the world of goods within. Between 1872 and 1874 the interior was remodelled by Louis-Charles Boileau. He collaborated with the young engineering firm of Gustave Eiffel, whose experience in bridging the landscape with iron railway trusses was now enlisted in the conquest of the deep space of an urban block by new techniques of selling. In place of the open courtyards required to permit daylight into earlier interiors, the new building focused around three skylit atria [116b] and remained open at night thanks to a full complement of gas lighting. A swooping metal stairway seemed literally suspended in the space, providing not only ever-panoramic vistas of merchandise, but making the shoppers themselves an integral part of the spectacle of a new world of luxury. A rival department store, 'À la ville de Saint-Denis', offered the thrill of ascending a three-storey skylit atrium on Léon Edoux's hydraulic elevator, unveiled a few years earlier at the International Exhibition of 1867.

Boileau, son of the architect of St-Eugène [111], realized that the new material negated all he had learned at the École des Beaux-Arts of the proportions, shadows, and manipulation of mass of grand public architectural design. 'Either we concede that it is impossible to create a monument with metal, or such a monument being unable to withstand serious comparison with stone buildings we should avoid once and for all imitating stone and consider it from an entirely new point of view.'[41] Henceforth, he concluded, architects would compose with voids rather than solids. Whereas Classical and Gothic design alike were based on adjusting solids to sculpt forms in light, in the delicate gossamer of iron-frame construction light itself would become the subject, manipulated to create reflections, sparkling effects, and even luminous clarity, 'like one plays with the lights of a chandelier by cutting differently shaped crystals'.[42] Architecture and commerce had indeed formed a new alliance. The interiorized world of the department store was developed by the next generation of retailers to create ever more fantastic interiors, veritable parallel universes of abundance in which retailing and design explored the manipulation of human desires and fantasies even as the new science of human psychology began to explore the realm of subjective experience. Émile Zola's quip that the department store 'was the cathedral of commerce … made for a population of customers',[43] gained an air of reality in 1874 when the new 'Printemps' department store on Paris's Boulevard Haussmann opened its doors for business after being blessed by the curate of the Madeleine.

The City Transformed, 1848–90

8

One of the effects of civilization (not to say one of the ingredients in it) … is, that the spectacle, and even the very idea of pain, is kept more and more out of the sight of those classes who enjoy in their fullness the benefits of civilization.

John Stuart Mill, 'Civilisation' (1836)

It was not simply the machines in the Palace of Industry on the Champs-Elysées which offered a spectacle of progress in the summer of 1855; Paris itself was being refashioned by new technologies of machinery and capital [**118**]. Under powerful gas lights, over 3,000 worked around the clock to join the Louvre and Tuileries palaces—separated for nearly a century by a dense and decaying quarter—into a grand palace/museum complex centred on a public garden [**119**]. Napoleon i's show street, the rue de Rivoli [**63**], had taken form over decades. His nephew Napoleon iii, along with his right-hand man, the Baron Georges Haussmann (1809–91), named Prefect of the Seine Département in June 1853, accelerated the process of reforming the city explored piecemeal by earlier governments. The scale of change introduced by the railway in the countryside in the 1840s was now unleashed on the city, which took a place in European consciousness as never before.

Determined to craft a showcase imperial capital, Haussmann and Napoleon iii offered tax exemptions for 20 years to speculators in a bid to complete in time for the 1855 fair the great cross-axis that was to be the backbone for remodelling the city under the banners of circulation, health, and security. The arcaded rue de Rivoli would be subsumed in a great east–west axis bisecting Paris from the barracks at Courbevoie in the west to the Place de la Bastille, perennial centre of insurrection, in the east. The new Boulevard de Strasbourg (today's Boulevard de Sébastopol) would link the railway on the city's northern fringe via the Ile de la Cité to the Porte d'Orléans on the south, clearing some of the city's densest quarters in its projected path. These projects fell short of their deadline, but influential foreign visitors were treated to the spectacle of a city refashioning itself from the Hôtel du Louvre, the largest of a new breed of grand luxury hotels which embellished Europe's large

117 Éduard Detaille

Opening of the Paris Opera House, 1875

Despite the profusion of ornament and richness of colour, Garnier argued that the Opéra's stairhall was complete only when it served as the prop for the spectacle of a whole society coming together for a moment of intense interaction in the minutes preceding the performance on stage. Unfinished when the Second Empire fell, the building was inaugurated under the regime of President MacMahon. Garnier stands in the centre of the landing, framed by caryatids and receiving the presidential procession.

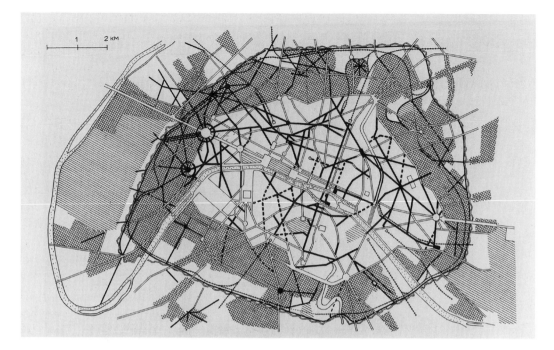

118

Plan of Haussmann's work in
Paris, c.1853

The original map which
Napoleon presented to the
new Prefect of the Seine upon
his appointment in June of
1853 is lost, but an 1867 map
given by the emperor to the
Prussian monarch William II
provides the best evidence of
the French emperor's own
involvement in redrawing
Paris's street network to
enhance circulation of
vehicles, goods, and
ultimately capital in a
modernized city.

cities as railway travel transported not only raw materials, finished
products, and labourers, but a new breed of urban consumers, the
tourists, across unprecedented distances. The hotel, designed by
Alfred Armand, was a project of the Pereire brothers, bankers and land
developers, who had launched their empire in the railway boom of the
1840s and snapped up most of the sites cleared by the state's expropria-
tions along the rue de Rivoli at preferential prices. Like Napoleon III
they were steeped in the Saint-Simonian ideology that remapping national territory and freeing up capital would not only modernize the
country but promote the general good.

Returning for the second Parisian 'Universal Exposition' in 1867,
visitors would be dazzled by the great elliptical building in which
Frédéric Le Play had brought the bounty of the world under the control of an ingenious organizational scheme. Radial axes were devoted
to different classes of manufactures, while the concentric rings of the
great glass and iron structure hosted displays of individual countries,
making taxonomic and national comparisons possible. The city, too,
with new radial roads connecting railway stations to the commercial
centre, gave the impression of being mastered by new standards of
order, cleanliness, efficiency, and beauty. Over 165 kilometres of new
streets—broad, straight, and furnished with pavements, drainage, gas
lighting, and newly planted trees—were punctuated by monumental
new churches, markets, and administrative buildings. With a six-fold
increase in private construction, apartment houses of unprecedented
refinement, of both exterior decorum and interior comfort, rapidly

lined the boulevards. The city that reformers dreamed of a century earlier [20] now breathed an air of progress so complete that even the municipal sewers were open for tours in specially designed wagons. The working classes had been largely chased from the centre, and thus from middle-class view, by escalating rents. It is estimated that over 350,000 Parisians were displaced in only 18 years.

By the time the Second Empire fell in 1870, nearly every major European capital—and many other cities which had swelled with industrialization and migrations from the countryside set in motion by railway networks—was being 'modernized' in rivalrous emulation. When the 1873 Universal Exhibition moved the spectacle of progress to Vienna, the Austrian capital was ready. The transformation of the old line of fortifications into a broad annular boulevard, the Ringstrasse, offered a model for other cities whose walls, effectively already breached by trains, were now to fall to the forces of development that the railway had unleashed. Increasing ten-fold the land area of Barcelona with a planned extension of gridded blocks, Ildefonso Cerdá coined the term 'urbanism' and authored the two-volume *General Theory of Urbanization* (1867), the first book to offer a body of theory, rather than simply a checklist of tasks, for designing cities. Cerdá's book had little influence outside his native Spain, however; the theory of nineteenth-century city building was encoded more in the language of contracts, bonds, and financial instruments that were the machines of the century's credit revolution. Alongside these invisible inventions, France's determination to remain a model of refinement—announced in the juxtaposition of fine arts and industry at the 1855 fair—succeeded so well that the image of the Parisian street and its architecture, both the grandiose buildings of state and the private architecture of the bourgeois apartment, joined the ranks of the city's luxury exports. By 1900 the prestige of French urbanity was international, imitated perhaps with even greater conviction in Bucharest or Buenos Aires, for instance, than among France's western European neighbours, as the École des

119 Eduard Baldus

The Louvre and Tuileries united, c.1855

Paris's transformation into a showplace of urban spatial order was circulated widely by the new technology of photography. At the Louvre the photographer Baldus was charged with recording the construction and photographing hundreds of plaster models considered for the rich sculptural decoration of this palace/museum complex which would celebrate Napoleon III's regime as a high point in the forward march of French culture.

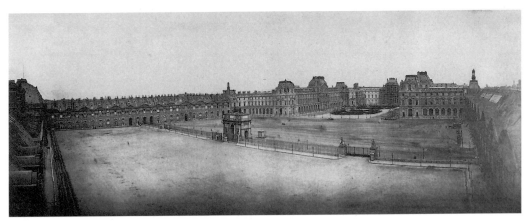

Beaux-Arts welcomed an ever greater flood of foreign students into its architectural ateliers.

Urban reform before Haussmann

Like the eclectic architectural imagery of Paris's new skyline, little in the formal repertoire of 'Haussmannism' was unprecedented, beyond the scale and breathtaking speed of the operation. Harmoniously ordered frontages of private dwellings forming geometrically aligned streets focused on a free-standing monument had been an ideal since the mid-eighteenth century [**19, 20, 61, 63**]. Parks as urban lungs and places for the moral improvement and distraction of the working classes from potential social unrest were lessons imbibed during Louis Napoleon's exile in London in the 1840s and imported to France in the wake of the 1848 Revolution. What was new was the sense that an urban whole, and with it a powerfully consistent visual form, could be infused into a city, with overlapping and well-functioning systems of circulation, leisure, and even sanitation. In the wake of the declaration of 1841 that the French rail system should rapidly connect Paris to all French borders, Paris was to be transformed by a network of streets, radiating from a series of *rond-points*, that would connect the ring of new railway stations to the centre and after 1860 integrate the annexed ring of industrializing villages around the city.

'Government is not a necessary ulcer', the future emperor declared in campaigning for election as President of the Republic in 1848. 'It is

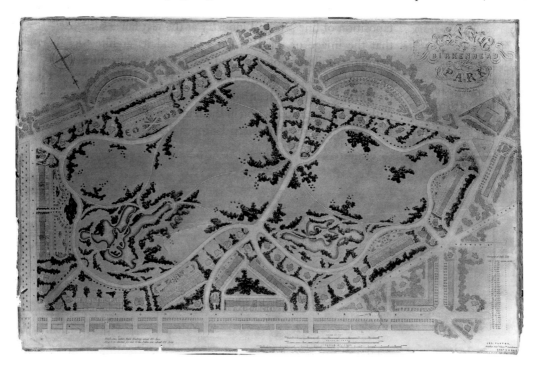

121 F.-A. Duquesny

Gare de l'Est, Paris, 1847–52
Duquesny's station design,
with its combination of a
masonry pediment and an
enormous glass lunette
announcing the round arched
span of the engineer Sérinet's
glass and iron shed behind,
was a very influential
interpretation of the railway
station as a modern portal to
the city. The monumental
scale of the lunette was
intended to dominate a major
axial boulevard connecting the
station to the heart of the city.

rather the beneficent motive of every social organism.'[1] Echoing Saint-Simonian understanding of the city as a veritable body, one indeed that could be cured, the statement also resounded with memories of devastating epidemics—19,000 had died in the 1848 outbreak of cholera—and of the barricades that had divided the city. London had shown the way, using street cuts such as New Oxford Street to clear slum districts while opening paths of circulation, in the wake of Edwin Chadwick's statistical study of the urban poor and of the Parliamentary Commission on the State of Large Towns and Populous Districts. Both reports declared a correlation between the health, and the morals, of the working classes and the physical environment of overcrowded speculative housing and insanitary streets. Legislation mandated minimum standards for dwellings in terms of sanitation, drainage, and ventilation, set up medical inspections, and launched campaigns of building urban sewers. Chadwick campaigned for public parks, while Engels's descriptions of the working-class slums of Manchester, soon seconded by the social realist literature of Dickens and others, made it impossible for the middle classes to ignore living conditions in working class-districts, even if their daily paths skirted direct confrontation with 'the other half'. In 1842 laws were passed allowing compulsory expropriation of unhealthy dwellings in the name of the greater public good. Two years later the municipality of Liverpool charged Paxton with laying out a spacious park in the working-class suburb of Birkenhead. On the site of a drained swamp, and bordered by houses, this adaptation of English picturesque gardens to public welfare was a direct response to the faith that nature was essential to urban health and a morally uplifting agent, a worthy rival in short to the temptations of the pub or the barricades [120].

In France the opening wedge for large-scale intervention in shaping cities was expropriation laws passed to facilitate laying out the railway, even if rail companies' desires to penetrate to the heart of the city were

122 Gabriel Veugny

Cité Napoléon, Paris,
1849–53

The architect Veugny's design
for sanitary workers' dwellings,
sponsored directly by Louis
Napoleon soon after his
election in December 1848,
was the first adaptation of the
utopian socialist ideals of a
phalanstry [**83**] to an existing
city. Its use of glass and iron
skylights to create an interior
street was innovative. Critics of
the regime claimed it put the
workers in barracks, viewed by
some as potentially explosive,
by others as disingenuously
philanthropic.

stopped short at the edge of the historic centres [**121**]. In the 1840s the
prefect Rambuteau responded to a debate over whether or not the government should intervene to arrest the westward migration of Paris's
commercial and financial centre. Since the mid-eighteenth century the
quagmire of narrow streets in the central market district, Les Halles,
had been discussed as the city's most pressing need [see **18**]. Now the
question was posed in larger political terms. Should the state or the
speculative market—and these were years in which economists such as
Jean-Baptiste Say were extolling Adam Smith's ideas of a free market as
a democratic and natural value—determine the form and destiny of the
city? Rambuteau launched a policy of using street improvements as an
instrument of the state's remodelling of urban space and its self-conscious channelling of private development. The street that today bears
his name was the forerunner of Haussmann's work a decade later, although by comparison with Second Empire boulevards it seems timid
in width and length. Not only did the rue Rambuteau markedly improve access to Les Halles, it was the first street in Paris to be festively
inaugurated and to sport an inscribed cornerstone—a symbolic threshold of the triumph of ordered open space created by the central power
over the marketplace's desire to build urban fabric to the maximum.

During the short-lived Second Republic, Louis Napoleon pursued a two-pronged policy of government-built workers' dwellings and legal and financial incentives to jump-start luxury real estate. The Cité Napoléon [**122**], intended as a prototype for public housing in each of Paris's administrative districts, offered a startlingly original prototype in which glass and iron skylights maximized air and light, even while iron gates, locked each evening, betrayed an overarching concern with reducing the threat of social unrest. But like the contemporary 'Model House for Families' in London, designed by Henry Roberts for the Society for Improving the Conditions of the Labouring Classes, supported by Prince Albert, it remained an isolated experiment. Until the twentieth century 'improved slum dwellings'—as they were called in Britain—would be the province of paternalistic entrepreneurs such as Sir Titus Salt at Saltaire near Bradford in Yorkshire (1851–76), the Krupps manufactory near Essen (1863–75), or the Meunier Chocolate Company at Noisel outside Paris (*c*.1874). After the declaration of the Empire in December 1852 and the dismissal months later of Berger, Haussmann's predecessor, for opposing debt-financed public works, Napoleon III and his advisers put their energies fully into crafting an alliance between the state and specially formed private land-holding and development companies. On the model of the Pereire brothers' company, formed to extend the rue de Rivoli, in which the state's and financiers' interests were mutually served by finely built ashlar masonry apartment houses, transformation was soon under way in the dense cores of Lyon, Marseille, and other provincial cities as well as Paris [**123**].

123 Adolphe Terris
(photographer)

Creation of the rue Impériale in Marseille

As cities throughout France were remodelled on the model of Haussmann's Paris, the works involved a massive reworking of the terrain. In Marseille a whole hill was levelled to create a broad and swift link between new steamship ports and the commercial centre of the city.

Launched under the banner of creating jobs—by the late 1850s one in five Parisians were working in the building trades—the system of floating loans against future increases in the value of improved land made Haussmann's works a veritable self-financing system of public works. In the 1860s, when liberal and legitimist opponents of the regime questioned the legality of these operations and the legislature annulled the state's right to retain the unredeveloped portions of expropriated properties, Napoleon III's advisers replied that the 'movement of capital … must be considered as the principal cause of the progress of public wealth in Paris'.[2] But critics had begun to link mushrooming shanty towns on the city's edge with the transformation of the centre of Paris into an elegant backdrop for the very moneyed classes who profited dramatically from urban transformation.

Remodelling Paris: the markets and the Rivoli–Strasbourg cross-axis

Napoleon III anticipated many of these criticisms. Even before the curtain was raised on the first of the boulevards that made movement a part of the urban aesthetic for the first time, the emperor demanded that work on the central markets be given priority over all the other new public buildings he hoped would leave the imprint of his regime on the cityscape [**124, 125**]. The 'Louvre of the People', as he called his vast rationalization of Paris's food supply, was the only major state project completed in time for the 1855 exhibition. In place of the labyrinth of outdoor markets in twisting streets little changed since the Middle Ages, Victor Baltard created a rationalized city within the city. Eight rectangular pavilions of glass and iron, maximizing ventilation and sanitation, were organized around a grid of broad covered streets, providing easy access for carts and pedestrians. Vaulted undercrofts were even provided in hopes of a connection to the main-line railway stations and

124 Victor Baltard

Les Halles, Paris, 1852–55

The new markets hummed with efficiency and order, their gridded internal streets poised as a model for the reshaping of the city beyond. Their frank industrial vocabulary provided a new model for utilitarian building in cities throughout Europe and for countless provincial markets in smaller French cities.

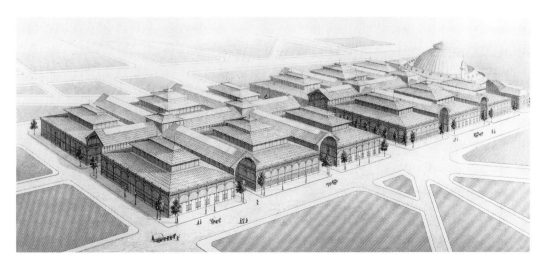

Unveiling of the Boulevard de Strasbourg, 1858 (today Sébastopol)

Haussmann later admitted that the path of the boulevard had not been determined solely by the axis of the Gare de l'Est, which it connected to the Ile de la Cité over two miles away: 'It was to tear open Old Paris, the district of the riots and barricades, by a wide, central thoroughfare which would pierce this almost impenetrable labyrinth from one side to the other.'

thus to a national network of goods. The whole was marvelled at by contemporaries; Zola even celebrated the newly ordered spectacle of abundance in his novel *Le Ventre de Paris*.

The Second Empire created not only a new alliance between the state and the market in crafting urban space and fostering an understanding of land itself as a commodity; it also negotiated a subtle hierarchy between the great monuments of the state and the residential fabric. Three years after Les Halles was completed, the façades of the Boulevard de Strasbourg (now Sébastopol) were unveiled [**125**] in a ceremony celebrating the dynamism of the private market in creating a harmonious backdrop to public monuments. The simplest legal guidelines governed the relation of façade height to the broad new street, the alignment of balconies, the set-back angle of the mansard roofs, and the use of fine stone on the principal façade [**126**]. These ensured that the work of numerous independent builders would yield those grand sweeping perspectives that endow even the least accomplished of the Second Empire's public buildings with a dramatic monumental presence. When one looks north on the Boulevard de Sébastopol, the trees shading the pavements provide a leafy frame to the vista of the Gare de l'Est, while to the south an even more theatrical view is staged. Unable to align the boulevard with a bridge across the Seine, Haussmann ordered the architect A.-W.-N Bailly, a pupil of Duban, to shift off-centre the crowning dome of his projected Tribunal de Commerce (1858–64) on the Ile de la Cité so that it might serve as a terminus to the vista which greets visitors alighting at the Gare de l'Est some two miles away. Nearly all the major monuments commissioned by the state would be shaped by such scenographic imperatives. At the head of the

Apartment house, rue de la
Chaussée d'Antin, *c.*1855
Apartment-house living had
been pioneered in Paris in the
eighteenth century, but under
the Second Empire it became
the building-block of a new
urban fabric. The ground floor
was let to shops, while the
apartments were arranged to
give even multiple dwellings
some of the allure of grand
living, from the monumentally
scaled *porte-cochère* to the
contrivance of principal rooms
en suite along the street
façade.

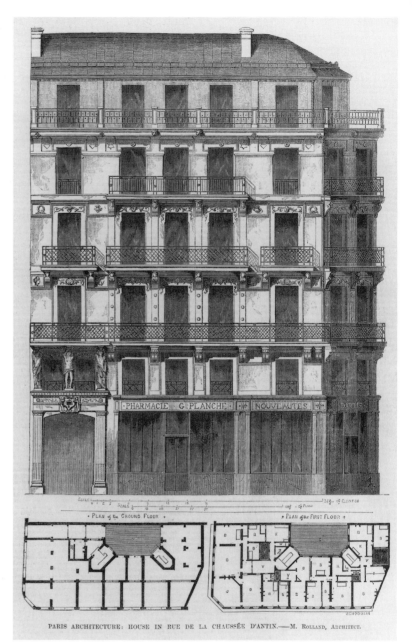

· PLAN of the GROUND FLOOR ·   · PLAN of the FIRST FLOOR ·

PARIS ARCHITECTURE: HOUSE IN RUE DE LA CHAUSSÉE D'ANTIN.—M. ROLLAND, ARCHITECT.

Boulevard de Magenta, Baltard exploited iron to maximize interior
space on one of the awkward polygonal building sites traced by
Haussmann's street network. The iron framework of the church of St-
Augustin (1860–71) is draped with a thin masonry envelope and supports a monumental dome scaled to the urban vista rather than to this
parish church for the luxury quarters developing in the city's north-
west. Gabriel Davioud's exuberant monumental fountain on the Place
St-Michel (1858–60) was calculated to close the vista on the Boulevard

du Palais which crosses the Ile de la Cité and to mask the angled departure of the Boulevard St-Michel, the left bank's grand new thoroughfare. The Boulevard St-Michel in turn was traced to align with a view of the newly recreated flèche of the Sainte-Chapelle. The Paris of postcards was emerging even as photography for the first time became inexpensive enough to compete on the souvenir market. A quip made a century earlier by Voltaire, that Paris would appear a grand city only once its historic monuments had been excavated from haphazard urban fabric, now guided the work of 'liberating' monuments from fabric as history came to reside in the monument, not the texture of the city. With the finishing touches of Alphand's carefully calibrated system of urban 'promenades'—a linked system of greenery on every scale, from single trees planted in traffic islands where boulevards cross to the replacement of the long straight paths of the Bois de Boulogne, a former hunting domain, with a picturesque pleasure-ground—Paris presented the image of the city as a scenic event, background, and destination for an expanding leisured class. Alphand's publication *The Promenades of Paris* (1867–73) detailed the inventions that made this possible, including special machines for transplanting mature trees, and provided models widely followed. It was the only text that set down something approaching a theory of Haussmannization.

Garnier's Opéra

The scenographic masterpiece of Haussmann's Paris, the luxury quarter of hotels, shops, clubs, and banks developed around the new Opéra (1862–75), was completed only after the curtain had fallen on the Second Empire at Sedan, the decisive battle of the Franco-Prussian War. Although Napoleon III would never appear in this building, calculated as a backdrop to his court, Charles Garnier (1825–98) orchestrated a microcosm of the values of an ascendant urban bourgeoisie that had come into its own during his reign [**117, 127**]. In 1869 Haussmann had been chased from the scene by the outcry over what Jules Ferry labelled 'Les Comtes Fantastiques d'Haussmann', a play both on the dual meaning of 'Comtes' in French—stories and accounts—and on Offenbach's popular opera *Contes d'Hoffmann* (*Tales of Hoffmann*).[3] Yet nothing testifies more to the durability of Haussmann's urban system than the harmonious relations—of scale, materials, and architectural language—of the urban archipelago of apartment, office, and hotel blocks, and the monumentally composed Beaux-Arts island of Garnier's Opéra. It was a model of urbanity imitated as much for its forms as its finances, a system ultimately eclipsed only after the First World War.

There is a fascinating counterpoint between the Opéra and the urban fabric, much of which was planned before Garnier's project was selected in 1861 in a particularly contested public competition. The sur-

rounding structures establish a new grand scale for the building-blocks of a city—products of the increasing power of the financial actors on the urban land market—even while they demurely take their place in the urban tissue. The identical pilastered façades of the two blocks that form the sides of the square in front of the Opéra offer not even a hint of the different functions behind—one an office building, the other a luxury hotel. Within its staid perimeter, the Grand Hotel, another creation of the Pereire–Armand team, contains several of the most luxurious and grandiose spaces of the Second Empire, all of them taking advantage of the spans made possible by an extensive iron frame completely hidden from view under limestone façades. The opera house, by contrast, is the consummate statement of the cherished principle of the École des Beaux-Arts that grand public buildings should be composed in both plan and elevation as lucid expressions of their component functions, set in a clear hierarchy. At the same time the plasticity of its handling, the high relief and gusto of its ornamental details, and Garnier's introduction of rich polychromy of coloured marbles, mosaics, and gilding, even on the exterior, represented for many a daring departure from academic decorum.

Seen from the opposite end of the broad Avenue de l'Opéra, cut to provide a processional approach from the Tuileries Palace and a connection to the St-Lazare station, gateway to the burgeoning western suburbs [127], the opera house is composed of three independent masses which build to a crescendo in the great pyramidal flyhouse housing stage machinery and crowned by a figure of Apollo. This beacon on the skyline—Apollo is also a lightning rod!—envelops the softer profile of the domed auditorium and the richly ornamented rectangular block of the foyer and stairhall, these scaled to closer vistas. Garnier's building is not simply a setting for opera; it is itself masterfully staged in urban space. The perspective is calculated so that the stagehouse and auditorium disappear from view as one enters the broad Place de l'Opéra. The square is no longer an enclosed space in the city, as in so many eighteenth-century squares, but the point of convergence of a whole series of broad avenues. Even as this space suggests a moment's repose, reinforced by the common cornice heights, new vistas open up towards the rotunda entrances on the Opéra's flanks and to grand buildings beyond—banks and department stores.

Garnier presented his design as the embodiment of an empirical and sensual approach to architecture in *The Theatre*, published in 1871 as construction resumed after the traumatic interlude of the Commune. But this polemical refusal of the rationalist call for material and structural expression of his one-time employer Viollet-le-Duc was anything but arbitrary. Garnier was adamant that iron should be exploited to create an architecture that allows free rein to the artist's imagination and his skill in making his architecture a vehicle for a society's dreams and fantasies. Arguing for the supremacy of the artist's eye and judgement, even taste, Garnier was none the less a perceptive student of human behaviour; his acuity might be envied even by practitioners of the new social sciences of the period, who hoped to theorize only after empirical observation. Like Semper's, Garnier's notion of architecture was grounded in a theory of representation, not however in the art of making but in the observation of the basic human pleasure in play-acting. 'Everything that happens in the world', he maintained, 'is but theatre and representation'.[4] Once again a primordial fire is postulated, but around this flame Garnier imagines social rituals taking form as an individual exploits the flame to create shadow pantomimes. Others gather around, first as an audience, gladly switching roles after a time. Despite the period's enormous progress in stage machinery, ventilation, gas lighting, and iron technology for construction—all of which could be marvelled at by professional visitors—for Garnier the fundamental and unchanging role of the architect was to accommodate society's pleasure in assuming roles and savouring spectacles, of seeing and being seen. If the avant-garde of the early twentieth century vilified the Opéra—Le Corbusier chief among them—it was because Garnier had catered to the status quo rather than using his art as an opening wedge for a better world.

128 Charles Garnier

Paris Opéra **a)** Sectional view
b) Exterior

Garnier's debt to Victor Louis's earlier staging of arrival and ascent at the Bordeaux theatre is clear [cf. **26**], but by the mid-nineteenth century the social spaces of circulation for intermission occupy fully as much space as the stagehouse and auditorium in this palace of representations. Garnier calculated separate paths for each class of users, but all converge in his grandiose stairhall.

Garnier imagined the building as both a functional and ritualistic accommodation of three classes of users [**128a, b**]. An elaborate pavilion was provided for the emperor, complete with a ramped carriage drive and a suite of lavish rooms for entertaining before progressing to the royal box, a trajectory that never crossed the path of other theatre-goers, although the emperor would never in fact appear there. For season-ticket subscribers and for those holding but an evening's ticket, Garnier provided separate spatial sequences. Subscribers could alight from their carriages at their own pavilion—pendant to the Imperial entrance—and make their way into an opulently ornamented circular space at the heart of the building—directly below the auditorium—reserved for their social exchanges. Glimpses of the main stairhall not only provided a rich view through layers of space—Garnier exploited the same principle throughout of wrapping each space of assembly with circulation space—but the reassurance of knowing the path ahead, a characteristically self-conscious psychological interpretation of the inherited logic of the academic art of planning. Mirrors on each of the columns not only exploited the flicker of the gas light as the first of the dazzling effects the art of architecture could contribute to the festivities, but also, as Garnier explained, allowed ladies to check their hair and dress one last time in the comfort of their own social class before stepping onto the stage of the great stairhall. There everyone would meet in the grand spectacle of arrival and during the promenades between acts, before returning to the places assigned them by ticket price.

'The auditorium seems to have been made for the staircase rather than the staircase for the auditorium … In this floor plan everything seems to have been sacrificed to introductions,' Viollet-le-Duc complained of Garnier's willingness to break the rules of academic composition, which demanded that the most important place receive the greatest opulence of decoration.[5] The auditorium seemed an anticlimax after the rich colours of an array of marbles and the layering of space and orchestration of oblique views that make the stairhall a veritable kaleidoscope of effects. But Garnier was unapologetic: 'the staircase *is* the Opéra, just as the Invalides is its cupola and Saint-Etienne du Mont its rood screen,' he replied.[6] He went on to say that the composition was only complete when it was filled with the splendour and movement of the crowd in full regalia. The test was not only the eye but also the body, for Garnier conceived a space in which architectural forms are in dialogue with the movement and sensations of an ambient visitor [**117, 129a, b**]. The design of the stairs themselves is characteristic of this approach. The lower steps swell gently outward to communicate subliminally the grandeur of the space and of the occasion. Midway up, the curvature is inverted as the steps now yield to the foot and endow the arrival on the landing before the portal to the finest seats, framed by marble caryatids, with an unhurried grace. The eighteenth-century art of sublimity is here on the threshold of the modern psychology of form. Garnier worked ceaselessly on site, testing with models of hundreds of works of sculpture, painting, and mosaic commissioned from leading artists—the sculptor Jean-Baptiste Carpeaux and the painter Paul Baudry among them—making adjustments of colour, scale, and angle to create a harmonious synthesis of effects.

Underneath its dazzling surface effects the opera house made skilful use of the latest technologies of iron construction—as the campaign of construction photography by Delamaet and Durandelle makes clear—but Garnier placed himself in bitter opposition to exposed iron, such as Viollet-le-Duc proposed for a modern French architecture [**114**]. 'I have a great fear of all definitive theories in the arts which are framed in an exclusivist manner,' he wrote, 'because if aesthetics becomes nothing more

than the execution of an over-reasoned formula, it will mark the death of imagination, the spontaneous, and even of the incorrect, which are not to be disdained in human creations.'[7] In later years he made himself a tireless campaigner for civic decorum over what he saw as a utilitarian threat to urban embellishment. He helped to organize the petition against Gustave Eiffel's great iron tower for the 1889 Universal Exposition and fought, unsuccessfully, to have Hector Guimard's art nouveau designs for cast-iron entrances to the new underground metropolitan railway replaced by stone monuments that could declare the city's commitment to the public sphere as a place of dignity and tradition.

A generation was trained at the Opéra, importing a new taste for colour, a sense of movement through space and tactile cues, and a quest for spatial richness in public space into the great flourishing of Beaux-Arts architecture in the final decades of the century. Paul Nénot, architect of the Sorbonne (1885–91), and Jean-Louis Pascal, who designed the masterful medical school at Bordeaux (1876–88), were among Garnier's assistants. The vast majority of theatres designed in the second half of the nineteenth century owe both their vigorous, even neo-Baroque, sense of form as well as their urban prominence in no small degree to the example of Haussmann and Garnier's collaboration. In addition to Garnier's own work on the festive Casino at Monte Carlo (1878–79), the building's exceptionally far-flung and long-lasting influence could be traced from the works of former assistants in the provinces, such as the theatres at Reims and Montpellier, to scaled-down adaptations from Cracow's Slowacki Theatre of 1893 (designed by Jan Zawiejski) to the opera at Constantin in French Algeria, and the Amazon Opera in Brazil.

The Viennese Ringstrasse

Emperor Franz Joseph's order to lay out a new city on the site of the fortifications ringing Vienna was carried out during decades of political and social transformation in the Habsburg Empire [130]. Even before an urban design competition focused international architectural attention on the Austrian capital in 1858, the sovereign had traced the outlines of a new alliance between market and crown. Land not set aside for new public institutions long needed by the city, a new opera house chief among them, or for much needed parks was to be sold for private development, the profits 'to establish a building fund … [to finance] public buildings and the transfer of such military facilities and buildings as are still necessary'.[8] With memories of the 1848 uprisings still fresh, efficient troop movements were, as in Paris, one of the advantages gained from the new broad, straight boulevards, connected to railway stations and new barracks. Laying the cornerstone of the first monument in 1856, the emperor also set the stage, unwittingly, for a fierce competition of values and power that was to play itself out through the style and placement of public buildings on the Ringstrasse, as the polygonal boulevard ringing the city's historic centre was soon called. Heinrich von Ferstel's design for a Neo-Gothic church to commemorate the emperor's fortune in escaping a Hungarian nationalist's bullet would be raised by public subscription as, in the emperor's words, 'a monument of patriotism and devotion of the people of Austria to the Imperial House' [130b]. By the time the building was completed 20 years later the Ringstrasse had become one of the last grand landscapes of stylistic eclecticism, with a Gothic city hall (1872–73), by Friedrich von Schmidt, asserting the rights of the municipality over the imperial prerogative to plan the national capital, Theophilus Hansen's Greek Parliament (1874–83), proclaiming the arrival of a legislative sharing of power as part of the constitution awarded the middle classes in 1866, and a grandly scaled Italian Renaissance university (1873–84) by Ferstel, evoking associations with the rise of secular humanist culture. Tellingly, as Carl Schorske has noted, these three landmarks of the ascendant liberal bourgeoisie were laid out on precisely the land still held in reserve in the first years of planning to serve as a military parade-ground.[9]

The Ringstrasse quickly emerged as the favoured setting for the new fluid relations between the rising strata of the bourgeoisie and the old aristocracy who mingled at the Opera (Siccardsburg and van der Null, 1861–69), the first building completed on the Ring, and the Burgtheater (Semper, 1874–88), and who enjoyed in both the wealth and the prestige

130 (page 258)

Vienna Ringstrasse, 1860
a) Plan
The creation of a new urban belt on the site of the fortifications and fire zone separating the old city centre and the suburbs which had grown up over the eighteenth century created a new kind of space of continuous movement and of the integration of a broad traffic artery, with planted parks and free-standing monumental public buildings.

b) View along the Ringstrasse, c.1888
The apotheosis of the nineteenth century's exploration of the associative value of historical style in giving form and meaning to the new institutions of the modern nation-state, the Ringstrasse juxtaposed a Grecian Parliament, northern Gothic Town Hall, a great Renaissance palazzo for the university, and a twin-towered Gothic church erected to commemorate a failed assassination attempt on Emperor Franz Joseph II.

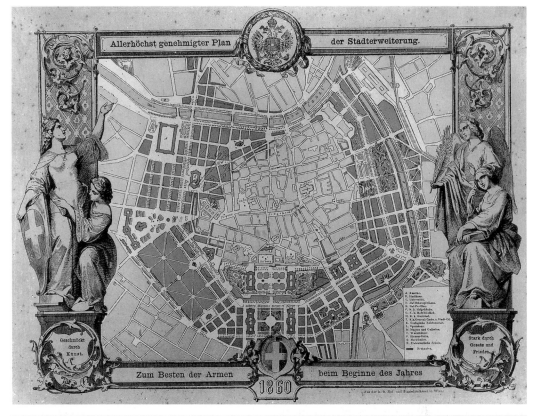

258 THE CITY TRANSFORMED, 1848-90

131 Semper

Project for the Museums district, Vienna, 1873

In this monumental project for expanding the palace and creating new museums of art and natural history, Semper was able to give form to his theory that monumental façades should be the theatrical backdrop to the rituals and institutions of urban life. The Renaissance for him coincided with the emergence of free city-states and bourgeois culture and he proposed it be further developed for modern times.

generated by the construction of the grand blocks of apartments that rose to share in the aura of the new cultural symbols. Significantly, the two theatres were the only buildings whose forms locked into the spatial flow of the boulevard itself, each designed with great loggias for promenading that took in at the same time privileged views of the urban spectacle on the boulevard. The other public buildings were set as free-standing monuments in the chain of parks developed at the new quarter's broadest points, coming into view sequentially and individually as one travelled along the 56-metre (184 ft)-wide boulevard, prototypes of the monument set in greenery which was to be repeated worldwide in coming decades as museums, opera houses, and administration buildings were connected with projects for tree-lined boulevards. One of the most innovative features of the road design was the provision of service roads for moving goods separately from the broad central roadway, left open for faster horse-drawn carriages and omnibuses.

By the time of the Universal Exposition in 1873 the Ringstrasse was a marvel of civic engineering, along with new quays along the Danube and a state-of-the art sewage network. On display at the Exposition were colossal renderings of a project of neo-imperial splendour that ran counter to the new model of urbanism emerging on the Ring [131].

Dissatisfied with the results of a limited competition for a museum complex to be placed just outside the old gate to the palace, Franz Joseph had called Semper from Zurich in 1869. Together with a young Viennese architect, Karl von Hasenauer, Semper drew up plans for a grand 'Culture Forum', in which a vast extension to the palace would be linked across the Ringstrasse by triumphal arches to the great domed blocks of pendant museums for art and natural history. Whereas in the 1840s, in projects for joining museum and opera house in Dresden, Semper had proposed to blur the distinction between court and city, in Vienna his forum was a revival of more traditional urban space defined by the great walls of buildings in counterpoint to the dynamic flow of the Ringstrasse. Even in its partially realized form, the verdant square between Vienna's museums offers a bounded space of stasis, and refocuses attention on the imperial Hofburg and on the great statue of Maria Theresa surrounded by major figures of the Austrian Enlightenment, a celebration of the partnership offered by the crown to the liberal bourgeoisie in the constitution of 1866.

Although Franz Joseph had set up a City Expansion Commission to oversee the building of the Ringstrasse, the discussion of the ideal form of a modern city sparked by the competition continued for decades, fostering the growth of the belief in German-speaking Europe after 1870 that city planning was a domain of professional knowledge. As the first building plots were being offered for sale, a controversy erupted over both the form of dwellings and the respective roles of marketplace and the state. Opposing the spread of the apartment house, already established as the form of middle-class dwelling in the dense inner city of Vienna, constrained for decades by its fortifications, architect Heinrich von Ferstel and art historian Rudolf von Eitelberger argued that the state should mandate the development of newly opened land with single-family houses set in gardens. 'The sale of these building sites should be undertaken with the interests of the community in mind ... The objective should be public welfare, and not short-term gains,' they argued.[10] Ironically enough they took their inspiration from speculative villa suburbs that had ringed London with the tentacular spread of the railway and the progressive separation of places of dwelling and work in middle-class life. While Ferstel succeeded in creating a 'cottage association' in 1872 and developed 300 homes in Vienna's Währing suburb, the market for luxury apartment houses prevailed, transforming much of the Ringstrasse into a dense quarter of majestically scaled middle-class apartment blocks [132]. These 'rental palaces' (Mietspaläste) borrowed the imagery of Vienna's Renaissance and Baroque palaces for façade details and such interior accoutrements as grand staircases even while floor plans tested architects' ingenuity in devising schemes to maximize the number of dwellings and profit on each site. Aesthetics and economics could not

132

Apartment houses on the
Reichsratstrasse, Vienna,
c.1875

The monumental façades of
the great 'rental palaces' gave
distinction to the apartment-
house blocks that filled the
plots opened up by the
Ringstrasse development. At
once dwelling and investment
for the middle class, who
enjoyed expanded political
representation in a
constitutional monarchy and
expanding economic power,
plans were invariably
contrived to place reception
rooms on the façade of the
building, making Ringstrasse
vistas a quantifiable
commodity.

be divorced, for the large-scale block responded not only to a speculative logic but allowed for the grandeur of imagery and scale that ensured maximum prestige and hence rental revenue. Plans invariably
placed reception rooms along the façade, making the Ringstrasse's vistas themselves a quantifiable commodity.

The Ensanche of Barcelona

By the time Barcelona's walls were razed in 1858, not only had the
Mediterranean port achieved the greatest population density of any
European city, but the urban crisis had inspired Ildefonso Cerdá
(1815–76), a trained architect and engineer, to devote his life and personal fortune to formulating a general theory of 'urbanization', which
he declared a new science. At first glance Cerdá's plan to decant the
enormous concentration of population, wealth, and commerce contained within Barcelona's defensive walls across the surrounding territory seems but an elaboration of those gridded cities the Spanish
empire had used to colonize the New World since the sixteenth century [**133**]. But for Cerdá the plan, with its superimposition of a great
diagonal cross-axis establishing a regional scale for a repeatable pattern
of city blocks with distinctive chamfered corners, embodied his notion
that it was possible to channel the forces of nineteenth-century speculative development towards a higher communitarian ideal, one indeed
formed in conscious critique of the Haussmannian model.

Arriving in Nîmes in June of 1844 Cerdá, employed as a civil engineer to improve Spain's roads, was overwhelmed by the sight of the
railway and the realization of the impact it was having on city and
countryside. It was as if in 'those long trains … whole errant populations had suddenly moved house'.[11] Cerdá dated his determination to

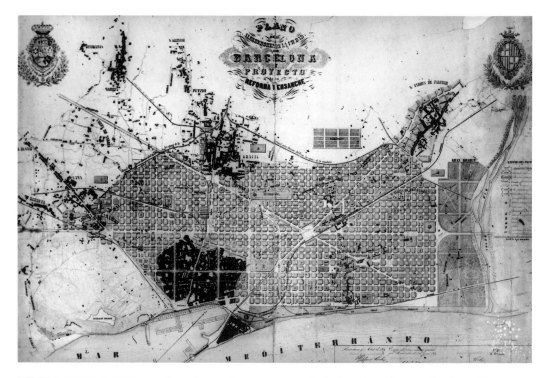

Ensanche of Barcelona, plan
as adopted in 1860

Cerdá conceived of all streets
as part of an endless
communication system,
insisting that all be straight
and equally wide. Individual
residential quarters were to be
the same throughout the city,
not only to accommodate all
social classes but to forge a
model of a city of infinite
expandability.

study cities to that moment, declaring that 'the application of steam as
a locomotive force marked for humanity the end of one era and the beginning of another'. He returned to Spain with the writings of Léonce
and Jean Reynaud, former Saint-Simonians who postulated that the
railway would promote the abolition of artificial boundaries, restructuring spatial relations in terms of networks of time and exchanges of
goods, and of the anarchist philosopher Pierre-Joseph Proudhon, who
had pronounced private property to be 'theft' when it was held by those
who did not work.[12]

Barcelona's port was booming with the arrival of the first commercial steam-ships even as the city's population had more than doubled in
a century within its walls. Cerdá joined his voice to growing popular
demand for demolishing the fortifications, whose only defenders by
mid-century were property-owners enjoying escalating rents on scarce
urban land. The social uprisings of July 1854 provided the final impetus
to convince the city fathers, who ordered the walls to be demolished
and agreed to organize a competition to solicit plans for city expansion
and beautification. Launched in 1858, but a few months after the an-
nouncement of Vienna's Ringstrasse competition, the Barcelona plan
attracted little attention outside Spain. But from the first the programme, as well as the proposed projects, was far more radical in responding to the request that the city be allowed to expand to its natural
topographical boundaries. Rather than designing an ideal urban quarter of monuments, contestants were invited to consider how planning

might be conceived as a process to last several generations. Cerdá did not enter the competition, but his lobbying in Madrid in favour of ideas he had long been formulating for his native Catalonia as a critique of what he viewed as the entrenched conservatism of local property-owners found support. His plan was adopted in 1860.

On lengthy visits to Paris between 1856 and 1858 Cerdá examined Haussmann's work with the same statistical completeness he had already applied to diagnosing Barcelona's ills, measuring street and pavement widths, noting distances between benches, trees, and even urinals. But although he was to be an advocate of an ideally dimensioned grid of spaces and services in the modern city, he insisted that a plan divorced of a social calculus could never serve more than the interests of a narrow class. 'No-one had even considered the question of providing comfortable accommodation for the great number of families who would be mercilessly evicted,' he complained of Haussmann's work, advocating in turn that planning a city must comprise both streets and houses.[13] 'The family house is an elementary city,' he noted, insisting that neither could be abandoned to the uncontrolled speculative market.[14] Cerdá imagined the city as an organism whose dynamic growth must be mastered rather than as an ideal form to be composed. Speaking of the city as Viollet-le-Duc was in those same years speaking of buildings, Cerdá introduced his *General Theory of Urbanization* with a promise: 'more than the materiality, I want to speak of the organism, the life, I should say, which animates the material city's material parts'.[15] Like any organism, a city is a constant interchange between principles of movement and stasis, terms that came both from his training in mechanical engineering and his readings in French positivist theory. Discussing the great square that Barcelona's city administration thought should serve as the link between the old town and the newly laid-out quarters, Cerdá proposed instead a grand railway station linking all lines at a single nodal point—a critique of the circle of individual stations that ringed Paris, London, and Vienna by the 1860s. Reflecting Jean Reynaud's idea of the city as a nodal point on a territorial grid, formulated in the Saint-Simonian *Encyclopédie Nouvelle* as early as the 1840s, the modern city would be a place of interchange in a world dissolved of borders and walls. At counterpoint to the streets as transportation corridors was the careful design of districts. With all blocks chamfered, the intersections of streets in Barcelona's plans provide places of assembly which Cerdá imagined as the community squares of the modern large city. In some places several blocks could be combined to form large public gardens— a correction of the grid introduced in these same years in the creation of Central Park in New York—but Cerdá's proposal was even more radical in that he proposed that each block be built on only two sides and then only with rows of houses no more than 24 metres (99 ft) deep; all the remaining area was to be developed as gardens, parks, or open space. The two rows could either be parallel or set at right angles, varied to create different patterns, introduce hierarchies of neighbourhoods, and create localized focal points around schools, churches, and market halls. In some cases, up to eight blocks might be combined to accommodate industry; but Cerdá condoned no radical separation of zones of work and living, as in the industrializing cities he had visited in France and England. While the formal aspects of Cerdá's plan served as models for other Spanish city 'expansions', including those of Madrid, Bilbao, and San Sebastian, even in Barcelona the market ultimately triumphed. City blocks were densely filled with apartment houses, mansions, and even blocks of flats for workers, all of which are closer to large-scale blocks of late nineteenth-century Berlin or Vienna than the controlled garden metropolis envisioned by Cerdá. By the time of his death in 1876 Cerdá was at work on a synthesis of his earlier theories of 'urbanization' and 'ruralization' into a global theory of national spatial planning, a veritable colonization of Spain's interior. This work served as a point of departure for the Madrid architect Arturo Soria y Mata's 1884 prototype of a linear city in which the new technologies of tram and train travel organized urban space in a model freed of traditional images of city form.

The rise of suburbs

In 1858 a 436-hectare site on the main route west from Paris to St-Germain was developed as a planned suburb, a veritable haven of domestic life from which most forms of trade and industry were banned. In emulation of the suburbs proliferating on the railway lines out of London, Le Vésinet [**134**] was a verdant nodal point on Paris's emerging suburban rail network. Around a small gridded 'village centre' with

---

The English suburb

The separation of middle-class residence from the commercial urban core was already characteristic of London's western and northern growth in the eighteenth century, but it was only in the nineteenth century that the suburb became associated with the aesthetic of free-standing buildings. J. C. Loudon became the most vociferous advocate of individual 'villas' of the type pioneered by Nash in the Park Villages [**62**] and Loudon's own 'semi-detached' villa at Porchester Terrace, Bayswater (1823–5), publishing numerous articles and handbooks, notably his widely used *The Suburban Gardener and Villa Companion* (1836–38). This appeared at the same time as the first railway lines out of central London began transforming patterns of the daily commute to work. Loudon believed that suburban life could accommodate both responsible citizenship and the crafting of a private universe set in the illusion of open nature. As Dyos and Reeder noted, 'the middle-class suburb was an ecological marvel. It gave access to the cheapest land … to those having most security of employment and leisure to afford the time and money spent travelling; it offered an arena for the manipulation of social distinctions … to those most adept at turning them into shapes on the ground …' ('Slums and Suburbs', in H. J. Dyos and Michael Wolff (eds), *The Victorian City: Images and Realities*, vol. 2, London, 1973, p. 369).

134

Panoramic view of the projected suburb at Le Vésinet, 1858

Minutes from St-Lazare railway station and all the modern urban functions around the Opéra, the nineteenth-century suburb was the dialectical opposite of the rationally planned city, set in a contrived nature which even obscured the boundaries of individual properties, although here houses sought a diversity in style and personality quite distinct from the anonymity of the Parisian apartment house.

church, market, and post office, ample house plots were laid out on curvilinear streets and set in picturesque landscape developed to create the illusion of living in ample countryside even while discreet hedges and garden walls denoted property lines. The first houses borrowed their imagery and forms from the French rural vernacular, especially the half-timbered Norman cottage destined for a long career in suburbs and seaside resorts, notably at Arcachon on the Atlantic coast, developed by the Pereire brothers in conjunction with new railway lines. The ideal of the suburb, pioneered by John Nash and others on the edge of London [62] around 1820, had its first heyday in direct connection with the dispersal and specialization of space made possible by new modes of transport. 'Villa quarters' rose on the fringes of nearly every European city, in particular in Germany where walls were progressively dismantled, as the setting of home life was increasingly distinguished from sectors of the city given over to the burgeoning world of the office, of places of entertainment, and of department stores—located on omnibus routes and near main-line stations—which drew customers from the city and beyond. New architectural types and the new distribution of urban activities went hand in hand in the nineteenth century.

Critics and the planned city

City modernization was codified as a 'science' in influential manuals by Reinhard Baumeister (*City Expansion in its Technical, Legal and Economic Aspects*, 1876) and Josef Stübben (*City Planning*, 1890), whose winning project in the 1880 competition to replan Cologne's former

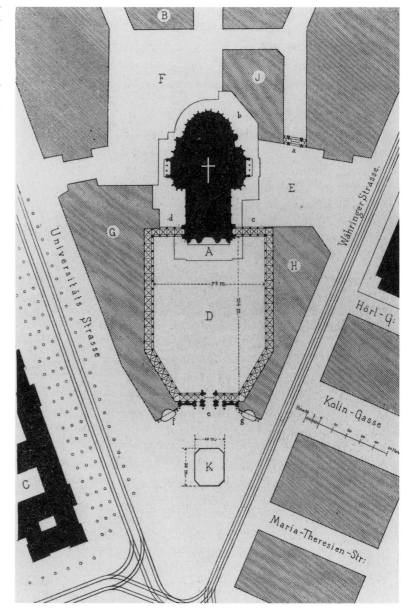

135 Camillo Sitte

Project for the transformation of the Votive Church Plaza, Vienna, from *City Building According to Artistic Principles* (1889)

To integrate free-standing monuments into the city fabric and to reform the vast open spaces of the Ringstrasse, Sitte drew up concrete proposals such as this one to flank the Votivkirche by lower buildings filling out to the street line and creating a sequence of outdoor spaces, including a great cloistered arcade.

fortifications led to a career in planning urban expansions in cities from Naples to Warsaw and Helsinki. Stübben praised Paris, noting that 'The city lies ... transparent before us ... it is just as easy to find one's way about as is a clearly designed house. This gives us a feeling of security and pleasantness ... something that the visitor in an unsystematically designed city will always miss.'[16] By then critics had launched an attack on the planned city, holding it responsible for that national and personal degeneration which became a common complaint of the *fin de siècle*. Scepticism of geometric order and regularity, already expressed in cartoons and spoofs on the monotony of Haussmann's works in the 1860s, found support in two influential works published at the height of nineteenth-century urban expansion, Camillo Sitte's *City Planning According to Artistic Principles* (Vienna, 1889) and Charles Buls's *The Aesthetic of Cities* (Brussels, 1893). Both the Viennese architect and the former mayor of Brussels—a city that had undergone a radical 'Haussmannization' in the 1860s and 1870s—attacked the systematic application of rational formulas in defence of the distinct artistic wholeness of individual cities as the work of time and generations. Sitte studied medieval and Baroque town plans throughout Europe, not to reform them but to learn their secrets, chief among them the idea of bounded and enclosed spaces as both aesthetically and psychologically more pleasing, and the appreciation of varied and unexpected viewpoints as adding interest and a sense of distinctive place. While he admitted that it was impossible to recreate in modern times what had grown up over time, he insisted none the less that public buildings and diverse functions should be integrated into the fabric of the town.

Sitte and Buls alike attacked architectural restoration in that spirit of Viollet-le-Duc which 'liberated' historical monuments from surrounding fabric, arguing that the fabric was as important to both memory and modern well-being as to individual monuments. While Sitte's visual categories are reminiscent of the English picturesque tradition, with its emphasis on the empirical, the originality of his work—and its resonance with contemporary concerns—was its preoccupation with the psychological resonance of urban space. Responding to theories formulated by the emerging field of psychology that the modern city posed dangers to the nervous state and mental health of its inhabitants, Sitte prescribed learning from historical cities, just as artists learned from nature, to make the new art of city building a therapeutic and restorative practice. For his native Vienna he even drew up proposals for restoring some of the qualities of close-knit, traditional urban fabric, scale, and thus sense of community to the Ringstrasse by adding additional building blocks to fill the voids and reconnect the monuments to the town and the individual [135]. Like Morris, Ruskin, and Webb in architecture, Sitte opened the debates on tradition and innovation, on art and community, and on the role of art in the psychic sense of the individual in society which were to be prominent themes of the art nouveau and the early modern movements.

The Crisis of Historicism, 1870–93

9

The cult of the monument vs the cultivation of the interior

An impassioned critique of historicist culture was voiced as early as 1874 by Friedrich Nietzsche, who diagnosed 'a malignant historical fervour' as one of the crippling symptoms of a modern culture burdened by archaeological erudition and faith in the laws of historical progression. In his seminal *The Use and Abuse of History*, the German philosopher described the loss of individual and communal subjectivity in the modern urban landscape of historical art and architecture in which man 'is turned into a restless, dilettante spectator'.[1] History had so permeated culture that it had overwhelmed 'the other spiritual powers, art and religion as the one sovereign'.[2] Nietzsche's prognosis was largely ignored in the renewed mandate to official art and architecture in the 1870s and 1880s to endow new political realities with the aura of tradition and permanence in the wake of political upheavals and wars which redrew the map of Europe after 1870. The unification of Italy and of Germany (which emerged as an industrial power to challenge the dualism of Britain and France), the strategic dispersal of power within the sprawling Habsburg Empire, and the struggles in France to erect the Third Republic on the debris of the Second Empire, would all enlist the existing arsenal of historicist architecture to fashion new bids for legitimacy.

Yet alongside an official architectural culture of escalating historical rhetoric, a series of new experiments was launched in domestic and commercial architecture which drew on new theories of art's potential to craft a realm for individual realization, a place even for an escape from those very masks of culture which Nietzsche decried as the character of public life in the century where historical consciousness had emptied individuals of subjectivity. The fervent experiments of avant-garde culture of the 1890s—experiments often described as the seedbed of modernism—had been anticipated in many ways in the 1870s and 1880s. Indeed, most of the salient features of the art nouveau had already been explored in the 1880s, from the wide-scale use of coloured glass and floriated decorative treatment of wrought and cast iron, notably in Paul Sédille's Printemps department store in Paris (1881), to the quest for a harmony of interior effects which broke down the distinctions between architecture and the decorative arts in the

136 Victor Horta

Tassel House, Brussels, stairhall, 1892

The daring celebration of iron in a domestic interior was accompanied by a new flowing conception of interior space. Space, light, decoration, and bodily movement through the house merged as rarely before. The 'whiplash' line, a signature of Belgian art nouveau, infused everything from wall painting to the design of light fixtures and structural iron, as Horta took up the idea of a total interior pioneered in England by Morris and his followers.

work of the English Arts and Crafts movement. What was new in the 1890s was a Europe-wide cult of youthful innovation, variously labelled 'Jugendstil' (youth style) in Germanic Central Europe, 'art nouveau' (new art) in France and Belgium, and 'Liberty' in Italy, where it evoked as much the political notion as an admiration for the Liberty store in London, a shrine of the Arts and Crafts movement and William Morris's philosophy which was to be a building-block of that anti-academicism and anti-historicism which grounded the art nouveau as a protest movement against the status quo.

Urban landmarks and the rhetoric of legitimacy

Europe's capitals were more than ever the arena of conflicting values played out in the built landscape of cities. In France, the political stand-off between secular and religious parties which characterized the return to parliamentary rule under the Third Republic after 1872 was emblazoned by 1889 in the Parisian skyline. The slowly rising domes of architect Paul Abadie's Sacre-Coeur atop Montmartre, a glistening white monument of expiation by which the Catholic church hoped to induce atonement for the materialist decades of the Second Empire, competed with the towering 300-metre (984 ft)-high pinnacle of iron erected with breathtaking rapidity by the engineer/builder Gustave Eiffel—the centrepiece of the Universal Exposition of 1889, the centenary of the French Revolution[137a]. The tower was decried by many as a crude work of engineering that broke the harmonious equilibrium of Haussmann's urbanism—notably by Charles Garnier, who spearheaded the campaign of artists and intellectuals against the 'useless and monstrous' tower 'unwanted even by commercial America'[3]—even as its state sponsors and the republican left celebrated it as a veritable crucifix of the secular faith in technological progress. Some even characterized it as the first embodiment of a new art, an 'art nouveau', echoing Eiffel's own claims that he had allowed forms without precedent to emerge from the demands and possibilities of construction in undisguised iron. Unlike the Sacre-Coeur, which skilfully combined a multitude of stylistic references to the past to imply that a medieval matrix of styles could sponsor a modern style, the great iron tower was freed from all references to the past, its forms determined uniquely by lines of tension, compression, and wind resistance.

No less a monument to the capacity of positive engineering science to rival history was the great hall of machines which stood next to the tower on the 1889 fairground. Ferdinand Dutert and Victor Contamin's Galerie des Machines offered with the broadest span yet achieved in iron construction not only proof positive of the Exposition Universelle's mandate to celebrate a century of progress since the French Revolution, but a sublime spatial experience that rivalled the Crystal Palace of 1851. Yet while historians of modernism

137
View of the Exposition
Universelle, 1889, Paris
a) *previous page*, the Eiffel
Tower **b)** The Palais des Beaux
Arts
Centrepiece of the 1889
World's Fair, Eiffel's tower's
original function to
commemorate the centenary
of the French Revolution soon
gave way to a host of other
messages, from celebrating
French economic and
technical achievement to
advertising Eiffel's own
company. Formigé's Palace,
with its rich polychromatic
effects achieved by exhibiting
a palette of other industrial
materials, most notably
ceramic tile, was to have a
more immediate impact on
public building.

long ago extracted these buildings from their context as landmarks in
the rise of a modern architecture freed from nostalgia and incorporat-
ing the daring of engineering developments, the 1880s and 1890s were
much more affected by architectural innovations in a host of other
buildings on the fairground. Jules Formigé's Palace of the Fine Arts,
which combined a metallic frame with a colourful mixture of materials, including polychrome brick and glazed terracotta, offered a hybrid palette which combined industrial progress with the Semperian
notion that architectural meaning could derive from a modern 'dressing' of structure and was more suggestive for integration in a host of
new urban building demands [**137b**].

Schools and the ideal of secular municipal administration

In less festive interpretations this vocabulary of mixed materials served as
the architectural grammar of the school-building programme launched
by the Third Republic, and even exercised a great influence on American
architects who were just then devising the first 'curtain walls' for enclosing the iron framework of commercial office buildings. While this
colourful palette would influence a new generation of commercial structures in France, its most visible application came in the hundreds of
schools which, by 1900, had transformed the daily landscape of cities and
villages across France. The passage in 1882 of the law requiring universal
secular education (the *Loi Ferry*, after the minister Jules Ferry) gave a
new focus to the rationalist programme of Viollet-le-Duc's disciples,

Even before state law required universal secular education, Viollet-le-Duc's followers had defined a new vocabulary for the school-building programme of the city of Paris. Narjoux, whose publications of municipal buildings ensured an international influence for French utilitarian architecture, created this dramatic sectional perspective to celebrate the maximization of light and ventilation in buildings clad with thin, sheer piers of polychromatic brick, punctuated with windows, and opened by ample structural iron.

who quickly made the ubiquitous schoolhouse with its clear conjugation of materials and construction into a triumphant expression of the secular democratic spirit of the industrial age, a fulfilment in a sense of the programme announced a half-century earlier by Saint-Simonianism (see chapter 6) [**138**].

France was not alone: programmes of school construction announced the triumph of secular and rational municipal administration in London, where by 1895 over 400 schools had been built in response to the Elementary Education Act of 1870, and Berlin, where the rational style of Schinkel's Bauakademie was adapted to provide elementary and secondary schools as well as a host of other municipal utilities with the stamp of rationality that heralded a new conception of government as a progressive force. In London E. R. Robson, architect to the School Board, adopted both the flexible stylistic language of the 'Queen Anne', pioneered in house architecture by Richard Norman Shaw and W. E. Nesfield, and its progressive associations. A major component of what came, by the end of the century, to be called the 'free style' on account of its relaxed attitude towards historical precedent and its celebration of individual sensibility, the Queen Anne style had been associated with progressive social attitudes first in Shaw's designs of the garden suburb of Bedford Park (1877–80) and then through its use for Cambridge's first women's college, Newnham College by Basil Champneys (1874–1910).

Public architecture in newer nations

Ideological battles between architecture as the instrument of a national consensus and a vision of the state as rational provider gave new potency to historical architectural styles in shaping the national agenda, particularly in politically 'young' countries where stylistic choices not

139 Giuseppe Sacconi

Rome, Monument to Victor Emmanuel II, 1884

The veritable embodiment of bombastic state representation, Sacconi's monument to the young Italian state's concern to assert the antiquity of its culture would rapidly become the target of avant-garde critiques. For Le Corbusier this modern Classicism—'the horrors of Rome' he called it in his seminal *Towards a New Architecture* of 1923—was a parody of the original.

only involved an editorial choice about the past, but offered a bid to suppress rival presents. After the capital of the new Italian state was moved from Florence—its role as capital from 1865 to 1870 coincided with extensive works of urban renewal—to Rome, the Italian architectural profession's energies were focused on crafting monumental images of the secular state to rival traditional Christian symbols. At the same time architects responded to the imperative to help craft a national identity from a mosaic of regional cultures; many adopted the notion that all of Italy shared a heritage of '*Romanità*' or Romanness, giving monumental Neoclassicism a new impulse. Great publicity surrounded the open competitions for a new Palace of Justice (1883) to be raised on a marshy site on the banks of the Tiber and a national monument to Victor Emmanuel (1882 and 1884) [**139**] on the edge of the Forum, both intended as secular rallying points for a new Italian consensus and as elements on the Roman skyline which could rival the prominence of the dome of St Peter's. Alternative views which looked to the medieval past were offered by architects such as Camillo Boito in Lombardy and the Veneto and Alfredo d'Andrade in Piedmont, but their styles soon took on the aura of regionalist rebuttals to the centralization of state culture and imagery in the Roman capital.

The closing decades of the century bore witness to numerous ambitious projects for central courts and national museums, aimed at providing highly visible institutions to focus national identity around the secular activities of justice and culture. Few efforts to secularize the cityscape could rival Joseph Poelaert's Palace of Justice (1866–83), which reorganized the cityscape of Brussels and responded to the efforts of Belgian politicians to foster a workable unity of Flemish and Walloon populations. Poelaert gave a brilliant personal and emotive interpretation of the official preference for a monumental Classicism, a style which deftly sidestepped the ongoing debates over national style, with partisans of Gothic and Renaissance pasts, in this young country where historical narrative was too easily partisan. In newly united Germany, Ludwig Hoffmann and Paul Dybwad's National Law Courts in Leipzig (1887–95) took up the monumental Classicism introduced with Paul Wallot's Berlin Reichstag as a style that could likewise transcend local traditions to forge a national cosmopolitan imagery. A contrary approach was pursued in the Amsterdam Rijksmuseum (1876–85), whose architect P. J. H. Cuypers, one of the most rigorous and inventive of Viollet-le-Duc's disciples, turned to the Dutch Renaissance for a stylistic matrix, evoking a period when national greatness and identity had first come to fruition. This refusal of both the Gothic and Classical Revivals in the first monumental building to rise in Amsterdam for centuries offered a monumental secular imagery that sidestepped troubling rifts between Protestants and Catholics. Style in this period, when regional identities were in rising tension with centralizing efforts, could be as much an instrument of diplomacy and consensus-building, such enterprises suggested, as of overt political dominance.

Stylistic rhetoric and the rise of advertising

By the end of the century it was not only national consensus that was being pursued through stylistic signs and historical associations in architecture. Business and industry also began to assert claims through the manipulation of architectural imagery, exploiting the urban prominence of buildings such as factories and warehouses with a nascent sense of advertising. It is no coincidence that the 1880s and 1890s, associated with the heyday of graphic invention in posters and handbills—one of the media that ensured the rapid dissemination of the fashion for the art nouveau after 1893—also gave birth to some of the most memorable uses of stylistic imaging for commercial architecture. Orientalizing architecture, with its rich colours and exotic forms of Moorish and Arab derivation, had long been exploited to connote luxury, notably in the famous engine-house for the waterworks at Sanssouci in Potsdam (1841–42) by Schinkel's pupil Ludwig Persius, where the smokestack is treated as a monumental minaret set at the cusp between the Classical town and the picturesque gardens of the royal domain. By the late nineteenth century even factories, long governed by a pragmatic utilitarianism, adopted historicist strategies for the economic potential of image recognition and salesmanship.

140

Templeton's Carpet Factory in Glasgow, 1889–92

By the 1890s the exotic languages of an expanded knowledge of world architecture was co-opted by the burgeoning art of advertising. Here references to the near east and Byzantium are used to connote the luxury of modern carpets.

Examples are particularly to be found in breweries, distilleries, and tobacco factories, where buildings served as advertising not only in the landscape but as images on product labels. In France vineyards built Revivalist châteaux to figure on bottle labels and give the aura of pedigree and antiquity as architecture became a medium of vintage! But few buildings are more spectacular in this regard than Templeton's Carpet Factory in Glasgow (1889–92) with its exuberant colour and jagged skyline and reminiscences of the Doge's Palace in Venice and the newly discovered polychromy of Assyrian and Persian architecture [140]. Here the wall as carpet was not so much a homage to Semper's theory of the textile origins of architectural ornament as an advertisement for the oriental origins of luxurious carpets! By the end of the century historical reference, on the wane in the world of official representation, was enjoying a renaissance in commercial architecture, where the period's exploration of the capacity of architecture to affect human behaviour was now to be exploited more for profit than for social engineering or national identity. Belatedly architecture joined the arsenal of the burgeoning art of advertising, which quickly exploited even the newest findings of the young field of visual psychology to fine-tune its message and appeal.

The domestic realm and the refuge of the psyche

One of the most salient shifts in the entire discussion of architecture in the decades after 1870 was a growing interest in exploring the psychology of form through the new disciplines of experimental neurological medicine and psychology. While late eighteenth-century sensationalist ideas (see chapter 3) were common currency by the early nineteenth century, the relation of form to states of mind was given a whole new emphasis and scientific grounding at the end of the century in two widely diverging areas. One was the rise of medical research on the nervous system, which allowed an increasingly direct correlation between external stimuli and the physical and emotional reactions of human subjects; the other was the emergence of empathy, and by 1890 Gestalt psychology, as a pursuit of aesthetic theory, particularly in Germany where a scientific basis for aesthetic judgement became a predominant concern of philosophical inquiry. Something of the renewal of interest in Baroque architecture in the 1880s and 1890s, particularly in southern Germany and Austria, must be attributed to the explorations by Robert Vischer, Heinrich Wölfflin, and others of the emotive powers of Baroque movement and space in a series of widely read works. Perhaps most suggestive of all was the theory that space rather than style was the fundamental link between the formal qualities of architecture and the overall character of any given moment in civilization. Whereas eighteenth-century sensationalism rapidly came to serve as a support for exploring the persuasive power of public buildings and for the discourse on reformative institutions, the emergence of modern physiological study coincided with a whole new attention to the realm of the private interior as a necessary retreat from the pressures of public life in the overlapping social, religious, and cultural discourses of the closing decades of the nineteenth century.

In France the public lectures of Jean-Martin Charcot at the Salpêtrière Hospital in the 1880s gave broad currency to concepts of individual and even national nervous health. The theory that the sensory overstimulation of the modern metropolis was a factor in the widely discussed fears of national degeneration, particularly acute in France in the wake of the Paris Commune and the defeat at the hands of the Prussians, was countered by proposals that the private interior should—as Deborah Silverman has argued in an innovative study of the origins of art nouveau design—'take on a new role as a soothing anaesthetizer of the citizen's overwrought nerves'.[4] Reinforced by the discourses on individuality as a means of achieving personal freedom in a modern society, the conception of the domestic interior was transformed in but a few years from a place primarily to assert status or historical ancestry—of the type pioneered in the eighteenth century by Walpole—to a place expressing personal feeling and fulfilment. In parallel, architectural history itself began to shift its focus from the history of church design as the paradigm for stylistic development to a fascination with the house as the most accurate mirror of the social development of specific cultures. Tinged with colonial discourses, this would inform the displays of ethnographic villages and panoramas of the history of human habitation that were among the most popular displays at the World's Fairs at the end of the century, notably the street of nations designed by Garnier in 1889 in the shadow of the very Eiffel Tower he reviled. By the 1890s developments in house design, in particular the innovations both technical and stylistic in the country and city houses of Shaw, Webb, Lethaby, and other 'free-style' practitioners in Britain, were to be singled out as the forerunners of a critique of reigning historicism. For Hermann Muthesius, an outspoken critic of official architectural culture in Germany, writing in *The English House* (1904), the English house offered not only a model for reforming the interiors and lifestyles of individual Germans, but a veritable paradigm of a new way of thinking about architecture that could break the pattern of historicist thought Nietzsche had so potently criticized in *The Use and Abuse of History*. The stage for the modern movement's preoccupation with the domestic realm as the true field for exploring the nature of modern consciousness, as well as its profound distrust of public architecture as an increasingly hollow exercise in rhetoric, was set. Its first great flourish came in the interiors of Antonio Gaudí in Barcelona, of Victor Horta and Henri van de Velde in Brussels, the early work of Hector Guimard in Paris, and by the end of the century the first designs of Josef Maria Olbrich in Vienna and of Charles Rennie Mackintosh in Glasgow.

Paradoxically it was the great publicity given to the freedom from convention in private interiors such as Horta's Tassel House of 1892, often seen as the veritable threshold of the art nouveau, that allowed architecture seen only by invited guests to be celebrated almost overnight as the makings of the first modern art with true freedom from historical reference. Behind an extraordinarily discreet façade, Horta exploited the technology of glass and iron construction he had learned from the great greenhouse structures built for the royal family at Laaken in the 1880s by his master, Alphonse Balat, to create an interior of unprecedented spatial fluidity. Here was a celebration of the fact that even within metropolitan conventions the individual psyche could be unleashed in the world of the interior. The famous staircase [136] revealed both Horta's willingness to free the imagination and to pursue the cues offered by such mentors as Viollet-le-Duc about the search for a new organic style. The tensile strength of iron is for the first time given an iconographical expression in Horta's combination of cast and wrought iron to *express* the fluidity of iron; and the whiplash line points to the numerous calls for architects to study the underlying generative principles of nature so that an architecture might be found that is at once freed from historic precedent and tied to a larger order.

Art nouveau's heyday lasted a scant 10 years, between Horta's Tassel House of 1892 in Brussels and the Turin World's Fair of 1902, in which the excesses of art nouveau ornament were broadly criticized. But it proved immensely popular and represented the first architectural style without historical precedent.

Earlier architects had turned to nature for inspiration, notably Ruskin's followers, but art nouveau architects took interest in the organic world of form as a principle of both structural form and spatial design. Viollet-le-Duc was another major source of inspiration, and accounts for many architects' celebration of revealed construction in exposed ironwork. The whiplash line was a superficial sign of style that could be traced from poster and book design in the 1880s to the decoration of Horta's houses in the early 1890s to furniture design, but more important was a shared set of principles and attitudes which infused even work whose rectilinear and abstract geometric exploration seem at odds with the organic. Charles Rennie Mackintosh was a pioneer in this regard, soon followed by the Viennese Secessionists. Mackintosh's Glasgow School of Art (1896) was tinged still with elements of the Scottish baronial tradition, evidence too that art nouveau often merged with elements of regionalism and national Romanticism. In Hungary and Poland, for instance, art nouveau quickly incorporated elements of a revival of interest in folk culture.

Art nouveau was a short-lived fashion, its forms exhausted within a decade by their commercial overexposure and aesthetic reaction. Yet this vibrant movement forms a bridge to the twentieth century, when the legacy of nineteenth-century design theory mingles with the culture of the avant-garde desire to celebrate a break with tradition. By the late 1890s the domestic interior had emerged paradoxically enough as a prime focus of public debate on the relationship between environment and modern consciousness, and it was here that art nouveau was to make its greatest challenges to convention.

Notes

Introduction

1. Nikolaus Pevsner, *Pioneers of the Modern Movement from William Morris to Walter Gropius* (1936); Sigfried Giedion, *Space, Time, and Architecture* (1941); and Emil Kaufman, *Von Ledoux bis Le Corbusier* (1933) and *Architecture in the Age of Reason* (1955).

Chapter 1

1. Marc-Antoine Laugier, *An Essay on Architecture* (2nd edn, 1755), trans. by Wolfgang and Anni Herrmann. Los Angeles: Hennessey & Ingalls, Inc., 1977, p. 12.
2. *Ibid.*
3. *Ibid.*, p. 19.
4. *Ibid.*, p. 8.
5. J. J. Winckelmann, *Reflections on the Imitation of the Painting and Sculpture of the Greeks*, published in Gert Schiff (ed.), *German Essays on Art History*. New York: Continuum Publishing Co., 1988, p. 1. This is my correction of the translation offered in this useful anthology. The full complexity of this quotation, with its play on imitation and inimitable, has rarely been commented upon.
6. J. B. Leroy, *Ruines des plus beaux monuments de la Grèce*, 2nd edn. Paris, 1770, p. v.
7. G. B. Piranesi, *Diverse maniere d'adornare i cammini ed ogni altra parte degli edifizi*. Rome, 1769.
8. Maximilien Brébion to Ch. Cl. de Flahaut de la Billardie, Comte d'Angiviller, 20 October, 1780, Paris, Archives Nationales O¹ 1694.
9. J. B. Leroy, *Histoire de la disposition et des formes différentes que les chrétiens ont données à leur temples*. Paris, 1764, p. 57.
10. From a letter from Adam to his family, 13 February 1755, quoted by John Fleming, *Robert Adam and His Circle in Edinburgh and Rome*. Cambridge, Mass.: Harvard University Press, 1962, p. 140.
11. Robert and James Adam, *Works in Architecture of Robert and James Adam*. London, 1773, p. 1.

Chapter 2

1. J.-F. Blondel, *De la distribution des maisons de plaisance, et de la décoration des édifices en général*. Paris, 1737, vol. 1, preface, p. iii.
2. Jürgen Habermas, *The Structural Transformation of the Public Sphere*. Cambridge, Mass., 1989, p. xi.
3. Pierre Patte, *Monuments érigés en France à la gloire de Louis XV*. Paris, 1765, p. 198.
4. Voltaire, 'Des Embellissements de Paris' (1749) in *Oeuvres de Voltaire*. Paris, 1830, vol. 29, pp. 99–111.
5. La Font de Saint-Yenne, *À l'ombre du grand Colbert*. Paris, 1751.
6. Barry Bergdoll, 'Un amphithéâtre pour Sainte-Geneviève', in Michel Le Moël (ed.), *L'Urbanisme Parisien au siècle des lumières*. Paris, 1997, pp. 152–61.
7. Laugier, *Essay on Architecture*. Paris, 1753. Trans. by Wolfgang and Anni Herrmann, 1977, p. 121.
8. Laugier, *Observations sur l'architecture*. Paris, 1765, p. 229.
9. John Gwynn, *London and Westminster Improved ...* London, 1766, p. 3.
10. *Ibid.*, p. 20.
11. *Ibid.*, p. 61.
12. Quoted in José-Augusto Franco, *Une ville des Lumières, la Lisbonne de Pombal*. Paris, 1965, pp. 229–30.
13. *Entretiens sur le fils naturel*. Paris, 1757. See for a commentary Jay Caplain in Denis Hollier (ed.), *A New History of French Literature*. Cambridge, Mass., 1989, pp. 471–766.
14. *Mercure de France*, cited in Henri Lagavre, 'Le Grand-Théâtre de Bordeaux devant l'opinion (1772–1785)', *Victor Louis et le théâtre*. Paris, 1982, pp. 48–9.
15. Jean-Louis de Cordemoy, *Nouveau traité de toute l'architecture ...* Paris, 1714.
16. Joseph Baretti, *A Guide through the Royal Academy*. London, 1781, p. 3.
17. John Newman, 'Somerset House and other Public Buildings', in John Harris and Michael Snodin (eds), *Sir William Chambers, Architect*

to George III. London, 1996, p. 114.

18. Quoted by John Newman, 'Somerset House' (1996), p. 118. On the use of the puff by Wedgwood and its development as a commercial strategy see Neil McKindrick et al., *The Birth of Consumer Society: The Commercialization of Eighteenth Century England.* London, 1982.

19. Robert Pool and John Cash, *Views of Dublin,* 1780, p. 12; quoted in E. MacPaland, *James Gandon, Vitruvius Hibernicus.* London: Zwemmer, 1985, p. 33.

Chapter 3

1. William Hogarth, *An Analysis of Beauty.* London, 1754. See Matthew Craske, *Art in Europe, 1700–1830.* Oxford, 1997.

2. Jean-Marie Morel, *Théorie des Jardins.* Paris, 1776.

3. Joseph Spence, *Anecdotes, Observations, and characters of books and men.* London, 1820; quoted in Kenneth Woodbridge, *The Stourhead Landscape.* London: The National Trust, 1978, p. 15.

4. Quoted in Caisse Nationale des Monuments Historiques et des Sites, *Jardins en France, 1760–1820.* Paris, 1978, p. 77.

5. Étienne-Louis Boullée, *Architecture, Essay on Art,* trans. by Helen Rosenau, *Boullée and Visionary Architecture.* London: Academy Editions, 1976, p. 107.

6. Boullée, *Architecture,* Rosenau edn (1976), pp. 73–4.

7. *Ibid.,* p. 86.

8. J.-F. Blondel, *Cours d'architecture.* Paris, 1771–77, I: 426–7, see also II: 626–7.

9. G. de Mably, *De la léglislation.* Paris, 1776, Book 3, p. 97; cited in R. Middleton, 'Sickness, Madness, and Crime as the Grounds of Form', *AA Files* 24 (1992), p. 24.

10. Pierre Cabanis, *Observations sur les Hôpitaux,* Paris, 1790.

11. Quoted in A. Vidler, *Claude-Nicolas Ledoux, Architecture and Social Reform at the End of the Ancien Régime.* Cambridge, Mass., 1990, p. 32.

12. *Ibid.,* p. 95.

13. For an illustration see Matthew Craske, *Art in Europe* (1997), fig. 106.

Chapter 4

1. Abbé Henri Grégoire in Corps législatif, *Rapport fait au Conseil des Cinque-Cents, sur les sceaux de la République, par Grégoire: Séance du 11 pluviôse an IV.*

2. Armand-Guy Kersaint, *Discours sur les monuments publics prononcé au Conseil du Département de Paris, le 15 décembre 1791 …*

(Paris, 1791), p. 1.

3. Rousseau, *Letter to d'Alembert on the Theatre* (1758), here cited trans. by James Leith, *Space and Revolution, Projects for Monuments, Squares, and Public Buildings in France, 1789–1799.* Montreal, 1991, p. 36.

4. A.-L.-T. Vaudoyer, *Idées d'un citoyen françois sur le lieu destiné à la sépulture des hommes illustres de la France.* Paris, 1791.

5. A.-C. Quatremère de Quincy, 'Character', as translated in 'Extracts from the *Encyclopédie Méthodique d'Architecture,* Antoine-Chrysostome Quatremère de Quincy, 1755–1849', in *9H 7* (1985), p. 34.

6. A.-C. Quatremère de Quincy, *Rapport fait au Directoire du Département de Paris, sur le dernier compte rendu de 17 novembre 1792, et sur l'état actuel du monument le deuxième jour du second mois de l'an II.* Paris, 1793, pp. 76–7.

7. J.-N.-L. Durand, *Précis des leçons données …* Paris, 1802, vol. 1, p. 18.

8. See John Brewer, *The Sinews of Power: War, Money and the English State 1688–1783.* London, 1989.

9. Martin Daunton, 'London and the World', in Celina Fox (ed.), *London—World City, 1800–1840.* New Haven: Yale University Press, 1992, p. 21.

10. Sir Francis Baring, *Observations on the Establishment of the Bank of England and on the Paper Circulation of the Country.* London, 1797, reprint New York, 1967, p. 42; Adam Smith, *The Wealth of Nations,* 1776.

11. These were probably derived from Raventine construction which Soane might have known from the publication by Ciampini, or later Seroux d'Agincourt.

12. Sir John Summerson, 'Soane: the Man and the Style', in *John Soane.* London: Architectural Design Monographs, 1983, p. 9; adapted from Summerson's *Sir John Soane,* London, 1952.

13. See Uvedale Price, *An Essay on the Picturesque,* Richard Payne Knight, *The Landscape,* and Humphry Repton, *Sketches and Hints on Landscape Gardening.*

14. C. R. Cockerell, 'An account of the Architectural Progress of the Bank of England', ms., p. 12, quoted in D. Abramson, *Money's Architecture.* Harvard Ph.D, 1993, p. 430.

15. Quoted in Werner Szambien, *De la Rue des Colonnes à la Rue de Rivoli.* Paris: DAAVP, 1992, p. 81.

16. *Parliamentary Papers* 1828, vol. 4, p. 387; quoted in J. Mordaunt Crook, 'Metropolitan Improvements: John Nash and the Picturesque', in Fox, *London—World City* (1992), p. 89.

Chapter 5

1. Fischer von Erlach, *Civil and Historical Architecture*, 1730, English edn, author's preface, as quoted in Eileen Harris with Nicholas Savage, *British Architectural Books and Their Writers*. Cambridge, 1990, p. 194.
2. J. Herder, *Fragments toward German literature*, 1787.
3. Georg Forster, *Ansichten vom Niederrhein, von Brabant, Flandern, Holland und England und Frankreich, im April, Mai und Junius 1790*. Berlin, 1791, p. 70. Trans. in Georg Germann, *The Gothic Revival*. London, 1972, p. 85.
4. Tieck, *Franz Sternbalds Wanderungen: eine altdeutsche Geschichte* (1798), Book III, Chp. 2, quoted and trans. in Germann, *Gothic Revival* (1972), p. 89.
5. Schlegel, *Kritische Friedrich-Schlege— Ausgabe 1. Ableitung IV: Ansichten und Ideen der christlichen Kunst*, ed. Hans Eichner. Munich, 1959.
6. J. G. Fichte, *Reden an die deutsche Nation*. Berlin, 1912, p. 125.
7. *Ibid.*, pp. 125–6.
8. Karl Friedrich Schinkel, quoted in Georg Friedrich Koch, 'Schinkels architektonische Entwürfe im gothischen Stil,1810–1815', *Zeitschrift für Kunstgeschichte* 32 (1969), 262–316 and trans. by Germann, *Gothic Revival* (1972), p. 91.
9. L. von Klenze, *Sammlung Architektonische Entwürfe*. Munich, 1830, 1st folio, foreword, p. 1. Also quoted by Oswald Hederer, *Leo von Klenze*. Munich, 1964, p. 16.
10. E. J. Hobsbawm, *Nations and Nationalism since 1780. Programme, Myth, Reality*. Cambridge, 1990, p. 91.
11. Linda Colley, *Britons, Forging the Nation 1707-1837*. London and New Haven, 1992, p. 365.
12. Hugh Trevor-Roper, 'The Invention of Tradition: The Highland Tradition of Scotland', in Eric Hobsbawm and Terence Ranger (eds), *The Invention of Tradition*. Cambridge, 1983, pp. 29–30.
13. Thomas Hope, *Observations on the Plans and Elevations designed by James Wyatt, architect, for Downing College, Cambridge, in a letter to Francis Anneseley, esq., M.P. by Thomas Hope*, 1804.
14. Benjamin Ferrey, *Recollections of A. W. N. Welby Pugin and his father Augustus Pugin*. London, 1861, p. 248.
15. A. W. N. Pugin, *The True Principles of Pointed or Christian Architecture*. London, 1841; reprint edn, London, 1973, p. 1.
16. *Ibid.*
17. As recalled by G. G. Scott, *Personal and Professional Recollections*. London, 1879, p. 203.
18. Pugin, *True Principles* (1973), p. 1.
19. Scott, *Personal and Professional Recollections*, p. 88.
20. Eugène-Emmanuel Viollet-le-Duc, 'Restauration', *Dictionnaire raisonné de l'architecture française du xie au xvie siècle* (1854–1868), here quoted from Barry Bergdoll (ed.), *The Foundations of Architecture: Selections from the* Dictionnaire Raisonné. New York, 1990, p. 195.
21. Ruskin, *Seven Lamps of Architecture*. London, 1849, ch. 6, section 10.

Chapter 6

1. Léon Vaudoyer, letter to A.-L.-T. Vaudoyer, 22 March 1830, quoted in B. Bergdoll, *Léon Vaudoyer, Historicism in the Age of Industry*. New York, 1994, p. 107.
2. Quatremère de Quincy, *De l'Imitation*. Paris, 1823, p. 80.
3. Neil Levine, 'The Book and the Building: Hugo's theory of architecture and Labrouste's Bibliothèque Ste-Geneviève', in Robin Middleton (ed.), *The Beaux-Arts and Nineteenth Century French Architecture*. London, 1982, pp. 138–173.
4. Hippolyte Fortoul, *De l'Art en Allemagne*. Paris, 1841, vol. 1, p. 177. For a commentary on this key phrase see B. Bergdoll, *Léon Vaudoyer* (1994), pp. 109ff.
5. Quoted in Norbert and Lieb, *München—Die Geschichte seiner Kunst*. Munich, 1971, p. 237.
6. Hippolyte Fortoul, *De l'Art en Allemagne*. Paris, 1840, vol. 2, pp. 169ff.
7. Leo von Klenze, *Versuch einer Wiederherstellung des toskanischen Tempels nach seinen historischen und technischen Analogien*, in *Denkschriften der Königlichen Akademie der Wissenschaften zu München für die Jahren 1821 und 1822*. Munich, 1824, p. 7.
8. Quoted in Hederer, *Leo von Klenz* (1964), p. 117.
9. Heinrich Hübsch, *In what style should we build?* (1828) trans. in Wolfgang Herrmann (ed.), *In what style should we build? The German Debate on Architectural Style*. Santa Monica, CA: Getty Center, 1992, p. 78.
10. James Fergusson, *History of the Modern Styles of Architecture*. London, 1862, here quoted 3rd edn, New York, 1891, vol. 2, pp. 206–7.
11. Karl Friedrich Schinkel, *Sammlung Architektonische Entwürfe … *Berlin, 1841.
12. J. W. Goethe, 'Nature: Aphoristic', English trans. from Agnes R. Arber, *Goethe's Botany: The Metamorphosis of Plants (1790)* and Tobler's *Ode to Nature (1782)*. Waltham, Mass., 1946,

p. 123.

13. Prince Maximilian, letter to Schinkel, and Schinkel, letter to Prince Maximilian, 24 January 1833; reprinted in Margarethe Kühn, *Schinkel Lebenswerk: Ausland: Bauten und Entwürfe*. Berlin, 1989, p. 4. See also Eberhard Drüeke, *Der Maximilianstil: Zum Stilbegriff der Architektur im 19. Jahrhundert*. Mittenwald, 1981, pp. 15–19.

14. Goerd Peschken, *Karl Friedrich Schinkel: Das architektonische Lehrbuch*. Berlin, 1979, p. 149.

15. Quoted in Mark Crinson, *Empire Building: Orientalism & Victorian Architecture*. London, 1996, p. 100.

16. *Principles of Church Restoration*, London, 1846, p. 9, quoted in David Brownlee, 'The First High Victorians: British Architectural Theory in the 1840s', *Architectura* 15 (1985), p. 37.

17. G.G. Scott, *A plea for the faithful restoration of our ancient churches*. London, 1850.

18. John Ruskin, 'The Lamp of Obedience', *Seven Lamps* (1849).

19. G. G. Scott, *Remarks on Secular and Domestic Architecture*. London, 1857, p. viii.

20. *Building News* 5 (11 June 1858): p. 589.

Chapter 7

1. *Times*, 12 June 1852, quoted in John Ruskin, *The Opening of the Crystal Palace considered in some of its relations to the prospects of art*. London, 1852.

2. E. L. Bucher, *Kulturhistorisches Skizzen aus der Industrieaustellung aller Völker*. Frankfurt, 1851, quoted by Sigfried Giedion, *Space, Time, and Architecture*. Cambridge, Mass., 1941, p. 251.

3. 'The Design of The Crystal Palace', *The Ecclesiologist* 12 (1851), pp. 269–70.

4. Ruskin, *The Opening of the Crystal Palace* (1852).

5. Ruskin, *Seven Lamps*; edn quoted is E. T. Cooke and Alexander Wedderburn, *The Works of John Ruskin*. London, 1903–12, vol. 8, p. 46.

6. Ruskin, *Stones of Venice* II (1853) in Cooke and Wedderburn, *The Works of John Ruskin*, (1903–12), vol. 10, p. 196.

7. *Ibid.*, p. 194.

8. Ruskin, *Seven Lamps*, (1853), p. 48.

9. *Ibid.*, p. 201.

10. *Ibid.*, p. 250.

11. As explained in Henry W. Acland and John Ruskin, *The Oxford Museum*. London, 1859, pp. 51–2.

12. *Building News* 6 (8 April 1859), p. 338, quoted in Eve Blau, *Ruskinian Gothic: The Architecture of Deane and Woodward, 1845–1861*.

Princeton, 1982, p. 61.

13. *Journal of Design* 5 (1851), p. 158, quoted in Giedion, *Space, Time, and Architecture* (1941), pp. 351–2.

14. Christopher Dresser, *The Art of Decorative Design*. London, 1862, pp.34–40.

15. Cited in Asa Briggs (ed.), *William Morris: Selected Writings and Designs*. Harmondsworth, 1962, p. 131.

16. Cited in Briggs, *William Morris*.

17. From a letter of 1883 quote in *ibid.*, p. 33.

18. William Morris, 'Prospectus' (1881) in Morris, *Works*, vol. 22, p. 5, and cited by Briggs, *William Morris*, p. 16.

19. Society for the Preservation of Ancient Buildings, *Thirteenth Annual Meeting of the Society, Report of the Committee …* London, 1890, p. 10. Quoted in Mark Swenarton, *Artisans and Architecture: The Ruskinian Tradition in Architectural Thought*. New York, 1988, p. 54.

20. Cited in Briggs, *William Morris* (1962).

21. Viollet-le-Duc, *Lectures on Architecture*, vol. I, p. 450.

22. Viollet-le-Duc, 'Style', *Dictionnaire raisonné*, vol. 8, 1858, as trans. in B. Bergdoll (ed.), *Viollet-le-Duc: The Foundations of Architecture …* New York, 1990, p. 240.

23. Viollet-le-Duc, *Dictionnaire*, vol. 2, p. 385.

24. Léon de Laborde, *De l'union des arts et de l'industrie*. 2 vols. Paris, 1856. For an analysis see Whitney Walton, *France at the Crystal Palace: Bourgeois Taste and Artisan Manufacture in the Nineteenth Century*. Berkeley, Calif. and Oxford, 1992.

25. Viollet-le-Duc, 'Restoration', *Dictionnaire*, as trans. in Bergdoll, *Viollet-le-Duc* (1990), p. 195.

26. Georges-Eugène Haussmann, *Mémoires*. Paris, 1890–93, cited here two-vol. edn, Paris, 1979, vol. 2, p. 228.

27. Viollet-le-Duc, 'Style', *Dictionnaire*, p. 253.

28. On this see the footnote to Viollet-le-Duc's eighth *Entretien*, Paris, 1858, vol. I, p. 323.

29. Viollet-le-Duc, *Entretiens sur l'Architecture* (1858), vol. I, p. 449.

30. Viollet-le-Duc, 'Rapport fait au Service des Edifices Diocésains …' 1855, Archives Nationales, Paris (F-19-7741), cited in Bergdoll, *Léon Vaudoyer* (1994), p. 254.

31. Viollet-le-Duc, 'Style', *Dictionnaire*, vol. 8, 1858 as trans. in Bergdoll, *Viollet-le-Duc* (1990), pp. 251–2.

32. Viollet-le-Duc, *Entretiens* (1858), vol. 2, p. 77.

33. Gottfried Semper, 'Science, Art, and Industry' (1852), as trans. in H. F. Mallgrave and W. Herrmann, *Gottfried Semper: The Four*

Elements of Architecture and Other Writings. Cambridge, 1989, p. 146.

34. *Ibid.*, p. 135.

35. Gottfried Semper, 'Prospectus, Comparative Theory of Building' (1852), as trans. in Mallgrave and Hermann, *Gottfried Semper* (1989), p. 170.

36. *Ibid.*

37. Semper, 'Science, Industry and Art' (1852), p. 134.

38. Semper, 'The Four Elements of Architecture' (1851), trans. in Mallgrave and Herrmann, *Gottfried Semper* (1989), p. 102.

39. Gottfried Semper, Preface to 'Vergleichende Baulehre (1850)', ms. 55, as trans. in Wolfgang Herrmann, *Gottfried Semper: In Search of Architecture.* Cambridge, Mass., 1984, p. 193.

40. Rosalind Williams, *Dream Worlds: Mass Consumption in Late Nineteenth Century France.* Berkeley, Calif., 1982, p. 9.

41. Boileau in *Encyclopédie d'architecture*, 1876, p. 120, cited in Bernard Marrey, *Les Grands Magasins des origines à 1939.* Paris, 1979, p. 76.

42. Quoted in Marrey, *Les Grands Magasins* (1979), p. 74.

43. Zola, *Au Bonheur des Dames*, 1882.

Chapter 8

1. Quoted in Louis Girard, *La Politique des Travaux Publiques du Second Empire.* Paris, 1952, p. 22.

2. A. Bailleux de Marisy, 'La Ville de Paris devant le Corps Législatif', p. 444, cited in Anthony Sutcliffe, *The Autumn of Central Paris.* Montreal, 1971, p. 31.

3. Jules Ferry, *Les Comtes Fantastiques d'Haussmann.* Paris, 1869.

4. Charles Garnier, *Le théâtre*, Paris, 1871.

5. Viollet-le-Duc, 'Le Nouvel Opéra', *Gazette des Architectes et du Bâtiment* 1 (1863), pp. 29–30, cited in Monika Steinhauser, *Die Architektur der Pariser Oper.* Munich, 1969, p. 104.

6. Charles Garnier, *Le nouvel Opéra de Paris.* Paris, 1878–81, vol. 1.

7. Garnier, *Le thèâtre.*

8. Originally published in the *Wiener Zeitung*, 25 December 1857, trans. in Thomas Hall, *Planning Europe's Capital Cities: Aspects of Nineteenth Century Urban Development.* London, 1997, p. 172.

9. Carl Schorske, *Fin de Siècle Vienna: Politics and Culture.* New York, 1980, p. 39.

10. *Das bürgerliche Wohnhaus und das Wiener Zinshaus.* Vienna, 1860.

11. I. Cerdá, *La Teoria general de la urbanizacion.* Madrid, 1867.

12. Pierre-Joseph Proudhon, *Qu'est-ce que la propriété?* (What is property?), Paris, 1840.

13. Cerdá, *Teoria general*, here cited French edition, *La théorie générale de l'urbanisation.* Paris, 1979.

14. *Ibid.*, p. 136.

15. *Ibid.*, p. 149.

16. Josef Stübben, 'Paris in Bezug auf Strassenbau und Stadterweiterung', *Zeitschrift für Bauwesen* 29 (1879), 383.

Chapter 9

1. Friedrich Nietzsche, *The Use and Abuse of History*, written 1873 and first published 1874, here quoted from trans. by Adrian Collins, Indianapolis: Bobbs-Merrill, 1949, pp. 4 and 28.

2. *Ibid.*, p. 52.

3. The petition is reproduced in Henri Loyrette, *Gustave Eiffel.* New York, 1985, p. 174.

4. Deborah Silverman, *Art Nouveau in Fin-de-Siècle France: Politics, Psychology, and Style.* Berkeley and London, 1989, p. 79.

	Art and architecture		Historical events
1737		**1737**	**Voltaire**, *Eléments de la Philosophie de Newton*
	1738 **William Kent** designs Rousham Gardens, near Oxford		
		1739	Discovery of **Herculaneum**
1740	1740 **Piranesi** moves from Venice to Rome and starts print business	**1740–8**	**War of Austrian Succession**
	Knobelsdorff designs Opera as first part of projected forum for Frederick the Great in Berlin		
	1743 **Blondel** founds private architecture school, Paris		
		1747	Foundation of the École des Ponts-et-Chaussées, Paris, under direction of **J.-R. Perronet**
			Montesquieu, *Spirit of Laws*
	1748 **Stuart & Revett** announce plans for *Antiquities of Athens*	**1748**	**Pompeii** excavated
	1749 **La Font de Saint-Yenne** calls for a new period of great public works in *À l'ombre du grand Colbert*	**1749**	**Buffon**, *Natural History* (36 vols, completed 1788)
	Walpole begins work at Strawberry Hill		
1750		**1750**	**Turgot** lectures at the Sorbonne on philosophical progress of the human mind; **Voltaire** accepts Frederick the Great's invitation to the court at Potsdam/Berlin
	1751 **Marquis de Marigny** appointed Director of Royal Buildings and begins reform of artistic taste in France	**1751**	**Diderot** publishes first volume of the *Encyclopédie*
	Abbé Laugier, *Essay on Architecture*		**Voltaire**, *The Century of Louis XIV*
	Contant d'Ivry begins St-Vaast, Arras		
	Soufflot, New Theatre, Lyon (completed 1756)		
	Peyre, project for a cathedral submitted to Accademia di San Luca, Rome		
		1754	**Condillac**, *Treatise on Sensations*
	1755 **Gabriel** designs Place Louis XV, Paris	**1755**	**Rousseau**, *Discourse on the Origin of Inequality*
	Winckelmann, *Reflections on the Imitation of Greek Works in Painting and Sculpture*		**Lisbon Earthquake** (1 November)
		1756	Outbreak of **Seven Years' War** (1756–63)
	1757 **Soufflot**'s first design for Ste-Geneviève, Paris, published	**1757**	**Frederick II** (the Great) wins victories for Prussia
			Edmund Burke, *A Philosophical Enquiry into the Origin of our Ideas of the Sublime and the Beautiful*
	1758 **Leroy**, *Ruins of the Most Beautiful Monuments of Greece*	**1758**	**Rousseau**, *Lettre sur les spectacles*
	James Stuart, Doric pavilion at Hagley Park, Worcestershire		
	1759 **William Chambers**, *Treatise on Civil Architecture*	**1759**	**Voltaire**, *Candide*
1760	1760 **Robert Adam** working at Kedleston and Syon Houses	**1760**	**George III**, King of Great Britain and Ireland (1760–1820)
	Robert Mylne, Blackfriars Bridge, London		
	1761 **Piranesi**, *Of the Magnificence and the Architecture of Rome*		
		1762	**Rousseau**, *Social Contract*
			Catherine the Great, Empress of Russia (1762–96)
	1763 **Le Camus de Mézières**, Wheat Market, Paris	**1763**	**Treaty of Paris**; France loses Québec, Britain's American and Indian acquisitions confirmed

	Art and architecture		Historical events	
1764	1764	Cornerstones of **Soufflot**'s Ste-Geneviève and **Contant d'Ivry**'s Madeleine laid in Paris	1764	Jesuits expelled from France
	1765	Work under way at Wörlitz, Germany, finished *c.*1794 **Piranesi**, *Parere su l'Architettura*	1765	**Catherine the Great** announces international competition for embellishment of St Petersburg in European journals **Voltaire**, *Philosophy of History*
	1766	**John Gwynn**, *London and Westminster Improved ...*	1766	Stamp Act imposed by Rockingham in 1765 on American colonies repealed in response to protests **Bougainville**'s voyage around the world (1766–79)
	1767	**J. D. Antoine**, Mint, Paris (construction 1771–75) Royal Crescent, Bath, by **John Wood**; **Craig**'s extension plan for Edinburgh	1767	**Catherine the Great** publishes *Instructions* westernizing Russian law
	1768	**Adam brothers** begin work on Adelphi, London	1768	**Cook**'s voyage in *Endeavour* charts New Zealand and eastern Australia
	1769	**Pierre Patte**, *Project for an Ideal Street* **Simon Du Ry**, Museum Fridericianum, Kassel (1769–76)	1769	Birth of **Napoleon** Improved steam engine using condenser patented by **James Watt**
1770			1770	Spinning jenny patented by **Hargreaves**
	1771	**Charles De Wailly** presents a view of staircase of new Comédie-Française at Salon		
	1772	**Payne Knight**, Downton Castle, Herefordshire **William Chambers**, *Dissertation on Oriental Gardening*	1772	**Goethe** publishes 'On German Architecture' in Herder's magazine on German art Paris's **Hôtel Dieu** burns (December)
	1773	**Victor Louis**, Grand Théâtre, Bordeaux		
	1774	Désert de Retz landscape garden, outside Paris	1774	**Priestley** discovers oxygen **Louis XVI**, King of France (1774–93)
	1775	**Ledoux** at work on Salines at Arc et Senans (1774–78)	1775	**American War of Independence** breaks out in New England
	1776	**Morel**, *Theory of Gardens* **William Chambers**, Somerset House, London, 1776–96 Bedford Square, London	1776	**Adam Smith**, *The Wealth of Nations*
	1777	**Adam**, Culzean Castle, Scotland (to 1790)	1777	*Sturm und Drang* literary movement in Germany **John Howard**, *The State of Prisons*
	1779	**Peyre and De Wailly**, Comédie-Française, Paris (1779–82)	1779	Coalbrookdale Bridge in English West Midlands is first cast-iron bridge
1780	1780	**Quatremère de Quincy**, *Encyclopédie méthodique d'architecture*	1780	**Gordon Riots** (anti-Catholic in Britain, followed by Catholic Relief Act of 1781)
	1781	**Gandon**, Custom House, Dublin	1781	**Kant**, *Critique of Pure Reason*
			1783	**Peace of Paris** ends American War of Independence **Montgolfier brothers**' first hot-air balloon flight, Paris
	1784	**J. F. Dauthe**, remodelling of St Nicholas, Leipzig **Boullée**, Newton cenotaph project		
			1785	**Watt**'s steam engine
	1786	**Gandon**, Four Courts, Dublin (1786–1802)		
	1788	**Soane** appointed architect of the Bank of England	1788	**Louis XVI** calls the States General at Versailles
	1789	**Langhans**, Brandenburg Gate, Berlin	1789	**French Revolution** (States General and storming of Bastille) First steam-driven mill, Manchester
1790			1790	**Kant**, *Critique of Judgement*
	1791	**Bentham**, Panopticon **Legrand & Molinos**, Feydeau theatre	1791	**Albion Grain Mills fire** in London (2 March)

	Art and architecture		Historical events	
1791	1791	Panthéon created from **Soufflot**'s Ste-Geneviève		
	1792	**Ledoux**, Hosten Houses, Paris	1792	**Republic** declared in France (September)
	1793	**Strutt**, Fireproof West Mill, Belper (1793–95)	1793	Commission des Artistes, Paris, to plan sale of confiscated church and aristocratic property
				Declaration of the Rights of Man and the Citizen (June)
	1794	Competitions of the Year II Controversy over the 'picturesque' between **Uvedale Price**, **Richard Payne Knight** and **Humphry Repton** Louvre Museum opens in former palace	1794	École Centrale (later École Polytechnique) founded to train engineers
	1795	**Lenoir**, Museum of French Monuments, Paris	1795	Metric system; State Council on Civic Buildings founded
			1793–5	**The Terror**, **Louis XVI** and **Marie Antoinette** guillotined (January); Britain declares war on France
	1796	Competition for a monument to Frederick the Great, Berlin	1796	French campaigns in Italy; Napoleon victor
	1797	**Weinbrenner**, first proposal for Market Square, Karlsruhe Rue des Colonnes, Paris	1797	**Schelling**, *Natural Philosophy*
			1798	**Malthus**, *An Essay on the Principle of Population*
			1799	Napoleon's coup d'état
1800	1800	**Durand**, *Portfolio and Parallel of Buildings of all Types Ancient and Modern*	1800	**J. G. Fichte**, The Destiny of Man
	1801	**Antolini**, project for Foro Bonaparte, Milan	1801	**Wilberforce**'s Act in Britain abolishes slavery
				Alexander I Tsar of Russia (1801–25)
	1802	Rue de Rivoli, Paris	1802	Concordat concluded between Napoleon and Pope
	1804	**William Wilkins**, Grange Park **Ledoux**, *Architecture* published with projects including ideal city of Chaux	1804	**Napoleon** crowned emperor in Paris; Napoleonic Code issued
	1805	**Rondelet**, *Theoretic and Practical Treatise on the Art of Building*	1805	**Nelson** wins **Battle of Trafalgar**; French defeat Austrians and Russians at Austerlitz
	1806	Iron dome, Wheat Market, Paris, by **Bélanger** **Napoleon**'s grand projects for Paris including Temple of Glory (Madeleine), Vendôme Column, Arc de Triomphe **Luigi Cagnola**, Arco del Sempione, Milan **Repton**, *Enquiry into the Changes of Taste in Landscape Gardening*	1806	**Holy Roman Empire** abolished; Prussians defeated at Jena
			1807	**Hegel**, *Phenomenology of Spirit*; Fichte, *Addresses to the German Nation*
			1808	Spanish rising against French; occupations begin **Peninsular War** (1808–14)
			1809	**Lamarck** publishes *Zoological Philospophy*
1810	1810	**Schinkel** publishes memorandum defending Gothic for Mausoleum of Queen Luise of Prussia		
	1811	Regent Street, London, begun by **John Nash**	1811	Krupp Factory at Essen; Luddites riot against machines in England
				George III mentally ill; **Prince Regent** installed (1811–20)
	1813	**Ludwig I of Bavaria** opens competition for a Walhalla (built 1816–34)	1813	**Robert Owen**, *A New View of Society*

	Art and architecture		Historical events
1815		**1815**	**Hundred Days**; Napoleon escapes from Elba but defeated by allies at **Waterloo**
	1816 Elgin Marbles brought to British Museum **Schinkel**, Neue Wache, Unter den Linden, Berlin (Guard House)	**1816**	**Peterloo Massacre**, Manchester
	1817 **Thomas Rickman**, *An Attempt to Discriminate the Styles of English Architecture*		
		1818	Parliament approves one million pounds to fund 600 new churches
		1819	Macadamized roads stimulate coach travel
1820	1820 **Taylor and Nodier** begin publishing *Voyages pittoresques et romantiques dans l'ancienne France*	1820	Abortive uprisings in Portugal, Sicily, Germany, and Spain **George IV** (1820–30) King in Britain
		1821	**Greek War of Independence** begins
		1822	**George IV**'s state visit to Edinburgh
	1823 **Smirke**, British Museum, and **Schinkel**, Altes Museum **Nash**, Park Village East, London		
	1825 **Schinkel**, Charlottenhof, Sanssouci, Potsdam	1825	**Ludwig I** ascends the throne in Bavaria; Nicholas I in Russia
	1826 **Wilkins** selected to design London University		
	1828 **Henri Labrouste**'s study of Paestum rocks the French Academy of Art **Heinrich Hübsch**, *In what style should we build?*	1828	**Hegel**, Lectures on Aesthetics at Berlin University Saint-Simonian *Predications*, Paris
	1829 **Charles Barry**, Travellers Club, Pall Mall, London, inaugurates neo-Renaissance	1829	Catholic emancipation in Britain **Fourier**, *Le nouveau monde industriel et sociétaire*
1830	1830 **Hittorff** announces his theories of polychromy on Greek temples in Sicily; **Leo von Klenze** begins Walhalla, near Regensburg	1830	Revolution in Paris issues in a period of liberal rule under **Louis-Philippe** (1830–48); Belgian independence **Otto of Bavaria** on the throne of Greece First railway line, Liverpool–Manchester
	1832 **Schinkel**, Bauakademie, Berlin (finished 1835)	1832	**Great Reform Bill**, England
	1833 **Félix Duban** appointed to remodel École des Beaux-Arts, Paris **Rohault de Fleury**, glass and iron greenhouses, Paris Jardin des Plantes		
	1834 **Wilkins**'s National Gallery, London	1834	**British Poor Law Amendment** Victor Considerant publishes his theory of the Phalanstery
	1835 **Pugin**, St Marie's Grange, near Salisbury	1835	**Municipal Corporations Act**, Britain
	1836 **Pugin**, *Contrasts* **Pugin and Barry** selected as architects of Houses of Parliament, London		
	1837 **Klenze**, Hermitage Museum, St Petersburg	1837	**Victoria** Queen of Great Britain and Ireland (1837–1901) Creation by Guizot of Commission on Historic Monuments, Paris
	1838 **Labrouste**, Bibliothèque Ste-Geneviève (1838–50)	1838	The People's Charter drawn up in London by Chartists
	1839 **Pugin**, St Giles, Cheadle; **Wild**, Christ Church Streatham **Bindesbøll**, Thorwaldsen Museum, Copenhagen (1839–48)	1839	**Auguste Comte**, *Cours de Philosophie Positiviste* **Daguerre** announces invention of photography
1840	1840 **Viollet-le-Duc** begins restoration of La Madeleine, Vézelay		
	1841 **Pugin**, *True Principles of Christian or Pointed Architecture*	1841	Declaration that French rail system should connect Paris to all borders
		1842	Law for compulsory expropriation of unhealthy dwellings, England

	Art and architecture		Historical events

1842

<table>
<tr><td></td><td></td><td>1842</td><td>Chadwick, Report on the Sanitary Condition of the Labouring People of Great Britain</td></tr>
<tr><td>1843</td><td>Viollet-le-Duc and Lassus win competition to restore Notre-Dame</td><td>1843</td><td>First telegraph office in London</td></tr>
<tr><td>1844</td><td>Paxton, Birkenhead Park, near Liverpool Nikolaikirche Competition, Hamburg</td><td>1844</td><td>Engels, The Condition of the Working Classes in England in 1844. Free Church of Scotland formed in protest against established Church of Scotland Alexander von Humboldt, Cosmos</td></tr>
<tr><td></td><td></td><td>1845</td><td>Potato Famine in Ireland</td></tr>
<tr><td>1846</td><td>Wild, St Mark, Alexandria, Egypt</td><td>1846</td><td>Repeal of Corn Laws; Peel resigns</td></tr>
<tr><td>1847</td><td>Duquesny, Gare de l'Est, Paris</td><td>1847</td><td>Pre-Raphaelite Brotherhood formed Risorgimento in Italy</td></tr>
<tr><td>1848</td><td>Maximilian of Bavaria opens competition for a new style of architecture</td><td>1848</td><td>Marx and Engels's Communist Manifesto</td></tr>
<tr><td>1849</td><td>Cité Napoléon, Paris, model housing (1849–53) William Butterfield, All Saints, Margaret Street, London (1849–59) Ruskin, Seven Lamps of Architecture</td><td>1848–9</td><td>Revolutions in Europe; Declaration of Second Republic in France (1848–52)</td></tr>
</table>

1851

<table>
<tr><td>1851</td><td>Ruskin, Stones of Venice (1851–53); Semper, The Four Elements of Architecture Paxton, Crystal Palace for Great Exhibition, Hyde Park, London</td><td>1851</td><td>Coup d'état in France by Louis-Napoleon</td></tr>
<tr><td>1852</td><td>Vaudoyer, Marseille Cathedral (1852–93) Deane & Woodward, Trinity College Museum, Dublin</td><td>1852</td><td>Sir Titus Salt founds Saltaire (workers' town) near Bradford, Yorkshire Declaration of Second Empire, Paris</td></tr>
<tr><td></td><td></td><td>1853</td><td>Baron Haussmann appointed prefect and begins Paris transformation Crimean War begins</td></tr>
<tr><td>1854</td><td>Viollet-le-Duc begins publishing Dictionnaire raisonné (1854–68)</td><td></td><td></td></tr>
<tr><td>1855</td><td>Les Halles, Paris by Baltard (1854–66); Palais des Beaux-Arts for Exposition Universelle of 1855, Paris</td><td>1855</td><td>Opening of railway to Lyon and Mediterranean</td></tr>
<tr><td>1856</td><td>Owen Jones, Grammar of Ornament</td><td>1856</td><td>France and Britain attack China, taking Tientsin and Peking</td></tr>
<tr><td>1857</td><td>Government Offices Competition, London</td><td></td><td></td></tr>
<tr><td></td><td></td><td>1858</td><td>Suez Company founded</td></tr>
<tr><td>1859</td><td>Philip Webb, Red House for William Morris</td><td>1859</td><td>Darwin, Origin of Species</td></tr>
</table>

1860

<table>
<tr><td>1860</td><td>Fuller & Johnson, Canadian Parliament, Ottawa Work begins on Viennese Ringstrasse Cerdá's plan for Barcelona extension adopted</td><td>1860</td><td>Combustion engine; Bessemer's mass production of steel Garibaldi victorious in southern Italy</td></tr>
<tr><td></td><td></td><td>1861</td><td>Death of Prince Albert Russia abolishes serfdom; American Civil War begins (1861–65) Victor Emmanuel II King of Italy (1861–78)</td></tr>
<tr><td>1862</td><td>Christopher Dresser, The Art of Decorative Design Joseph Poelaert, Palais de Justice, Brussels (1862–83)</td><td>1862</td><td>Otto von Bismarck becomes president of German Diet</td></tr>
<tr><td>1863</td><td>Garnier begins construction of Paris Opéra Gottfried Semper, Der Stil; Viollet-le-Duc, Lectures on Architecture (1863–72)</td><td></td><td></td></tr>
</table>

Art and architecture	**Historical events**

Art and architecture	Historical events
	1864 First International formed in London (Karl Marx organizes)
1865 Extensive urban renewal in Florence, temporary capital of Italy	
1866 Law Courts Competition, London, won by G. E. Street, built 1874–82	1866 Austro-Prussian War Nobel invents dynamite
1867 Exposition Universelle, Paris Cerdá General Theory of Urbanization	1867 Austro-Hungarian Compromise; coronation of Emperor Franz-Joseph I, Budapest Marx, Capital, vol. 1
1868 Scott, St Pancras Station Hotel, London; Waterhouse, Town Hall, Manchester	
	1869 Fall of Haussmann

Art and architecture	Historical events
	1870 Franco-Prussian War, Fall of Second Empire, Commune in Paris
1871 Saulnier, Meunier Factory and Model Town, Noisel-sur-Marne	1871 British trade unions gain legality French Third Republic suppresses Commune and loses Alsace Lorraine to Germany
1872 Alexandre Laplanche, Au Bon Marché, department store, Paris Friedrich von Schmidt, Town Hall, Vienna	1872 Bismarck opposes Catholic church in Kulturkampf
1873 Semper, Project for Museums District in Vienna	
1874 Von Hansen, Austrian Parliament, Vienna (1874–83)	1874 Nietzsche, The Use and Abuse of History First Impressionist Exhibition, Paris
1875 Félix Narjoux, rue de Tanger school, Paris	
1876 Philip Webb, Smeaton Manor, Yorkshire	1876 Alexander Bell, telephone
1877 Morris and Webb found Society for the Protection of Ancient Buildings Shaw, Bedford Park, London P. J. H. Cuipers, Rijksmuseum, Amsterdam (1877–85)	1877 Russo-Turkish War, 1877–78; Queen Victoria Empress of India Pasteur discovers origins of infectious disease
1878 Garnier, Casino, Monte Carlo (1878–79)	1878 Edison, incandescent light bulb
	1879 Land League formed in Ireland

Art and architecture	Historical events
1880 Josef Stübben wins competition for Cologne urban expansion Cologne Cathedral dedicated in great neo-medieval pageant	1880 Gladstone British Prime Minister (1880–85), First Boer War (1880–81)
	1881 Jewish pogroms in Eastern Europe
1882 Soria y Mata, The Linear City Competition for Hungarian Parliament Building, Budapest Competition for Victor Emmanuel Monument, Rome	1882 Ferry Law in France requiring universal primary education Triple Alliance: Germany, Austrian–Hungary, Italy
1883 William Morris declares himself a socialist Competition for the Palace of Justice, Rome	1883 Social insurance in Germany
	1884 Third British Reform Act
1885 Nénot, Sorbonne, Paris (1885–91)	1885 Motor car (Benz) and motorcycle (Daimler)
1887 Hoffmann & Dybwad, National Courts, Leipzig (1887–95)	1887 Queen Victoria's Golden Jubilee and Trafalgar Square Riots (Bloody Sunday) Automatic telephone
1888 Port Sunlight, England	1888 Wilhelm II Emperor of Germany (1888–1918) London County Council formed

	Art and architecture	**Historical events**
1889	**1889** **Camillo Sitte**, *City Planning According to Artistic Principles* Universal Exhibition, Paris, with Eiffel Tower and **Dutret**'s Gallery of Machines Templeton's Carpet Factory, Glasgow	**1889** **Second International** in Paris
1890	**1890** **Josef Stübben**, *City Planning*	
		1891 Young Turk movement founded in Geneva
	1892 **Victor Horta**, Tassel House, Brussels **1893** **Zawiejski**, Slowacki Theatre, Cracow **Charles Buls**, *The Aesthetic of Cities* published in Brussels	**1893** Diesel engine
		1895 **Marconi** invents radio-telegraphy

Glossary

Note: This glossary contains technical and stylistic terms specifically referred to in the text. References to other terms within the glossary appear in **bold**. For a more complete guide to architectural terminology, with helpful illustrations, readers should consult either John Fleming, Hugh Honour, and Nikolaus Pevsner, *A Dictionary of Architecture* (Penguin Books, 1966) or Cyril Harris, *Historic Architecture Sourcebook* (New York: McGraw-Hill, Inc., 1977).

amphitheatre the elliptical or circular space of the ancient Greek and Roman theatre, generally formed of rising tiers of seats. By extension, any semicircular open space.

architecture parlante (French, 'speaking architecture') the notion that a building's forms, either component volumes or decorative embellishments, so closely portray aspects of the function that the building communicates its purpose, and thus meaning, with the clarity of spoken language. Although generally used to refer to the search for symbolic forms in relation to new building types by the French architects Boullée, Ledoux, and their followers in the 1780s and 1790s, it seems the term was only coined, and initially in derision, in the 1840s.

art nouveau a loose cluster of movements in the 1890s that sought to derive a vocabulary for the arts in the most inclusive sense, from graphic arts and ceramics to architecture, through a turn to an abstract language of form derived from the whiplash line of nature first explored in the 1880s by Mackmurdo in England and in the early 1890s by Obrist in Germany and Victor Horta in Brussels. In contrast to the curvilinear modes explored in France, Belgium, and Germany, a rectilinear mode of abstraction was explored by Mackintosh in Scotland and Hoffmann in Vienna which shared the anti-academic, anti-historicist philosophy of the earlier curvilinear decorative style even while exploring an entirely different formal vocabulary.

basilica refers to the long oblong buildings of the ancient Romans used for public assembly, often surrounded by aisles and galleries and featuring an apse opposite the entrance. Once adapted by the Early Christians for worship, the basilica's apse was now moved to one of the short ends to create the characteristic directional form of the Christian church interior.

bay a vertical division or module of a building, often marked either by fenestration, the Classical orders (columns or pilasters), or a single arch of an arcade. In vaulted architecture a bay refers to a unit of vaulting including the vertical elevations and the ceiling.

building type refers to a specific purpose or function of a building and its related form or physiognomy. Temples, churches, palaces, and amphitheatres are building types that date back to ancient times; while railway stations, public museums, and department stores are characteristic new building types of modern times.

caryatid a column in the form of a sculpted female figure, of which the most famous ancient example is the Erechtheum on the Athenian acropolis. May also be used as an **engaged** figure.

castellated refers to a building whose roof line bears the crenellations typically associated with medieval castles.

catenary an elliptically shaped arch which gains its strength from its precise geometric form. The catenary can be generated mathematically, but its form derives from the catenary curve, formed by a flexible cord hung between two points of a porch. This is inverted, or flipped, to form the arch.

cella the principal chamber of a Classical temple housing the cult image. Generally windowless, the cella was fronted by the **portico**.

circus in Roman architecture a long oblong building with rounded ends, and often tiered seating, used for racing events. In the eighteenth century the type was taken over in ranges of housing and town planning.

coffered refers to the interior decoration of a ceiling or a vault with a regular grid of sunken square or polygonal ornamental panels. The classic example is to be found in the Roman Pantheon, which served as a model for many Renaissance and eighteenth and nineteenth-century adaptations.

coliseum the arcaded, multi-storey, open-air arena devised by the Romans for gladiatorial events; by extension any enclosed elliptical building or urban space.

colonette a diminutive column either in height or in width, generally used to describe the columnar elements of medieval architectural design which depart entirely from the system of proportions which governed the dimensions and dimensional relations of Classical columns.

colonnade a row of columns carrying an entablature, generally made up of equally spaced units.

Corinthian one of the three orders of columns devised by the Greeks, the Corinthian is characterized by its elegant, elaborate capital of acanthus leaves and its tall proportions in comparison with the squatter **Doric** or **Ionic** orders.

cornice the crowning element of a Classical entablature or the crowning projecting set of mouldings along the top of a building or wall.

crypt a chamber or vault beneath the main floor of a church, often, but not always, subterranean. In the Christian tradition crypts are particularly associated with the cult of relics.

cryptoporticus in Roman architecture, an enclosed gallery formed of walls punctured with openings rather than colonnades. In the eighteenth century the term was applied to any covered subterranean passage, as in Kent's design of the gardens at Rousham.

dégagement French term for a free-standing element, either a component of a building which stands free of a larger structure (i.e. a column as opposed to a pilaster), or a building as a free-standing object in a city.

Doric the first of the orders in both Greek and Roman architecture, the Doric order is characterized by the simplicity of its forms, its simple 'pillow-like' capital, and its sturdy proportions. The Greek Doric order was baseless and generally fluted and generally of squatter proportions, height to width, than the Roman.

engaged an element that is physically part of the wall, from which it might project in relief, as in an engaged column which is locked into the masonry structure of the wall behind.

entablature the spanning element of a Classical order, consisting generally of three principal parts—the **architrave**, **frieze**, and **cornice**.

forum (pl. **fora**) in Roman town planning a precinct around a temple or group of temples, often bordered by open colonnades or arcades. By the eighteenth century the forum connoted not simply the physical form of the Roman open space but the public life that took place there.

frieze properly speaking, the middle of the three component mouldings of a Classical **entablature**. Often ornamented with a motif of garlands or interlaced floral ornaments known as rinceaux, the term frieze is thus often also used for any running moulding denoting the separation of floors on a façade or crowning the ornamental treatment of interior walls in room decoration.

Gallican of or related to France, used in church history to refer to the theory whereby the French church was an autonomous authority, independent of papal or Roman authority because of its own antiquity in ancient Gaul.

Gothick a deliberately antiquarian spelling to refer to the eighteenth century's romanticized, even picturesque freedom in reviving the forms of Gothic architecture for modern buildings. Often Gothick also connotes the associations of the Gothic in eighteenth-century literature with gloom, mystery, and the obscure.

Graeco-Gothic the search for a synthesis of the essence of the two great systems of western architecture, the Greek and the Gothic, in which Classical columns carry vaults of medieval lightness and technical achievement. The Graeco-Gothic was a particularly progressive element of Neoclassical aesthetics, especially in France.

ha-ha a ditch with a wall on its inner side below ground level, separating the ornamental part of a house's garden from its adjacent agricultural fields, which prevented livestock from approaching the house but, unlike a fence or garden wall, remained invisible from a distance, thus creating the illusion of a seamless unity of garden and prospect. The origins of the term have long been disputed and subject to numerous theories.

hall church a church in which the side aisles are of the same height as the central vessel or nave.

intrados the inner curve or underside of an arch, also called soffit.

Ionic an order of columns in both Greek and Roman architecture characterized by its voluted capital and its elegant proportions.

Mannerist used to describe principally Italian architecture of the sixteenth century in which Classical motifs were used often in contradiction or exaggeration of their original meaning; by extension applied to any style in which a self-conscious, sometimes even ironic attitude towards the decorative elements and component parts can be detected. In Italian architecture Mannerism is generally associated with the work of Michelangelo, Giulio Romano, and their followers.

Neoclassicism the revival of interest in the architecture of Greece and Rome in the decades after 1750 led only rarely to literal copying of ancient buildings; rather, the movement began as a reaction against what were seen as the excesses of late Baroque and Rococo architecture. Theorists and designers argued that in returning to a strict adherence to Greek principles they were instilling a respect for nature and reason in architecture, in parallel with the reform of all human institutions.

order(s) in Classical architecture an order is a system of design which comprises the elements of a column and its related **entablature** as well as a range of acceptable proportions. The three principal orders of the Greeks were the **Doric** , **Ionic**, and **Corinthian**, to which the Romans added the **Tuscan** and the Composite. In the Renaissance and later the possibility of a sixth order, often a national order, was often discussed. At least from the time of Vitruvius the different orders were also associated with different characters of buildings and often even supposed to be gendered—the Doric connoting masculinity, the Ionic held to be feminine. In addition they were arranged in a hierarchical sequence of elegance and majesty from the Doric to the Corinthian.

Palladian, Palladianism a style derived from the work of the sixteenth-century Italian architect Andrea Palladio, whose *Four Books on Architecture* was one of the most widely emulated source-books for architecture in the eighteenth and nineteenth centuries. Palladianism was first programmatically put forth as an architectural reform in Britain after 1730 in the circle of Lord Burlington and Colin Campbell, who looked back as much to the Italian master as they did to his first English disciple, Inigo Jones. For many art historians the English Palladian Revival, or Neo-Palladianism, is the first phase of eighteenth-century **Neoclassicism** .

parterre in a theatre the area of the audience immediately in front of the stage, often on a gradient, as opposed to seats arranged in tiers or balconies above the stage. While in the Elizabethan tradition the parterre area was given over to standing, in the French theatre of the eighteenth century the parterre was seated and quickly took on higher class distinctions.

pediment the triangular gable end of a roof, generally above a **portico** of columns in Classical or Neoclassical architecture. The term is also applied to the use of a similar motif above windows or doors, where it may take on any of a variety of forms, from the triangular to the semicircular.

Perpendicular a term used to refer to a late phase of English Gothic architecture, *c.*1330–50, characterized by emphasis on straight horizontals and verticals, slender dividing piers, and regular patterns of fenestration. Fan vaults were much favoured, as in King's College Chapel, Cambridge and the chapel of Henry VII at Westminster Abbey.

pier a solid masonry support, either free-standing or clustered as in medieval design, i.e. compound pier.

pilaster a shallow relief pier generally treated as a flat column in relief on a wall surface. Unlike columns, these often serve no structural purpose but are used for rhythm or to articulate a space and/or frame elements, particularly openings. An essential element of Classical Roman and Renaissance architectural design, the pilaster was widely questioned in rigorist Neoclassical theory, notably by Laugier and Lodoli, but still used widely in Neoclassical design.

polychromy literally multi-coloured, refers to the use of coloured surfaces in buildings, either through the appliqué of different materials or through applied paint on stucco.

portico a porch generally formed by a **colonnade** of Classical columns supporting an **entablature** and **pediment**.

propylaeum in Greek architecture an entrance gate formed by an open colonnade, generally giving entrance to a precinct, such as the Acropolis at Athens.

proscenium in modern theatre design the space between the curtain and the orchestra defined by a monumental frame or arch which marks the separation between audience and spectacle.

Residenz German term referring to the principal palace of a ruler; by extension, to the capital city or principal seat.

Romanticism the term had its origins in literature in the seventeenth century and referred to a revival of interest in medieval romances, but by the end of the eighteenth century it had emerged in various guises in the visual arts as well as in literature with diverse and even contradictory tenets. As early as 1924 Arthur Lovejoy warned that one could only speak of 'romanticisms' in the plural. In any case, the movement that knew its heyday from *c.*1780 to *c.*1830 had at its heart a reaction to Enlightenment reason and thus an appeal to emotion, sentiment, and subjectivity. It brought with it an embrace of relative truths, national specificities, and an interest in a variety of styles, both for their national and exotic appeal.

scagliola a material composed of plaster and marble chips or other coloured matter to imitate marble.

spandrel the area of solid material adjacent to an arch, or the area between two arches or two vaults.

stoa in Greek architecture a free-standing **colonnade**, generally composed of an unbroken rear wall and an open colonnade facing a public area such as the agora.

trabeation the use of a system of post-and-lintel construction, or more specifically in Greek architecture of the rectilinear structural and visual principle of columnar architecture.

Tuscan an order of columns introduced by the Romans and thought to be derived ultimately from the Etruscans. The simplest of the Roman orders, it was unfluted, carried a simple capital closely related to the Doric, and was governed by a sturdy aesthetic of proportional relations.

undercroft a vaulted room, sometimes underground, below the main space of a church, chapel, or palace hall (cf. **crypt**).

Further Reading

NB: This bibliography comprises principally English language titles. Foreign language titles have been included only when they can be used by the beginning student to great advantage for their illustrations or documentary material or when they are of such seminal importance that they cannot be ignored.

There are few surveys of architectural production that span the period and the continental scope of this volume. For, as evoked in the Introduction, most considerations of the late eighteenth and nineteenth century were, until quite recently, preoccupied with revealing the roots of twentieth-century modernism. The most prominent exception is **Robin Middleton and David Watkin**, *Neoclassical and Nineteenth Century Architecture* (New York, 1981), which should be used in the original hardback edition that alone contains the excellent biographical dictionary of major architects discussed and a rich bibliographical guide to monographic literature before 1977. **François Loyer**'s *Architecture of the Industrial Age, 1789–1914* (New York, 1983) is a highly personal and episodic account rich in unusual pictorial material and bristling with insights, while **Claude Mignot**'s *Architecture of the Nineteenth Century in Europe* (New York, 1984) is a reliable and comprehensive survey—its organization of much of its material according to building types is a fine complement to **Sir Nikolaus Pevsner**'s dry but useful *History of Building Types* (Princeton, 1976) and to the nineteenth-century chapters of **Henry-Russell Hitchcock**'s *Architecture: Nineteenth and Twentieth Centuries* in the Pelican History of Art (Harmondsworth, 1958, most recently updated 1977). Their overt polemical agendas notwithstanding, there is still much to be obtained from the accounts of **Pevsner** in *Pioneers of Modern Design* (London, 1936), particularly useful for its account of decorative arts reform and of international recognition of British accomplishments in domestic

architecture in the second half of the nineteenth century, and from **Sigfried Giedion**'s *Space, Time and Architecture* (Cambridge, Mass., originally published 1941; 5th rev. and enlarged edn, 1967), still useful for its summary of technological developments, a theme expanded with great originality in his *Mechanization Takes Command*, (New York, 1948), which addresses an issue that the scope of the present volume could not encompass. Technological determinants are combined with a distinctly Marxist reading of developments in town planning in the first volume of **Leonardo Benevolo**'s *History of Modern Architecture* (London, 1971). No less polemical is **Alberto Perez-Gomez**'s *Architecture and the Crisis of Modern Society* (Cambridge, Mass., 1983), whose central thesis of rationalization in architecture as a progressive erosion of its metaphysical and expressive capacities remains a stimulating and challenging argument.

Otherwise the best accounts of the period are more in-depth surveys of either a particular country or movement. For Britain one should consult **John Summerson**, *Architecture in Britain, 1530–1830* (Harmondsworth, 6th edn, 1977) and the excellent survey on *Victorian Architecture* by **Roger Dixon and Stefan Muthesius** (London, 1978). In addition to the three-volume *Histoire de l'architecture française* (vol. 2—From the Renaissance to the Revolution, by **Jean-Marie Perouse de Montclos**, Paris, 1989, vol. 3—From the Revolution to the Present, by **François Loyer**, Paris, 1999), one should consult **Allan Braham**, *The Architecture of the French Enlightenment* (London, 1980) and **Wend von Kalnein**, *Architecture in France in the Eighteenth Century* (New Haven, 1995). There is no adequate account of French nineteenth-century architecture in English, although histories of the Academy and several key buildings are considered in **Arthur Drexler** (ed.), *The Architecture of the Ecole des*

Beaux-Arts (London and New York, 1977). **David Watkin and Tilman Mellinghof**, *German Architecture and the Classical Ideal* (London, 1987), which covers Neoclassical architecture from 1750 to 1845 throughout the German states, is largely descriptive in tone but a useful guide, although it entirely overlooks non-Classical imagery, notably the important Gothic Revival and Rundbogenstil of the same period. No less descriptive is **Carrol V. Meeks**, *Italian Architecture, 1750–1914* (New Haven, 1966), which remains the only survey account in English of this little-known period in Italian architecture, although it should be read in conjunction with the appropriate chapters in **Joseph Rykwert**, *The First Moderns*. Iberian architecture of the nineteenth century has been little studied, even by Spanish and Portuguese historians. Work on Scandinavian architecture in English is confined largely to guidebooks. Synthetic appraisals of architecture in the former communist bloc is only beginning. The period 1750–1890 is well covered in **Dora Wiebenson and József Sisa** (eds), *The Architecture of Historic Hungary* (Cambridge, Mass., 1998), and a very brief account of the period in Poland is available in **Stefan Muthesius**, *Art, Architecture, and Design in Poland: an introduction* (Konigstein im Tanus, 1994) but there are as yet no good English-language surveys of eighteenth- and nineteenth-century architecture in other Central and Eastern European countries and the Balkans. **Ioannes N. Traulos**, *Neo-classical Architecture in Greece* (Athens, 1967) is largely a pictorial survey.

The development of architectural theory in this period is treated in a number of excellent works, most particularly **Hanno-Walter Kruft**'s indispensable *A History of Architectural Theory from Vitruvius to the Present* (London, 1994) and **Nikolaus Pevsner**'s *Some Architectural Writers of the Nineteenth Century* (Oxford, 1972). **Peter Collins**, *Changing Ideals in Modern Architecture 1750–1950* (London, 1965) should be used with caution for it has a tendency to schematize complex ideas in its quest for categories. Unfortunately only a fragment of the period is covered in the superlative and engaging accounts of English eighteenth-century architectural theory and publishing available in **Eileen Harris and Nicholas Savage**, *British Architectural Books and Writers, 1556–1785* (Cambridge, 1990). Also useful, but limited to the holdings of the libraries they celebrate, are the two volumes thus far

published of The Mark J. Millard Architectural Collection: **Dora Wiebenson and Claire Baines**, vol. 1, *French Books: Sixteenth through Nineteenth Centuries* and **Robin Middleton and Nicholas Savage**, vol. 2, *English Books*, as well as **Adolf K. Placzek and Angela Giral**, *Avery's Choice: Five Centuries of Great Architectural Books* (New York, 1997).

A number of works give synthetic accounts of developments in town planning and town planning theory. **Leonardo Benevolo**'s *The Origins of Modern Town Planning* (Cambridge, Mass., 1968) is particularly good on utopian planning and on early sanitation legislation with an emphasis on the first half of the nineteenth century, while **Françoise Choay**'s *The Modern City: Planning in the Nineteenth Century* (New York, 1969) remains a valuable survey of the second half of the century. **Anthony Suttcliffe**, *The Rise of Modern Urban Planning, 1800–1914* (London, 1980) is a useful collection of essays, while the individual chapters of **Thomas Hall**, *Planning Europe's Capital Cities, Aspects of Nineteenth Century Urban Development* (London, 1997) provide excellent summaries and sources.

Chapter 1: Neoclassicism
Primary texts
Adam, Robert and James Adam, *The Works in Architecture of Robert and James Adam, Esquires*. 3 vols (London, 1773–1822).
Laugier, Marc-Antoine, *An Essay on Architecture*. Trans. with an introduction by Wolfgang and Anni Herrmann (Los Angeles, 1977).
Piranesi, Giovanni Battista, *Della magnificenza ed architettura de' Romani* (Rome, 1761; reprint edn, Milan, 1993).
Piranesi, Giovanni Battista, *The polemical works, Rome, 1757, 1761, 1765, 1769*. Edited with an introduction by John Wilton-Ely (Farnborough, Hants, 1972).
Stuart, J. and N. Revett, *The Antiquities of Athens*. 4 vols (London, 1762–1816).
Winckelmann, Johann Joachim, *On the Imitation of the Painting and Sculpture of the Greeks* (translated by Henry Fuseli), reprinted in Gert Schiff (ed.), *German Essays on Art History* (New York, 1988) pp. 1–17.

Secondary texts
Beard, Geoffrey, *The Work of Robert Adam* (New York, 1978).
Black, Jeremy, *The British and the Grand Tour* (London, 1985).
Braham, Allan, *The Architecture of the French Enlightenment* (London, 1980).

Egbert, D. D., *The Beaux-Arts Tradition in French Architecture* (Princeton, 1980).

Eriksen, Sven, *Early Neoclassicism in France* (London, 1974).

Etlin, Richard A., *Symbolic Space, French Enlightenment Architecture and Its Legacy* (Chicago, 1994).

Fleming, John, *Robert Adam and his Circle in Edinburgh & Rome* (Cambridge, Mass., 1962) is still one of the most perceptive accounts of Adam's early career and his attitudes towards antiquities.

Gallet, Michael, *Parisian Domestic Architecture of the Eighteenth Century* (London, 1972).

Gordon, Alden R., 'Jérôme-Charles Bellicard's Italian Notebook of 1750–51: The Discoveries at Herculaneum and Observations on Ancient and Modern Architecture', *Metropolitan Museum Journal* 25 (1990): 49–142. Bellicard accompanied Soufflot and Marigny on their important tour of Italy.

Harrington, Kevin, *Changing Ideals of Architecture in the Encyclopédie, 1750–1776* (Ann Arbor, Mich., 1985).

Harris, John and Michael Snodin (eds), *Sir William Chambers, Architect to George III* (New Haven and London, 1996).

Hermann, Wolfgang, *Laugier and Eighteenth Century French Theory* (London, 1962).

Middleton, Robin, 'The Abbé de Cordemoy and the Graeco-Gothic Ideal: A Prelude to Romantic Classicism', *Journal of the Warburg and Courtauld Institutes* 25 (1962): 278–320; 26 (1963): 90–123 remains the classic and definitive account of the origins and spread of the Graeco-Gothic synthesis.

Nyberg, Dorothea, 'La Sainte Antiquité: Focus of an Eighteenth-Century Architectural Debate', in Douglas Fraser, Howard Hibbard, and Milton J. Lewine (eds), *Essays in the History of Architecture Presented to Rudolf Wittkower* (London, 1967), pp. 159–69.

Perlove, Shelley Karen, 'Piranesi's *Tomb of the Scipios* of *Le Antichità Romane* and Marc-Antoine Laugier's Primitive Hut', *Gazette des Beaux-Arts* 113 (March 1989): 115–20.

Picon, Antoine, *French Architects and Engineers in the Age of Enlightenment* (Cambridge, 1992).

Podro, Michael, *The Critical Historians of Art* (New Haven and London, 1982) for a good discussion of Winckelmann.

Rabreau, Daniel, 'La Basilique Sainte-Geneviève de Soufflot', pp. 37–96 in Barry Bergdoll (ed.), *Le Panthéon: Symbole des révolutions* (Paris, 1989) is the single best treatment of the design, evolution, and political context and meanings of Soufflot's building.

Rykwert, Joseph, *On Adam's House in Paradise: the idea of the primitive hut in architectural history* (New York, 1972).

Rykwert, Joseph, *The First Moderns: The Architects of the Eighteenth Century* (Cambridge, Mass., 1980) is particularly valuable for its discussion of the Italian rigorists in relation to the better-known trends of French Enlightenment theory.

Scott, Ian Jonathan, *Piranesi* (London and New York, 1975).

Scott, Katie, *The Rococo Interior: Decoration and Social Spaces in Early Eighteenth Century Paris* (London and New Haven, 1995) should be used in conjunction with the classic account by **Fiske Kimball**, *The Creation of the Rococo* (Philadelphia, 1943).

Serra, Joselita Raspi (ed.), *Paestum and the Doric Revival, 1750–1830* (Florence, 1986).

Stillman, Damie, *English Neo-classical Architecture*, 2 vols (London, 1988). This two-volume survey is one of the few works to address the full range of building types, including new kinds of commercial spaces. Although it is not a history *per se* of the commercialization of eighteenth-century architectural practice in Britain, it contains much valuable information for a future business history of architecture.

Shvidkovskii, D.O., *The Empress and the Architect: British architects and gardens at the court of Catherine the Great* (New Haven, Conn., 1996).

Tait, A. A., *Robert Adam: Drawings and the Imagination* (Cambridge, 1993).

Vidler, Anthony, *The Writing of the Walls: Architectural Theory in the Late Enlightenment* (Princeton, 1987) for the second part on 'Interpretations of History'.

Watkin, David, *Athenian Stuart, Pioneer of the Greek Revival* (London, 1982).

Watkin, David, *Sir John Soane: Enlightenment Thought and the Royal Academy Lectures* (Cambridge, 1996). A study of the intellectual sources of Soane's ideas in both design and pedagogy, this monumental work provides a synoptic view of major figures and themes in eighteenth-century British, French, and Italian architectural theory.

Wiebenson, Dora, *Sources of Greek Revival Architecture* (London, 1969) is a reliable account of archaeological travel and the bibliographical revolution.

Wilton, Andrew and Ilaria Bignamini, *Grand Tour: The lure of Italy in the eighteenth century* (London, 1996).

Wilton-Ely, John, *The Mind and Art of Giovanni Battista Piranesi* (London, 1978).
Wittkower, Rudolph, 'Piranesi's Architectural Creed', *Journal of the Warburg Institute* 2 (1938), reprinted in *Studies in the Italian Baroque* (London, 1975), pp. 235–46.

Chapter 2: What is Enlightenment?
Primary texts
Gwynn, John, *London and Westminster Improved … to which is prefixed a Discourse on Public Magnificence* (London, 1766).
Laugier, Marc-Antoine, *Essay on Architecture* (Paris, 1753) Chp. 5: 'On the Embellisment of Towns'.
Peyre, Marie-Joseph, *Oeuvres d'Architecture* (Paris, 1765; reprint Zaragoza, Spain, 1996). Primarily a folio of architectural projects, it should be consulted for its illustrations even by those without French, since its Europe-wide influence was enormous.
Ralph, James, *A Critical Review of the Publick Buildings, Statues and Ornaments in, and about London and Westminster …* (London, 1734; reprint edition Farnborough, Hants, 1971).

Secondary texts
Benhamou, Reed, 'Continuing Education and other innovations: an eighteenth century case study', *Studies in Eighteenth Century Culture* 15 (1986): 67–76 is a valuable study of Blondel's teaching to be read in conjunction with Richard Etlin's discussion in *Symbolic Space* (see chp. 1).
Bergdoll, Barry, 'Competing in the Academy and the Marketplace: European Architectural Competions, 1401–1927', in Hélène Lipstadt (ed.), *The Experimental Tradition: Essays on Competitions in Architecture* (New York, 1989), pp. 21–52.
Chartier, Roger, *The Cultural Origins of the French Revolution* (Durham, NC and London, 1991).
Cleary, Richard, *The Place Royale and Urban Design in the Ancient Regime* (Cambridge, 1999).
Crow, Thomas, *Painters and Public Life in Eighteenth-Century Paris* (New Haven, 1985) is both an excellent model for a future study of the rise of architectural criticism in Enlightenment France and includes extensive discussion of La Font de Saint-Yenne's role as an art critic.
Egorov, I. A., *The Architectural Planning of St. Petersburg, Its development in the 18th and 19th centuries* (Athens, Ohio, 1969).
Franca, José-Augusto, *Une ville des Lumières: la Lisbonne de Pombal* (Paris, 1965).

Habermas, Jürgen, *The Structural Transformation of the Public Sphere, an Inquiry into a category of bourgeois society* (Cambridge, Mass., 1989). Presents important material and positions in relationship to the development of a reading public and a public sphere in the closing decades of the eighteenth century.
MacPaland, Edward, *James Gandon, Vitruvius Hibernicus* (London, 1985).
McKindrick, Neil et al., *The Birth of Consumer Society: The Commercialization of Eighteenth Century England* (London, 1982).
Middleton, Robin, 'Diversity but Hygienic Please: Pierre Patte's Arcades Verdict', in *Daedalos* 24 (15 June 1987): 72–9.
Muthesius, Stefan, *The English Terraced House* (London, 1982).
Neumeyer, Alfred, 'Monuments to "Genius" in German Classicism', *Journal of the Warburg and Courtauld Institutes* 2 (1938): 159–63. Remains one of the only accounts of Gilly's Friedrich the Great monument in the context of Romantic hero-worship.
Olsen, Donald, *Town Planning in London: The Eighteenth and Nineteenth Centuries* (New Haven, 1982).
Picon, Antoine, 'Pierre Patte and the Concept of the Rational Town', chp. 8 in *French Architects and Engineers in the Age of the Enlightenment* (Cambridge, 1992).
Rabreau, Daniel, 'The Theatre-monument: a century of "French" typology, 1750–1850', *Zodiac* 2 (September 1989): 44–69.
Rabreau, Daniel and Monika Steinhauser, 'Le Théâtre de l'Odéon de Charles De Wailly et Marie-Joseph Peyre, 1767–1782', *Revue de l'Art* 19 (1973): 8–49 remains the classic article, with a richly documented history of the design evolution and politics of this seminal project.
Schorske, Carl, 'The idea of the City in European Thought: Voltaire to Spengler', in Oscar Handlin and John Burchard (eds), *The Historian and the City* (Cambridge, Mass., 1963), pp. 95–114.
Stillman, Damie, *English Neo-classical Architecture* (London, 1988).
Summerson, Sir John, *Georgian London* (London, 1978).
Sutcliffe, Antony, *Paris: An Architectural History* (New Haven, 1993) offers a convenient overview in English of the development of eighteenth-century Paris but it is to be used with care, as it is flawed by numerous errors.
Vidler, Anthony, 'Scenes of the Street: Transformations in Ideal and Reality, 1750–1871', in Stanford Anderson (ed.), *On Streets* (Cambridge, Mass., 1978), pp. 29–106.
Wurnow, Robert, *Communities of Discourse:*

Ideology and Social Structure in the Reformation, Enlightenment and European Socialism (Cambridge, Mass., 1989).

Chapter 3: Experimental Architecture
Primary texts

Boullée, Etienne-Louis, *An Essay on Art* (*c.*1794), trans. in Helen Rosenau, *Boullée and Visionary Architecture* (London, 1976).

Burke, Sir Edmund, *A Philosophical Enquiry into the Origin of our Ideas of the Sublime and the Beautiful* (London, 1757).

Condillac, Abbé Bonnot de, *Traité des Sensations* (Paris, 1754), translated as *Condillac's Treatise on Sensations* by Geraldine Carr (London, 1930).

Hunt, John Dixon and Peter Willis, *The Genius of the Place: The English Landscape Garden, 1620–1820* (Cambridge, Mass., 1988). An anthology of texts.

Le Camus de Mézières, Nicolas, *The Genius of Architecture; or the analogy of that art with our sensations, 1780*. English edition translated by David Britt and introduced by Robin Middleton (Santa Monica, 1992).

Locke, John, *An Essay Concerning Human Understanding* (London, 1689).

Ledoux, Claude-Nicolas, *Architecture Considered in Relation to Art, Morals, and Legislation*. Reprint edn with English commentary (Princeton Architecture Books, 1983).

Ledoux, Claude-Nicolas, *Architecture de Ledoux: Inédits pour un tome* III (Paris, 1991). Edition of the long-lost volume of plates for Ledoux's third volume, on domestic design, for his great folio *Architecture*, with an introduction by Michel Gallet.

Secondary texts

Bender, John, *Imagining the Penitentiary: Fiction and the Architecture of Mind in Eighteenth-Century England* (Chicago, 1987).

Bressani, Martin, 'Etienne-Louis Boullée: empiricism and the cenotaph for Newton', *Architectura* 23, no. 1 (1993): 37–57.

Carter, George, *Humphry Repton, Landscape Gardener, 1752–1818* (Norwich, 1982).

Curl, James Stevens, *The Art and Architecture of Freemasonry: an introduction* (London, 1991).

Evans, Robin, *The Fabrication of Virtue: English prison architecture, 1750–1840* (Cambridge, 1982).

For the Friends of Nature and Art: The Garden Kingdom of Prince Franz von Anhalt-Dessau (Ostfildern-Ruit, 1997).

Foucault, Michel, *The Birth of the Clinic; an archaeology of medical perception* (trans. of

Naissance de la clinique, New York, 1973).

Foucault, Michel, *Discipline and Punish: the birth of the prison* (trans. of *Surveiller et punir*, New York, 1977).

Hipple, Walter John, *The Beautiful, the Sublime and the Picturesque in Eighteenth Century British Aesthetic Theory* (Carbondale, Ill., 1957). Remains a classic.

Hunt, John Dixon, *Gardens and the Picturesque: studies in the history of landscape architecture* (Cambridge, Mass., 1992).

Hunt, John Dixon, *The Figure in the Landscape: poetry, painting, and gardening during the eighteenth century* (Baltimore, 1976).

Hussey, Christopher, *The Picturesque: Studies in a point of a view* (London, 1927, revised edition, Hamden, Conn., 1967).

Markus, Thomas A., *Buildings and Power: Freedom and Control in the Origin of Modern Building Types* (London, 1993).

Middleton, Robin, 'Sickness, Madness and Crime as the Grounds of Form', *AA Files* 24 (1992): 16–30 and 25 (1993): 14–29.

Middleton, Robin, 'Boullée and the Exotic', *AA Files* 19 (1990): 35–49.

O'Neal, John C., *The Authority of Experience: Sensationist Theory in the French Enlightenment* (Penn State, 1996). Largely literary in focus but a good survey and very suggestive for thinking about architecture.

Robinson, Sidney, *Inquiry into the Picturesque* (Chicago, 1991).

Stroud, Dorothy, *Capability Brown* (London, 1984).

Stroud, Dorothy, *George Dance, Architect 1741–1825* (London, 1971).

Stroud, Dorothy, *Humphry Repton* (London, 1962).

Vidler, Anthony, *Claude Nicolas Ledoux: architecture and social reform at the end of the ancien régime* (London and Cambridge, Mass., 1990).

Vidler, Anthony, *The Writing of the Walls: architectural theory in the late enlightenment* (New York, 1987). Part one treats the building types taken up by the discourse on institutions: prisons, hospitals, and factories.

Watkin, David, *The English Vision: the picturesque in architecture, landscape, and garden design* (London, 1982).

Wiebenson, Dora, *The Picturesque Garden in France* (Princeton, 1978).

Woodbridge, Kenneth, *Landscape and Antiquity: aspects of English culture at Stourhead, 1718 to 1838* (London, 1970).

Chapter 4: Revolutionary Architecture

Primary texts

Durand, J. -N. -L., *Summary of courses offered at the École Polytechnique* (1802–05). A translation with an introduction by Antoine Picon will be published by the Getty Center, Santa Monica, California, in 2000.

Durand, J. -N. -L., *Portfolio and parallel of buildings of all types ancient and modern* (1800).

Quatremère de Quincy, A. -C., Translations from the *Dictionnaire d'Architecture* in *9H7* (1985) and 'Type', in *Oppositions* 4 (1977), introduced by Anthony Vidler.

Secondary texts

Abramson, Daniel, 'Money's Architecture: The building of the Bank of England, 1731–1833', Ph.D. Dissertation, Harvard University, 1993.

Bannister, T., 'The First Iron Framed Buildings in England', *Architectural Review* 107 (1950): 231–46.

Bergdoll, Barry, 'Friedrich Weinbrenner and Neoclassical Karlsruhe: A Vision Tempered by Reality', in *Friedrich Weinbrenner, 1766–1825* (London, 1982).

Bergdoll, Barry, 'Panoramic Patriotism: Charles De Wailly's proposal for the Pantheon, c.1797', in Nanni Baltzer et al. (eds), *Forsters Kaleidoscope* (Zurich: ETH, forthcoming).

Crook, J. M. and M. H. Port, *The History of the King's Works*. Vol. 6 (1752–1851) (London, 1973).

Deming, Mark, 'Le Panthéon Révolutionnaire', in Barry Bergdoll (ed.) *Le Panthéon: Symbole des Révolutions* (Paris, 1991), pp. 97–150. Remains the best text on the creation of the revolutionary Panthéon.

Fox, Celina (ed.), *London—World City, 1800–1840* (New Haven, 1992).

Hunt, Lynn, *Politics, Culture, and Class in the French Revolution* (Berkeley, 1984).

Johnson, H. R., 'William Strutt's Cotton Mills', *Transactions of the Newcomen Society* 30 (1955–57): 179–205.

Kennedy, Emmet, *A Cultural History of the French Revolution* (New Haven, 1989).

Lavin, Sylvia, *Quatremère de Quincy and the Invention of a Modern Language of Architecture* (Cambridge, Mass., 1991).

Leith, James A., *The Idea of Art as Propaganda in France, 1750–1799* (Toronto, 1965).

Leith, James A., *Space and Revolution: Projects for monuments, squares, and public buildings in France, 1789–1799* (Montreal, 1991). Those with French should also consult Jean-Pierre Mouilleseaux and Annie Jacques, *Les Architectes de la Liberté* (Paris, 1989) and Philippe Bordes and Régis Michel, *Aux Armes aux Arts!: Les Arts et la Révolution, 1789–1799* (Paris, 1989).

Luke, Yvonne, 'The Politics of Participation: Quatremère de Quincy and the Theory and Practice of "Concours Publics" in Revolutionary France, 1791–1795', *Oxford Art Journal* X-1 (1987): 15–43.

Mansbridge, Michael, *John Nash: a complete catalogue, 1752–1835* (London, 1991).

McClellan, Andrew, *Inventing the Louvre: Art, Politics, and the Origins of the Modern Museum in Eighteenth Century Paris* (Cambridge, 1994).

Morachiello, Paolo and Georges Teyssot, 'State, town and the colonization of the territory during the First Empire', *Lotus International* 24 (1979): 24–39.

Ozouf, Mona, *Festivals and the French Revolution* (Cambridge, Mass., 1988).

Ozouf, Mona, 'The Pantheon or the Ecole Normale des Morts', in Pierre Nora (ed.), *Realms of Memory* (New York, 1996).

Richards, J. M., *The Functional Traditon in Early Industrial Building* (London, 1958).

Richardson, Margaret and May Anne Stevens (eds.), *John Soane, Architect: Master of Space and Light* (London, 1999).

Sawyer, Sean, 'Sir John Soane's symbolic Westminster: the apotheosis of George III', *Architectural History* 39 (1996): 54–76.

Schumann-Bacia, Eva, *John Soane and the Bank of England* (New York, 1991).

Skempton, A. W., 'Samuel Wyatt and the Albion Mill', *Architectural History* 14 (1971): 53–73.

Summerson, John, 'Soane: the Man and the Style', in *John Soane* (London, 1983); adapted from Summerson's *Sir John Soane* (London, 1952).

Summerson, John, 'The Evolution of Soane's Bank Stock Office in the Bank of England', in *The Unromantic Castle and other Essays* (London, 1990), pp. 143–56.

Summerson, Sir John, *The Life and Work of John Nash, Architect* (London, 1980).

Szambien, Werner, *J.N.L. Durand* (Paris, 1983).

Temple, Nigel, *John Nash and the Village Picturesque* (London, 1979).

Villari, Sergio, *J.N.L. Durand (1760–1834): Art and Science of Architecture* (New York, 1990).

Chapter 5: Nationalism and Stylistic Debates

Primary texts

Eastlake, Charles Locke, *A History of the Gothic Revival: An Attempt to Show How the Taste for Medieval Architecture which lingered in England during the last two centuries has since been encouraged and developed* (London, 1872). Reprint edn (Leicester, 1971).

Ferrey, Benjamin, *Recollections of A.W.N. Pugin and his father Augustus Pugin* (London, 1861). Reprint edn with introduction by Clive and Jane Wainwright (London, 1978).

Goethe, Johann, 'On German Architecture' (1772), in John Gage (ed.), *Goethe on Art* (London, 1980).

Pugin, A. W. N., *True Principles of Pointed or Christian Architecture* (1841; reprint, New York, 1973).

Pugin, A. W. N., *Apology for the Revival of Christian Architecture* (1843).

Pugin, A. W. N., *Contrasts; or a parallel between the noble edifices of the Middle Ages and Corresponding Buildings of the Present Day; shewing the Present Decay of Taste*, 2nd edn (London, 1841). Modern critical edn by H. -R. Hitchcock (Leicester, 1969).

Rickman, Thomas, *An Attempt to Discriminate the Styles of English Architecture* (London, 1817).

Walpole, Horace, *Description of the Villa of Mr. Horace Walpole … at Strawberry Hill near Twickenham, Middlesex …* (1784 and subsequent edns; facsimile edn London, 1964).

Secondary texts

Anderson, Benedict, *Imagined Communities: Reflections on the Origin and Spread of Nationalism* (rev. edn, London, 1991).

Atterbury, Paul (ed.), *Pugin: Master of the Gothic Revival* (London and New Haven, 1995).

Atterbury, Paul, and Clive Wainwright (eds), *Pugin: A Gothic Passion* (London and New Haven, 1994).

Bergdoll, Barry, *Karl Friedrich Schinkel: An Architecture for Prussia* (New York, 1994).

Brooks, Chris, *The Gothic Revival* (London, 1999).

Brooks, Chris and Andrew Saint (eds), *The Victorian Church, Architecture and Society* (Manchester, 1995).

Clark, Kenneth, *The Gothic Revival: An Essay in the History of Taste*. 3rd edn (London, 1962).

Cole, David, *The Work of Sir Gilbert Scott* (London, 1980).

Colley, Linda, *Britons, Forging the Nation, 1707–1837* (New Haven and London, 1992).

Crook, J. Mordaunt, *The British Museum* (London, 1972).

Crook, J. Mordaunt, *The Greek Revival: Neoclassical Attitudes In British Architecture 1760–1870* (London, 1972).

Crook, J. Mordaunt, *John Carter and the Mind of the Gothic Revival* (London, 1995).

Csorba, László, József Sisa, and Zoltán Szalay, *The Hungarian Parliament* (Budapest, 1993).

Fawcett, Jane (ed.), *Seven Victorian Architects* (London, 1976).

Ferriday, Peter, *Victorian Architecture* (London, 1963).

Fessas-Emmanouil, Helen, *Public Architecture in Modern Greece, 1827–1992* (Athens, 1993).

Germann, Georg, *Gothic Revival in Europe and Britian: Sources, Influences and Ideas* (London, 1972).

Hitchcock, Henry-Russell, *Early Victorian Architecture in Britian*. 2 vols (New Haven, 1954).

Hobsbawm, Eric and Terence Ranger (eds), *The Invention of Tradition* (Cambridge, 1983). A very suggestive approach for reconsidering the roles of revivals in nineteenth-century architecture.

Hobsbawm, Eric, *Nations and Nationalism since 1780. Programme, Myth, Reality* (Cambridge, 1990).

Lewis, Michael, *The Politics of the German Gothic Revival: Auguste Reichensperger* (New York, 1993).

Lewis, W. S., 'The Genesis of Strawberry Hill', *Metropolitan Museum Studies* 5 (1934–36): 57–92.

Liscombe, R. W., *William Wilkins, 1778–1839* (Cambridge, 1980).

Macauley, James, *The Gothic Revival, 1745–1845* (Glasgow, 1975). Treats in particular the lesser-known history of the Gothic Revival in Northern England and Scotland.

Macleod, Robert, *Style and Society: Architectural ideology in Britain 1835–1914* (London, 1971).

Port, M. H., (ed.), *The Houses of Parliament* (New Haven and London, 1976).

Port, M. H., *Six Hundred New Churches: a study of the church building commission, 1818–1856* (London, 1961).

Robson-Scott, W. D., *The Literary Background of the Gothic Revival in Germany* (Oxford, 1965).

Schorske, Carl, 'Medieval Revival and Its Modern Content: Coleridge, Pugin, and Disraeli', in *Thinking with History: Explorations in the Passage to Modernism*

(Princeton, 1998), pp. 71–89.

Seton-Watson, Hugh, *Nations and States. An Enquiry into the Origins of Nations and the Politics of Nationalism* (Boulder, Col., 1977).

Sicca, Cinzia Maria, *Committed to Classicism: The Buildings of Downing College Cambridge* (Cambridge, 1987).

Stanton, Phoebe, 'The Sources of Pugin's *Contrasts*', in Sir John Summerson (ed.), *Concerning Architecture* (London, 1968).

Stanton, Phoebe, *Pugin* (London, 1971).

Travlos, John and George Manousakis, *Neoclassical Architecture in Greece* (Athens, 1967).

Wainwright, Clive, *The Romantic Interior: The British Collector at Home, 1750–1850* (New Haven and London, 1989). Includes an excellent discussion of Strawberry Hill.

Watkin, David, *The Triumph of the Classical: Cambridge Architecture, 1804–1834* (Cambridge, 1977)

Watkin, David, *Thomas Hope 1769–1831 and the Neo-Classical Idea* (London, 1968).

White, James F., *The Cambridge Movement, The Ecclesiologists and the Gothic Revival* (Cambridge, 1962).

Williams, Raymond, *Culture and Society, 1780–1950* (New York, 1960). Perceptive treatment of the Pugin–Ruskin–Morris line in British architectural/ethical thinking.

Wilton-Ely, John, 'The Genesis and Evolution of Fonthill Abbey', *Architectural History* 23 (1980): 40–51.

Wright, Gwendolyn, *The Formation of National Collections of Art and Archaeology* (Washington, DC, 1996).

Youngson, A. J., *The Making of Classical Edinburgh* (Edinburgh, 1966).

Chapter 6: Historicism and New Building Types

Primary texts

Hübsch, Heinrich, *In what style should we build?* (Karlsruhe, 1828), trans. with other texts in Hermann, Wolfgang and Harry Francis Mallgrave, *In What Style should we Build? the German debate on architectural style* (Santa Monica, Calif., 1992).

Schinkel, Karl Friedrich, *Collection of Architectural Designs* (Berlin, 1819–40). English edn edited by Kenneth Hazlett, Stephen O'Malley, and Christopher Rudolph (Chicago, 1981).

Scott, Sir George Gilbert, *Personal and Professional Recollections* (London, 1879).

Scott, Sir George Gilbert, *Remarks on Secular and Domestic Architecture, Present and Future* (London, 1857).

Street, George Edmund, 'On the Proper Characteristics of a Town Church' (1850), and 'The True Principles of Architecture, and the Possibility of Development' (1852), *The Ecclesiologist* 11 (1850): 227–33 and 13 (1852): 247–62.

Street, George Edmund, *Brick and Marble Architecture in the Middle Ages* (London, 1855).

Thomson, Alexander, *The Light of Truth and Beauty, the Lectures of Alexander 'Greek' Thomson, Architect 1817–1875*, edited by Gavin Stamp (Glasgow, 1999).

Secondary texts

Benevolo, Leonardo, *The Origins of Modern Town Planning* (London and Cambridge, Mass., 1971) is especially good on the role of utopian socialist thought.

Bergdoll, Barry, 'Archaeology vs. History: Heinrich Hübsch's Critique of Neo-classicism and the Beginnings of Historicism in German Architectural Theory', *Oxford Art Journal* 5 (1983) 2: 3–12.

Bergdoll, Barry, *Karl Friedrich Schinkel: an Architecture for Prussia* (New York, 1994).

Bindman, David and Gottfried Riemann (eds), *Karl Friedrich Schinkel, 'The English Journey': Journal of a Visit to France and England in 1826* (New Haven and London, 1993).

Brownlee, David B., 'The First High Victorians: British Architectural Theory in the 1840s', *Architectura* 15 (1985): 33–46.

Brownlee, David B., *The Law Courts: The Architecture of George Edmund Street* (Cambridge, Mass. and London, 1984).

Brownlee, David B., '*Neugriechisch/Néo-Grec*: The German Vocabulary of French Romantic Architecture', *Journal of the Society of Architectural Historians* 50 (1991): 18–21.

Crinson, Mark, *Empire Building: Orientalism and Victorian Architecture* (London, 1996).

Crook, J. Mordaunt, *The Dilemma of Style: Architectural Ideas from the Picturesque to the Post-Modern* (London, 1987). A survey of the problems of eclecticism in architecture.

Crook, J. Mordaunt, *William Burges and the High Victorian Dream* (London and Chicago, 1981).

Dixon, Roger and Stefan Muthesius, *Victorian Architecture*, 2nd edn (London, 1985).

Drexler, Arthur (ed.), *The Architecture of the Ecole des Beaux-Arts* (New York and London, 1977). Especially for Neil Levine's seminal article on Henri Labrouste's Paestum studies and the Bibliothèque Sainte-Geneviève.

Hersey, George, *High Victorian Gothic* (Baltimore and London, 1972).

McFadzean, Ronald, *The Life and Work of Alexander Thomson* (London, 1979).

McWilliam, Neil, 'David d'Angers and the Pantheon Commission: Politics and Public Works under the July Monarchy', *Art History* 5 (1982): 426–46.

McWilliam, Neil, *Dreams of Happiness, Social Art and the French Left, 1830–1850* (Princeton, 1993). Deals exclusively with the art theory but lays out much of the essential background for understanding French utopian socialist architecture.

Meeks, Carrol M. V., *The Railroad Station, an architectural history* (New Haven, 1956).

Middleton, Robin (ed.), *The Beaux-Arts and Nineteenth-century French Architecture* (London and Cambridge, Mass., 1982).

Middleton, Robin, 'The Rationalist Interpretations of Léonce Reynaud and Viollet-le-Duc', *AA Files* 11 (1986): 29–48.

Muthesius, Stefan, *The High Victorian Movement in Architecture* (London, 1972).

Orbach, Julian, *Victorian Architecture in Britain* (London, 1987). A Blue Guide to Victorian architecture which provides an indispensable gazetteer and is peppered with intelligent and original insights.

Physick, John and Michael Darby, '*Marble Halls': Drawings and Models for Victorian Public Buildings* (London, 1973).

Schönemann, Heinz, *Karl Friedrich Schinkel: Charlottenhof, Potsdam-Sanssouci* (Stuttgart, 1997).

Smart, C. M., *Muscular Churches: Ecclesiastical Architecture of the High Victorian Period* (Fayetteville, Ark., 1989).

Stamp, Gavin, *Alexander 'Greek' Thomson* (London, 1999).

Stamp, Gavin and Sam McKinstry (eds), *Greek Thomson* (Edinburgh, 1994).

Summerson, Sir John, *Victorian Architecture in England: Four Studies in Evaluation* (New York, 1970).

Taylor, Katherine Fischer, *In the Theater of Criminal Justice, The Palais de Justice in Second Empire Paris* (Princeton, 1993).

Thompson, Paul, *William Butterfield, Victorian Architect* (London, 1971).

Van Zanten, A. L., 'The Palace and the Temple: Two Utopian Architectural Visions of the 1830s', *Art History* 2, no. 2 (June 1979): 179–200.

Van Zanten, David, 'Félix Duban and the buildings of the Ecole des Beaux-Arts', *Journal of the Society of Architectural Historians* 37 (1978): 64–84. Those with French should now consult Françoise Hamon and Sylvain Bellenger, *Félix Duban* (Paris, 1996).

Van Zanten, David, *Designing Paris: The Architecture of Duban, Labrouste, Duc, and Vaudoyer* (Cambridge, Mass., 1987).

Van Zanten, David, *The Architectural Polychromy of the 1830s* (New York, 1977).

Watkin, David and Tilman Mellinghof, *German Architecture and the Classical Ideal* (London, 1987) remains the only account of Bavarian Neoclassical architecture in English.

Zukowsky, John (ed.), *Karl Friedrich Schinkel: The Drama of Architecture* (Chicago, 1994).

Chapter 7: New Technology and Architectural Form

Primary texts

Acland, Henry W. and John Ruskin, *The Oxford Museum* (London, 1859).

Dresser, Christopher, *The Art of Decorative Design* (London, 1862).

Morris, William, *News from Nowhere and selected writings and designs.* Edited by Asa Briggs (New York, 1986).

Ruskin, John, *The Opening of the Crystal Palace considered in some of its relations to the prospects of art* (London, 1852). Reprinted in E. T. Cook and A. Wedderburn, *The Works of John Ruskin.* 39 vols (London, 1903-12).

Ruskin, John, *The Seven Lamps of Architecture* (London, 1849).

Ruskin, John, *The Stones of Venice.* 3 vols (London, 1851–53).

Semper, Gottfried, *The Four Elements of Architecture and Other Writings.* Trans. by Harry Francis Mallgrave and Wolfgang Herrmann (Cambridge, 1989).

Viollet-le-Duc, Eugène-Emmanuel, *The Foundations of Architecture: Selections from the Dictionnaire Raisonné of Viollet-le-Duc* (New York, 1990).

Viollet-le-Duc, Eugène-Emmanuel, *Lectures on Architecture.* English trans. by Benjamin Bucknall (London, 1877–81). Modern edn (New York, 1987).

Secondary texts

Allwood, John, *The Great Exhibitions* (London, 1977).

Baker, Malcolm and Brenda Richardson, *A Grand Design: The Art of the Victoria and Albert Museum* (New York, 1997).

Bergdoll, Barry, *Léon Vaudoyer, Historicism in the Age of Industry* (New York, 1994).

Blau, Eve, *Ruskinian Gothic: The Architecture of Deane and Woodward, 1845–1861* (Princeton, 1982).

Boe, Alf, *From Gothic Revival to Functional Form: A Study in Victorian Theories of Design* (Oslo, 1957).

Bressani, Martin, 'Notes on Viollet-le-Duc's Philosophy of History: Dialectics and Technology', *Journal of the Society of Architectural Historians* 48 (1989): 327–50.

Bressani, Martin, 'The life of stone: Viollet-le-Duc's physiology of architecture', *ANY* 14 (1996): 22–27.

Brooks, Michael W., *John Ruskin and Victorian Architecture* (New Brunswick, N. J. and London, 1987).

Chadwick, George F., *The Works of Sir Joseph Paxton* (London, 1961).

Darby, Michael, *The Islamic Perspective: an aspect of British Architecture and Design in the Nineteenth Century* (London, 1983).

Darby, Michael and David van Zanten, 'Owen Jones's Iron Buildings of the 1850s', *Architectura* 4 (1974): 53–75.

Davey, Peter, *Arts and Crafts Architecture* (London, 1995).

Durant, Stuart, *Christopher Dresser* (London and New York, 1993).

Garrigan, Kristine Ottesen, *Ruskin on Architecture, His Thought and Influence* (Madison, Wisc., 1973).

Greenhalgh, Paul, *Ephemeral Vista: The Expositions Universelles, Great Exhibitions and World's Fairs* (Manchester, 1988).

Halén, Widar, *Christopher Dresser* (London, 1993).

Hearn, M. F., *The Architectural Theory of Viollet-le-Duc: readings and commentaries* (Cambridge, Mass., 1990).

Herrmann, Wolfgang, *Gottfried Semper: In Search of Architecture* (Cambridge, Mass. and London, 1984). Includes trans. of important Semper manuscripts and a discussion of the relation between Semper and Bötticher's thought.

Hunt, John Dixon (ed.), *The Ruskin Polygon: essays on the imagination of John Ruskin* (Manchester, 1982).

Mallgrave, Harry Francis, *Gottfried Semper, Architect of the Nineteenth Century* (New Haven and London, 1996).

Marrey, Bernard, *Les Grands Magasins des origines à 1939* (Paris, 1979). This remains the best account of the development of the Parisian department store. Richly illustrated, it should be consulted by students even without French.

Muthesius, Stefan, ' "The Iron Problem" in the 1850s', *Architectural History* 13 (1970): 58–63.

O'Connell, Lauren M., 'A Rationalist Nationalist Architecture: Viollet-le-Duc's Modest Proposal for Russia', *Journal of the Society of Architectural Historians* 52 (1993): 436–52.

Schwarzer, Mitchell, *German Architectural Theory and the Search for Modern Identity* (Cambridge and New York, 1995).

Soros, Susan Weber (ed.) *E. W. Godwin, Aesthetic Movement Architect and Designer* (New Haven, 1999).

Summerson, Sir John, 'Viollet-le-Duc and the rational point of view', in *Heavenly Mansions* (New York, 1948).

Swenarton, Mark, *Artisans and Architecture: The Ruskinian Tradition in Architectural Thought* (New York, 1988).

Unrau, John, *Looking at Architecture with Ruskin* (London, 1978).

Wainwright, Clive, 'Principles true and false: Pugin and the foundation of the Museum of Manufactures', *The Burlington Magazine* 136 (1994): 357–64.

Wittemore, Leila, 'Theater of the Bazaar: Women and the Architecture of Fashion in 19th Century Paris', *A/R/C* 1 (1995): 15–25.

Yanni, Carla, *Nature's Museums: Victorian Science & the Architecture of Display* (Baltimore and London, 1999).

Chapter 8. The City Transformed

Primary texts

Alphand, *Les Promenades de Paris* (Paris, 1867–73; reprint edition, Princeton Architectural Books, 1989).

Cerdá, Ildefonso, *The five bases of the General Theory of Urbanization.* edited by Arturo Soria Puig (Madrid, 1999).

Sitte, Camillo, *City Planning According to Artistic Principles* (1889). Trans. in George R. Collins and Christiane Crasemann Collins, *Camillo Sitte: The Birth of Modern City Planning* (New York, 1986).

Secondary texts

Bullock, Nicholas and James Read, *The Movement for Housing Reform in Germany and France 1840–1914* (Cambridge, 1985).

Choay, Françoise, *The Modern City: Planning in the Nineteenth Century* (New York, 1969).

Evenson, Norma, *Paris: A Century of Change, 1878–1978* (New Haven and London, 1979).

Haiko, Peter, *Vienna, 1850–1930: Architecture* (New York, 1992).

Harvey, David, 'Paris 1852–1870', in *Consciousness and the Urban Experience* (Baltimore, 1985).

Jordan, David, *Transforming Paris: The Life and Labors of Baron Haussmann* (New York, 1995).

Ladd, Brian, *Urban Planning and Civic Order in Germany, 1860–1914* (Cambridge, Mass., 1990).

Loyer, François, *Paris Nineteenth Century: Architecture and Urbanism* (New York, 1988).

Mead, Christopher, *Charles Garnier's Paris Opera: Architectural Empathy and the Renaissance of French Classicism* (New York, 1991).

Moravánsky, Akos, *Competing Visions: Aesthetic Invention and Social Imagination in Central European Architecture, 1867–1918* (Cambridge, Mass., 1998).

Pinkney, David, *Napoleon III and the Rebuilding of Paris* (Princeton, 1958).

Schorske, Carl, *Fin-de-Siècle Vienna: Politics and Culture* (New York, 1981). The seminal interpretation offered here of the Ringstrasse should now be read in conjunction with the author's reconsideration of his position in 'Museum in Contested Space: The Sword, the Scepter, and the Ring', in Schorske, *Thinking with History: Explorations in the Passage to Modernism* (Princeton, 1998), pp. 104–22.

Simo, Melanie Louise, *Loudon and the Landscape, From Country Seat to Metropolis* (London, 1988).

Soria, Arturo, 'Ildefonso Cerdá's general theory of *urbanización*', *Town Planning Review* 66 (Jan. 1995): 15–39.

Suttcliffe, Anthony, *The Autumn of Central Paris: The Defeat of Town Planning, 1850–1950* (Montreal and London, 1971).

Van Zanten, David, *Building Paris: Architectural Institutions and the Transformation of the French Capital, 1830–1870* (New York and Cambridge, 1994).

Williams, Guy R., *London in the Country, The Growth of Suburbia* (London, 1975).

Chapter 9: The Crisis of Historicism
Primary texts

Mallgrave, Harry F. and Eleftherios Ikonomou (eds), *Empathy, Form, and Space: Problems in German Aesthetics, 1873–1893* (Santa Monica, Calif., 1994). Contains key texts by Robert Vischer, Heinrich Wölfflin, and August Schmarsov.

Nietzsche, Friedrich, *The Use and Abuse of History* (1874). Trans. by Adrian Collins (Indianapolis, 1949).

Secondary texts

Dal Co, Francesco, *Figures of Architecture and Thought: German Architectural Culture, 1880–1920* (New York, 1990).

Girouard, Mark, *Sweetness and Light: The Queen Anne Movement, 1860–1900* (Oxford, 1977).

Harvey, David, 'Monument and Myth: The Building of the Basilica of the Sacred Heart', in *The Urban Experience* (New York, 1989), pp. 200–28.

Loyrette, Henri, *Gustave Eiffel* (New York, 1985).

Mallgrave, Harry (ed.), *Otto Wagner: Reflections on the Raiment of Modernity* (Santa Monica, Calif., 1993). Especially important for the essay by Duncan Berry.

Russell, Frank (ed.), *Art Nouveau Architecture* (New York, 1979).

Saint, Andrew, *Richard Norman Shaw* (New Haven and London, 1976).

Schwarzer, Mitchell, 'The Emergence of Architectural Space: August Schmarsov's Theory of *Raumgestaltung*', *Assemblage* 15 (1991): 49–61.

Silverman, Deborah, *Art Nouveau in Fin-de-Siècle France: Politics, Psychology and Style* (Berkeley and London, 1989).

Silverman, Deborah, 'The Paris Exhibition of 1889: Architecture and the Crisis of Individualism', *Oppositions* 8 (1977): 70–91.

Stamp, Gavin and Andre Goulancourt, *The English House, 1860–1914. The Flowering of English Domestic Architecture* (London, 1986).

Picture Credits

The publisher would like to thank the following individuals and institutions who have kindly given permission to reproduce the illustrations listed below.

1. Charles Eisen: frontispiece for the second edition of Marc-Antoine (Abbé) Laugier's *Essay on Architecture* (Paris 1755). Royal Institute of British Architects [RIBA] Library, London/photo A.C. Cooper.
2. Johann Friedrich Dauthe: Nikolaikirche, Leipzig, 1784. Bildarchiv Foto Marburg.
3. Gabriel-Pierre-Martin Dumont: the Temple of Neptune, Paestum, 1764. Bibliothèque Nationale, Paris.
4. James Stuart sketching on the Acropolis, 1751, from J. Stuart and N. Revett, *Antiquities of Athens*, ii (1787). British Library, London (459.g.14).
5. James Stuart: Doric Temple at Hagley, Worcestershire, 1758. Country Life Picture Library, London.
6. Julien David Leroy: view of the Propylaea from *Les ruines des plus beaux monuments de la Grèce*. (Paris, 1758). British Library, London (1899.g.30).
7. Giovanni Battista Piranesi: Tomb of the Scipios, from *Antichità Romane*, ii (1756). British Library, London (147.i.6).
8. Giovanni Battista Piranesi: preparatory study for *Parere su l'architettura*, c.1765. Pen, with brown and Indian ink over red chalk. Kunstbibliothek, Berlin/photo. Bildarchiv Preussischer Kulturbesitz.
9. Giovanni Battista Piranesi: Temple of Neptune as illustrated in *Différentes vues de quelques restes ... de l'ancienne ville de Pesto* (1778). Photo Conway Library, Courtauld Institute of Art, London.
10. J.-G. Soufflot: perspective view of the projected church of Ste-Geneviève, Paris, 1757, as engraved by J.C. Bellicard. Musée Carnavalet, Paris/Photothèque Musées de la Ville de Paris.
11. J.-G. Soufflot: church of Ste-Geneviève (now Panthéon), Paris, 1757–89. Interior. Photo A.F. Kersting, London.
12. J.-G. Soufflot: section of the 1764 project for the church of Ste-Geneviève, Paris. Archives Nationales, Paris (N.IV Seine/1093, 11).
13. J.-G. Soufflot: Ste-Geneviève, Paris. Section through the masonry of the pediment. From A.-J.-B. Rondelet, *Traité theorique et pratique de l'art de bâtir* (1802–17). RIBA, London/photo A.C. Cooper.
14. Julien David Leroy: engraved plate illustrating the development of the Christian church, Paris, 1764. From *Histoire de la disposition et des formes différentes que les chrétiens ont données à leurs temples ...* (1764) Avery Architectural and Fine Arts Library, Columbia University in the City of New York.
15. J.-G. Soufflot. Ste-Geneviève, section of final project, c.1770. Archives Nationales, (N.III Seine/1093, 3), Paris.
16. Robert Adam. Kedleston Hall. (a) South garden elevation. Photo A.F. Kersting, London. (b) Plan. Courtesy the National Trust.
17. Robert Adam. Syon House, Middlesex. (a) View of the entrance hall. Photo A.F. Kersting, London; (b) Ante-chamber. Photo A.F. Kersting; (c) Plan. Courtesy of Duke of Northumberland.
18. Pierre Patte. Composite map of Paris with rival plans submitted in 1748 for siting and designing a Place Louis XV, 1765. From Pierre Patte, *Monumens ériges en France ...* (1765). RIBA Library, London/photo A.C. Cooper.
19. G.L. Le Rouge. Engraving of the Place Louis XV (today de la Concorde) as inaugurated in 1763 to the designs of the royal architect Anges-Jacques Gabriel. Musée Carnavalet, Paris/Photothèque des Musées de la Ville de Paris/photo Ladet.
20. Pierre Patte. Project for an ideal street, 1769. From *Mémoires sur les objets les plus importans de l'architecture* (1769). RIBA

Library, London/photo A.C. Cooper.
21. Aerial view of the centre of Lisbon.
Arquivo Fotográfico, Departemento da
Patrimonio Cultural, Lisbon.
22. Nicolas Le Camus de Mezières. Halle au
Blé. Site plan as engraved in the architect's
folio presentation of the design, with partial
elevation and section. From *Récueil des
differens plans et dessins concernant la nouvelle
Halle des Grains* (1769). RIBA Library,
London/photo A.C. Cooper.
23. M.-J. Peyre. Project for a cathedral and two
palaces. (a) Perspective view; (b) Plan. From
M.-J. Peyre, *Oeuvres d'architecture* (1765).
RIBA Library, London/photo A.C. Cooper
24. Charles De Wailly. Section of the
Comédie-Française, Paris/ Photothèque des
Musées de la Ville de Paris/Berthier.
25. Charles De Wailly and M.-J. Peyre. Aerial
view of the Comédie-Française and its
quarter, Paris, 1779–82. Photo Roger–Viollet,
Paris.
26. Victor Louis. Stairhall of the Grand
Théâtre in Bordeaux, 1773–80. Photo Achim
Bednorz, Cologne.
27. William Chambers. River façade of the
new Mint (Hôtel des Monnaies), Paris. RIBA
Drawings Collection, London/photo A.C.
Cooper.
28. Jacques Gondoin. School of Surgery, Paris.
(a) Street view. Photo Achim Bednorz,
Cologne; (b) Plan. (c) View of the anatomy
theatre. From Jacques Gondoin, *Descriptions
des écoles de chirurgerie* (1780). RIBA Library,
London/photo A.C. Cooper.
29. Jean-Louis Desprez (1743–1804). Idealized
view of Somerset House, London, with St
Paul's Cathedral and Blackfriars Bridge. Pen
and watercolour. 57.8 x 177 cm. Yale Center for
British Art, Paul Mellon Collection
(B1977.14.6146), New Haven, CT/photo
Richard Caspole.
30. Jean-Louis Desprez (1743–1804). The
courtyard of Somerset House, London,
1776–96. Pen, ink and wash. 70 x 129 cm.
Trustees of Sir John Soane's Museum,
London.
31. View of the Forum Fredricianum, Berlin.
Engraving after K.F. Schinkel, 1830. Photo
AKG London.
32. Friedrich Gilly. Design for a monument to
Frederick the Great to be erected in
Berlin, 1797. Kupferstichkabinett, Staatliches
Museen, Berlin/photo Bildarchiv Preussischer
Kulturbesitz.
33. Plan of the gardens at Rousham. After
R. Middleton and D. Watkin, *Neoclassical
and Nineteenth-Century Architecture* (Milan:

Electa, 1977; New York: Abrams, 1980).
34. The Gardens at Stourhead. (a) Plan;
(b) View from the village, looking across the
lake towards the Pantheon, *c*.1775. Watercolour
by Coplestone Warre Bampfylde. Stourhead
House, Warminster/photo The Art Archive,
London.
35. Erménonville: view of the Island of Poplars
with Rousseau's cenotaph from the Temple of
Philosophy, designed by Girardin, 1766–70.
From *Promenade ou itinéraire de Jardins
d'Erménonville* (1788). British Library
(576.f.11), London.
36. Worlitz, near Dessau, Germany. (a) copy of
the Coalbrookdale cast-iron bridge.
(b) Plan. Engraving by J.S. Probst after
J.C. Neumark, 1784. Photos Kulturstiftung
DessauWorlitz.
37. Entrance to the Désert de Retz, in the
Forest of Marly near Chambourçy, *c*.1775.
From G. Le Rouge, *Détails de nouveaux jardins
à la mode*, ii (1776-88). British Library
(34.f.11–12), London.
38. Robert Adam. Culzean Castle, Scotland,
1777–90. Photo A.F. Kersting, London.
39. Etienne-Louis Boullée. Cenotaph for
Newton, *c*.1784. (a) Night view of exterior.
(b) Daytime view of interior. Bibliothèque
Nationale (Estampes, HA.57,7–8), Paris.
40. Etienne-Louis Boullée. Interior of the
Metropole on the feast of the Fête Dieu,
c.1781. Bibliothèque Nationale (Estampes,
HA.56,8), Paris.
41. Etienne-Louis Boullée. Design for the
Royal Library, interior. Bibliothèque
Nationale (Estampes, HA.56,36), Paris.
42. George Dance. Newgate Prison, London.
1768–75. Photograph 1900. © Crown
Copyright. National Monuments Record,
London.
43. Giovanni Battista Piranesi. Imaginary
Prison from *Carceri d'invenzione* (2/*c*.1760).
Photo Conway Library, Courtauld Institute of
Art, London.
44. Jeremy Bentham. 'Panopticon', *c*.1791.
Bentham Papers (115/44). Manuscripts and
Rare Books, University College London.
45. Bernard Poyet. Radial hospital plan. Plan,
elevation and section for the Hôtel-Dieu on
the Île des Cygnes, 1785. Pen and black ink and
black and pink wash on laid paper. Sheet
59.2 x 45.6 cm. Collection Centre Canadien
d'Architecture/Canadian Centre for
Architecture (DR1987:0115), Montreal.
46. Pavilion plan hospital. From J.-N.-L.
Durand, *Récueil et parallèle des edifices
de tout genres anciens et modernes* (1799–1810).
RIBA Library, London/photo A.C. Cooper.

47. Claude-Nicolas Ledoux. Hôtel Thélusson, Paris, 1778. From C.-N. Ledoux, *L'architecture considerée* (1804). RIBA Library, London/photo A.C. Cooper.

48. Claude-Nicolas Ledoux. Project for Chaux. From C.-N. Ledoux, *L'architecture considerée* (1804). British Library (559*.H.20), London.

49. Claude-Nicolas Ledoux. 'Pacifière' for Chaux. From L.-C. Ledoux, *L'architecture considerée* (1804). British Library (559*.H.20), London.

50. Pierre-François Palloy. Monument to the Revolution to be erected on the site of the demolished prison of the Bastille, 1789. From *Adresse, et projet général ... présenté a l'Assemblé nationale et au roi des français* (Paris, 1792). Bibliothèque Nationale, Paris.

51. Jacques-Guillaume Legrand and Jacques Molinos. Project for a national palace to be erected over the incomplete foundations of the royal church of the Madeleine, 1792. Musée Carnavalet, Paris/Photothèque des Musées de la Ville de Paris/Ledet.

52. Bird's-eye view of the Festival of Federation, 14 July 1790. Engraving by Choquet after Chaillot. Musée Carnavalet, Paris/Photothèque des Musées de la Ville de Paris/Habouzit.

53. Charles De Wailly. Project to transform the Panthéon, 1797. Pen and grey ink and brown and grey wash on laid paper. Sheet 24.4 x 19.7 cm. Collection Centre Canadien d'Architecture/Canadian Centre for Architecture (DR1995:0061), Montreal.

54. Jean-Nicolas-Louis Durand and Jacques-Thomas Thibault. Project for a Temple of Equality submitted in the Competitions of the Year II (1794). Drawing by Leo von Klenze. Staatliche Graphische Sammlung (INV.27000), Munich.

55. Louis Cassas. Gallery of Architecture opened in the Rue de Seine, Paris, c.1806. From L.P. Baltard, *Athenaeum* (1806). British Library (PP.1655), London.

56. Early nineteenth-century mule shop. From E. Baines, *History of Cotton Manufacture* (1835). British Library (1044.g.23), London.

57. Joseph Gandy. Rendering of Soane's Bank Stock Office, 1798. Pen and watercolour. 42.8 x 94.1 cm. Trustees of Sir John Soane's Museum, London.

58. Sir John Soane. Plan of the Bank of England, London, 1794–1810. Trustees of Sir Sir John Soane's Museum, London.

59. Sir John Soane. Tivoli Corner, Bank of England, 1807. Pen and watercolour. 31.9 x 91.7 cm. Trustees of Sir John Soane's Museum, London.

60. Joseph Gandy. The Bank of England Imagined in Ruins, 1830. Watercolour. 72.5 x 129 cm. Trustees of Sir John Soane's Museum, London.

61. Friedrich Gilly. View of the Rue des Colonnes in Paris, 1798. Universitäts-bibliothek, Technische Universität Berlin. Original lost in World War II. From A. Rietdorf, *Gilly: Wiedergeburt der Architektur* (Berlin: Hans von Hugo Verlag, 1940).

62. John Nash. Park Village East, London, 1823–24. Public Record Office (MPEEI/911), Kew.

63. Charles Percier and Pierre-Louis Fontaine. Rue de Rivoli, Paris, 1802–c.1825). From A.C. Pugin, *Paris and its Environs Displayed in a Series of Picturesque Views*, i (1829–31). RIBA Library, London/photo A.C. Cooper.

64. (a) Map of Regent Street and Regent's Park complex. After R. Middleton and D. Watkin, *Neoclassical and Nineteenth-Century Architecture* (Milan: Electa, 1977; New York: Abrams, 1980). (b) View of Regent Street. *From Metropolitan Improvements, or London in the 19th century ... from original drawings by Thomas Shepherd* (1827). RIBA Library, London/photo A.C. Cooper.

65. Friedrich Weinbrenner. Market Square, Karlsruhe, c.1815. Lithograph by Karl Muller, 1828. Landesbildstelle Baden (no.19011), Karlsruhe.

66. John Foulston. View of Devonport, near Plymouth, 1820s. Watercolour. City Museum and Art Gallery, Plymouth/photo Robert Chapman.

67. Horace Walpole. Strawberry Hill, Twickenham, London, begun c.1750. (a) Exterior view. (b) The Long Gallery. (c) Plan. From H. Walpole, *A Description of the Villa of Mr Horace Walpole* (1784 edn). RIBA Library, London/photo A.C. Cooper.

68. The collapse of Fonthill Abbey on Christmas Day, 1825. Lithograph by W. Westall after J. Buckler. Beckford Tower Trust Collection, Bath.

69. (a) Cologne Cathedral as it appeared in the early nineteenth century. (b) Tony Avenarius. Ceremony for the dedication of Cologne Cathedral, 1880, with model of building and allegorical figure of Germania. Rheinisches Bildarchiv (nos. 134661 and 180492), Cologne.

70. Karl Friedrich Schinkel. Project for a cathedral to the Wars of Liberation, 1814. Kupferstichkabinett, Staatliches Museen, Berlin/photo Bildarchiv Preussischer Kulturbesitz.

71. Leo von Klenze. Painting showing

Walhalla (near Regensburg) and the Salvator-kirche, 1839. Historisches Museum/photo Museen der Stadt Regensburg.

72. Leo von Klenze. Königsplatz, Munich with Glyptothek (1816–34) and Propylaeum (1834). Stadtmuseum (INV.P.13.682), Munich.

73. Aerial view of Edinburgh showing Calton Hill with the incomplete colonnade of the projected Scottish National Monument. Skyscan Balloon Photography Copyright, Toddington.

74. Aerial view of Whitehall with Houses of Parliament and the National Gallery on Trafalgar Square. Skyscan Balloon Photography Copyright, Toddington.

75. A.W.N. Pugin. 'Contrasted Chapels', a plate from *Contrasts* (1836). RIBA Library, London/photo A.C. Cooper.

76. A.W.N. Pugin. Contrasted towns in 1440 and 1840. Plate added to the second edition of *Contrasts* (1840). RIBA Library, London/photo A.C. Cooper.

77. A.W.N. Pugin. Poster advertising an architectural competition from *Contrasts* (1836). RIBA Library, London/photo A.C. Cooper.

78. A.W.N. Pugin. St Giles, Cheadle, interior, 1839–44. Photo Martin Charles, Isleworth.

79. Charles Barry. Plan of the Houses of Parliament. From the *Illustrated London News* (30 September 1843). Photo Mary Evans Picture Library, Blackheath.

80. Pugin's own house, St Mary's Grange, near Salisbury, 1835. Photo P.D. Higgins.

81. Imre Steindl. Parliament House, Budapest, 1885–1904. Photo A.F. Kersting, London.

82. Sir George Gilbert Scott. Midland Grand Hotel, St Pancras Station, London, 1868–74. Photo Alan Chandler/Architectural Association Photo Library, London.

83. Victor Considerant's Phalanstery, published in 1834. From *Description du phalanstère et considerations sociales sur l'architectonique* (2/1840). Bibliothèque Nationale, Paris.

84. Henri Labrouste. Temple of Hera I at Paestum, 1828–29. École Nationale Supérieure des Beaux-Arts, Paris.

85. Jacques Ignace Hittorff. Reconstruction of the Temple of Empedocles, Selinunte. From *Restitution du Temple d'Empédocle* (1851). British Library (650.c.29; atlas), London.

86. Prosper Morey, after Félix Duban. Drawing of the École des Beaux-Arts, Paris. Archives Nationales (CP/VA/VIII/2), Paris.

87. Henri Labrouste. Bibliothèque Ste-Geneviève, 1838–50. (a) Exterior view.

(b) Reading Room on the second floor. Photos Roger–Viollet, Paris. (c) Plan of second floor.

88. Heinrich Hübsch. Pump room, Baden-Baden., 1837–40. Landesbildstelle Baden (NO.2600), Karlsruhe.

89. Heinrich Hübsch. St Cyriakus, Bulach, near Karlsruhe, 1828–37. Views of exterior and interior as published in the architect's own Bauwerke. Institut für Baugeschichte, Universität Karlsruhe.

90. Heinrich Hübsch. Experiments with vaulting forms derived from the use of hanging models, c.1838, from his *Bauwerke*. *Institut für Baugeschichte*, Universität Karlsruhe.

91. Karl Friedrich Schinkel. Schauspielhaus (Theatre), Berlin, 1819–21. Aquatint by Jugel after Schinkel, 1825. Photo AKG London.

92. Karl Friedrich Schinkel. *Langes Blatt*. Pencil, pen and watercolour. 33.5 x 149.3 cm. Kupferstichkabinett, Staatliches Museen, Berlin/photo Bildarchiv Preussischer Kulturbesitz/photo Jörg P. Anders.

93. Eduard Gärtner. View of the Bauakademie, Berlin, 1868. Oil on canvas. 63 x 82 cm. Nationalgalerie, Berlin/photo Bildarchiv Preussischer Kulturbesitz/photo Jörg P. Anders.

94. James Wild. Christ Church, Streatham, 1839–41. National Monuments Record, London. © Crown copyright NMR.

95. William Butterfield. All Saints, Margaret Street, London, 1849–59. (a) Exterior view. Photo Martin Charles, Isleworth. (b) Plan. After R. Middleton and D. Watkin, *Neoclassical and Nineteenth-Century Architecture* (Milan: Electa, 1977; New York: Abrams, 1980).

96. Sir George Gilbert Scott. View of staircase, Midland Grand Hotel, St Pancras Station, London. Arcaid, London/photo Nicholas Kane.

97. Alexander Thomson. St Vincent Street Church, Glasgow. National Monuments Record, Scotland.

98. M.G.B. Bindesbøll. Thorvaldesen Museum, Copenhagen, 1839–48. Photo Paul Larsen, Lechlade.

99. Thomas Deane and Benjamin Woodward. Trinity College Museum, Dublin, 1852–57. Photo Audio-Visual and Media Service, University of Dublin, Trinity College.

100. Aerial view of King's Cross and St Pancras stations, London. © London Aerial Photography.

101. Crystal Palace, London, 1851. Engraving

by Armytage. Mary Evans Picture Library, Blackheath.

102. Hector Horeau. Proposal for covering the projected Avenue de l'Opéra, Paris *c.*1862. Académie d'Architecture (1.202), Paris.

103. Glaziers' wagons at the Crystal Palace. Engraving from the *Illustrated London News* (4 January 1851). Mary Evans Picture Library, Blackheath.

104. Charles Downe. Working drawings for Paxton's Crystal Palace. From G.F. Chadwick, *The Works of Sir Joseph Paxton* (London: Architectural Press, 1961).

105. John Ruskin. Fondaco dei Turchi, Venice, 1853. Watercolour. Ruskin Museum, Coniston/ photo Bridgeman Art Library, London.

106. James O'Shea carving a jamb of a first-floor window of the University of Oxford Museum, *c.*1860. Photo University of Oxford Museum.

107. Central Court of the University of Oxford Museum. Photo A.F. Kersting, London.

108. Joseph Paxton. Victoria Regia. (a) Paxton's special glass house. Engraving from the *Illustrated London News* (17 November 1849). Mary Evans Picture Library, London. (b) Engraving of the underside of a leaf, from W. Jackson and W. Fitch, *Victoria Regia, or, Illustrations of the Royal Water-Lily* (1851). Photo courtesy of the Trustees of the Chatsworth Settlement, Devonshire Collections, Chatsworth.

109. Owen Jones. 'Moresque Ornament', details of mosaics from the Alhambra Palace. Lithographic plate (no. 153) from *The Grammar of Ornament* (London, 1856).

110. Philip Webb. Red House, stairhall, near Bexleyheath, Kent, 1860s. Photo Martin Charles, Isleworth.

111. Louis-Auguste Boileau. Ste-Eugène–Ste-Cécile, Paris, 1854–55. Photo Roger–Viollet, Paris.

112. Léon Vaudoyer. Marseille Cathedral, 1852–90. Photo Achim Bednorz, Cologne.

113. Viollet-le-Duc. Springing point of the arch from the article 'Construction' of the *Dictionnaire Raisonné de l'Architecture* (1858). RIBA Library, London/photo A.C. Cooper.

114. Viollet-le-Duc. Concert hall, *c.*1866, from *Entretiens sur l'Architecture* (1858). RIBA Library, London/photo A.C. Cooper.

115. Gottfried Semper. Caribbean Hut, from *Der Stil*, 1862.

116. Alexander Laplanche. Au Bon Marché, Paris, 1872. (a) Exterior. (b) Interior. Photos Roger–Viollet, Paris.

117. Eduard Détaille. Opening of the Paris Opera House, 5 January 1875. Musée de Versailles et de Trianon/photo Bridgeman Art Library (Giraudon), London.

118. Plan of Haussmann's work in Paris, *c.*1853. From L. Benevolo, *History of Modern Architecture.* (Rome: Laterza, 1993)

119. Eduard Baldus. The Louvre and Tuileries United, *c.*1855. The Getty Research Institute for the History of Art and the Humanities (Bonnemaison Panorama Collection), Los Angeles.

120. Joseph Paxton. Birkenhead Park near Liverpool, 1844. Williamson Art Gallery and Museum, Birkenhead.

121. F.-A. Duquesny. Gare de l'Est, Paris, 1847–52. Photo Roger–Viollet, Paris.

122. Gabriel Veugny. Cité Napoléon, 1849–53. Section. Musée des Arts Décoratifs, Paris/photo Jean-Loup Charmet.

123. Adolphe Terris. Creation of the rue Impériale in Marseille. From M. Culot and D. Drocourt, *Marseille: La Passione des Contrastes* (Brussels: Mardega, and Paris: Institut Français d'Urbanisme, 1991).

124. Victor Baltard. Les Halles, Paris, 1852–55. Engraving from F. Narjoux, *Paris: Monuments éléves par la ville, 1850–80*, ii (1883). British Library (1735.b.20), London.

125. Unveiling of the Boulevard Strasbourg, 1858 (today Sébastopol). Engraving from *L'illustration* (12 August 1858). Photo Mary Evans Picture Library, Blackheath.

126. Apartment House, Boulevard de Strasbourg, *c.*1855. From *The Builder*, xvi, 159 (6 March 1858). RIBA Library, London/photo A.C. Cooper.

127. Charles Garnier. New Opéra, 1863–75. Aerial view. Photo Roger–Viollet, Paris.

128. Charles Garnier. Paris Opéra. (a) Exterior. Engraving. Musée Carnavalet, Paris/photo Bulloz. (b) Sectional view, 1863–75. From *Le Journal Illustré* (28 February 1875). Photo Bibliothèque Nationale, Paris.

129. Charles Garnier. Paris Opéra. Details of the staircase. From Charles Garnier, Le nouvel Opéra de Paris (1878). British Library (TAB.690.D), London.

130. Vienna Ringstrasse, 1860. (a) Plan view. Engraving. (b) View along the Ringstrasse, *c.*1888. Historisches Museum der Stadt Wien (INV.67.989 and 68.013).

131. Gottfried Semper and Karl von Hasenauer. Project for the Museums district, Vienna, 1873. Illustration by Girard and Rehlender for the Universal Exposition of 1873. Landesamt für Denkmalpflege Sachsen, Dresden.

132. Apartment houses on the Reichsrat-strasse, Vienna, *c.*1875. Historisches Museum

der Stadt Wien (INV.105.018/17).

133. Ildefonso Cerdà. Ensanche of Barcelona, plan as adopted in 1860. Institut Municipal de Historia, Barcelona/photo Institut Amatller d'Art Hispànic.

134. Panoramic view of the projected suburb at Le Vésinet, 1858. Bibliothèque Municipal du Vésinet, Le Vésinet.

135. Camillo Sitte. Project for the transformation of the votive Church Plaza, Vienna, from *Der Städtebau nach seinen künstlerichen Grundsätzen.*

136. Victor Horta. Hôtel Tassel, Brussels. Stairhall, 1892. Photo Bastin and Evrard, Brussels.

137. Views of the Exposition Universelle, 1889, Paris. (a) The Eiffel Tower. (b) The Palais des Beaux-Arts. Photos Roger–Viollet, Paris.

138. Félix Narjoux. Rue de Tanger School, 1875–77. From F. Narjoux, *Paris: Monuments élevés par la ville 1850–80*, ii (1883). British Library (1735.B.20)

139. Guiseppe Sacconi. Rome, Monument to Victor Emmanuel II, 1884. Photo Richard Glover/Arcaid, Kingston-upon-Thames.

140. Templeton's Carpet Factory in Glasgow, 1889–92. National Monuments Record, Scotland.

The publisher and the author apologize for any errors or omissions in the above list. If contacted they will be pleased to rectify these at the earliest opportunity.

Index